# IN DEFENSE OF THE LAND ETHIC

SUNY Series in Philosophy and Biology

David Edward Shaner, Editor
Furman University

# IN DEFENSE OF THE LAND ETHIC

## Essays in Environmental Philosophy

## *J. Baird Callicott*

State University of New York Press

Published by
State University of New York Press, Albany

©1989 State University of New York

For information, address State University of New York
Press, State University Plaza, Albany, N.Y., 12246

Library of Congress Cataloging in Publication Data

Callicott, J. Baird.
    In defense of the land ethic : essays in
    environmental philosophy / J. Baird Callicott. 1941.
        p.   cm.—(SUNY series in philosophy and biology)
    Includes index.
    ISBN 0-88706-899-5.    ISBN 0-88706-900-2 (pbk.)
    1. Human ecology—Moral and ethical aspects. 2. Environmental protection—
Moral and ethical aspects. 3. Leopold, Aldo, 1887-1948.    I. Title.   II. Series.
GF80.C35 1988                                                                    88-7039
179'.1—d19                                                                          CIP

10 9 8 7 6 5 4 3 2

*For my mother and father,*
*Evelyne E. and Burton H. Callicott*

# Contents

# Acknowledgements

For critical advice during the making of this volume, I thank Frances Moore Lappé, Bryan G. Norton, Holmes Rolston, III, Claudia Card, Alice Van Deburg, William Eastman, David Edward Shaner, and Eugene C. Hargrove, who also suggested its title. For critical advice on individual essays in this collection, I thank Richard Watson, Don Marietta, Tom Regan, Thomas W. Overholt, Jeffrey Olen, Arthur L. Herman, Frances Moore Lappé, Bryan G. Norton, Holmes Rolston, III, Eugene C. Hargrove, and an assortment of anonymous referees. For secretarial assistance with the book as a whole and with each of its essays individually, I thank Carolee Cote. I would also like to express my thanks to William Eastman, Diane Ganeles, and Jackie Remlinger for their help and expertise in producing this book.

I thank Eugene C. Hargrove for permission to reprint from *Environmental Ethics*: "Elements of an Environmental Ethic: Moral Considerability and the Biotic Community" (vol. 1 [1979], pp. 71-81); "Animal Liberation: A Triangular Affair" (vol. 2 [1980], pp. 311-328); "Hume's *Is/Ought* Dichotomy and the Relation of Ecology to Leopold's Land Ethic" (vol. 4 [1982], pp. 173-174); "Traditional American Indian and Western European Attitudes Toward Nature: An Overview" (vol. 4 [1982], pp. 293-318); "Intrinsic Value, Quantum Theory, and Environmental Ethics" (vol. 7 [1985], pp. 357-375); "Review of Tom Regan, *The Case for Animal Rights*" (vol. 7 [1985], pp. 365-372); and "The Metaphysical Implications of Ecology" (vol. 9 [1986], pp. 300-315).

"Aldo Leopold on Education, as Educator, and His Land Ethic in the Context of Contemporary Environmental Education" first appeared in the *Journal of Environmental Education*, vol. 14, no. 1, (1982), pp. 34-41; published by Heldref Publications, 4000 Albemarle St., N.W., Washington, D.C. 20016; copyright 1982. It is reprinted with permission of the Helen Dwight Reid Educational Foundation.

I thank Max Schnepf for permission to reprint "Leopold's Land Aesthetic" (copyright 1982, the Soil Conservation Society of America) from the *Journal of Soil and Water Conservation* 38 (1983), pp. 329-332.

"On the Intrinsic Value of Nonhuman Species" first appeared in

Bryan G. Norton, ed., *The Preservation of Species: The Value of Biological Diversity* (copyright 1986, Princeton University Press), pp. 138-172, reprinted with permission of Princeton University Press.

"The Conceptual Foundations of the Land Ethic" was first published in 1987 in Madison Wisconsin by the University of Wisconsin Press in J. Baird Callicott, ed., *Companion to A Sand County Almanac: Interpretive and Critical Essays*, pp. 186-217.

"Moral Considerability and Extraterrestrial Life" is from *Beyond Spaceship Earth: Environmental Ethics and the Solar System*, edited by Eugene C. Hargrove; copyright 1986 by Eugene C. Hargrove; reprinted with permission of Sierra Club Books.

# Introduction: The Real Work[1]

## I
## Environmental Philosophy: Its Origins and Types

My life's work as a philosopher began in earnest when I settled into my first university post during the mid-sixties. It was an exciting time, especially on college and university campuses; and a dangerous time, especially in the South, where I happened to find my first real job. Three serious social phenomena stood out as a challenge and opportunity for an idealistic young academician: the Civil Rights movement, the peace movement, and the environmental movement. Of these three, the greatest philosophical opportunity and the biggest intellectual challenge seemed to me to be presented by the "quiet crisis" (in Stewart Udall's memorable phrase)—the environmental crisis.

My involvement in the Southern Civil Rights and peace movements was not appreciated by my employers; and so in 1969 I found myself a new job in the central sand country of Wisconsin. I was unaware at the time that I had alighted at the spiritual epicenter of the dawning ecological consciousness—and conscience.

The School of Conservation (now the College of Natural Resources) gave Wisconsin State University–Stevens Point (now the University of Wisconsin–Stevens Point) its distinct personality. Shortly after joining the philosophy department, I proposed to develop a completely new course called "Environmental Ethics." It was designed to attract the large population of students majoring in forestry, wildlife management, and the like and, incidentally, to permit me to explore my hunch that ecology was a treasure trove of philosophically revolutionary ideas. As time went on a few other academic philosophers developed similar courses here and there. Thus, at first, environmental philosophy amounted to little more than relevancy offerings in the curricula of sundry colleges and universities where resident philosophers happened to be motivated to develop and teach them. Among environmental philosophers there was no community and little communication until Eugene C. Hargrove established *Environmental Ethics: An Interdisciplinary Journal Dedicated to the Philosophical Aspects of Environmental Problems*

1

late in the decade (the first volume appeared in 1979).

By then, those of us who had been working away in relative isolation had formed quite different conceptions of what environmental ethics and philosophy was all about. Some approached it as a species of applied ethics—epitomized by biomedical ethics and business ethics—which emerged in similar circumstances at about the same time.[2] From this point of view, new and exotic technologies—like nuclear power and genetic engineering—had created new and exotic environmental hazards for *human beings,* which earlier moral sages could not have imagined (or which the leading contemporary metaethicists would not deign to consider). The task of environmental philosophy, accordingly, is to apply the environmental philosopher's preferred standard moral theory—Kant's deontology, Bentham's utilitarianism, Mill's utilitarianism, Rawls's theory of justice, or whatever— to the novel moral situations created by the new technologies which had so dramatically and so dangerously altered "man's" environment. Since Western moral philosophy has been overwhelmingly if not entirely anthropocentric—i.e., focused exclusively on human welfare and the intrinsic value of human beings (or human experiences)—the environment enters into ethics, upon such an approach to environmental ethics, only as the arena of human interaction. The environment is treated as, so to speak, a value-neutral vector between human moral agent and human moral patient.

Conceived as a type of applied ethics, environmental ethics is usually issue-oriented. One might consider, for example, the generation of acidic gases by coal-fired electric utilities and other smokestack industries and try to puzzle out who's to balme for acid rain and how justly to compensate those whose "natural resources" have been damaged by it. Or one might consider the siting of nuclear facilities and the morality of imposing unequal involuntary risks on different segments of a country's population. In addition to distinctly moral questions, issues like acid rain and nuclear plant-siting involve complex technical questions (like the reaction of aerosols in the presence of sunlight and the carcinogenic potential of low-level radiation emissions), complex economic questions (like the cost effectiveness of stack scrubbers and the exact multiplier factor to assign each tourist dollar), and complex questions of international law and public security.

Other environmental philosophers feared that in the quagmire of formulae, equations, tables, graphs, legal technicalities, and the relative moral merits of libertarianism, utilitarianism, and egalitarianism surrounding environmental issues, the deeper philosophical problem of the value of the natural environment in its own right and our duties, if any, to nature itself was ignored. Feeling that the most fundamental moral matters would go begging if environmental ethics remained merely a novel application of normal Western moral theory to new and complex environmental issues, they attempted to extend conventional Western moral theory so that it would include *non*human beings among the direct beneficiaries of ethics.[3] But the elasticity of conventional Western moral theory is limited. Hence, the most plausible extensions ended with animals—and even then, not all animals were included.[4] Environmental ethics, conceived as an incremental extension of morality beyond the species barrier, is, thus, pretty much coincidental with animal welfare ethics—popularly known as "animal liberation."[5]

Like environmental-ethics-as-applied-ethics, animal liberation is firmly attached to the usual ways and means of mainstream modern Western moral theory. But unlike environmental-ethics-as-applied-ethics, it does not concentrate on the complex technical, economic, and political aspects of environmental issues as a new arena for the application of tried and true moral precepts. Rather, its central concern is how best to extend the first principles of conventional moral theory to wider circles of moral patients by familiar methods of moral reasoning. Animal liberation thus has a decidedly theoretical cast— making it more distinctly philosophical than an interdisciplinary mix of philosophy, public policy, economics, engineering, and environmental science in equal measures.

An extensionist might begin with his or her preferred traditional moral theory—Kant's deontology, Bentham's utilitarianism, Mill's utilitarianism, Rawls's theory of justice, or whatever—and ask how it might be stretched to bring nonhuman beings, fellow vertebrates usually, under the umbrella of moral considerability. Or proceeding in reverse fashion, an extensionist might begin with the moral intuition that somehow animals and perhaps other living beings ought to be extended moral consideration and ask which among the available alternatives in Western moral philosophy offers the most promising theoretical rationale for doing so.

A third contingent of environmental philosophers saw in the environmental crisis a profound repudiation by the environment itself of modern Western civilization's attitudes and values toward nature. Thus, nothing less than a sweeping philosophical overhaul—not just of ethics, but of the whole Western world view—is mandated. These philosophers, among whom I count myself, have been called "ecocentrists" since we have advocated a shift in the locus of intrinsic value from individuals (whether individual human beings or individual higher "lower animals") to terrestrial nature—the ecosystem—as a whole.[6] Like extensionists, ecocentric environmental philosophers are more preoccupied with cognitive than with technical, economic, and political questions. But unlike extensionists, ecocentrists are more concerned to criticize than to expand conventional Western moral philosophy (and metaphysics as well). Our goal is to build, from the ground up, new ethical (and metaphysical) paradigms.

This is a most expansive, ambitious and, I'm sure some will say, pretentious conception of environmental ethics. But even though it seems to be the most radical of all, it is, from an even more extreme point of view, relatively conservative. More radical still are the self-styled Deep Ecologists, on the one hand, and some Asianists and comparative philosophers, on the other, who suggest, in one way or another, that philosophy itself, the rational method, is a part of the problem, not the solution:[7] Ecocentric philosophers are like Wittgenstein's fly—still in the bottle—if we imagine that we can *think* our way out of the environmental crisis, they argue.[8]

The ecocentric approach to environmental ethics is conservative, even classical, in another sense: it calls philosophy back to its abdicated place and role in Western cultural history. Twentieth-century philosophy has suffered from physics envy. Twentieth-century academic philosophers have sought to stake out for themselves a piece of intellectual turf—before it was all claimed by one or another of the sciences—and to outfit themselves with an arcana, complete with a jargon and symbolic mode of expression, all their own. As a result, philosophers have become increasingly isolated and irrelevant in the larger intellectual community, and as the century wanes, the discipline has become among the most fractious and scholastic.

Meanwhile, the world in which we live changes at a dizzying pace. The global landscape has become thoroughly mechanized and saturated with all sorts of synthetic substances. The global human population has trebled in less than a century. An episode of extinction rivaling in rate and magnitude the die-off of the dinosaurs is taking place under our noses; in the span of one century—a blink of the eye in geologic measures of time—one-tenth of the species that existed when mankind inherited the Earth will have been eradicated. The physical sciences have looked to the very edge of the universe, to the beginning of time, and into the finest structure of matter. In the course of that looking, our most fundamental ideas of space, time, matter, and motion, and the nature of our knowledge thereof have been radically altered.

Today the need is greater than ever for philosophers to do what they once did—to redefine the world picture in response to irretrievably transformed human experience and to the flood of new information and ideas pouring forth from the sciences; to inquire what new way we human beings might imagine our place and role in nature; and to figure out how these big new ideas might change our values and realign our sense of duty and obligation.

## II
### Aldo Leopold: Seminal Environmental Philosopher

Other thinkers, during the twentieth century, have partially filled the intellectual vacuum created by the preoccupation of the majority of those who identify themselves as philosophers with special problems far removed from the real world and from the general questions inspiring Western thinkers since Socrates. Albert Schweitzer, Arthur Koestler, Aldous Huxley, Albert Einstein, Werner Heisenberg, Benjamin Whorf, Claude Levi-Strauss, Alan Watts; and more recently, Gary Snyder, Marshall McLuhan, R. D. Laing, Paul Shepard, Carl Sagan, Fritjof Capra, E. F. Schumacher, William Irwin Thompson, Frances Moore Lappé, Wendell Berry, Edward O. Wilson, and Stephen Jay Gould come randomly to mind.

Aldo Leopold was one such thoughtful amateur. As a high-minded and idealistic young forest ranger, Leopold struggled to grasp the dynamics of "game," woods, range, water, and soil in Arizona and New Mexico.[9] His understanding of the land matured apace with the science of ecology. In Leopold's integrative thinking, ecology was never just another specialized science nor merely a tool and fund of information for the efficient exploitation of natural resources. It was, rather, a profound new way of perceiving and cognitively organizing the natural world, validated by his own extensive field experience. Moreover, Leopold found his values changing as his ecological understanding deepened and therefore suggested that ecology was also pregnant with profound ethical precepts.

But precisely because Leopold's acquaintance with the history and methods of philosophy was only that of a roundly educated gentleman, the metaphysical and axiological implications of ecology are incompletely expressed in his literary legacy, however true his insights. Leopold's compressed writing style further compounds the incipience of his ecological philosophy. He believed in the virtue of straightforward, pithy prose. Leopold's laconic philosophical essays rarely run longer than a dozen pages. *A Sand County Almanac*, at first glance a mere miscellany, moreover, presents the distilled essence of Leopold's ecological vision not discursively, as a schooled philosopher might, but by the accumulated weight of description, example, illustration, and commentary finally capped by summary argumentation in the book's climactic essay, "The Land Ethic."

When I first became acquainted with it in the early seventies, I found in Aldo Leopold's *A Sand County Almanac* just what the doctor ordered for an emerging contemporary environmental ethic. As an environmental philosopher of the third kind—an ecocentric revisionist—I felt that Leopold's *A Sand County Almanac* was a touchstone, a seminal classic. And I wanted to flesh out the arguments which Leopold himself only evoked and to connect his ideas, especially his ethical ideas, with the antecedents in the history of Western philosophy echoing in his rich literary allusions.

Through the essays assembled in this book I have attempted, over nearly a decade, more fully to develop, articulate, historicize, and defend "The Land Ethic." A number of my colleagues and friends urged me to collect them in a single volume, not only as a convenience, but because they are thematically connected and together present a unified environmental philosophy.

For presentation here, I have sorted the essays into topical groups. Within each section the essays are arranged chronologically; so each theme or topic exhibits parallel development. I have resisted the temptation to substantively revise, for this volume, some of the things I wrote and tone down others, especially in the earlier pieces. Here and there I have made a slight emendation in the style or corrected a typographical error that found its way into print. Because each essay once stood on its own, standing together they occasionally overlap and repeat. Nevertheless, each contributes something unique to a whole fabric of thought.

### III
### These Essays: Their Organization and Several Occasions

*Part I.* My work is probably most closely associated with an environmental critique of animal liberation/rights and thus I am probably best known for driving a wedge between animal welfare and environmental ethics. In any case, "Animal Liberation: A Triangular Affair," first published in *Environmental Ethics* in 1980 is my most famous—or infamous—essay, depending upon your point of view. This is the one that I would most like to revise (censor) for this publication. It was intended to provoke controversy and provoke controversy it certainly has.

Due in large measure to the industry and philosophical acuity of Peter Singer and Tom Regan, extensionism seemed, at the beginning of the eighties, poised to completely take over environmental ethics. The debate appeared to me to have become increasingly polar—between the anthropocentrists (the "moral humanists" as I called them) and the animal liberationists (the "humane moralists"). I wanted to attract attention to what then seemed to me to be the neglected third party to the controversy, the more radical ecocentric point of view, classically championed by Aldo Leopold. I succeeded—too well. It is especially important to me, therefore, not only to have the opportunity to put this essay in the same volume with my more tempered and considered interpretations and extrapolations of Aldo Leopold's land ethic, but also to put this essay in the same section with my more tempered and inclusive account of animal welfare ethics.

The process of rebuilding the bridges which I had set aflame began with my review essay of Tom Regan's *The Case for Animal Rights* published in *Environmental Ethics* in 1985. Although the review is critical of Regan's counterattack on ecocentric environmental ethics, it points, at the end, to an approach to a theoretical reunification of animal welfare and environmental ethics. In "Animal Liberation and Environmental Ethics: Back Together Again" I attempt to follow up on the theoretical program of reconciliation suggested in the review of Regan. This paper was presented to the Society for the Study of Ethics and Animals meeting in conjunction with the Pacific Division of the American Philosophical Association in Portland, Oregon, in March 1988 and was published in *Between the Species* later the same year. These three papers on animal liberation/rights and environmental ethics constitute the first section of this book.

*Part II.* The next section develops a holistic environmental ethic based upon Aldo Leopold's land ethic. Its first essay, "Elements of an Environmental Ethic: Moral Considerability and the Biotic Community," was written in 1977 as the invited lecture to the Wisconsin Philosophical Association and was published in the inaugural issue of *Environmental Ethics*. It too clearly reveals my concern to express in a professionally respectable vocabulary—complete with logical symbols and numbered propositions—the basic tenets of the land ethic.

I wrote the second essay of the second section, "The Conceptual Foundations of the Land Ethic," in 1985. It represents my best effort to set out thoroughly and systematically the cognitive elements and logic of Leopold's land ethic, that is, to present the land ethic in full philosophical regalia. It was published in *Companion to A Sand County Almanac: Interpretive and Critical Essays,* an anthology of twelve essays written by ten scholars which I edited for the University of Wisconsin Press in celebration of the centennial of Aldo Leopold's birth.

This section ends with "The Metaphysical Implications of Ecology," presented to the Society for Asian and Comparative Philosophy meeting in conjunction with the Eastern Division of the American Philosophical Association in Washington in 1986. It was published later the same year in a special issue of *Environmental Ethics* devoted to conceptual resources for environmental philosophy in Asian traditions of thought (which was coordinated with a complementary special issue of *Philosophy East and West*). This paper locates Aldo Leopold's land ethic in its most expansive cognitive matrix—an integrative systemic ecological/quantum theoretical paradigm—to which the land ethic is related as figure to ground.

*Part III.* The two most revolutionary features of the land ethic are, first, the shift in emphasis from part to whole—from individual to community—and, second, the shift in emphasis from human beings to nature, from anthropocentrism to ecocentrism. The former is the overall theme of part II of this volume, the latter of part III. Ethical holism and ecocentrism present, respectively, equally monumental theoretical challenges to an environmental philosopher because they buck the current of nearly the whole history of Western moral thought. In combination, a holistic *and* ecocentric ethic would appear practically to defy any attempt at expression continuous with the Western ethical heritage.

I wrote "Hume's *Is/Ought* Dichotomy and the Relation of Ecology to Leopold's Land Ethic," the first essay of the third part of this collection, for a conference on environmental ethics and contemporary ethical theory held at the University of Georgia in 1981. It was published the following year in *Environmental Ethics*. It tackles a central but circumscribed problem for any ethic that purports to be informed by science, the problem of deriving value from fact, ought from is—the problem, as it is sometimes characterized, of the naturalistic fallacy. In wrestling with this problem, which was first posed by David Hume in the eighteenth century, it occurred to me that in Hume's ethics might be found a value theory that could transcend anthropocentrism. It also became clear to me that, happily, Hume's value theory was actually at the core of Leopold's land ethic, having been absorbed by Leopold through Darwin, who had borrowed extensively from both Hume and Hume's younger contemporary, Adam Smith.

I prepared "On the Intrinsic Value of Nonhuman Species" for the University of Maryland Philosophy and Public Policy's working group on species preservation which met during 1981–82. It eventually appeared in 1986 in *The Preservation of Species*, edited by Bryan G. Norton and published by Princeton University Press. In it I explore a number of historical approaches to value theory in the Western tradition and suggest that, among existing alternatives, the Hume-Darwin-Leopold approach is the best suited for an ecocentric environmental ethic.

In "Intrinsic Value, Quantum Theory, and Environmental Ethics" I try to go beyond the historical axiology originating with Hume, grounded in evolutionary theory by Darwin, and extended to the biotic community by Leopold. Quantum theory has pulled the cognitive rug out from under the Hume-Darwin-Leopold approach to the intrinsic or inherent value of nature. This paper outlines two alternative theories of the inherent or intrinsic value of nature in light of and inspired by the New Physics. I presented it to a conference on new directions in environmental ethics held at the University of Georgia in 1984, and it was published the following year in *Environmental Ethics*.

*Part IV.* Popular environmental literature regularly attributes to traditional American Indian peoples—as an object lesson for contemporary Western civilization—one or another form of land wisdom. With few exceptions, however, professional ethnographers and anthropologists consider the American-Indian-as-ecological-guru to be neo-romantic nonsense, a post-sixties edition of the Noble Savage with an environmental spin. The fourth section of this volume develops the hypothesis that American Indians, some of them at least, did actually espouse an environmental ethic and that in abstract structure it was similar to the land ethic.

Thomas W. Overholt and I wrote a textbook entitled *Clothed-in-Fur and Other Tales: An Introduction to an Ojibwa World View* for our course at the University of Wisconsin–Stevens Point, American Indian Environmental Philosophies. While doing the research for that book I was surprised to discover that the traditional Ojibwa (and other subarctic peoples) represented their natural environments by means of an essentially social model, which although mythic in substance, was identical in form to the ecological model of a biotic community—the key concept of the land ethic. In "Traditional American Indian and Western European Attitudes Toward Nature: An Overview," published in *Environmental Ethics* in 1982, I attempted to draw out the parallel between the traditional Ojibwa land ethic and Aldo Leopold's land ethic, and to argue, in passing, that certain critics of the notion that American Indian world views represented a useful resource for contemporary environmental ethics were mistaken. "American Indian Land Wisdom?: Sorting Out the Issues" was presented to a symposium entitled "Plains Indian Cultures: Past and Present Meanings" at the University of Nebraska in 1986 and was published three years later in *Struggle for the Land: Indigenous Understanding and Industrial Empire*, edited by Paul A. Olson. It refines and extends the argument of the earlier paper.

*Part V.* For the final section of this book, I have drawn on my

Wisconsin neighbors and neighborhood to create a more concrete portrait of both the philosopher and the countryside of Wisconsin's sand counties. "Aldo Leopold on Education, as Educator, and His Land Ethic in the Context of Contemporary Environmental Education" was written as the keynote address for the Midwest Environmental Education Association meetings in 1981 and published the following year in the *Journal of Environmental Education*. Aldo Leopold was not just "interested" in education. One could argue, as indeed I do argue in this essay, that for Leopold universal ecological education is the key to realizing the land ethic—in policy and practice as well as in theory. I wrote "Leopold's Land Aesthetic" for a conference sponsored by the Humanities and Agriculture Program of the University of Florida entitled "Agriculture, Change, and Human Values" in 1982. It was published the following year in the *Journal of Soil and Water Conservation*. Among Leopold's least-appreciated contributions is his prescient critique of industrial agriculture and advocacy of a sustainable agriculture or "agroecology"—anticipating the contemporary work of Wendell Berry, Wes Jackson, and Marty Strange. In "Leopold's Land Aesthetic" I have tried to abstract the environmental aesthetic of *A Sand County Almanac*—in Leopold's own view, a theme equal in importance to environmental ethics —and illustrate it in context of a working central-Wisconsin farmstead.

Eugene C. Hargrove inadvertently afforded me the opportunity to vent my irritation with the contemporary romance of space exploration and space travel when he invited me to present a paper at his "space conference," Environmental Ethics and the Solar System. It took place at the University of Georgia in 1985. I here include "Moral Considerability and Extraterrestrial Life"—which appeared the following year in Sierra Club Books' edition of selected papers from that conference entitled *Beyond Spaceship Earth*—not primarily to gain more converts to "terracentricism" or "Earth chauvinism," but to indicate the important limits of the land ethic. An ethic that embraces everything in effect embraces nothing. The land ethic may seem fatally promiscuous in its inclusion of "soils, waters, plants, and animals," individually and collectively—until we consider extraterrestrial entities. I try to show how and why it doesn't include them. This essay highlights the importance of what in some of the others I have called "the Copernican conceptual element" of the land ethic. And, because it clearly exhibits the limitations of the land ethic, it makes a fitting finale for this collection.

## IV
## The Outlook

The approach to environmental philosophy that these essays commend and explore radically departs from normal modern moral philosophy. It grows, rather, out of modern biological thought about the environing natural world and about human nature. Kant and Bentham are the fountainheads of normal modern moral philosophy. A biocentric—not ecocentric—environmental ethic, along essentially Kantian lines, has recently been developed by Paul Taylor.[10] Bentham, founding father of utilitarianism, is the ultimate source and inspiration for both anthropocentric environmental ethics (especially the classical American conservation ethic) and for extensionist environmental ethics. Aldo Leopold's land ethic is firmly rooted in natural history—in evolution and ecology. Its clearest antecedent is Charles Darwin's construction of morality in *The Descent of Man*. It is especially fitting and elegant, I think, for an ethic with a broad biological concern or orientation—an ecocentric ethic —to have a firm biological foundation and to be rooted in an evolutionary and ecological understanding of nature and human psychology and behavior.

The contemporary successor to Darwin's account of ethics is today called sociobiology. Many of these essays refer to and touch upon sociobiology, but do not provide, certainly, anything like an adequate and rigorous derivation of environmental ethics from sociobiology. The distinctly ethical implications of sociobiology have been, sadly, misunderstood and misrepresented, in my opinion, both by its advocates and by its critics. Rightly understood and positively presented, I think that sociobiology offers a tremendous resource for moral philosophy generally and for environmental ethics especially. Thus, I think that these essays, through what they most conspicuously lack, suggest an important direction for future research in environmental ethics—the rigorous derivation of an environmental ethic from contemporary sociobiology and ecology.

The full development of an evolutionary and ecological environment aesthetic represents a second important direction for research globally suggested by the papers included here. For Aldo Leopold an appropriate land aesthetic was just as important as an adequate land ethic. In comparison to ethics, the attention given to natural aesthetics by the community of environmental and ecological philosophers has been roughly proportional to the attention it has received in this book.

Although the notion of environmental philosophy animating these essays is grand, I certainly do not pretend that they do more than point to the real work of contemporary philosophy. The Western philosophical tradition, to which I feel a deep loyalty, is critical to the core. I put these essays forward not only as a defense of Leopold's seminal environmental ethic, but as an invitation to critical exploration along the trail he charted. If they contribute in some measure to a reorientation of contemporary philosophical thought, I shall be more than satisfied.

# I

# Animal Liberation
# and Environmental Ethics

# 1

## Animal Liberation: A Triangular Affair

### Environmental Ethics and Animal Liberation

Partly because it is so new to Western philosophy (or at least heretofore only scarcely represented) *environmental ethics* has no precisely fixed conventional definition in glossaries of philosophical terminology. Aldo Leopold, however, is universally recognized as the father or founding genius of recent environmental ethics. His "land ethic" has become a modern classic and may be treated as the standard example, the paradigm case, as it were, of what an environmental ethic is. Environmental ethics then can be defined ostensively by using Leopold's land ethic as the exemplary type. I do not mean to suggest that all environmental ethics should necessarily conform to Leopold's paradigm, but the extent to which an ethical system resembles Leopold's land ethic might be used, for want of anything better, as a criterion to measure the extent to which it is or is not of the environmental sort.

It is Leopold's opinion, and certainly an overall review of the prevailing traditions of Western ethics, both popular and philosophical, generally confirms it, that traditional Western systems of ethics have not accorded moral standing to nonhuman beings.[1] Animals and plants, soils and waters, which Leopold includes in his community of ethical beneficiaries, have traditionally enjoyed no moral standing, no rights, no respect, in sharp contrast to human persons whose rights and interests ideally must be fairly and equally considered if our actions are to be considered "ethical" or "moral." One fundamental and novel feature of the Leopold land ethic, therefore, is the extension of *direct* ethical considerability from people to nonhuman natural entities.

At first glance, the recent ethical movement usually labeled "animal liberation" or "animal rights" seems to be squarely and centrally a kind of environmental ethics.[2] The more uncompromising among the animal liberationists have demanded equal moral consideration on behalf of cows, pigs, chickens, and other apparently enslaved and oppressed nonhuman animals.[3] The theoreticians of this new hyper-egalitarianism have coined such terms as *speciesism* (on analogy with *racism* and *sexism*) and *human chauvinism* (on analogy with *male chauvinism*), and have made animal liberation seem, perhaps not improperly, the next and most daring development of political liberalism.[4] Aldo Leopold also draws upon metaphors of political liberalism when he tells us that his land ethic "changes the role of *Homo sapiens* from conqueror of the land community to plain member and citizen of it."[5] For animal liberationists it is as if the ideological battles for equal rights and equal consideration for women and for racial minorities have been all but won, and the next and greatest challenge is to purchase equality, first theoretically and then practically, for all (actually only *some*) animals, regardless of species. This more rhetorically implied than fully articulated historical progression of moral rights from fewer to greater numbers of "persons" (allowing that animals may also be persons) as advocated by animal liberationists, also parallels Leopold's scenario in "The Land Ethic" of the historical extension of "ethical criteria" to more and more "fields of conduct" and to larger and larger groups of people during the past three thousand or so years.[6] As Leopold develops it, the land ethic is a cultural "evolutionary possibility," the next "step in a sequence."[7] For Leopold, however, the next step is much more sweeping, much more inclusive than the animal liberationists envision, since it "enlarges the boundaries of the [moral] community to include soils, waters, [and] plants ..." as well as animals.[8] Thus, the animal liberation movement *could* be construed as partitioning Leopold's perhaps undigestable and totally inclusive environmental ethic into a series of more assimilable stages: today animal rights, tomorrow equal rights for plants, and after that full moral standing for rocks, soil, and other earthy compounds, and perhaps sometime in the still more remote future, liberty and equality for water and other elemental bodies.

Put just this way, however, there is something jarring about such a graduated progression in the exfoliation of a more inclusive environmental ethic, something that seems absurd. A more or less reasonable case might be made for rights for some animals, but when we come to plants, soils, and waters, the frontier between plausibility and absurdity appears to have been crossed. Yet, there is no doubt that Leopold sincerely proposes that *land* (in his inclusive sense) be ethically regarded. The beech and chestnut, for example, have in his view as much "biotic right" to life as the wolf and the deer, and the effects of human actions on mountains and streams for Leopold is an ethical concern as genuine and serious as the comfort and longevity of battery hens.[9] In fact, Leopold to all appearances never considered the treatment of battery hens on a factory farm or steers in a feed lot to be a pressing moral issue. He seems much more concerned about the integrity of the farm woodlot and the effects of clear-cutting steep slopes on neighboring streams.

Animal liberationists put their ethic into practice (and display their devotion to it) by becoming vegetarians, and the moral complexites of vegetarianism have been thoroughly debated in the recent literature as an adjunct issue to animal rights.[10] (No one, however, has yet expressed, as among Butler's Erewhonians, qualms about eating plants, though such sentiments might be expected to be latently present if the rights of plants are next to be defended.) Aldo Leopold, by contrast, did not even condemn hunting animals, let alone eating them, nor did he personally abandon hunting, for which he had had an enthusiasm since boyhood, upon becoming convinced that his ethical responsibilities extended beyond the human sphere.[11] There are several interpretations for this behavioral peculiarity. One is that Leopold did not see that his land ethic actually ought to prohibit hunting, cruelly killing, and eating animals. A corollary of this interpretation is that Leopold was so unperspicacious as deservedly to be thought stupid—a conclusion hardly comporting with the intellectual subtlety he usually evinces in most other respects. If not stupid, then perhaps Leopold was hypocritical. But if a hypocrite, we should expect him to conceal his proclivity for blood sports and flesh eating and to treat them as shameful vices to be indulged secretively. As it is, bound together between the same covers with "The Land Ethic" are his unabashed reminiscences of killing and consuming *game*.[12] This term (like *stock*) when used of animals, moreover, appears to be morally equivalent to referring to a sexually appealing young woman as a "piece" or to a strong, young black man as a "buck"—if animal rights, that is, are to considered as on a par with women's rights and the rights of formerly enslaved races. A third interpretation of Leopold's approbation of regulated and disciplined sport hunting (and a fortiori meat eating) is that it is a form of human and animal behavior not inconsistent with the land ethic as he conceived it. A corollary of this interpretation is that Leopold's land ethic and the environmental ethic of the animal liberation movement rest upon very different theoretical foundations, and that they are thus two very different forms of environmental ethics.

The urgent concern of animal liberationists for the suffering of domestic animals, toward which Leopold manifests an attitude which can only be described as indifference, and the urgent concern of Leopold, on the other hand, for the disappearance of species of plants as well as animals and for soil erosion and stream pollution, appear to be symptoms not only of very different ethical perspectives, but of profoundly different cosmic visions as well. The neat similarities, noted at the beginning of this discussion, between the environmental ethic of the animal liberation movement and the classical Leopold land ethic appear in light of these observations to be rather superficial and to conceal substrata of thought and value which are not at all similar. The theoretical foundations of the animal liberation movement and those of the Leopold land ethic may even turn out not to be companionable, complementary, or mutually consistent. The animal liberationists may thus find themselves not only engaged in controversy with the many conservative philosophers upholding *apartheid* between man and "beast," but also faced with an unexpected dissent from another, very different, system of environmental ethics.[13] Animal liberation and animal rights may well prove to be a triangular rather than, as it has so far been represented in the philosophical community, a polar controversy.

### Ethical Humanism and Humane Moralism

The orthodox response of "ethical humanism" (as this philosophical perspective may be styled) to the suggestion that nonhuman animals should be accorded moral standing is that such animals are not worthy of this high perquisite. Only human beings are rational, or capable of having interests, or possess *self*-awareness, or have linguistic abilities, or can represent the future, it is variously argued.[14] These essential attributes taken singly or in various combinations make people somehow exclusively deserving of moral consideration. The so-called "lower animals," it is insisted, lack the crucial qualification for ethical considerability and so may be treated (albeit humanely, according to some, so as not to brutalize man) as things or means, not as persons or as ends.[15]

The theoreticians of the animal liberation movement ("humane moralists" as they may be called) typically reply as follows.[16] Not all human beings qualify as worthy of moral regard, according to the various criteria specified. Therefore, by parity of reasoning, human persons who do not so qualify as moral patients may be treated, as animals often are, as mere things or means (for example, used in vivisection experiments, disposed of if their existence is inconvenient, eaten, hunted, and so forth). But the ethical humanists would be morally outraged if irrational and inarticulate infants, for example, were used in painful or lethal medical experiments, or if severely retarded people were hunted for pleasure. Thus, the double-dealing, the hypocrisy, of ethical humanism appears to be exposed.[17] Ethical humanism, though claiming to discriminate between worthy and unworthy ethical patients on the basis of objective criteria impartially applied, turns out after all, it seems, to be *speciesism,* a philosophically indefensible prejudice (analogous to racial prejudice) against animals. The tails side of this argument is that some animals, usually the "higher" lower animals (cetaceans, other primates and so forth), as ethological studies seem to indicate, may meet the criteria specified for moral worth, although the ethical humanists, even so, are not prepared to grant them full dignity and the rights of persons. In short, the ethical humanists' various criteria for moral standing do not include all or only human beings, humane moralists argue, although in practice ethical humanism wishes to make the class of morally considerable beings coextensive with the class of human beings.

The humane moralists, for their part, insist upon *sentience* as the only relevant capacity a being need possess to enjoy full moral standing. If animals, they argue, are conscious entities who, though deprived of reason, speech, forethought or even *self*-awareness (however that may be judged), are capable of suffering, then their suffering should be as much a matter of ethical concern as that of our fellow human beings, or strictly speaking, as our very own. What, after all, has rationality or any of the other allegedly uniquely human capacities to do with ethical standing? Why, in other words, should beings who reason or use speech (and so forth) qualify for moral status, and those who do not fail to qualify?[18] Isn't this just like saying that only persons with white skin should be free, or that only persons who beget and not those who bear should own property? The criterion seems utterly unrelated to the benefit for which it selects. On the other hand, the capacity to suffer is, it seems, a more relevant criterion for moral standing because—as Bentham and Mill, notable among modern philosophers, and Epicurus, among the ancients, aver—pain is evil, and its opposite, pleasure and freedom from pain, good. As moral agents (and this seems axiomatic), we have a duty to behave in such a way that the effect of our actions is to promote and procure good, so far as possible, and to reduce and minimize evil. That would amount to an obligation to produce pleasure and reduce pain. Now pain is pain wherever and by whomever it is suffered. As a moral agent, I should not consider my pleasure and pain to be of greater consequence in determining a course of action than that of other persons. Thus, by the same token, if animals suffer pain—and among philosophers only strict Cartesians would deny that they do—then we are morally obliged to consider their suffering as much an evil to be minimized by conscientious moral agents as human suffering.[19] Certainly actions of ours which contribute to the suffering of animals, such as hunting them, butchering and eating them, and experimenting on them, are on these assumptions morally reprehensible. Hence, a person who regards himself or herself as not aiming in life to live most selfishly, conveniently, or profitably, but rightly and in accord with practical principle, if convinced by these arguments, should, among other things, cease to eat the flesh of animals, to hunt them, to wear fur and leather clothing and bone ornaments and other articles made from the bodies of animals, to eat eggs and drink milk, if the animal producers of these commodities are retained under inhumane circumstances, and to patronize zoos (as sources of psychological if not physical torment of animals). On the other hand, since certain very simple animals are almost certainly insensible to pleasure and pain, they may and indeed should be treated as morally inconsequential. Nor is there any *moral* reason why trees should be respected or rivers or mountains or anything which is, though living or tributary to life processes, unconscious. The humane moralists, like the moral humanists, draw a firm distinction between those beings worthy of moral consideration and those not. They simply insist upon a different but quite definite cut-off point on the spectrum of natural entities, and accompany their criterion with arguments to show that it is more ethically defensible (granting certain assumptions) and more consistently applicable than that of the moral humanists.[20]

## The First Principle of the Land Ethic

The fundamental principle of humane moralism, as we see, is Benthamic. Good is equivalent to pleasure and, more pertinently, evil is equivalent to pain. The presently booming controversy between moral humanists and humane moralists appears, when all the learned dust has settled, to be esentially internecine; at least, the lines of battle are drawn along familiar watersheds of the conceptual terrain.[21] A classical ethical theory, Bentham's, has been refitted and pressed into service to meet relatively new and unprecedented ethically relevant situations—the problems raised especially by factory farming and ever more exotic and frequently ill-conceived scientific research employing animal subjects. Then, those with Thomist, Kantian, Lockean, Moorean, and so forth ethical affiliations have heard the bugle and have risen to arms. It is no wonder that so many academic philosophers have been drawn into the fray. The issues have an apparent newness about them; moreover, they are socially and politically avant-garde. But there is no serious challenge to cherished first principles.[22] Hence, without having to undertake any creative ethical reflection or exploration, or any reexamination of historical ethical theory, a fresh debate has been stirred up. The familiar historical positions have simply been re-trenched, applied, and exercised.

But what about the third (and certainly minority) party to the animal liberation debate? What sort of reasonable and coherent moral theory would at once urge that animals (and plants and soils and waters) be included in the same class with people as beings to whom ethical consideration is owed and yet not object to some of them being slaughtered (whether painlessly or not) and eaten, others hunted, trapped, and in various other ways seemingly cruelly used? Aldo Leopold provides a concise statement of what might be called the categorical imperative or principal precept of the land ethic: "A thing is right when it tends to preserve the integrity, stability, and beauty of the biotic community. It is wrong when it tends otherwise."[23] What is especially noteworthy, and that to which attention should be directed in this proposition, is the idea that the good of the biotic *community* is the ultimate measure of the moral value, the rightness or wrongness, of actions. Thus, to hunt and kill a white-tailed deer in certain districts may not only be ethically permissible, it might actually be a moral requirement, necessary to protect the local environment, taken as a whole, from the disintegrating effects of a cervid population explosion. On the other hand, rare and endangered animals like the lynx should be especially nurtured and preserved. The lynx, cougar, and other wild feline predators, from the neo-Benthamite perspective (if consistently and evenhandedly applied) should be regarded as merciless, wanton, and incorrigible murderers of their fellow creatures, who not only kill, it should be added, but cruelly toy with their victims, thus increasing the measure of pain in the world. From the perspective of the land ethic, predators generally should be nurtured and preserved as critically important members of the biotic communities to which they are native. Certain plants similarly, may be overwhelmingly important to the stability, integrity, and beauty of biotic communities, while some animals, such as domestic sheep (allowed perhaps by egalitarian and humane herdspersons to graze freely and to reproduce themselves without being harvested for lamb and mutton) could be a pestilential threat to the natural floral community of a given locale. Thus, the land ethic is logically coherent in demanding at once that moral consider-ation be given to plants as well as to animals and yet in permitting animals to be killed, trees felled, and so on. In every case the effect upon ecological systems is the decisive factor in the determination of the ethical quality of actions. Well-meaning actions from the point of view of neo-Benthamite ethics may be regarded as morally wanton from the point of view of land ethics, and vice versa. An example of the former, in addition to those already mentioned, is turning dairy cows out to pasture in a woodlot situated on a steep slope overlooking a trout stream (for the sake of the shady comfort and dietary variety of the cattle) with ruinous impact upon the floral and wildlife community native to the woods, the fish and benthic orgamisms of the stream, and the microbic life and the physiochemical structure of the soil itself. An example of the latter is trapping or otherwise removing beaver (to all appearances very sensitive and intelligent animals) and their dams to eliminate siltation in an otherwise free-flowing and clear-running stream (for the sake of the complex community of insects, native fish, heron, osprey, and other avian predators of aquatic life which on the anthropocentric scale of consciousness are "lower" life forms than beaver).

### The Land Ethic and the Ecological Point of View

The philosophical context of the land ethic and its conceptual foundation is clearly the body of empirical experience and theory which is summed up in the term *ecology*. The specter of the naturalistic fallacy hovers around any claim to discover values in facts (and/or, probably, in scientific theories as well), but notwithstanding the naturalistic fallacy (or the fact/value lacuna), which is essentially a logical problem for formal ethics, there appears very often to be at least a strongly compelling psychological connection between the way the world is imagined or conceived and what state of things is held to be good or bad, what ways of behaving are right or wrong, and what responsibilities and obligations we, as moral agents, acknowledge.[24]

Since ecology focuses upon the relationships between and among things, it inclines its students toward a more holistic vision of the world. Before the rather recent emergence of ecology as a science the landscape appeared to be, one might say, a collection of objects, some of them alive, some conscious, but all the same, an aggregate, a plurality of separate individuals. With this atomistic representation of things it is no wonder that moral issues might be understood as competing and mutually contradictory clashes of the "rights" of separate individuals, each separately pursuing its "interests." Ecology has made it possible to apprehend the same landscape as an articulate unity (without the least hint of mysticism or ineffability). Ordinary organic bodies have articulated and discernible parts (limbs, various organs, myriad cells); yet, because of the character of the network of relations among those parts, they form in a perfectly familiar sense a second-order whole. Ecology makes it possible to see land, similarly, as a unified system of integrally related parts, as, so to speak, a third-order organic whole.[25]

Another analogy that has helped ecologists to convey the particular holism which their science brings to reflective attention is that land is integrated as a human community is integrated. The various parts of the "biotic community" (individual animals and plants) depend upon one another *economically* so that the system as such acquires distinct characteristics of its own. Just as it is possible to characterize and define collectively peasant societies, agrarian communities, industrial complexes, capitalist, communist, and socialist economic systems, and so on, ecology characterizes and defines various biomes as desert, savanna, wetland, tundra, woodland, and other communities, each with its particular "professions," or "niches."

Now we may think that among the duties we as moral agents have toward ourselves is the duty of self-preservation, which may be interpreted as a duty to maintain our own organic integrity. It is not uncommon in historical moral theory, further, to find that in addition to those peculiar responsibilities we have in relation both to ourselves and to other persons severally, we also have a duty to behave in ways that do not harm the fabric of society per se. The land ethic, in similar fashion, calls our attention to the recently discovered integrity—in other words, the unity—of the biota and posits duties binding upon moral agents in relation to that whole. Whatever the strictly formal logical connections between the concept of a social community and moral responsibility, there appears to be a strong psychological bond between that idea and conscience. Hence, the representation of the natural environment as, in Leopold's terms, "one humming community" (or, less consistently in his discussion, a third-order organic being) brings into play, whether rationally or not, those stirrings of conscience which we feel in relation to delicately complex, functioning social and organic systems.[26]

The neo-Benthamite humane moralists have, to be sure, digested one of the metaphysical implications of modern biology. They insist that human beings must be understood continuously with the rest of organic nature. People are (and are only) animals, and much of the rhetorical energy of the animal liberation movement is spent in fighting a rear guard action for this aspect of Darwinism against those philosophers who still cling to the dream of a special metaphysical status for people in the order of "creation." To this extent the animal liberation movement is biologically enlightened and argues from the taxonomical and evolutionary continuity of man and beast to moral standing for some nonhuman animals. Indeed, pain, in their view the very substance of evil, is something that is conspicuously common to people and other sensitive animals, something that we as people experience not in virtue of our metasimian cerebral capabilities, but because of our participation in a more generally animal, limbic-based consciousness. *If* it is pain and suffering that is the ultimate evil besetting human life, and this not in virtue of our humanity but in virtue of our animality, then it seems only fair to promote freedom from pain for those animals who share with us in this mode of experience and to grant them rights similar to ours as a means to this end.

Recent ethological studies of other primates, cetaceans, and so on, are not infrequently cited to drive the point home, but the biological information of the animal liberation movement seems to extend no further than this—the continuity of human with other animal life forms. The more recent ecological perspective especially seems to be ignored by humane moralists. The holistic outlook of ecology and the associated value premium conferred upon the biotic community, its beauty, integrity, and stability may simply not have penetrated the thinking of the animal liberationists, or it could be that to include it would involve an intolerable contradiction with the Benthamite foundations of their ethical theory. Bentham's view of the "interests of the community" was bluntly reductive. With his characteristic bluster, Bentham wrote, "The community is a fictitious *body* composed of the individual persons who are considered as constituting as it were its *members*. The interest of the community then is what?—the sum of the interests of the several members who compose it."[27] Betham's very simile—the community is like a body composed of members—gives the lie to his reduction of its interests to the sum of its parts taken severally. The interests of a person are not those of his or her cells summed up and averaged out. Our organic health and well-being, for example, requires vigorous exercise and metabolic stimulation which cause stress and often pain to various parts of the body and a more rapid turnover in the life cycle of our individual cells. For the sake of the person taken as whole, some parts may be, as it were, unfairly sacrificed. On the level of social organization, the interests of society may not always coincide with the sum of the interests of its parts. Discipline, sacrifice, and individual restraint are often necessary in the social sphere to maintain social integrity as within the bodily organism. A society, indeed, is particularly vulnerable to disintegration when its members become preoccupied totally with their own particular interests, and ignore those distinct and independent interests of the community as a whole. One example, unfortunately, our own society, is altogether too close at hand to be examined with strict academic detachment. The United States seems to pursue uncritically a social policy of reductive utilitarianism, aimed at promoting the happiness of all its members severally. Each special interest accordingly clamors more loudly to be satisfied while the community as a whole becomes noticeably more and more infirm economically, environmentally, and politically.

The humane moralists, whether or not they are consciously and deliberately following Bentham on this particular, nevertheless, in point of fact, are committed to the welfare of certain kinds of animals distributively or reductively in applying their moral concern for nonhuman beings.[28] They lament the treatment of animals, most frequently farm and laboratory animals, and plead the special interests of these beings. We might ask, from the perspective of the land ethic, what the effect upon the natural environment taken as whole would be if domestic animals were actually liberated? There is, almost certainly, very little real danger that this might actually happen, but it would be instructive to speculate on the ecological consequences.

## Ethical Holism

Before we take up this question, however, some points of interest remain to be considered on the matter of a holistic versus a reductive environmental ethic. To pit the one against the other as I have done without further qualification would be mistaken. A society is constituted by its members, an organic body by its cells, and the ecosystem by the plants, animals, minerals, fluids, and gases which compose it. One cannot affect a system as a whole without affecting at least some of its components. An environmental ethic which takes as its *summum bonum* the integrity, stability, and beauty of the biotic community is not conferring moral standing on something *else* besides plants, animals, soils, and waters. Rather, the former, the good of the community as a whole, serves as a standard for the assessment of the relative value and relative ordering of its constitutive parts and therefore provides a means of adjudicating the often mutually contradictory demands of the parts considered separately for *equal* consideration. If diversity does indeed contribute to stability, then specimens of rare and endangered species, for example, have a prima facie claim to preferential consideration from the perspective of the land ethic. Animals of those species, which, like the honey bee, function in ways critically important to the economy of nature, moreover, would be granted a greater claim to moral attention than psychologically more complex and sensitive ones, say, rabbits and voles, which seem to be plentiful, globally distributed, reproductively efficient, and only routinely integrated into the natural economy. Animals and plants, mountains, rivers, seas, the atmosphere are the immediate practical beneficiaries of the land ethic. The well-being of the biotic community, the biosphere as a whole, cannot be logically separated from their survival and welfare.

Some suspicion may arise at this point that the land ethic is ultimately grounded in human interests, not in those of nonhuman natural entities. Just as we might prefer a sound and attractive house to one in the opposite condition, so the "goodness" of a whole, stable, and beautiful environment seems rather to be of the instrumental, not the intrinsic, variety. The question of ultimate value is a very sticky one for environmental as well as for all ethics and cannot be fully addressed here. It is my view that there can be no value apart from an evaluator, that all value is as it were in the eye of the beholder. The value that is attributed to the ecosystem, therefore, is humanly dependent or (allowing that other living things may take a certain delight in the well-being of the whole of things, or that the gods may) at least dependent upon some variety of morally and aesthetically sensitive consciousness. Granting this, however, there is a further, very crucial distinction to be drawn. It is possible that while things may only have value because we (or someone) values them, they may nonetheless be valued for themselves as well as for the contribution they might make to the realization of our (or someone's) interests. Children are valued for themselves by most parents. Money, on the other hand, has only an instrumental or indirect value. Which sort of value has the health of the biotic community and its members severally for Leopold and the land ethic? It is especially difficult to separate these two general sorts of value, the one of moral significance, the other merely selfish, when something that may be valued in both ways at once is the subject of consideration. Are pets, for example, well-treated, like children, for the sake of themselves, or, like mechanical appliances, because of the sort of services they provide their owners? Is a healthy biotic community something we value because we are so utterly and (to the biologically well-informed) so obviously dependent upon it not only for our happiness but for our very survival, or may we also perceive it disinterestedly as having an independent worth? Leopold insists upon a noninstrumental value for the biotic community and *mutatis mutandis* for its constituents. According to Leopold, collective enlightened self-interest on the part of human beings does not go far enough; the land ethic in his opinion (and no doubt this reflects his own moral intuitions) requires "love, respect, and admiration for land, and a high regard for its value." The land ethic, in Leopold's view, creates "obligations over and above self-interest." And, "obligations have no meaning without conscience, and the problem we face is the extension of social conscience from people to land."[29] If, in other words, any genuine ethic is possible, if it is possible to value *people* for the sake of themselves, then it is equally possible to value *land* in the same way.

Some indication of the genuinely biocentric value orientation of ethical environmentalism is indicated in what otherwise might appear to be gratuitous misanthropy. The biospheric perspective does not exempt *Homo sapiens* from moral evaluation in relation to the well-being of the community of nature taken as a whole. The preciousness of individual deer, as of any other specimen, is inversely proportional to the population of the species. Environmentalists, however reluctantly and painfully, do not omit to apply the same logic to their own kind. As omnivores, the population of human beings should, perhaps, be roughly twice that of bears, allowing for differences of size. A global population of more than four billion persons and showing no signs of an orderly decline presents an alarming prospect to humanists, but it is at present a global disaster (the more per capita prosperity, indeed, the more disastrous it appears) for the biotic community. If the land ethic were only a means of managing nature for the sake of man, misleadingly phrased in moral terminology, then man would be considered as having an ultimate value essentially different from that of his "resources." The extent of misanthropy in modern environmentalism thus may be taken as a measure of the degree to which it is biocentric. Edward Abbey in his enormously popular *Desert Solitaire* bluntly states that he would sooner shoot a man than a snake.[30] Abbey may not be simply depraved; this is perhaps only his way of dramatically making the point that the human population has become so disproportionate from the biological point of view that if one had to choose between a specimen of Homo sapiens and a specimen of a rare even if unattractive species, the choice would be moot. Among academicians, Garrett Hardin, a human ecologist by discipline who has written extensively on ethics, environmental and otherwise, has shocked philosophers schooled in the preciousness of human life with his "lifeboat" and "survival" ethics and his "wilderness economics." In context of the latter, Hardin recommends limiting access to wilderness by criteria of hardiness and woodcraft and would permit no emergency roads or airborne rescue vehicles to violate the pristine purity of wilderness areas. If a wilderness adventurer should have a serious accident, Hardin recommends that he or she get out on his or her own or die in the attempt. Danger, from the strictly human-centered, psychological perspective, is part of the wilderness experience, Hardin argues, but in all probability his more important concern is to protect from mechanization the remnants of wild country that remain even if the price paid is the incidental loss of human life, which, from the perspective once more of the biologist, is a commodity altogether too common in relation to wildlife and to wild landscapes.[31] Hardin's recommendation of harsh policies in relation to desperate, starving nations is based strictly upon a utilitarian calculus, but reading between the lines, one can also detect the biologist's chagrin concerning the ecological dislocations which a human population explosion have already created and which if permitted to continue unchecked could permanently impoverish (if not altogether extinguish) an already stressed and overburdened economy of nature.[32]

Finally, it may be wondered if anything ought properly be denominated an "ethic" which on the basis of an impersonal, not to say abstract, good, "the integrity, stability, and beauty of the biotic community," permits and even requires *preferential* consideration. A "decision procedure," to give it for the moment a neutral rubric, which lavishes loving and expensive care on whooping cranes and (from the Benthamite point of view, villainous) timber wolves while simultaneously calculating the correct quotas for "harvesting" mallards and ruffed grouse should hardly be dignified, it might be argued, by the term *ethic*. Modern systems of ethics have, it must be admitted, considered the principle of the equality of persons to be inviolable. This is true, for example, of both major shools of modern ethics, the utilitarian school going back to Bentham and Mill, and the deontological, originating with Kant. The land ethic manifestly does not accord equal moral worth to each and every member of the biotic community; the moral worth of individuals (including, take note, human individuals) is relative, to be assessed in accordance with the particular relation of each to the collective entity which Leopold called "land."

There is, however, a classical Western ethic, with the best philosophical credentials, which assumes a similar holistic posture (with respect to the social moral sphere). I have in mind Plato's moral and social philosophy. Indeed, two of the same analogies figuring in the conceptual foundations of the Leopold land ethic appear in Plato's value theory.[33] From the ecological perspective, according to Leopold as I have pointed out, land is like an organic body or like a human society. According to Plato, body, soul, and society have similar structures and corresponding virtues.[34] The goodness of each is a function of its structure or organization and the relative value of the parts or constituents of each is calculated according to the contribution made to the integrity, stability, and beauty of each whole.[35] In the *Republic*, Plato, in the very name of virtue and justice, is notorious for, among other things, requiring infanticide for a child whose only offense was being born without the sanction of the state, making presents to the enemy of guardians who allow themselves to be captured alive in combat, and radically restricting the practice of medicine to the dressing of wounds and the curing of seasonal maladies on the principle that the infirm and chronically ill not only lead miserable lives but contribute nothing to the good of the polity.[36] Plato, indeed, seems to regard individual human life and certainly human pain and suffering with complete indifference. On the other hand, he shrinks from nothing so long as it seems to him to be in the interest of the community. Among the apparently inhuman recommendations that he makes to better the community are a program of eugenics involving a phony lottery (so that those whose natural desires are frustrated, while breeding proceeds from the best stock as in a kennel or stable, will blame chance, not the design of the rulers), the destruction of the pair bond and nuclear family (in the interests of greater military and bureaucratic efficiency and group solidarity), and the utter abolition of private property.[37]

When challenged with the complaint that he is ignoring individual human happiness (and the happiness of those belonging to the most privileged class at that), he replies that it is the well-being of the community as a whole, not that of any person or special class at which his legislation aims.[38] This principle is readily accepted, first of all, in our attitude toward the body, he reminds us—the separate interests of the parts of which we acknowledge to be subordinate to the health and well-being of the whole—and secondly, assuming that we accept his faculty psychology, in our attitude toward the soul, whose multitude of desires must be disciplined, restrained, and, in the case of some, altogether repressed in the interest of personal virtue and a well-ordered and morally responsible life.

Given these formal similarities to Plato's moral philosophy, we may conclude that the land ethic—with its holistic good and its assignment of differential values to the several parts of the environment irrespective of their intelligence, sensibility, degree of complexity, or any other characteristic discernible in the parts considered separately —is somewhat foreign to modern systems of ethical philosophy, but perfectly familiar in the broader context of classical Western ethical philosophy. If, therefore, Plato's system of public and private justice is properly an "ethical" system, then so is the land ethic in relation to environmental virtue and excellence.[39]

## Reappraising Domestication

Among the last philosophical remarks penned by Aldo Leopold before his untimely death in 1948 is the following: "Perhaps such a shift of values [as implied by the attempt to weld together the concepts of ethics and ecology] can be achieved by reappraising things unnatural, tame, and confined in terms of things natural, wild, and free."[40] John

Muir, in a similar spirit of reappraisal, had noted earlier the difference between the wild mountain sheep of the Sierra and the ubiquitous domestic variety. The latter, which Muir described as "hooved locusts," were only, in his estimation, "half alive" in comparison with their natural and autonomous counterparts.[41] One of the more distressing aspects of the animal liberation movement is the failure of almost all its exponents to draw a sharp distinction between the very different plights (and rights) of wild and domestic animals.[42] But this distinction lies at the very center of the land ethic. Domestic animals are creations of man. They are living artifacts, but artifacts nevertheless, and they constitute yet another mode of extension of the works of man into the ecosystem. From the perspective of the land ethic a herd of cattle, sheep, or pigs is as much or more a ruinous blight on the landscape as a fleet of four-wheel-drive off-road vehicles. There is thus something profoundly incoherent (and insensitive as well) in the complaint of some animal liberationists that the "natural behavior" of chickens and bobby calves is cruelly frustrated on factory farms. It would make almost as much sense to speak of the natural behavior of tables and chairs.

Here a serious disanalogy (which no one to my knowledge has yet pointed out) becomes clearly evident between the liberation of blacks from slavery (and more recently, from civil inequality) and the liberation of animals from a similar sort of subordination and servitude. Black slaves remained, as it were, metaphysically autonomous: they were by nature if not by convention free beings quite capable of living on their own. They could not be enslaved for more than a historial interlude; the strength of the force of their freedom was too great. They could, in other words, be retained only by a continuous counterforce, and only temporarily. This is equally true of caged wild animals. African cheetas in American and European zoos are captive, not indentured, beings. But this is not true of cows, pigs, sheep, and chickens. They have been bred to docility, tractability, stupidity, and dependency. It is literally meaningless to suggest that they be liberated. It is, to speak in hyperbole, a logical impossibility.

Certainly it is a practical impossibility. Imagine what would happen if the people of the world became morally persuaded that domestic animals were to be regarded as oppressed and enslaved persons and accordingly set free. In one scenario we might imagine that like former American black slaves they would receive the equivalent of forty acres and a mule and be turned out to survive on their own. Feral cattle and sheep would hang around farm outbuildings waiting forlornly to be sheltered and fed, or would graze aimlessly through their abandoned and deteriorating pastures. Most would starve or freeze as soon as winter settled in. Reproduction, which had been assisted over many countless generations by their former owners, might be altogether impossible in the feral state for some varieties, and the care of infants would be an art not so much lost as never acquired. And so in a very short time, after much suffering and agony, these species would become abruptly extinct. Or, in another scenario beginning with the same simple emancipation from human association, survivors of the first massive die-off of untended livestock might begin to recover some of their remote wild ancestral genetic traits and become smaller, leaner, heartier, and smarter versions of their former selves. An actual contemporary example is afforded by the feral mustangs ranging over parts of the American West. In time such animals as these would become (just as the mustangs are now) competitors both with their former human masters and (with perhaps more tragic consequences) indigenous wildlife for food and living space.

Foreseeing these and other untoward consequences of immediate and unplanned liberation of livestock, a human population grown morally more perfect than at present might decide that they had a duty, accumulated over thousands of years, to continue to house and feed as before their former animal slaves (whom they had rendered genetically unfit to care for themselves), but not to butcher them or make other ill use of them, including frustrating their "natural" behavior, their right to copulate freely, reproduce, and enjoy the delights of being parents. People, no longer having meat to eat, would require more vegetables, cereals, and other plant foods, but the institutionalized animal incompetents would still consume all the hay and grains (and more since they would no longer be slaughtered) than they did formerly. This would require clearing more land and bringing it into agricultural production with further loss of wildlife habitat and ecological destruction. Another possible scenario might be a decision on the part of people not literally to liberate domestic animals but simply to cease to breed and raise them. When the last livestock have been killed and eaten (or permitted to die "natural" deaths), people would become vegetarians and domestic livestock species would thus be rendered deliberately extinct (just as they had been deliberately created). But there is surely some irony in an outcome in which the beneficiaries of a humane extension of conscience are destroyed in the process of being saved.[43]

The land ethic, it should be emphasized, as Leopold has sketched it, provides for the *rights* of nonhuman natural beings to a share in the life processes of the biotic community. The conceptual foundation of such rights, however, is less conventional than natural, based as one might say, upon evolutionary and ecological entitlement. Wild animals and native plants have a particular place in nature, according to the land ethic, which domestic animals (because they are products of human art and represent an extended presence of human beings in the natural world) do not have. The land ethic, in sum, is as much opposed, though on different grounds, to commercial traffic in wildlife, zoos, the slaughter of whales and other marine mammals, and so forth, as is the humane ethic. Concern for animal (and plant) rights and well-being is as fundamental to the land ethic as to the humane ethic, but the difference between naturally evolved and humanly bred species is an essential consideration for the one, though not for the other.

The "shift of values" which results from our "reappraising things unnatural, tame, and confined in terms of things natural, wild, and free" is especially dramatic when we reflect upon the definitions of *good* and *evil* espoused by Bentham and Mill and uncritically accepted by their contemporary followers. Pain and pleasure seem to have nothing at all to do with good and evil if our appraisal is taken from the vantage point of ecological biology. Pain in particular is primarily information. In animals, it informs the central nervous system of stress, irritation, or trauma in outlying regions of the organism. A certain level of pain under optimal organic circumstances is indeed desirable as an indicator of exertion—of the degree of exertion needed to maintain fitness, to stay in shape, and of a level of exertion beyond which it would be dangerous to go. An arctic wolf in pursuit of a caribou may experience pain in her feet or chest because of the rigors of the chase. There is nothing bad or wrong in that. Or, consider a case of injury. Suppose that a person in the course of a wilderness excursion sprains an ankle. Pain informs him or her of the injury and by its intensity the amount of further stress the ankle may endure in the course of getting to safety. Would it be better if pain were not experienced upon injury or, taking advantage of recent technology, anaesthetized? Pleasure appears to be, for the most part (unfortunately it is not always so) a reward accompanying those activities which contribute to organic maintenance, such as the pleasures associated with eating, drinking, grooming, and so on, or those which contribute to social solidarity like the pleasures of dancing, conversation, teasing, and so forth, or those which contribute to the continuation of the species, such as the pleasures of sexual activity and of being parents. The doctrine that life is the happier the freer it is from pain and that the happiest life conceivable is one in which there is continuous pleasure uninterrupted by pain is biologically preposterous. A living mammal which experienced no pain would be one which had a lethal dysfunction of the nervous system. The idea that pain is evil and ought to be minimized or eliminated is as primitive a notion as that of a tyrant who puts to death messengers bearing bad news on the supposition that thus his well-being and security is improved.[44]

More seriously still, the value commitments of the humane movement seem at bottom to betray a world-denying or rather a life-loathing philosophy. The natural world as actually constituted is one in which one being lives at the expense of others.[45] Each organism, in Darwin's metaphor, struggles to maintain it own organic integrity. The more complex animals seem to experience (judging from our own case, and reasoning from analogy) appropriate and adaptive psychological accompaniments to organic existence. There is a palpable passion for self-preservation. There are desire, pleasure in the satisfaction of desires, acute agony attending injury, frustration, and chronic dread of death. But these experiences are the psychological substance of living. To live *is* to be anxious about life, to feel pain and pleasure in a fitting mixture, and sooner or later to die. That is the way the system works. If nature as a whole is good, then pain and death are also good. Environmental ethics in general require people to play fair in the natural system. The neo-Benthamites have in a sense taken the uncourageous approach. People have attempted to exempt themselves from the life/death reciprocities of natural processes and from ecological limitations in the name of a prophylactic ethic of maximizing rewards (pleasure) and minimizing unwelcome information (pain). To be fair, the humane moralists seem to suggest that we should attempt to project the same values into the nonhuman animal world and to widen the charmed circle—no matter that it would be biologically unrealistic to do so or biologically ruinous if, per impossible, such an environmental ethic were implemented.

There is another approach. Rather than imposing our alienation from nature and natural processes and cycles of life on other animals, we human beings could reaffirm our participation in nature by accepting life as it is given without a sugar coating. Instead of imposing artificial legalities, rights, and so on on nature, we might take the opposite course and accept and affirm natural biological laws, principles, and limitations in the human personal and social spheres. Such appears to have been the posture toward life of tribal peoples in the past. The chase was relished with its dangers, rigors, and hardships as well as its rewards; animal flesh was respectfully consumed; a tolerance for pain was cultivated; virtue and magnanimity were prized; lithic, floral, and faunal spirits were worshipped; population was routinely optimized by sexual continency, abortion, infanticide, and stylized warfare; and other life forms, although certainly appropriated, were respected as fellow players in a magnificent and awesome, if not altogether idyllic, drama of life. It is impossible today to return to the symbiotic relationship of Stone Age man to the natural environment, but the ethos of this by far the longest era of human existence could be abstracted and integrated with a future human culture seeking a viable and mutually beneficial relationship with nature. Personal, social, and environmental health would, accordingly, receive a premium value rather than comfort, self-indulgent pleasure, and anaesthetic insulation from pain. Sickness would be regarded as a worse evil than death. The pursuit of health or wellness at the personal, social, and environmental levels would require self-discipline in the form of simple diet, vigorous exercise, conservation, and social responsibility.

Leopold's prescription for the realization and implementation of the land ethic—the reappraisal of things unnatural, tame, and confined in terms of things natural, wild, and free—does not stop, in other words, with a reappraisal of nonhuman domestic animals in terms of their wild (or willed) counterparts; the human ones should be similarly reappraised. This means, among other things, the reappraisal of the comparatively recent values and concerns of "civilized" *Homo sapiens* in terms of those of our "savage" ancestors.[46] Civilization has insulated and alienated us from the rigors and challenges of the natural environment. The hidden agenda of the humane ethic is the imposition of the anti-natural prophylactic ethos of comfort and soft pleasure on an even wider scale. The land ethic, on the other hand, requires a shrinkage, if at all possible, of the domestic sphere; it rejoices in a recrudescence of wilderness and a renaissance of tribal cultural experience.

The converse of those goods and evils, axiomatic to the humane ethic, may be illustrated and focused by the consideration of a single issue raised by the humane morality: a vegetarian diet. Savage people seem to have had, if the attitudes and values of surviving tribal cultures are representative, something like an intuitive grasp of ecological relationships and certainly a morally charged appreciation of eating. There is nothing more intimate than eating, more symbolic of the connectedness of life, and more mysterious. What we eat and how we eat is by no means an insignificant ethical concern.

From the ecological point of view, for human beings universally to become vegetarians is tantamount to a shift of trophic niche from omnivore with carnivorous preferences to herbivore. The shift is a downward one on the trophic pyramid, which in effect shortens those food chains terminating with man. It represents an increase in the efficiency of the conversion of solar energy from plant to human biomass, and thus, by bypassing animal intermediates, increases available food resources for human beings. The human population would probably, as past trends overwhelmingly suggest, expand in accordance with the potential thus afforded. The net result would be fewer nonhuman beings and more human beings, who, of course, have requirements of life far more elaborate than even those of domestic animals, requirements which would tax other "natural resources" (trees for shelter, minerals mined at the expense of topsoil and its vegetation, and so on) more than under present circumstances. A vegetarian human population is therefore *probably* ecologically cata-strophic.

Meat eating as implied by the foregoing remarks may be more *ecologically* responsible than a wholly vegetable diet. Meat, however, purchased at the supermarket, externally packaged and internally laced with petrochemicals, fattened in feed lots, slaughtered imperson-ally, and, in general, mechanically processed from artificial insemina-tion to microwave roaster, is an affront not only to physical metabolism and bodily health but to conscience as well. From the perspective of the land ethic, the immoral aspect of the factory farm has to do far less with the suffering and killing of nonhuman animals than with the monstrous transformation of living things from an organic to a mechanical mode of being. Animals, beginning with the Neolithic Revolution, have been debased through selective breeding, but they have nevertheless remained animals. With the Industrial Revolution an even more pro-found and terrifying transformation has overwhelmed them. They have become, in Ruth Harrison's most apt description, "animal machines." The very presence of animals, so emblematic of delicate, complex organic tissue, surrounded by machines, connected to machines, penetrated by machines in research laboratories or crowded together in space-age "production facilities" is surely the more real and visceral source of our outrage at vivisection and factory farming than the contemplation of the quantity of pain that these unfortunate beings experience. I wish to denounce as loudly as the neo-Benthamites this ghastly abuse of animal life, but also to stress that the pain and suffering of research and agribusiness animals is not greater than that endured by free-living wildlife as a consequence of predation, disease, starvation, and cold—indicating that there is something immoral about vivisection and factory farming which is not an ingredient in the natural lives and deaths of wild beings. That immoral something is the transmogrification of organic to mechanical processes.

Ethical vegetarianism to all appearances insists upon the human consumption of plants (in a paradoxical moral gesture toward those animals whose very existence is dependent upon human carnivorous-ness), even when the tomatoes are grown hydroponically, the lettuce generously coated with chlorinated hydrocarbons, the potatoes pumped up with chemical fertilizers, and the cereals stored with the help of chemical preservatives. The land ethic takes as much exception to the transmogrification of plants by mechanico-chemical means as to that of animals. The important thing, I would think, is not to eat vegetables as opposed to animal flesh, but to resist factory farming in all its manifestations, including especially its liberal application of pesticides, herbicides, and chemical fertilizers to maximize the production of vegetable crops.

The land ethic, with its ecological perspective, helps us to recognize and affirm the organic integrity of self and the untenability of a firm distinction between self and environment. On the ethical question of what to eat, it answers, not vegetables instead of animals, but organically as opposed to mechanico-chemically produced food. Purists like Leopold prefer, in his expression, to get their "meat from God," that is, to hunt and consume wildlife and to gather wild plant foods, and thus to live within the parameters of the aboriginal human ecological niche.[47] Second best is eating from one's own orchard, garden, henhouse, pigpen, and barnyard. Third best is buying or bartering organic foods from one's neighbors and friends.

## Conclusion

Philosophical controversy concerning animal liberation/rights has been most frequently represented as a polar dispute between traditional moral humanists and seemingly avant-garde humane moralists. Further, animal liberation has been assumed to be closely allied with environmental ethics, possibly because in Leopold's classical formulation moral standing and indeed rights (of some unspecified sort) are accorded nonhuman beings, among them animals. The purpose of this discussion has been to distinguish sharply environmental ethics from the animal liberation/rights movement both in theory and practical application and to suggest, thereupon, that there is an underrepresented, but very important, point of view respecting the problem of the moral status of nonhuman animals. The debate over animal liberation, in short, should be conceived as triangular, not polar, with land ethics or environmental ethics, the third and, in my judgment, the most creative, interesting, and practicable alternative. Indeed, from this third point of view moral humanism and humane moralism appear to have much more in common with one another than either have with environmental or land ethics. On reflection one might even be led to suspect that the noisy debate between these parties has served to drown out the much deeper challenge to "business-as-usual" ethical philosophy represented by Leopold and his exponents, and to keep ethical philosophy firmly anchored to familiar modern paradigms.

Moral humanism and humane moralism, to restate succinctly the most salient conclusions of this essay, are *atomistic* or distributive in their theory of moral value, while environmental ethics (again, at least, as set out in Leopold's outline) is *holistic* or collective. Modern ethical theory, in other words, has consistently located moral value in individuals and set out certain metaphysical reasons for including some individuals and excluding others. Humane moralism remains firmly within this modern convention and centers its attention on the competing criteria for moral standing and rights holding, while environmental ethics locates ultimate value in the biotic community and assigns differential moral value to the constitutive individuals relatively to that standard. This is perhaps the most fundamental theoretical difference between environmental ethics and the ethics of animal liberation.

Allied to this difference are many others. One of the more conspicuous is that in environmental ethics, plants are included within the parameters of the ethical theory as well as animals. Indeed, inanimate entities such as oceans and lakes, mountains, forest, and wetlands are assigned a greater value than individual animals and in a way quite different from systems which accord them moral considerability through a further multiplication of competing individual loci of value and holders of rights.

There are intractable practical differences between environmental ethics and the animal liberation movement. Very different moral obligations follow in respect, most importantly, to domestic animals, the principal beneficiaries of the humane ethic. Environmental ethics sets a very low priority on domestic animals as they very frequently contribute to the erosion of the integrity, stability, and beauty of the biotic communities into which they have been insinuated. On the other hand, animal liberation, if pursued at the practical as well as rhetorical level, would have ruinous consequences on plants, soils, and waters, consequences which could not be directly reckoned according to humane moral theory. As this last remark suggests, the animal liberation/animal rights movement is in the final analysis utterly unpracticable. An imagined society in which all animals capable of sensibility received equal consideration or held rights to equal consideration would be so ludicrous that it might be more appropriately and effectively treated in satire than in philosophical discussion. The land ethic, by contrast, even though its ethical purview is very much wider, is nevertheless eminently practicable, since, by reference to a single good, competing individual claims may be adjudicated and relative values and priorities assigned to the myriad components of the biotic community. This is not to suggest that the implementation of environmental ethics as social policy would be easy. Implementation of the land ethic would require discipline, sacrifice, retrenchment, and massive economic reform, tantamount to a virtual revolution in prevailing attitudes and lifestyles. Nevertheless, it provides a unified and coherent practical principle and thus a decision procedure at the practical level which a distributive or atomistic ethic may achieve only artificially and so imprecisely as to be practically indeterminate.

# 2

## Review of Tom Regan,
### *The Case for Animal Rights*

Over the last decade Tom Regan has contributed numerous essays to animal welfare ethics. Most of them were recently collected and published as *All That Dwell Therein* by the University of California Press.[1] *The Case for Animal Rights* (Berkeley: University of California Press, 1983) goes over the same ground, but represents Regan's cumulative, exhaustive, and systematized doctrine.

*The Case for Animal Rights* has been roundly reviewed in many other journals (including *The New York Review of Books*) and generally praised as a serious and significant work of moral philosophy.[2] Hence, I do not attempt here to cover the whole book or evaluate its overall philosophical merits except to say that it is a magnificent professional achievement by one of our ablest colleagues. It is coherently conceived and organized, finely textured, and thorough. If you love furry creatures and savor magisterial philosophical prose and detailed philosophical argument, then you'll like this book. I concentrate in this reivew on those particulars of the book especially interesting from an environmental point of view—the implications of Regan's theory of animal rights for environmental ethics and policy.

We don't have to speculate. Toward the end of his book Regan devotes a few pages to issues of environmental and ecological concern —endangered species, the theoretical foundations of environmental ethics, and hunting and trapping. Before turning to these issues, however, I need to summarize what I understand to be Regan's key concepts.

Not all animals have moral rights. Regan's moral base class is more restricted than Peter Singer's—his chief internecine rival in the field of animal welfare ethics—who doesn't regard *all* animals as equal either. Singer called for equal consideration of the divers interests of all *sentient* animals. According to Regan, however, only those animals who have "inherent value" have rights. And only those animals who meet the "subject-of-a-life criterion" have inherent value. To be a subject-of-a-life involves, among other things, being self-conscious and having the capacity to believe, desire, conceive the future, entertain goals, and act deliberately. The only animals Regan is sure meet all these qualifications are "mentally normal mammals of a year or more" (p. 78).

The case for animal rights turns out to be, thus, the case for mammal rights. Nevertheless, Regan insists on using the word *animal* throughout his discussion, even though what he really means, as he himself notes, is "mammal,"on the grounds of "economy of expression" (p. 78). This is puzzling since both words contain six letters. Why wasn't this book called *The Case for Mammal Rights?* Biologically literate readers with broader concerns (as well as philosophers concerned with precision, no less than economy, of expression) will immediately be put on the alert.

## II

Regan tells us "how [and how not] to worry about endangered species" (p. 359). His discussion of endangered species is astounding for two reasons—its candor and its naiveté. Regan to his credit does not hedge or attempt to disguise the fact that the "rights view" he recommends provides no rights (nor, for that matter, any discernible moral status whatever) for species per se: "Species are not individuals [contrary to David Hull and others who have thought deeply about his matter], and the rights view does not recognize the moral rights of species to anything, including survival" (p. 359).[3]

Perhaps some attempt could be made to adapt the rights view so that it might more positively address what has emerged as the primary and most desperate environmental concern of our time—biocide: abrupt, massive, wholesale anthropogenic species extinction. Perhaps it could by analogy with "minority rights," special rights which attach, not to minority groups per se, but which devolve upon individuals by virtue of their being members of minority groups. An individual member of a minority group, many people think, has a right to be hired, for example, in preference to an equally qualified member of a non-minority group. Similarly, perhaps a member of a rare and endangered species, like the black-footed ferret, might have a right, an individual right, to analogous preferential treatment in circumstances of direct conflict of interest with a member of an abundant species, like the domestic sheep. Regan expressly denies that his theory can be so amplified:

That an individual animal is among the last remaining members of a species confers no further right on that animal, and its rights not to be harmed must be weighed equitably with the rights of any others who have this right. If, in a prevention situation, we had to choose between saving the last two members of an endangered species [the last two Furbish louseworts, let us say] or saving another individual [for example, a cotton-tail rabbit] who belonged to a species that was plentiful but whose death would be a greater prima facie harm to that individual than the harm that death would be to the two [plants], then the rights view requires that we save that individual [the rabbit]. (p. 359)

So much for affirmative action in the area of species conservation. Adding insult to injury, Regan goes on to say that even if it were a matter of sacrificing "the last thousand or million members" of a species, members who do not qualify for rights, to prevent grave harm to a single individual mammal, then according to his theory, such a sacrifice would be mandated.

Regan is not opposed to saving endangered species so long as we do so for the right reason, which is, ironically, not to save species, but to prevent harm befalling individual rights-holding members of species. Thus, the Greenpeace effort to "save the whales" (my example, not his) is morally worthwhile and laudable from Regan's rights point of view, not as a desperate struggle against the extinction of whales, which apparently is of no moral consequence whatever, but because it prevents individual whales from being brutally harpooned and dying slow agonizing deaths. Species conservation should be regarded essentially as a nonmoral aesthetic and ecosystemic bonus following upon the protection of mammals' rights.

What is biologically naive in this indirect ethic for species conservation is Regan's inattention to the fact that the vast majority of endangered species are not comprised of rights-holding mammals. The vast majority are plants and invertebrates. Regan bubbles along talking about how "any and all harm done to rare or endangered animals ... is wrong" without so much as mentioning rare and endangered plants or, for that matter, even apparently thinking about all the animals (his persistent use of "animals" to refer only to furry creatures does, I admit, consistently irritate me because I think it is consistently misleading)— butterflies, beetles, mollusks, crustaceans, birds, fish, and amphibians —that fall outside his very restrictive qualifications for rights bearers.

### III

Regan's moral zeal does not generally dispose him to rhetorical temperance in condemning widespread and wholesale disregard of "animal" rights. But when he comes to consider Aldo Leopold's holistic land ethic, which would override an animal's rights to deal more directly and effectively with such pressing moral issues as biocide, he pulls all stops, drops rational argument altogether, and resorts to name calling. Because it is holistic, the land ethic, according to Regan, "might be fairly dubbed 'environmental fascism.'" And "environmental fascism and the rights view are like oil and water: they don't mix" (p. 362). Well, who would ever want to be an environmental fascist?! So much then for the seminal and classic paradigm for all subsequent *environmental* ethics.

As an alternative to Leopold's fascist approach to environmental ethics, Regan recommends that "environmentalists" take the rights view a step or two further than he has taken it. He toys with the idea that "collections or systems of natural objects might have inherent value" and thus possess the primary qualification, according to his theory, for holding rights (p. 362). But he suggests that it would be pretty far-fetched to imagine that wholes have rights, that is, that "moral rights could be meaningfully attributed to the *collection* of trees or the ecosystem" (p. 362).

Regan, of course, has bought into the myth of the real existence of rights—a confusion, as Wittgenstein might have diagnosed it, arising from language mesmerization. "Right(s)" is a noun. So we are tempted to ask what real, but metaphysical, *thing(s)* it labels. Like shoes, teeth, feathers, souls, and other things, some beings seem to have them and others don't. To construct a theory of moral rights, from this point of view, is to attempt to discover the true nature of rights and to identify the entities which naturally possess them. But "right(s)" is actually an expressive locution masquerading as a substantive. (That is the secret of its talismanic power.) "Right(s)" formulations are used to *state* claims. As opposed to mineral rights, water rights, property rights, civil rights, legal rights, and so forth, "moral rights" is used to claim moral consideration—for oneself or for other less articulate beings.

Even though "paradigmatic right-holders are individuals" (p. 362), it is not difficult *meaningfully* to assert moral rights on behalf of wholes like the whooping crane or the Bridger wilderness. People meaningfully assert all the time that nonindividuals—unions, corporations, states (as in "states' rights"), nations, sports teams, species, and ecosystems—have various rights, including moral rights. Only the occasional philosopher pretends to be puzzled about what is meant.

Upon the strength of such brief and facile considerations, Regan goes on to suggest that the most promising approach to environmental ethics is to make "the case that individual inanimate natural objects (e.g., *this* redwood) have inherent value and a basic moral right to treatment respectful of that value.... Were we to show proper respect for the rights of the individuals who make up the biotic community, would not the *community* be preserved (pp. 362-63)?"

As Mark Sagoff recently remarked, "This is an empirical question, the answer to which is 'no'."[4] To take an illustration familiar to almost everyone, if the right of individual whitetail deer to live unmolested were respected, the biotic communities which they help to make up would not be preserved. On the contrary, without some provision for "thinning the herd"—a euphemism for killing deer—plant members of some communities would be seriously damaged, some beyond recovery. Regan might object that I have missed his point in singling out one species among the myriad that compose a biotic community. Perhaps he means that if the rights of each individual of every species were simultaneously respected, then the community would be preserved. But to attempt to safeguard the rights of each and every individual member of an ecosystem would be to attempt to stop practically all trophic processes beyond photosynthesis—and even then we would somehow have to attempt to deal ethically with the individual life-threatening and hence rights-violating competition among plants for sunlight.

Nature, as Sagoff points out, is not fair; it does not respect the rights of individuals. An ethic for the preservation of nature, therefore, could hardly get off on the right foot if at the start it condemns as unjust and immoral the trophic asymmetries laying at the heart of evolutionary and ecological processes. An environmental ethic, therefore, could not be generated, as it were, by an invisible hand, from a further extension of rights (on the basis of some yet-to-be-worked-out theory) to "individual inanimate natural objects."

## IV

Although Regan generally condemns hunting and trapping, he has nothing whatever to say about fishing, nor does he bother to delve into the moral differences of bird as opposed to mammal hunting—another convenience of using the term *animal* in a loose, substandard way.

Regan runs through the usual utilities hunting affords human beings. And he dismisses them with his more or less standard argument, namely that is it morally inappropriate to aggregate preference satisfactions and weigh them against rights. Rights trump utilitarian felicity ledgers.

To the argument that hunting actually serves to reduce rather than increase animal suffering by sparing animals an agonizing death they or their conspecifics might otherwise suffer by starvation or the other vicissitudes of wild life, Regan offers both adventitious and essential rebuttal. First, since hunting and trapping are public sports pursued mostly by bumbling amateurs, as a matter of fact, not all deaths dealt by hunters and trappers are quick and clean. And second, hunting is not a humane tool of wildlife management, as apologists claim; rather wildlife management is an inhumane tool of hunting designed to produce a surplus "game crop" and so increases rather than lessens animal suffering inflicted both by sportspersons and nature.

These are adventitious considerations since both may be remedied. Hunting and trapping could beome more restricted, well regulated, and professionalized (as, for example, in Germany), and wildlife management could become reoriented toward genuinely benefiting wildlife rather than serving the interests of hunter and trapper wildlife consumers.

Still, Regan thinks, the ends, however benign and humane, cannot justify the means. Hunting and trapping simply violate the rights of individuals. And "policies that lessen the total amount of harm at the cost of violating the rights of individuals . . . are wrong" (p. 356).

What, then, should be the goal of wildlife management if not to serve the interests of human wildlife consumers or to humanely reduce wildlife suffering? Not even mentioning the possible goals of ecological diversity, integrity, and stability, he answers: "It should be to protect wild animals from those who would violate their rights . . . [,] to defend wild animals in the possession of their rights, providing them with the opportunity to live their own life, by their own lights as best they can, spared that human predation that goes by the name of 'sport'" (p. 357).

An obvious question immediately comes to mind. Why should wildlife management stop at preventing "human predation"? According to Regan, wildlife managers should become policemen who protect "wild animals from those who would violate their rights." But from the subject-of-a-life's point of view his or her rights are equally and indifferently violated upon being killed and eaten whether "those" who do so are human hunters or wolves. Regan's answer is that "animals are not moral agents and so can have none of the same duties moral agents have, including the duties to respect the rights of other animals. The wolves who eat the caribou do no moral wrong, though the harm they cause is real enough" (p. 357). This answer is not adequate. A wolf is an agent, not a natural force like a tidal wave or an earthquake, since, as a mammal, it has all the capacities Regan claims for subjects-of-a-life, though *perhaps* it is not a *moral* agent. An agent's moral competency is a relevant consideration in redressing his or her offense, but it is not a relevant consideration in protecting a patient's rights.

Consider an analogy. Though many people who are in fact moral agents attempt to avoid prosecution and/or punishment (sometimes successfully) by "pleading insanity," there are people—because of genetic defect or physical or psychological trauma—who are genuinely not responsible for their actions. They are not moral agents any more (and maybe even less) than wolves are, and so, quite properly, cannot be held to account for their behavior. Thus, they are not brought to trial and punished for their conduct. But, they are not permitted to remain free in society. We get them off the street and incarcerate them comfortably and respectfully in institutions, since, whether they are moral agents or not, if they remained free in society and continued to behave as before, they would certainly violate the rights of other people. Imagine the authorities explaining to the parents of a small child tortured and killed by a certifiably brain-damaged sadist that, even though he had a history of this sort of thing he is not properly a moral agent and so can violate no one's rights, and therefore has to be allowed to remain at large pursuing a course of action to which he is impelled by drives he cannot control.

But this is only an analogy and argument by analogy may be regarded as less weighty than logical analysis. Regan's permission of animal predation, however, stands in direct contradiction to his theory of animal rights. He says, "Since animals can pose innocent threats and because we are sometimes justified in overriding their rights when they do...,one cannot assume that all hunting and trapping are wrong" (p. 353). "Pose innocent threats" to whom? To people, as he explains. But Regan's whole case for animal rights turns on the principle that basic moral rights are enjoyed equally by all who are entitled to them: "As a matter of strict justice, then, we are required to give equal respect to those individuals who have equal inherent value ... whether they be humans or animals" (p. 264). And "all who possess [basic moral] rights possess them equally" (p. 327). Since some animals can and do pose innocent threats to other (rights holding) animals, as a matter of strict justice, we ought to deal with such threats no differently than we would if they were threats to (rights holding) humans. If we ought to protect humans' rights not to be preyed on by both human and animal predators, then we ought to protect animals' rights not to be preyed upon by both human and animal predators. In short, then, Regan's theory of animal rights implies a policy of humane predator extermination, since predators, however innocently, violate the rights of their victims.

Regan appears to recognize that the Achilles' heel of his elaborate case for animal rights is just this issue—predator policy. He is not willing to embrace the implications of his theory regarding predators and, as Steve Sapontzis actually does, recommend as a morally better world, a world purged of carnivores, a world of plants and herbivores.[5] Somewhat desperately Regan concludes that "wildlife managers should be principally concerned with letting animals be, keeping human predators out of their affairs, allowing these 'other nations' to carve out their own destiny" (p. 361).

Regan's allusion to Henry Beston's reconfiguration of our image of animals is ironic in this context. Beston's point is that we have incorrectly cast animals in our own image and then condescendingly judged them imperfect or incomplete: "We *patronize* them for their incompleteness, for their tragic fate of having taken form so far below ourselves."[6] But this is precisely what animal liberation and animal rights has now for more than a decade persisted in doing. The primary moral fulcrum of animal liberation/rights has been the "argument from marginal cases," as Regan has called it.[7] If marginal human beings (i.e., the severely retarded) are entitled to equal consideration and/or basic moral rights, as most people think, then so are animals who are at a similar mental level. This argument quite directly and deliberately equates animals with imbeciles, with imperfect and incomplete humans.[8]

Animal rights, à la Regan, does nothing if it does not draw some animals (mammals) into a single community with humans. Either they are members of other nations with their own lives to live and laws to live by or they are honorary mentally deficient and morally incompetent members of the human community, entangled, to both their benefit and peril, with such human artifices as rights and correlative restraints. (Beston, to whom Regan approvingly refers, takes the former alternative: "[Do not] expect Nature to answer to your human values as to come into your house and sit in a chair [like domestic cats and dogs]. The economy of nature . . . *has an ethic of its own.*"[9])

Mary Midgley has pointed the way out of this dilemma. Some animals, she remarks, have from time immemorial been members of a "mixed community" with human beings.[10] These are domestic animals. Bentham's "insuperable line" should be drawn not by reference to psychological capacities and subjective experiences, but by reference to actual social participation. Animal rights is not a preposterous notion if restricted to domestic animals. We expect dogs and cats to live peaceably in the same household even though they are "natural enemies." We expect similar restraint among barnyard mammals and fowl. We actually segregate incorrigible rogues and vicious domestic animals to safeguard the rights of the more peaceable ones. And many domestic animals often actually seem to understand not only their rights as honorary participants in a human civil order, but their obligations as well. To extend rights to wild animals, as Sagoff and Rodman have both pointed out, would be in effect to domesticate them.

After all, animal liberation and animal rights has historically been much more concerned with domestic than wild animals—pets, farm, and laboratory animals (which, most unfortunately, sometimes include animals stolen from the wild). If the case for animal rights would be theoretically restructured to divide animal rights holders from non-holders along the domestic/wild axis rather than subject-/non-subject-of-a-life axis, then its reconciliation with environmental ethics could be envisioned. Both would rest upon a common concept—the community concept. And the very different ethical implications of either would be governed by the different kinds of communities humans and animals comprise—the "mixed" human-domestic community, on the one hand, and the natural, wild biotic community, on the other.

# 3

## Animal Liberation and Environmental Ethics: Back Together Again

Probably more than any other one thing, my article "Animal Liberation: A Triangular Affair" has led to an increasingly acrimonious estrangement between advocates of individualistic animal welfare ethics and advocates of holistic ecocentric ethics.[1] I think this estrangement is regrettable because it is divisive. Animal welfare ethicists and environmental ethicists have overlapping concerns. From a practical point of view, it would be far wiser to make common cause against a common enemy—the destructive forces at work ravaging the non-human world—than to continue squabbling among ourselves.

Not long after the schism emerged, that is, not long after the appearance of "Triangular Affair," Mary Anne Warren took a positive step toward reconciliation. She insisted that ecocentric environmental ethics and animal welfare ethics were "complementary," not contradictory.[2]

Warren's approach is thoroughly pluralistic. She argues that animals, like human beings, have rights. But she also argues that animals do not enjoy the *same* rights as human beings and that the rights of animals are not *equal* to human rights. And she argues, further, that animal rights and human rights are grounded in different psychological capacities. A holistic environmental ethic, Warren suggests, rests upon still other foundations—the instrumental value of "natural resources" to us and to future generations and the "intrinsic value" we (or at least some of us) intuitively find in plants, species, "mountains, oceans, and the like."[3]

Warren recommends, in short, a wholly reasonable ethical eclecticism. Human beings have strong rights because we are autonomous; animals have weaker rights because they are sentient; the environment should be used with respect—even though it may not have rights—because it is a whole and unified thing which we value in a variety of ways. Conflicts will certainly arise among all the foci of the human/animal/environment triangle—an example cited by Warren concerns

49

introduced feral goats which threaten native plant species on New Zealand—but well-meaning people can muddle through the moral wilderness, balancing and compromising the competing interests and incommensurable values. In general, Warren concludes, "Only by *combining* the environmentalist and animal rights perspectives can we take account of the full range of moral considerations which ought to guide our interactions with the nonhuman world."[4]

However reasonable, there is something philosophically unsatisfying in Warren's ethical eclecticism. Moral philosophy historically has striven for theoretical unity and closure—often at considerable sacrifice of moral common sense. Consider, for example, Kant's deontological dismissal of the moral value of actions tainted with "inclination," even when the inclination in question is wholly altruistic. Or consider the morally outrageous consequences that some utilitarians have been led to accept in order faithfully to adhere to the theoretical foundations of utilitarianism.

In striving for theoretical unity and consistency, moral philosophy is not unlike natural philosophy. When a variety of apparently disparate phenomena (e.g., falling bodies, planetary motions, and tides) can be embraced by a single idea (gravity), the natural philosopher feels that a deep (though perhaps not ultimate) truth about nature has been struck. Similarly in moral philosophy, we strive to explain the commonly held welter of practical precepts and moral intuitions by appeal to one (or at most a very few theoretically related) imperative(s), principle(s), summary maxim(s), or Golden Rule(s). And if we succeed we feel that we have discovered something true and deep about morality.

The moral philosopher's love for theoretical unity, coherency, and self-consistency may represent more than a matter of mere intellectual taste. There is a practical reason to prefer theoretical unity in moral philosophy just as there is in natural philosophy. Probably more than anything else, the failure of the Ptolemaic system of astronomy—with its hodgepodge of ad hoc devices—accurately to predict the positions of the planets led Copernicus to unify the celestial phenomena by introducing a single radical assumption: that the sun, not the earth, is at the center of it all. In moral philosophy, when competing moral claims cannot be articulated in the same terms, they cannot be decisively compared and resolved. Ethical eclecticism leads, it would seem inevitably, to moral incommensurability in hard cases. So we are compelled to go back to the theoretical drawing board.

To achieve something more than a mere coalition of convenience—to achieve, rather, a lasting alliance—between animal welfare ethics and ecocentric environmental ethics will require the development of a moral theory that embraces both programs *and* that provides a framework for the adjudication of the very real conflicts between human welfare, animal welfare, and ecological integrity. It is the purpose of this essay to suggest such a theory on terms, shall we say, favorable to ecocentric environmental ethics, just as Tom Regan has suggested such a theory on terms favorable to animal welfare ethics.

Regan proposes a "rights-based environmental ethic" consistent with and, indeed, launched from his "rights view" version of animal welfare ethics. He himself has not worked out the grounds for the rights of individual trees and other non-"subjects-of-a-life," but he urges environmental ethicists seriously to take up the challenge. Writes Regan,

> The implications of the successful development of a rights-based environmental ethic, one that made the case that individual inanimate objects (e.g. *this* redwood) have inherent value and a basic moral right to treatment respectful of that value, should be welcomed by environmentalists. ... A rights-based environmental ethic remains a live option, one that, though far from being established, merits continued exploration. ... Were we to show proper respect for the rights of individuals who make up the biotic community, would not the *community* be preserved?[5]

To this (actually rhetorical) question Mark Sagoff replied, "I believe [that] this is an empirical question, the answer to which is 'no'. The environmentalist is concerned about preserving evolutionary processes, e.g., natural selection, whether these processes have deep enough respect for the rights of individuals...," or not [6] Nature, as Sagoff points out, is not fair; it does not respect the rights of individuals. To attempt to safeguard the rights of each and every individual member of an ecosystem would, correspondingly, be to attempt to stop practically all trophic processes beyond photosynthesis—and even then we would somehow have to deal ethically with the individual life-threatening and hence rights-violating competition among plants for sunlight. An ethic for the preservation of nature, therefore, could hardly get off on the right foot if, at the start, it condemns as unjust and immoral the trophic asymmetries lying at the heart of evolutionary and ecological processes. An environmental ethic cannot be generated, as it were by an invisible hand, from a further extension of rights (on the basis of some yet-to-be-worked-out-theory) to "individual inanimate objects."

I have another, and I think better, proposal which was suggested to me by the work of Mary Midgley.

Midgley, in her book *Animals and Why They Matter*, grounds the mattering—that is, in more familiar contemporary philosophical terminology, the moral considerability—of animals in what she calls "the mixed community":

> All human communities have involved animals. The animals . . .
> became tame, not just through fear of violence, but because they were
> able to form individual bonds with those who tamed them by coming
> to understand the social signals addressed to them. . . . They were able
> to do this, not only because the people taming them were social
> beings, but because they themselves were so as well.[7]

Midgley goes on to draw out a number of consequences from this pregnant and profound observation. Since we and the animals who belong to our mixed human-animal community are coevolved social beings participating in a single society, we and they share certain feelings that attend upon and enable sociability—sympathy, compassion, trust, love, and so on. Her main point is to show that it is preposterous to believe, with those whom she identifies as "Behaviourists," that animal members of our mixed community are mere automata, devoid of a rich subjective life. And her subordinate point is to show that the species-barrier to human-animal social interaction is both artificial and unhistorical. We have enjoyed, and there is no good philosophical reason why we should not continue to enjoy, interspecies social relationships and intimacy. Says Midgley, "the problem here is not about anthropomorphism, but about Behaviourism, and it arises already on the human scene. The barrier [between subjects] does not fall between us and the dog. It falls between you and me. . . . Natural sympathy, as Hume rightly said, has a basis in common humanity. Does it therefore follow that it stops at the species-barrier?"[8]

Midgley, curiously, does not go on to elaborate a positive moral theory which incorporates to the best advantage the very thorough and convincing case she has made for the existence of a wide variety of animal consciousness—from that of dogs to that of work elephants— each with its species' peculiarities, but each broadly based in, shall we say, a common bio-sociality. Midgley certainly does not go on to argue, à la Peter Singer, that the "sentiency" ambient among animal members of the mixed community, which she has so fully and forcefully defended, should constitute a *criterion* for equal moral consideration; nor does she argue, à la Tom Regan, that having a rich subjective life entitles domestic animals to equal moral *rights*. Her approving mention of Hume, however, and her emphasis on social affections and sympathy suggest to me that, if pressed, Midgley would sketch a Humean ethical theory to make moral hay of her defense of the subjectivity of animals and the possibility of intersubjective interaction between species.

David Hume's moral theory is distinguished from the prevailing modern alternatives—utilitarianism and deontology—primarily by two features: (1) Morality is grounded in feelings, not reason; although reason has its role to play in ethics, it is part of the supporting cast. And (2) altruism is as primitive as egoism; it is not reducible either to enlightened self-interest or to duty.

A pertinent contrast to Hume's understanding of ethics is afforded by Peter Singer. In *Animal Liberation* he heaped scorn on "sentimental appeals for sympathy" toward animals and avowed that his animal welfare ethic was grounded exclusively in "basic moral principles which we all accept; and the application of these principles to victims . . . is demanded by reason, not emotion."⁹ Singer follows the usual theoretical approach of normal modern moral philosophy—elegantly described by Kenneth Goodpaster—which has been to generalize egoism.¹⁰ Baldly stated, it comes to this: I insist upon moral consideration from others or moral rights for myself. My entitlement to moral standing or moral rights may be plausibly defended by appeal to a psychological characteristic or capacity possessed by me which is arguably relevant to ethical treatment. But then "others" are entitled to equal moral consideration to the extent that they possess, in equal measure, the same psychological characteristic. I may not love others (in this connection, Singer wants us to know that he keeps no pets) or sympathize with them; indeed I may be entirely indifferent to their concerns or even actively dislike them. Still, I am compelled by the logic of my own moral claim upon others to grudgingly grant their similar claims upon me.

Hume took a different course. He argued that both our moral judgments and our actions are rooted in altruistic feelings or sentiments that are very often opposed to "self-love." Writes Hume, "So far from thinking that men have no affection for anything beyond themselves, I am of opinion that tho' it be rare to meet with one, who loves any single person better than himself; yet 'tis rare to meet with one, in whom all the kind affections, taken together, do not over-balance all the selfish."¹¹ According to Hume, these kind affections are the soil in which our morals are rooted and from which they take their nourishment.

Aldo Leopold, in "The Land Ethic" of *A Sand County Almanac,* evidently patterned his own concept of an "ethical sequence" on Charles Darwin's discussion of the evolution of ethics in *The Descent of Man,* and Darwin cites both Hume's *Treatise* and Adam Smith's *Theory of the Moral Sentiments* as the philosophical antecedents of his own "natural history" of ethics. I have argued in a variety of venues and in considerable detail that, therefore, Hume's moral theory is the historical ancestor of Aldo

Leopold's land ethic, the modern ethic of choice of the environmental movement and of many contemporary environmental philosophers.[12] What's more, the moral fulcrum of the Leopold land ethic is the ecological concept of the "biotic community."

Mary Midgley's suggested animal welfare ethic and Aldo Leopold's seminal environmental ethic thus share a common, fundamentally Humean understanding of ethics as grounded in altruistic feelings. And they share a common ethical bridge between the human and nonhuman domains in the concept of community—Midgley's "mixed community" and Leopold's "biotic community." Combining these two conceptions of a metahuman moral community we have the basis of a unified animal-environmental ethical theory.

Hume regarded the social feelings upon which the edifice of ethics is erected to be a brute fact of human nature. Darwin explained how we came to have such feelings, as he explained so many other curious natural facts, by appeal to the evolutionary principle of natural selection.

Darwin's biosocial reduction of Hume's moral theory is particularly ingenious since, at first glance, altruism seems, from an evolutionary point of view, anomalous and paradoxical. Given the ceaseless struggle for the limited means to life lying at the heart of Darwin's conception of nature, concern for others and deferential behavior would appear to be maladaptive tendencies quickly eliminated from a gene pool, should they ever chance to emerge. Or so it would seem— until we consider the survival-reproductive advantages of social membership. Concern for others and self-restraint are necessary for social amalgamation and integration, Darwin argued. "Ethical" behavior is, in effect, the dues an individual pays to join a social group; and the survival advantages of group membership to individuals more than compensate them for the personal sacrifices required by morality. Since most animals, including most human beings, are not sufficiently intelligent to make a benefit-cost analysis of their social actions, we are outfitted, Darwin theorized, with "social instincts" impelling us toward socially conducive moral behavior.

What is right and what is wrong, Darwin suggests, reflects, more or less, the specific organizational structure of society—since ethics have evolved to facilitate social cohesion. The "ethics" of a hierarchically structured pack of wolves, for example, require celibacy of most its members. The ethics of apolitical and egalitarian human tribal societies require members periodically to redistribute their wealth. Who is and who is not an appropriate beneficiary of one's moral sympathies, similarly, reflects the *perceived* boundaries of social membership. In our dealings with those whom we regard as members, the rules apply; in our dealings with those whom we regard as outsiders, we do as we please.

Midgley's marvelous insight is that, however exclusive of other human beings the perceived boundaries of historical human societies may have been, they all, nevertheless, have included some animals— aboriginally man's hunting partner, the dog; and, after the Neolithic Revolution, a variety of herd, farm, and work animals: everything from the cow and pig to the Asian elephant and water buffalo. Consonant with my analysis in "A Triangular Affair," Midgley suggests therefore that a big part of the immorality of the treatment of animals in the current industrial phase of human civilization is that we have broken trust with erstwhile fellow members of our traditionally mixed communities. Animals have been depersonalized and mechanized and that goes a long way toward explaining the moral revulsion we all feel toward the factory farm and animal research laboratory.

How we ought and ought not treat one another (including animals) is determined, according to the logic of biosocial moral theory, by the nature and organization of communities. Even to those deeply sympathetic to the plight of animals there is something deeply amiss in the concept of *equal* moral consideration or *equal* moral rights for animals, required by the logic of extending the prevailing modern moral paradigms, just as there is something deeply amiss in the idea of requiring equal consideration for all human beings regardless of social relationship.

Peter Singer, once again, provides a revealing example of the latter as well as of the former. He argues that he has failed in his duty because he does not donate the greatest portion of his modest income to help alleviate the suffering of starving people living halfway around the world, *even though* to do so would impoverish not only himself, but his own children.[13] Suffering is suffering, no matter whose it may be, and it is the duty of a moral agent to be impartial in weighing the suffering of one against the suffering of another. Since the starving suffer more from his withholding money from them than his children would suffer were he to impoverish them short of starvation, Singer concludes that therefore he should give the greater portion of his income to the starving.

From Midgley's biosocial point of view, we are members of nested communities each of which has a different structure and therefore different moral requirements. At the center is the immediate family. I have a duty not only to feed, clothe, and shelter my own children, I also have a duty to bestow affection on them. But to bestow a similar affection on the neighbors' kids is not only not my duty, it would be considered anything from odd to criminal were I to behave so. Similarly, I have obligations to my neighbors which I do not have to my less proximate fellow citizens—to watch their houses while they are on vacation, for example, or to go to the grocery for them when they are sick or disabled. I have obligations to my fellow citizens which I do not have toward human beings in general *and* I have obligations to human beings in general which I do not have toward animals in general.

These subtly shaded social-moral relationships are complex and overlapping. Pets, for example, are—properly so, Midgley argues—surrogate family members and merit treatment not owed either to less intimately related animals, for example to barnyard animals, *or*, for that matter, to less intimately related human beings.

Barnyard animals, over hundreds of generations, have been genetically engineered (by the old-fashioned method of selective breeding) to play certain roles in the mixed community. To condemn the morality of these roles—as we rightly condemn human slavery and penury—is to condemn the very being of these creatures. The animal welfare ethic of the mixed community, thus, would not censure using draft animals for work or even slaughtering meat animals for food so long as the keeping and using of such animals was not in violation—as factory farming clearly is—of a kind of evolved and unspoken social contract between man and beast.

But it is not my intention here to attempt to detail our duties to the various classes of the animal members of mixed communities. Rather, I wish to argue that whatever our various duties to various kinds of domestic animals may, from this point of view, turn out to be, they differ in a general and profound way from our duties toward the wild animal members of the biotic community.

One of the principal frustrations with the familiar utilitarian and deontological approaches to animal liberation that I have experienced, as an environmental ethicist, is the absence of a well-grounded distinction between our proper ethical relations with, on the one hand, domestic and, on the other, wild animals. According to the conventional approach, cattle and antelope, pigs and porcupines, bears and battery hens are entitled to equal moral consideration and/or equal rights.

The Midgley-Leopold biosocial moral theory, by contrast, clearly provides the missing distinction. Domestic animals are members of the mixed community and ought to enjoy, therefore, all the rights and privileges, whatever they may turn out to be, attendant upon that membership. Wild animals are, by definition, not members of the mixed community and therefore should not lie on the same spectrum of graded moral standing as family members, neighbors, fellow citizens, fellow human beings, pets, and other domestic animals.

Wild animals, rather, are members of the biotic community. The structure of the biotic community is described by ecology. The duties and obligations of a biotic community ethic or "land ethic," as Leopold called it, may, accordingly, be derived from an ecological description of nature—just as our duties and obligations to members of the mixed community can be derived from a description of the mixed community.

Most generally and abstractly described, the ecosystem is, to quote Leopold, "a fountain of energy flowing through a circuit of soils, plants, and animals."[14] The currency, in other words, of the economy of nature is solar energy captured upon incidence by green plants and thereafter transferred from animal organism to animal organism—not from hand to hand, like coined money, but, so to speak, from stomach to stomach. The most fundamental fact of life in the biotic community is eating . . . *and being eaten.* Each species is adapted to a trophic niche; each is a link in a food chain, and a knot in a food web. Whatever moral entitlements a being may have as a member of the biotic community, *not* among them is the right to life. Rather, each being should be respected and left alone to pursue its modus vivendi—even if its way of life causes harm to other beings, including other sentient beings. The integrity, stability, and beauty of the biotic community depend upon *all* members, in their appropriate numbers, functioning in their co-evolved life ways.

Among the most disturbing implications drawn from conventional indiscriminate animal liberation/rights theory is that, were it possible for us to do so, we ought to protect innocent vegetarian animals from their carnivorous predators.[15] Nothing could be more contrary to the ethics of the biotic community than this suggestion. Not only would the (humane) eradication of predators destroy the community, it would destroy the species which are the intended beneficiaries of this misplaced morality. Many prey species depend upon predators to optimize their populations. And, at a deeper level, we must remember that the alertness, speed, grace, and all the other qualities we most admire in herbivorous animals—all the qualities, indeed, which make them subjects-of-a-life and thus worthy of moral consideration and/or rights—were evolved in direct response to their carnivorous symbionts.[16]

The Humean biosocial moral theory differently applied to larger-than-human communities by Midgley and Leopold has, unlike the more familiar approach of generalizing egoism, historically provided for a holistic as well as an individualistic moral orientation. We care, in other words, for our communities per se, over and above their individual members—for our families per se, for our country, and for mankind. As Midgley might say, *they* "matter" to us as well. Hence, according to Hume, "we must renounce the theory which accounts for every moral sentiment by the principle of self-love. We must adopt a more *publick affection* and allow that the interests of society are not, *even on their own account,* entirely indifferent to us."[17]

Darwin's holism is even more pronounced:

> We have now seen that actions are regarded by savages, and were probably so regarded by primeval man, as good or bad, solely as they obviously affect the welfare of the tribe—not that of the species, nor that of the individual member of the tribe. This conclusion agrees well with the belief that the so-called moral sense is aboriginally derived from social instincts, for both relate exclusively to the community.[18]

And the holistic dimension of Aldo Leopold's land ethic all but overwhelms the individualistic. Leopold provides only "respect" for individual members of the biotic community, but "biotic rights" for species and, in the last analysis, "the integrity, beauty, and stability of the biotic community" is the measure of right and wrong actions affecting the environment.

The hyperholism of the land ethic is also itself a function of an ecological description of the biotic community. But since the biosocial moral paradigm provides for various coexisting, cooperating, and competing ethics—each corresponding to our nested overlapping community entanglements—our holistic environmental obligations are not preemptive. We are still subject to all the other more particular and individually oriented duties to the members of our various more circumscribed and intimate communities. And since they are closer to home, they come first. In general, obligations to family come before obligations to more remotely related fellow humans. For example, *pace* Singer, one should not impoverish one's own children just short of starvation in order to aid actually starving people on another continent. But neither should one promote or even acquiesce in human starvation, no matter how distant, to achieve environmental goals—as some overzealous environmental activists have actually urged. Similarly, one should not allow a wild predator to help herself to one's free-range chickens, members of one's immediate mixed community. But neither should one interfere, other things being equal, in the interaction of the wild members of the biotic community.

So the acknowledgment of a holistic environmental ethic does not entail that we abrogate our familiar moral obligations to family members, to fellow citizens, to all mankind, *nor* to fellow members, individually, of the mixed community, that is, to domesticate animals. On the other hand, the outer orbits of our various moral spheres exert a gravitational tug on the inner ones. One may well deprive one's children of a trip to Disneyland or give them fewer toys at Christmas in order to aid starving people on another continent. Similarly, one may well make certain sacrifices oneself or impose certain restrictions on the animal members of one's mixed community for the sake of ecological integrity. Dairy cattle, for example, can be very destructive of certain plant communities and should be fenced out of them when other pasture or fodder is available—despite their own preferences and the economic interests of dairy farmers.

Animal liberation and environmental ethics may thus be united under a common theoretical umbrella—even though, as with all the laminated layers of our social-ethical accretions, they may occasionally come into conflict. But since they may be embraced by a common theoretical structure, we are provided a means, in principle, to assign priorities and relative weights and thus to resolve such conflicts in a systematic way.

# II

# A Holistic Environmental Ethic

# 4

## Elements of an Environmental Ethic:
## Moral Considerability and the Biotic Community

### I

An environmental ethic is supposed to govern human relations with nonhuman natural entities. It would, for example, prohibit or censure as wrong certain modes of conduct affecting animals and plants. According to an environmental ethic, it may be wrong to mutilate a tree, or pollute a river, or develop a wilderness.

In ordinary ethical discourse (ordinary, that is, in Western circles) not only does it make perfectly good sense to say, "it is wrong to mutilate trees," or "one should not pollute rivers," such moral statements are commonly uttered and readily understood, and, increasingly, more often than not, they elicit agreement. Therefore, it seems, at least prima facie, that familiar Western ethical concepts set out people's relations to the natural environment and condemn as wrong actions, for example, as setting a forest on fire.

In a paper entitled "Is There a Need for a New, an Environmental, Ethic?" Richard Routley argues that "The dominant Western ethical tradition" excludes an environmental ethic in principle  thereby requiring us to develop one on a nontraditional basis.[1] According to Routley's analysis, the moral turpitude involved in such wanton behavior as burning down a stand of virgin California redwoods, or (Routley's example) extirpating a species of great whales, lies in the effect of those actions upon other *people*. Hence, redwoods and whales are objects of ethical concern only indirectly, that is, only insofar as other human interests or rights may be affected.

To demonstrate this, Routley presents some ingenious limiting case paradigms, involving situations so construed as to eliminate consideration of other people, but not of trees, whales, or other nonhuman natural entities. For example, Routley asks us to consider the "last man" ("who lays about him eliminating, as far as he can, every living thing, animal or plant") or "the last people."[2] Suppose that after the proliferation of nuclear power plants it is discovered that radiation side

63

effects have blocked any chance of human reproduction. In bitterness, the last generation of people set about systematically destroying all life on the planet. Since future persons, posterity, are in principle removed from consideration, Routley argues that, *according to dominant Western ethical traditions,* what the last people do to the natural environment is not wrong or morally censurable.[3]

Assuming that Routley is right in maintaining that there is a need for a wholly new *environmental* ethic to limit behavior in such situations, let us ask what such an ethic might be like.

The following is an attempt to outline an environmental ethic according to which it would be clearly and indisputably wrong for human beings to act in the manner Routley describes in his examples. Just as there are a number of alternative ethical systems which set out proper and improper relations among persons and provide an explanation and justification thereof, so surely there must also be a number of possible conceptual elements from which we might derive directives of conduct with regard to nature. The environmental ethic that follows is an elaboration of that adumbrated by Aldo Leopold in 1933, and republished, in substantially revised form, in 1949.[4]

## II

Leopold's environmental ethic is based in part on the following closely related statements: (i) "All ethics so far evolved rest upon a single premise: that the individual is a member of a community of interdependent parts;"[5] (ii) "An ethic, ecologically, is a limitation on freedom of action in the struggle for existence. An ethic, philosophically, is a differentation of social from antisocial conduct. These are two definitions of the same thing. The thing has its origin in the tendency of interdependent individuals or groups to evolve modes of cooperation."[6]

What Leopold seems to be asserting is that there is some intimate connection between cooperation among individuals in groups, on the one hand, and ethics, on the other, where the term *ethics* is understood to indicate more or less voluntary systems of behavioral inhibition or restraint. As a first approximation of a logically explicit statement of this connection, I suggest the following: if one is a member of a cooperative group, community, or society, then one is subject to ethical or moral-like limitations on his freedom of action. Or, letting C stand for "belongs to a community" and E for "is subject to ethical limitations," Leopold might be understood to assert:

(1)      $(x)(Cx \supset Ex)$.

So expressed, (1) seems false straightaway. We can think of dozens of biological countercases; for example, *W* may be a member of a cooperative community, a termitarium, but it would seem presumptuous to suppose that *W* was subject to either moral or moral-like limitations on his freedom of action, limitations, that is, which are voluntarily assumed and socially sanctioned, since termites, like all other social insects, appear to do nothing at all voluntarily.

Thus, the relationship that Leopold claims to exist between ethics and social participation, if such a connection indeed obtains, must be more carefully stated so as to take account of the social insects and other manifestly nonethical animal societies. Termites, although almost certainly not subject to ethical or moral-like limitations, are certainly subject to social constraints on their activities, just as certainly as they are members of cooperative communities. It may be true that membership in a community implies limitations on freedom of action in the struggle for existence, while it may not be true that all such limitations are of a moral or moral-like modality. An ethic, when seen against the vast and overwhelming variety of the biological world, may be regarded as only one sort of means among many of achieving social integrity and thus the possibility of combined or cooperative industry. Ethics are peculiarly (though perhaps not uniquely) the human means of achieving social organization.

The history of the principle expressed by Leopold begins with the beginnings of modern biology and was expressly advanced and argued for by Charles Darwin in *The Descent of Man*.[7] Ethics and other systems of social restraint, according to Darwin, have evolved through natural selection. In brief, the increment of fitness (or survival/reproductive advantage) gained through membership in a community on the average is greater than the increment of fitness lost through being subject to ethics or to some other system of social limitation. A more social animal, although intraspecifically less aggressive and more diffident, is better adapted in many cases than a solitary animal. If the creature is a mammal, and especially if it is a *Homo sapiens*, being subject to moral limitations or something like that is, as it were, the dues paid in order to be part of a society.

Hence, we may beel confident that

(1a)     $(x) [Cx \supset (Ex \lor G_1x \lor G_2x \lor ... G_nx)]$,

where the new token *G* represents some system of moral-like limitations *or* some other mode of social limitation on individual freedom to which the individual animal, *x*, is subject, such as an instinctive set of responses to behavioral signals, or to pheromones, and so forth, the indefinite variety of which is indicated by the subscripts, *1-n*.

Among many species, to express Darwin's sociobiological reduction of ethics and other forms of social limitation more formally, $C_{(f)}$ )

$S_{(f)}$, where $f$ represents a suitable quantitative expression of fitness, $C$ a social way of life, and $S$ a solitary way of life. As $S_{(f)} / C_{(f)}$ approaches 1 then social organization and moral-like limitations become looser and lesser respectively. As $S_{(f)} / C_{(f)}$ approaches 0 then social organization and moral-like limitations become greater and more complex (relative to the organic complexity of the species involved). Furthermore, if $S_{(f)} / C_{(f)} \rangle 1$, then being a social animal subject to moral-like limitations will almost certainly be maladaptive. Therefore, if (1a) is true, then its converse is also true:

(1b)    $(x) [(Ex \ v \ G_1x \ v...etc.) \supset Cx]$.

If an individual animal is subject to ethical or other socially related behavioral limitations, then he is also, necessarily, a member of a community, since without the overbalancing gain in fitness consequent upon being a member of a community or a cooperative group pursuing life's struggle in common, he would suffer the loss of fitness devolving from restrained behavior and his genes would be winnowed from the species' gene pool by the operation of the principle of natural selection.

The sociobiological argument for (1a) and (1b) may be buttressed by another consideration. If (1a) and (1b) are generally true, then we should expect that $C$ and $E$ are covariant, that is, that the specific limitations to which an individual is subject will vary with the specific form of community organization to which he belongs. Taken together, (1a) and (1b) entail:

(1c)    $(x) [Cx \equiv (Ex \ v \ G_1x...etc.)]$.

To be a member of a community is materially equivalent to being subject to ethical limitations, *or* some system of moral-like restraints, *or* some other system involving limitations on individual behavior sufficient for social organization to be maintained. Dropping the scruple expressed by the addition of ...$vG_1x$, etc., and considering ethics exclusively in the context of human societies, an ethic is, as it were, a description of social organization—the internal description of the structure of a community by its own members. For example, consider the commandment, "Honor thy father and mother." This is the internally perceived equivalent of an objective, so to speak, sociological description of a typical human society organized in such a way that the pair bond and the nuclear family are central. If (1c) is true, then we should observe a direct correlation and covariance between the specific social structure of a given human group and its ethical precepts. We might predict, for example, that in a genuinely patrilineal society sexual morality would be more strict and the sanctions more severe, especially for females, than in a purely matrilineal society in which the identity of the male parent is inconsequential to the determination of status in the group. We might predict that as a society undergoes transition from one form to another, say from a tribal to a national structure, its ethical precepts will undergo parallel transformations. Anthropological and ethological studies could therefore conceivably confirm the correlation between ethics and community organization which Leopold regarded as axiomatic, and which Darwin took pains earlier on to argue for elaborately, and which Edward O. Wilson has recently expressed in a formal theory.[8]

## III

Leopold continues: "The land ethic simply enlarges the boundaries of the community to include soils, waters, plants, and animals, or collectively: the land."[9] Since *land ethic* can be taken as a popular equivalent for Routley's euphuistic *environmental ethic*, Leopold is thus suggesting that an environmental ethic would extend the term *community* (that is, our community) to include among its referents the nonhuman natural entities which he broadly describes as the *land*. Thus, if one is a member of the environmental community, then one is also subject to an environmental ethic, that is:

(2)    $(x) (LCx \supset LEx)$,

where *LC* represents "is a member of the land community (or environmental community)" and *LE* represents "is subject to environmental (or land) ethical limitations."

But not only are animals included within the perimeter of this community, so are plants—according to Leopold, even soils and waters. As members of the land or environmental community, are they then subject to reciprocal ethical limitations? Have trees duties? Have rocks obligations? May the very rain not fall where it will? As thus understood, an environmental ethic is absurd.[10]

Leopold certainly does not intend any such inference as this. Rather, what he wishes us to conclude is (i) that *we* are members of a human community (now grown from the savage clan to the "family of Man," and in reference to which we have evolved ethical limitations upon our conduct), (ii) that *we* are also members of a biotic, or land, or ecological community, and (iii) that accordingly, *we* should evolve or assume environmental ethical limitations upon *our* conduct.

If this environmental ethic is to be expressed in a clear and universal form, what is needed is a restrictive clause. We wish to "enlarge the boundaries of the community" to include nonhuman natural entities as beneficiaries of moral obligations, but without imposing upon them mutual or reciprocal obligations, duties, or moral limitations, which it would be impossible for them to bear and absurd for us to suppose that they might. On the other hand, I don't want to be merely arbitrary and single out people as being subject to a special burden (a kind of negative species chauvinism or, alternatively, a sort of generalization of the now largely abandoned idea of the "white man's burden"). We need rather a criterion that limits ethical obligations, duties, and so on to those beings who can in fact assume them—and which is expressed in a general way that leaves open, as an empirical question, what it includes or excludes. Such a criterion, happily, is immediately available. As I noted in the previous section, ethical and moral-like limitations are not the only systems of social limitation species have evolved. Ethics is only one such modality among many. Therefore, it is appropriate, and neither arbitrary nor prejudicial, to require ethical behavior consistent with an environmental ethic only of those beings who are otherwise subject to ethical limitations or other closely analogous moral-like social restraints. Hence, with a clear conscience that we are being fair, we may write:

(2a)      $(x) [(LCx \cdot Ex) \supset LEx]$.

For any natural being, human or otherwise, if he is a member of the land community *and* he is subject to (other) ethical limitations, then he is subject to environmental ethical limitations.

For those philosophers who maintain a strict policy of biological *apartheid,* no animal will meet both conditions specified for being subject to an environmental ethic. People, they will agree, are subject to ethical limitations, but for this very reason and others having to do with certain metaphysical and theological suppositions, people are *not* members of the biotic community. In addition, the same philosophers will argue that "brute beasts" are not in any way subject to ethical or moral-like limitations (behavioral evidence to the contrary notwithstanding) since, in their view, such limitations are a perquisite of people.

For those philosophers who are biologically more democratic, more than one species may meet both conditions. People are obviously moral animals, animals subject to ethical limitations, and, to these philosophers, it is equally obvious that people are members of the biotic (land or ecological) community. Moreover, they may believe that other species also meet both conditions. For example, *Orcinus orca* lives an intensely social life in permanently established pods. They hunt cooperatively, and are usually diffident while feeding. Their behavior is thus—in conformity generally with proposition (1a)—modified by ethical or moral-like limitations, and by definition they are also members of the biotic community. Thus, according to our theory Orcas should be as equally subject to an environmental ethic as ourselves. Whether Orcas do or do not behave accordingly is an indifferent question so far as our theory is concerned, since, although subject to environmental ethics, like most people they may ignore or avoid environmental duties. But, it would not be absurd to investigate Orca behavior empirically in relation to the environment for the purpose of discovering a certain wantonness or the lack of it in the Orca's exploitation of their resources.

## IV

A sociobiological interpretation and analysis of ethics such as Leopold's may provide a means of navigating through some of the more turbid waters of contemporary ethical theory. On the one hand is the Scylla of the "naturalistic fallacy" and on the other the Charybdis of imperatives, commandments, duties, obligations, the mute necessity of which some may be able to intuit ("nonnaturally") while others may not.

From a scientific point of view, that is, from a detached and analytic perspective, ethics and other moral-like systems of behavioral inhibition are functional in the same way in which any behavioral disposition is functional. An ethic enables some animals to integrate socially. Other animals, most notably the social insects, accomplish the same integration and orchestration of individuals by a completely different means; just as, for example, the bee communicates information to other bees by a means altogether different from that typical of mammals.

Thus, from this point of view, ethics are utilitarian, a means to an end—not an end which we may choose, but an end which is given by nature itself, remorselessly imposed by the principle of natural selection. If *inclusive fitness* is the given end of organic activity, and if social integration is in some cases the means thereto, then ethics, and other modalities of social restraint as a means to the formation of a society, are *generally* derived. In the terminology bequeathed to philosophy by Kant, they have something similar to the status of assertorial hypotheticals. If further specification of the type of society required to best adapt to available resources and natural enemies is given, among human beings and the "higher" mammals, specific restraints may be specifically derived. For example, for hunting/gathering people, a division of labor along sex lines may be more efficient than some other principle of division. As a means to this, certain mores and taboos evolve and eventually acquire the status of commandments, duties, or imperatives. "Thou shalt not covet thy neighbor's wife" serves to reduce quarreling among males, which thus facilitates cooperative hunting by the male members of the society upon which may turn the fitness of the group and a fortiori its individual members. Peculiarities in the restrained behavior among wolves might be explained in a similar manner.

Leopold notes, however, that "the path to social expediency is not discernible to the average individual."[11] Hence, from the internal point of view, the point of view of membership in a given society, ethical imperatives appear to be categorical, or apodeictic, and not prudential. If an environmental ethic is to be an ethic proper, not a complication of familiar prudential considerations based exclusively upon attention to human values (a new ecological enlightenment to guide collective and personal self-interest), it has to be internally articulated in such a way as to confer more than mere instrumental value upon nonhuman natural entities. Leopold remarks that "land-use ethics are still governed wholly by economic self-interest...[but]...obligations have no meaning without conscience, and the problem we face is the extension of social conscience from people to land. No important change in ethics was ever accomplished without a change in our intellectual emphasis, loyalties, affections, and convictions."[12] He further insists that "it is inconceivable to me that an ethical relation to land can exist without love, respect, and admiration for land, and a high regard for its value. By value, I of course mean...value in the philosophical sense."[13]

The function of an ethic, therefore, is one thing; its form and method quite another. In the best tradition of classical philosophical ethics, Leopold distills a general maxim, an overarching imperative, for the governance of conduct in respect to the environment: "A thing is right when it tends to preserve the integrity, stability, and beauty of the biotic community. It is wrong when it tends otherwise."[14]

The twentieth-century discovery of a biotic community has helped us realize the need (a prudential need) for an environmental ethic. To address this need, however, an ethic derived from utilitarianism does not, according to Leopold (and others), go far enough. A proper ethic, a distinctly environmental ethic—founded perhaps upon love and respect, upon an expanded moral sentiment—may be the only effective way to reestablish harmony between people and the biotic community as a whole, to which people also belong.

### V

In the only extended discussion to date [1979] of environmental ethics by a professional philosopher, *Man's Responsibility for Nature: Ecological Problems and Western Traditions,* John Passmore pounces on the idea of a land community when taken to have moral implications. He writes, "We sometimes now meet with the suggestion ... that animals do in fact form, with men, a single community, and so can properly be said to have rights. Indeed, Aldo Leopold has gone further than this: 'when we see land as a community to which we belong,' he writes, 'we may begin to use it with love and respect.' ... Ecologically, no doubt, men do form a community with plants, animals, soil, in the sense that a particular life-cycle will involve all four of them. But if it is essential to a community that the members of it have common interests and recognize mutual obligations then men, plants, animals, and soil do *not* form a community. Bacteria and men do not recognize mutual obligations, nor do they have common interests. In the only sense in which belonging to a community generates ethical obligation, they do not belong to the same community."[15]

Passmore specifies two necessary conditions for the existence of a community with moral import: (i) recognition of mutual obligations, and (ii) the sharing of common interests. I deny that the first is a necessary condition. Criminals are members of the human community but do not recognize mutual obligations, nor do the feebleminded, the senile, the insane, infants, the comatose, and so forth. The second condition is met by all candidates. Bacteria (whom Passmore must consider a very alien form of life) and people do have common interests. Indeed, in the case of some bacteria and all people the cooperative mutual dependency is so great that it could be called a biological symbiosis in the strictest sense. But all living things are united ecologically, and all share the common interest of life itself, the desire to live and to be let alone.

## VI

Still, doubt may linger regarding the legitimacy of the concept of an ecological community with ethical import. Is it more than a mere metaphor? Perhaps Passmore's criticisms can be easily dispatched, but there may be other flaws in the idea which he may have overlooked. To be reassured that the biotic-moral community is neither a will-of-the-wisp nor a wind egg, the similarities and differences between it and social paradigms should be explored. A full discussion of this problem goes beyond the scope of this paper; nevertheless, a few tentative observations may be helpful. The most conspicuous difference between an ecological community and a society is that the latter is usually composed of members all belonging to the same species. There are, I suppose, some exceptions to this rule, even among people, but they are exceptions and they are problematic. (For example, some American Indians do speak as if they are closely akin to some species of animal or plant and domestic animals and pets are sometimes treated as if they had some social standing.) But the differenct between a biotic community, which in its most expansive sense includes all living things ("plants and animals") and even nonliving things ("soils and waters"0, and human communities and other animal societies is fundamental. Therefore, the term 'ecological community' has at best an analogical sense.

From the perspective of natural selection, animal societies arise as a means to more efficient reproduction, to more efficient defense, and to a more efficient economy. Social organization may serve other functions but these are central and universal. For the first two functions there are few unequivocal analogues in the biotic community. Honey bees may be an essential part of the reproductive processes of many flowering plants, but this inter-specific reproductive dependency is not typical in nature. Sharks may incidentally protect the pilot fish who swim with them, but this is not a common kind of biocenosis. The biotic community is, on the other hand, an economic system par excellence. Indeed we could plausibly say that ecology is principally, if not altogether, the study of the economy of nature. Each of the myriad living forms, while pursuing its own interests, performs a function which contributes to the overall flow of materials, services, and energy within the system. Plants, while nourishing themselves on air, water, and minerals, fix solar energy in a form usable by some animals. They also produce free oxygen as a byproduct. Grazing animals, as they feed directly on plants, begin the process of recycling plant nutrients, restoring carbon dioxide to the air and minerals to the soil, a process completed by worms and bacteria. In general, each thing has a certain role or function in the natural economy to which it becomes adapted, and ecologists speak of *producers, consumers, decomposers,* and fit each to its "niche" in the ecosystem. To say, as Leopold says, that we are members of a land community therefore is to say that just as we are economically dependent on other people—farmers in Iowa, factory workers in Tokyo, and so forth—so are we also dependent upon phytoplankton, forests, earthworms, honey bees, bacteria, and so forth, in a way that is formally the same. If an ethic is the human mode of recognition and facilitation of reciprocity in the former case, then why should it not be for the latter as well?

## VII

Finally, we may ask, does our environmental ethic meet the Routley test for environmental ethics? If the ecological community and the human community are analogues, one to the other, in respect to a general economic form, that is, if the ecological community is the macrocosmos and the human community the microcosmos in respect to economy, then we may consider the following allegory as decisive. In Routley's "last people" example let us substitute the last of the Detroit tycoons. Sometime, in the not-so-distant future, after fossil fuels have all been spent and energy in any form is at a premium, the private automobile becomes a thing of the past. In bitterness the last of the Detroit automobile manufacturers set about destroying all the people they can lay hand upon, men, women, and children. If the conduct of the last of the Detroit tycoons is wrong, then in accordance with our environmental ethic, the conduct of Routley's last people is also clearly wrong.

# 5

## The Conceptual Foundations of the Land Ethic

*The two great cultural advances of the past century were the Darwinian theory and the development of geology.... Just as important, however, as the origin of plants, animals, and soil is the question of how they operate as a community. That task has fallen to the new science of ecology, which is daily uncovering a web of interdependencies so intricate as to amaze—were he here —even Darwin himself, who, of all men, should have least cause to tremble before the veil.*

—Aldo Leopold, fragment 6B16,
no. 36, Leopold Papers, University
of Wisconsin—Madison Archives

### I

As Wallace Stegner observes, *A Sand County Almanac* is considered "almost a holy book in conservation circles," and Aldo Leopold a prophet, "an American Isaiah." And as Curt Meine points out, "The Land Ethic" is the climatic essay of *Sand County*, "the upshot of 'The Upshot.'"[1] One might, therefore, fairly say that the recommendation and justification of moral obligations on the part of people to nature is what the prophetic *A Sand County Almanac* is all about.

But, with few exceptions, "The Land Ethic" has not been favorably received by contemporary academic philosophers. Most have ignored it. Of those who have not, most have been either nonplussed or hostile. Distinguished Australian philosopher John Passmore dismissed it out of hand, in the first book-length academic discussion of the new philosophical subdiscipline called "environmental ethics."[2] In a more recent and more deliberate discussion, the equally distinguished Australian philosopher H. J. McCloskey patronized Aldo Leopold and saddled "The Land Ethic" with various far-fetched "interpretations." He concludes that "there is a real problem in attributing a coherent meaning to Leopold's statements, one that exhibits his land ethic as representing a major advance in ethics rather than a retrogression to a

75

morality of a kind held by various primitive peoples."[3] Echoing McCloskey, English philosopher Robin Attfield went out of his way to impugn the philosophical respectability of "The Land Ethic." And Canadian philosopher L. W. Sumner has called it "dangerous nonsense."[4] Among those philosophers more favorably disposed, "The Land Ethic" has usually been simply quoted, as if it were little more than a noble, but naive, moral plea, altogether lacking a supporting theoretical framework—that is, foundational principles and premises which lead, by compelling argument, to ethical precepts.

The professional neglect, confusion, and (in some cases) contempt for "The Land Ethic" may, in my judgment, be attributed to three things: (1) Leopold's extremely condensed prose style in which an entire conceptual complex may be conveyed in a few sentences, or even in a phrase or two; (2) his departure from the assumptions and paradigms of contemporary philosophical ethics; and (3) the unsettling practical implications to which a land ethic appears to lead. "The Land Ethic," in short, is, from a philosophical point of view, abbreviated, unfamiliar, and radical.

Here I first examine and elaborate the compactly expressed abstract elements of the land ethic and expose the "logic" which binds them into a proper, but revolutionary, moral theory. I then discuss the controversial features of the land ethic and defend them against actual and potential criticism. I hope to show that the land ethic cannot be ignored as merely the groundless emotive exhortations of a moonstruck conservationist or dismissed as entailing wildly untoward practical consequences. It poses, rather, a serious intellectual challenge to business-as-usual moral philosophy.

## II

"The Land Ethic" opens with a charming and poetic evocation of Homer's Greece, the point of which is to suggest that today land is just as routinely and remorsely enslaved as human beings then were. A panoramic glance backward to our most distant cultural origins, Leopold suggests, reveals a slow but steady moral development over three millennia. More of our relationships and activities ("fields of conduct") have fallen under the aegis of moral principles ("ethical criteria") as civilization has grown and matured. If moral growth and development continue, as not only a synoptic review of history, but recent past experience suggest that it will, future generations will censure today's casual and universal environmental bondage as today we censure the casual and universal human bondage of three thousand years ago.[5]

A cynically inclined critic might scoff at Leopold's sanguine portrayal of human history. Slavery survived as an institution in the "civilized" West, more particularly in the morally self-congratulatory United States, until a mere generation before Leopold's own birth. And Western history from imperial Athens and Rome to the Spanish Inquisition and the Third Reich has been a disgraceful series of wars, persecutions, tyrannies, pogroms, and other atrocities.

The history of moral practice, however, is not identical with the history of moral consciousness. Morality is not descriptive; it is prescriptive or normative. In light of this distinction, it is clear that today, despite rising rates of violent crime in the United States and institutional abuses of human rights in Iran, Chile, Ethiopia, Guatemala, South Africa, and many other places, and despite persistent organized social injustice and oppression in still others, moral consciousness is expanding more rapidly now than ever before. Civil rights, human rights, women's liberation, children's liberation, animal liberation, and so forth, all indicate, as expressions of newly emergent moral ideals, that ethical consciousness (as distinct from practice) has if anything recently accelerated—thus confirming Leopold's historical observation.

## III

Leopold next points out that "this extension of ethics, so far studied only by philosophers"—and therefore, the implication is clear, not very satisfactorily studied—"is actually a process in ecological evolution" (p. 202). What Leopold is saying here, simply, is that we may understand the history of ethics, fancifully alluded to by means of the Odysseus vignette, in biological as well as philosophical terms. From a biological point of view, an ethic is "a limitation on freedom of action in the struggle for existence" (p. 202).

I had this passage in mind when I remarked that Leopold manages to convey a whole network of ideas in a couple of phrases. The phrase "struggle for existence" unmistakably calls to mind Darwinian evolution as the conceptual context in which a biological account of the origin and development of ethics must ultimately be located. And at once it points up a paradox: Given the unremitting competitive "struggle for existence" how could "limitations of freedom of action" ever have been conserved and spread through a population of Homo sapiens or their evolutionary progenitors?

For a biological account of ethics, as Harvard social entomologist

Edward O. Wilson has recently written, "the central theoretical problem ... [is] how can altruism [elaborately articulated as morality or ethics in the human species], which by definition reduces personal fitness, possibly evolve by natural selection?"[6] According to modern sociobiology, the answer lies in kinship. But according to Darwin— who had tackled this problem himself "exclusively from the side of natural history" in *The Descent of Man*—the answer lies in society.[7] And it was Darwin's classical account (and its diverse variations), from the side of natural history, which informed Leopold's thinking in the late 1940s.

Let me put the problem in perspective. How, we are asking, did ethics originate and, once in existence, grow in scope and complexity?

The oldest answer in living human memory is theological. God (or the gods) imposes morality on people. And God (or the gods) sanctions it. A most vivid and graphic example of this kind of account occurs in the Bible when Moses goes up on Mount Sinai to receive the Ten Commandments directly from God. That text also clearly illustrates the divine sanctions (plagues, pestilences, droughts, military defeats, and so forth) for moral disobedience. Ongoing revelation of the divine will, of course, as handily and as simply explains subsequent moral growth and development.

Western philosophy, on the other hand, is almost unanimous in the opinion that the origin of ethics in human experience has somehow to do with human reason. Reason figures centrally and pivotally in the "social contract theory" of the origin and nature of morals in all its ancient, modern, and contemporary expressions from Protagoras, to Hobbes, to Rawls. Reason is the wellspring of virtue, according to both Plato and Aristotle, and of categorical imperatives, according to Kant. In short, the weight of Western philosophy inclines to the view that we are moral beings because we are rational beings. The ongoing sophistication of reason and the progressive illumination it sheds upon the good and the right explain "the ethical sequence," the historical growth and development of morality, noticed by Leopold.

An evolutionary natural historian, however, cannot be satisfied with either of these general accounts of the origin and development of ethics. The idea that God gave morals to man is ruled out in principle— as any supernatural explanation of a natural phenomenon is ruled out in principle in natural science. And while morality might *in principle* be a function of human reason (as, say, mathematical calculation clearly is), to suppose that it is so *in fact* would be to put the cart before the horse. Reason appears to be a delicate, variable, and recently emerged faculty. It cannot, under any circumstances, be supposed to have evolved in the absence of complex linguistic capabilities which depend, in turn, for their evolution upon a highly developed social matrix. But we cannot have become social beings unless we assumed limitations on freedom of action in the struggle for existence. Hence we must have become ethical before we became rational.

Darwin, probably in consequence of reflections somewhat like these, turned to a minority tradition of modern philosophy for a moral psychology consistent with and useful to a general evolutionary account of ethical phenomena. A century earlier, Scottish philosophers David Hume and Adam Smith had argued that ethics rest upon feelings or "sentiments"—which, to be sure, may be both amplified and informed by reason.[8] And since in the animal kingdom feelings or sentiments are arguably far more common or widespread than reason, they would be a far more likely starting point for an evolutionary account of the origin and growth of ethics.

Darwin's account, to which Leopold unmistakably (if elliptically) alludes in "The Land Ethic," begins with the parental and filial affections common, perhaps, to all mammals.[9] Bonds of affection and sympathy between parents and offspring permitted the formation of small, closely kin social groups, Darwin argued. Should the parental and filial affections bonding family members chance to extend to less closely related individuals, that would permit an enlargement of the family group. And should the newly extended community more successfully defend itself and/or more efficiently provision itself, the inclusive fitness of its members severally would be increased, Darwin reasoned. Thus the more diffuse familial affections, which Darwin (echoing Hume and Smith) calls the "social sentiments," would be spread throughout a population.[10]

Morality, properly speaking—that is, morality as opposed to mere altruistic instinct—requires, in Darwin's terms, "intellectual powers" sufficient to recall the past and imagine the future, "the power of language" sufficient to express "common opinion," and "habituation" to patterns of behavior deemed, by common opinion, to be socially acceptable and beneficial.[11] Even so, ethics proper, in Darwin's account, remains firmly rooted in moral feelings or social sentiments which were—no less than physical faculties, he expressly avers—naturally selected, by the advantages for survival and especially for successful reproduction, afforded by society.[12]

The protosociobiological perspective on ethical phenomena, to which Leopold as a natural historian was heir, leads him to a generalization which is remarkably explicit in his condensed and often merely resonant rendering of Darwin's more deliberate and extended paradigm: Since "the thing [ethics] has its origin in the tendency of interdependent individuals or groups to evolve modes of co-operation,

... all ethics so far evolved rest upon a single premise: that the individual is a member of a community of interdependent parts" (p. 202-3).

Hence, we may expect to find that the scope and specific content of ethics will reflect both the perceived boundaries and actual structure or organization of a cooperative community or society. *Ethics and society or community are correlative.* This single, simple principle constitutes a powerful tool for the analysis of moral natural history, for the anticipation of future moral development (including, ultimately, the land ethic), and for systematically deriving the specific precepts, the prescriptions and proscriptions, of an emergent and culturally unprecedented ethic like a land or environmental ethic.

## IV

Anthropological studies of ethics reveal that in fact the boundaries of the moral community are generally coextensive with the perceived boundaries of society.[13] And the peculiar (and, from the urbane point of view, sometimes inverted) representation of virtue and vice in tribal society—the virtue, for example, of sharing to the point of personal destitution and the vice of privacy and private property—reflects and fosters the life way of tribal peoples.[14] Darwin, in his leisurely, anecdotal discussion, paints a vivid picture of the intensity, peculiarity, and sharp circumscription of "savage" mores: "A savage will risk his life to save that of a member of the same community, but will be wholly indifferent about a stranger."[15] As Darwin portrays them, tribespeople are at once paragons of virtue "within the limits of the same tribe" and enthusiastic thieves, manslaughterers, and torturers without.[16]

For purposes of more effective defense against common enemies, or because of increased population density, or in response to innovations in subsistence methods and technologies, or for some mix of these or other forces, human societies have grown in extent or scope and changed in form or structure. Nations—like the Iroquois nation or the Sioux nation—came into being upon the merger of previously separate and mutually hostile tribes. Animals and plants were domesticated and erstwhile hunter-gatherers become herders and farmers. Permanent habitations were established. Trade, craft, and (later) industry flourished. With each change in society came corresponding and correlative changes in ethics. The moral community expanded to become coextensive with the newly drawn boundaries of societies and the representation of virtue and vice, right and wrong, good and evil, changed to accommodate, foster, and preserve the economic and institutional organization of emergent social orders.

Today we are witnessing the painful birth of a human supercommunity, global in scope. Modern transportation and communication technologies, international economic interdependencies, international economic entities, and nuclear arms have brought into being a "global village." It has not yet become fully formed and it is at tension—a very dangerous tension—with its predecessor, the nation-state. Its eventual institutional structure, a global federalism or whatever it may turn out to be, is at this point completely unpredictable. Interestingly, however, a corresponding global human ethic—the "human rights" ethic, as it is popularly called—has been more definitely articulated.

Most educated people today pay lip service at least to the ethical precept that all members of the human species, regardless of race, creed, or national origin, are endowed with certain fundamental rights which it is wrong not to respect. According to the evolutionary scenario set out by Darwin, the contemporary moral ideal of human rights is a response to a perception however vague and indefinite—that mankind worldwide is united into one society, one community, however indeterminate or yet institutionally unorganized. As Darwin presciently wrote:

> As man advances in civilization, and small tribes are united into larger communities, the simplest reason would tell each individual that he ought to extend his social instincts and sympathies to all the members of the same nation, though personally unknown to him. This point being once reached, there is only an artificial barrier to prevent his sympathies extending to the men of all nations and races. If, indeed, such men are separated from him by great differences of appearance or habits, experience unfortunately shows us how long it is, before we look at them as our fellow-creatures [17]

According to Leopold, the next step in this sequence beyond the still incomplete ethic of universal humanity, a step that is clearly discernible on the horizon, is the land ethic. The "community concept" has, so far, propelled the development of ethics from the savage clan to the family of man. "The land ethic simply enlarges the boundary of the community to include soils, waters, plants, and animals, or collectively: the land" (p. 204).

As the foreword to *Sand County* makes plain, the overarching thematic principle of the book is the inculcation of the idea—through narrative description, discursive exposition, abstractive generalization, and occasional preachment—"that land is a community" (viii). The community concept is "the basic concept of ecology" (viii). Once land is popularly perceived as a biotic community—as it is professionally perceived in ecology—a correlative land ethic will emerge in the collective cultural consciousness.

## V

Although anticipated as far back as the mid-eighteenth century—in the notion of an "economy of nature"—the concept of the biotic community was more fully and deliberately developed as a working model or paradigm for ecology by Charles Elton in the 1920s.[18] The natural world is organized as an intricate corporate society in which plants and animals occupy "niches," or as Elton alternatively called them, "roles" or "professions," in the economy of nature.[19] As in a feudal community, little or no socioeconomic mobility (upward or otherwise) exists in the biotic community. One is born to one's trade.

Human society, Leopold argues, is founded, in large part, upon mutual security and economic interdependency and preserved only by limitations on freedom of action in the struggle for existence—that is, by ethical constraints. Since the biotic community exhibits, as modern ecology reveals, an analogous structure, it too can be preserved, given the newly amplified impact of "mechanized man," only by analogous limitations on freedom of action—that is, by a land ethic (viii). A land ethic, furthermore, is not only "an ecological necessity," but an "evolutionary possibility" because a moral response to the natural environment—Darwin's social sympathies, sentiments, and instincts translated and codified into a body of principles and precepts—would be automatically triggered in human beings by ecology's social representation of nature (p. 203).

Therefore, the key to the emergence of a land ethic is, simply, universal ecological literacy.

## VI

The land ethic rests upon three scientific cornerstones: (1) evolutionary and (2) ecological biology set in a background of (3) Copernican astronomy. Evolutionary theory provides the conceptual link between ethics and social organization and development. It provides a sense of "kinship with fellow-creatures" as well, "fellow-voyagers" with us in the "odyssey of evolution" (p. 109). It establishes a diachronic link between people and nonhuman nature.

Ecological theory provides a synchronic link—the community concept—a sense of social integration of human and nonhuman nature. Human beings, plants, animals, soils, and waters are "all interlocked in one humming community of cooperations and competitions, one biota."[20] The simplest reason, to paraphrase Darwin, should, therefore, tell each individual that he or she ought to extend his or her social instincts and sympathies to all the members of the biotic community though different from him or her in appearance or habits.

And although Leopold never directly mentions it in *A Sand County Almanac*, the Copernican perspective, the perception of the earth as "a small planet" in an immense and utterly hostile universe beyond, contributes, perhaps subconsciously, but nevertheless very powerfully, to our sense of kinship, community, and interdependence with fellow denizens of the earth household. It scales the earth down to something like a cozy island paradise in a desert ocean.

Here in outline, then, are the conceptual and logical foundations of the land ethic: Its conceptual elements are a Copernican cosmology, a Darwinian protosociobiological natural history of ethics, Darwinian ties of kinship among all forms of life on earth, and an Eltonian model of the structure of biocenoses all overlaid on a Humean-Smithian moral psychology. Its logic is that natural selection has endowed human beings with an affective moral response to perceived bonds of kinship and community membership and identity; that today the natural environment, the land, is represented as a community, the biotic community; and that, therefore, an environmental or land ethic is both possible—the biopsychological and cognitive conditions are in place—and necessary, since human beings collectively have acquired the power to destroy the integrity, diversity, and stability of the environing and supporting economy of nature. In the remainder of this essay I discuss special features and problems of the land ethic germane to moral philosophy.

The most salient feature of Leopold's land ethic is its provision of what Kenneth Goodpaster has carefully called "moral considerability" for the biotic community per se, not just for fellow members of the biotic community:[21]

> In short, a land ethic changes the role of *Homo sapiens* from conqueror of the land-community to plain member and citizen of it. It implies respect for his fellow-members, *and also respect for the community as such.* (p. 204, emphasis added)

The land ethic, thus, has a holistic as well as an individualistic cast.

Indeed, as "The Land Ethic" develops, the focus of moral concern shifts gradually away from plants, animals, soils, and waters severally to the biotic community collectively. Toward the middle, in the subsection called 'Substitutes for a Land Ethic,' Leopold invokes the "biotic rights" of *species*—as the context indicates—of wildflowers, songbirds, and predators. In 'The Outlook,' the climactic section of "The Land Ethic," nonhuman natural entities, first appearing as fellow members, then considered in profile as species, are not so much as mentioned in what might be called the "summary moral maxim" of the land ethic: "A thing is right when it tends to preserve the integrity, stability, and beauty of the biotic community. It is wrong when it tends otherwise" (p. 224–25).

By this measure of right and wrong, not only would it be wrong for a farmer, in the interest of higher profits, to clear the woods off a 75 percent slope, turn his cows into the clearing and dump its rainfall, rocks, and soil into the community creek, it would also be wrong for the federal fish and wildlife agency, in the interest of individual animal welfare, to permit populations of deer, rabbits, feral burros, or whatever to increase unchecked and thus to threaten the integrity, stability, and beauty of the biotic communities of which they are members. The land ethic not only provides moral considerability for the biotic community per se, but ethical consideration of its individual members is preempted by concern for the preservation of the integrity, stability, and beauty of the biotic community. The land ethic, thus, not only has a holistic aspect; it is holistic with a vengeance.

The holism of the land ethic, more than any other feature, sets it apart from the predominant paradigm of modern moral philosophy. It is, therefore, the feature of the land ethic which requires the most patient theoretical anaylsis and the most sensitive practical interpretation.


## VII

As Kenneth Goodpaster pointed out, mainstream modern ethical philosophy has take egoism as its point of departure and reached a wider circle of moral entitlement by a process of generalization:[22] I am sure that *I,* the enveloped ego, am intrinsically or inherently valuable and thus that *my* interests ought to be considered, taken into account, by "others" when their actions may substantively affect *me.* My own claim to moral consideration, according to the conventional wisdom, ultimately rests upon a psychological capacity—rationality or sentiency were the classical candidates of Kant and Bentham, respectively —which is arguably valuable in itself and which thus qualifies *me* for moral standing.[23] However, then I am forced grudgingly to grant the same moral consideration I demand from others, on this basis, to those others who can also claim to possess the same general psychological characteristic.

A criterion of moral value and consideration is thus identified. Goodpaster convincingly argues that mainstream modern moral theory is based, when all the learned dust has settled, on this simple paradigm of ethical justification and logic exemplified by the Benthamic and Kantian prototypes.[24] If the criterion of moral values and consideration is pitched low enough—as it is in Bentham's criterion of sentiency—a wide variety of animals are admitted to moral entitlement.[25] If the criterion of moral value and consideration is pushed lower still—as it is in Albert Schweitzer's reverence-for-life ethic—all minimally conative things (plants as well as animals) would be extended moral considerability.[26] The contemporary animal liberation/rights, and reverence-for-life/life-principle ethics are, at bottom, simply direct applications of the modern classical paradigm of moral argument. But this standard modern model of ethical theory provides no possibility whatever for the moral consideration of wholes—of threatened population of animals and plants, or of endemic, rare, or endangered species, or of biotic communities, or most expansively, of the biosphere in its totality—since wholes per se have no psychological experience of any kind. [27] Because mainstream modern moral theory has been "psychocentric," it has been radically and intractably individualistic or "atomistic" in its fundamental theoretical orientation.

Hume, Smith, and Darwin diverged from the prevailing theoretical model by recognizing that altruism is as fundamental and autochthonous in human nature as is egoism. According to their analysis, moral value is not identified with a natural quality objectively present in morally considerable beings—as reason and/or sentiency is objectively present in people and/or animals—it is, as it were, projected by valuing subjects.[28]

Hume and Darwin, furthermore, recognize inborn moral sentiments which have society as such as their natural object. Hume insists that "we must renounce the theory which accounts for every moral sentiment by the principle of self-love. We must adopt a more *publick affection* and allow that the *interests of society* are not, *even on their own account*, entirely indifferent to us."[29] And Darwin, somewhat ironically (since "Darwinian evolution" very often means natural selection operating exclusively with respect to individuals), sometimes writes as if morality had no other object than the commonweal, the welfare of the community as a corporate entity:

> We have now seen that actions are regarded by savages, and were probably so regarded by primeval man, as good or bad, solely as they obviously affect the welfare of the tribe,—not that of the species, nor that of the individual member of the tribe. This conclusion agrees well

with the belief that the so-called moral sense is aboriginally derived from social instincts, for both relate at first exclusively to the community.[30]

Theoretically then, the biotic community owns what Leopold, in the lead paragraph of 'The Outlook,' calls "value in the philosophical sense"—that is, direct moral considerability—because it is a newly discovered proper object of a specially evolved "publick affection" or "moral sense" which all psychologically normal human beings have inherited from a long line of ancestral social primates (p. 223). [31]

## VIII

In the land ethic, as in all earlier stages of social-ethical evolution, there exists a tension between the good of the community as a whole and the "rights" of its individual members considered severally. While 'The Ethical Sequence' section of "The Land Ethic" clearly evokes Darwin's classical biosocial account of the origin and extension of morals, Leopold is actually more explicitly concerned, in that section, with the interplay between the holistic and individualistic moral sentiments—between sympathy and fellow-feeling on the one hand, and public affection for the commonweal on the other:

> The first ethics dealt with the relation between individuals; the Mosaic Decalogue is an example. Later accretions dealt with the relation between the individual and society. The Golden Rule tries to integrate the individual to society; democracy to integrate social organization to the individual. (p. 202–3)

Actually, it is doubtful that the first ethics dealt with the relation between individuals and not at all with the relation between the individual and society. (This, along with the remark that ethics replaced an "original free-for-all competition," suggests that Leopold's Darwinian line of thought has been uncritically tainted with Hobbesean elements [p. 202]. Of course, Hobbes's "state of nature," in which there prevailed a war of each against all, is absurd from an evolutionary point of view.) A century of ethnographic studies seems to confirm, rather, Darwin's conjecture that the relative weight of the holistic component is greater in tribal ethics—the tribal ethic of the Hebrews recorded in the Old Testament constitutes a vivid case in point—than in more recent accretions. The Golden Rule, on the other hand, does not mention, in any of its formulations, society per se. Rather, its primary concern seems to be "others," that is, other human individuals. Democracy, with its stress on individual liberties and rights, seems to further rather than counter-vail the individualistic thrust of the Golden Rule.

In any case, the conceptual foundations of the land ethic provide a well-informed, self-consistent theoretical basis for including both fellow members of the biotic community and the biotic community itself (considered as a corporate entity) within the purview of morals. The pre-emptive emphasis, however, on the welfare of the community as a whole, in Leopold's articulation of the land ethic, while certainly consistent with its Humean-Darwinian theoretical foundations, is not determined by them alone. The overriding holism of the land ethic results, rather, more from the way our moral sensibilities are informed by ecology.

## IX

Ecological thought, historically, has tended to be holistic in outlook.[32] Ecology is the study of the relationships of organisms to one another and to the elemental environment. These relationships bind the *relata*—plants, animals, soils, and waters—into a seamless fabric. The ontological primacy of objects and the ontological subordination of relationships characteristic of classical Western science is, in fact, reversed in ecology.[33] Ecological relationships determine the nature of organisms rather than the other way around. A species is what it is because it has adapted to a niche in the ecosystem. The whole, the system itself, thus, literally and quite straightforwardly shapes and forms its component species.

Antedating Charles Elton's community model of ecology was F. E. Clements and S. A. Forbes's organism model.[34] Plants and animals, soils and waters, according to this paradigm, are integrated into one super-organism. Species are, as it were, its organs; specimens its cells. Although Elton's community paradigm (later modified, as we shall see, by Arthur Tansley's ecosystem idea) is the principal and morally fertile ecological concept of "The Land Ethic," the more radically holistic superorganism paradigm of Clements and Forbes resonates in "The Land Ethic" as an audible overtone. In the peroration of 'Land Health and the A-B Cleavage,' for example, which immediately precedes 'The Outlook,' Leopold insists that

> in all these cleavages, we see repeated the same basic paradoxes: man the conqueror *versus* man the biotic citizen; science the sharpener of his sword *versus* science the searchlight on his universe; land the slave and servant *versus* land the collective organism. (p. 223)

And on more than one occasion Leopold, in the latter quarter of "The Land Ethic," talks about the "health" and "disease" of the land—terms which are at once descriptive and normative and which, taken literally, characterize only organisms proper.

In an early essay, "Some Fundamentals of Conservation in the Southwest," Leopold speculatively flirted with the intensely holistic superorganism model of the environment as a paradigm pregnant with moral implications:

> It is at least not impossible to regard the earth's parts—soil, mountains, rivers, atmosphere, etc.—as organs or parts of organs, of *a coordinated whole*, each part with a definite function. And if we could see *this whole, as a whole*, through a great period of time, we might perceive not only organs with coordinated functions, but possibly also that process of consumption and replacement which in biology we call metabolism, or growth. In such a case we would have all the visible attributes of a living thing, which we do not realize to be such because it is too big, and its life processes too slow. And there would also follow that invisible attribute—a soul or consciousness—which... many philosophers of all ages ascribe to all living things and aggregates thereof, including the "dead" earth.
>
> Possibly in our intuitive perceptions, which may be truer than our science and less impeded by words than our philosophies, we realize the indivisibility of the earth—its soil, mountains, rivers, forests, climate, plants, and animals—and *respect it collectively* not only as a useful servant but as a living being, vastly less alive than ourselves, but vastly greater than ourselves in time and space.... Philosophy, then, suggests one reason why we cannot destroy the earth with moral impunity; namely, that the "dead" earth is an organism possessing a certain kind and degree of life, which we intuitively respect as such.[35]

Had Leopold retained this overall theoretical approach in "The Land Ethic," the land ethic would doubtless have enjoyed more critical attention from philosophers. The moral foundations of a land or, as he might then have called it, "earth" ethic, would rest upon the hypothesis that the Earth is alive and ensouled—possessing inherent psychological characteristics, logically parallel to reason and sentiency. This notion of a conative whole earth could plausibly have served as a general criterion of intrinsic worth and moral considerability, in the familiar format of mainstream moral thought.

Part of the reason, therefore, that "The Land Ethic" emphasizes more and more the integrity, stability, and beauty of the environment as a whole, and less and less the biotic right of individual plants and animals to life, liberty, and the pursuit of happiness, is that the superorganism ecological paradigm invites one, much more than does the community paradigm, to hypostatize, to reify the whole, and to sub-ordinate its individual members.

In any case, as we see, rereading "The Land Ethic" in light of "Some Fundamentals," the whole Earth organism image of nature is vestigially present in Leopold's later thinking. Leopold may have abandoned the "earth ethic" because ecology had abandoned the organism analogy in favor of the community analogy as a working theoretical paradigm. And the community model was more suitably given moral implications by the social/sentimental ethical natural history of Hume and Darwin.

Meanwhile, the biotic community ecological paradigm itself had acquired, by the late thirties and forties, a more holistic cast of its own. In 1935 British ecologist Arthur Tansley pointed out that from the per-spective of physics the "currency" of the "economy of nature" is energy.[36] Tansley suggested that Elton's qualitative and descriptive food chains, food webs, trophic niches, and biosocial professions could be quantitatively expressed by means of a thermodynamic flow model. It is Tansley's state-of-the-art thermodynamic paradigm of the environ-ment that Leopold explicitly sets out as a "mental image of land" in relation to which "we can be ethical" (p. 214). And it is the ecosystemic model of land which informs the cardinal practical precepts of the land ethic.

'The Land Pyramid' is the pivotal section of "The Land Ethic"—the section which effects a complete transition from concern for "fellow-members" to the "community as such." It is also its longest and most technical section. A description of the "ecosystem" (Tansley's deliber-ately nonmetaphorical term) begins with the sun. Solar energy "flows through a circuit called the biota" (p. 215). It enters the biota through the leaves of green plants and courses through plant-eating animals, and then on to omnivores and carnivores. At last the tiny fraction of solar energy converted to biomass by green plants remaining in the corpse of a predator, animal feces, plant detritus, or other dead organic material is garnered by decomposers—worms, fungi, and bacteria. They recycle the participating elements and degrade into entropic equilibrium any remaining energy. According to this paradigm

> land, then, is not merely soil; it is a fountain of energy flowing through a circuit of soils, plants, and animals. Food chains are the living channels which conduct energy upward; death and decay return it to the soil. The circuit is not closed; ... but it is a sustained circuit, like a slowly augmented revolving fund of life. (p. 216)

In this exceedingly abstract (albeit poetically expressed) model of nature, process precedes substance and energy is more fundamental than matter. Individual plants and animals become less autonomous beings than ephemeral structures in a patterned flux of energy. According to Yale biophysicist Harold Morowitz,

> viewed from the point of view of modern [ecology], each living thing ... is a dissipative structure, that is it does not endure in and of itself but only as a result of the continual flow of energy in the system. An example might be instructive. Consider a vortex in a stream of flowing water. The vortex is a structure made of an ever-changing group of water molecules. It does not exist as an entity in the classical Western sense; it exists only because of the flow of water through the stream. In the same sense, the structures out of which biological entities are made are transient, unstable entities with constantly changing molecules, dependent on a constant flow of energy from food in order to maintain form and structure.... From this point of view the reality of individuals is problematic because they do not exist per se but only as local perturbations in this universal flow.[37]

Though less bluntly stated and made more palatable by the unfailing charm of his prose, Leopold's proffered mental image of land is just as expansive, systemic, and distanced as Morowitz's. The maintenance of "the complex structure of the land and its smooth functioning as an energy unit" emerges in 'The Land Pyramid' as the *summum bonum* of the land ethic (p. 216).

## X

From this good Leopold derives several practical principles slightly less general, and therefore more substantive, than the summary moral maxim of the land ethic distilled in 'The Outlook.' "The trend of evolution [not its "goal," since evolution is ateleological] is to elaborate and diversify the biota" (p. 216). Hence, among our cardinal duties is the duty to preserve what species we can, especially those at the apex of the pyramid—the top carnivores. "In the beginning, the pyramid of life was low and squat; the food chains short and simple. Evolution has added layer after layer, link after link" (pp. 215–16). Human activities today, especially those, like systematic deforestation in the tropics, resulting in abrupt massive extinctions of species, are in effect "devolutionary"; they flatten the biotic pyramid; they choke off some of the channels and gorge others (those which terminate in our own species).[38]

The land ethic does not enshrine the ecological status quo and devalue the dynamic dimension of nature. Leopold explains that "evolution is a long series of self-induced changes, the net result of which has been to elaborate the flow mechanism and to lengthen the circuit. Evolutionary changes, however, are usually slow and local. Man's invention of tools has enabled him to make changes of unprecedented violence, rapidly, and scope" (pp. 216–17). "Natural" species extinction, that is, species extinction in the normal course of evolution, occurs when a species is replaced by competitive exclusion or evolves into another form.[39] Normally speciation outpaces extinction. Mankind inherited a richer, more diverse world than had ever existed before in the 3.5 billion-year odyssey of life on Earth.[40] What is wrong with anthropogenic species extirpation and extinction is the *rate* at which it is occurring and the *result*: biological impoverishment instead of enrichment.

Leopold goes on here to condemn, in terms of its impact on the ecosystem, "the world-wide pooling of faunas and floras," that is, the indiscriminate introduction of exotic and domestic species and the dislocation of native and endemic species, mining the soil for its stored biotic energy, leading ultimately to diminished fertility and to erosion; and polluting and damming water courses (p. 217).

According to the land ethic, therefore: Thou shalt not extirpate or render species extinct; thou shalt exercise great caution in introducing exotic and domestic species into local exosystems, in exacting energy from the soil and releasing it into the biota, and in damming or polluting water courses; and thou shalt be especially solicitous of predatory birds and mammals. Here in brief are the express moral precepts of the land ethic. They are all explicitly informed—not to say derived—from the energy circuit model of the environment.

## XI

The living channels—food chains—through which energy courses are composed of individual plants and animals. A central, stark fact lies at the heart of ecological processes: Energy, the currency of the economy nature, passes from one organism to another, not from hand to hand, like coined money, but, so to speak, from stomach to stomach. Eating *and being eaten*, living *and dying* are what make the biotic community hum.

The precepts of the land ethic, like those of all previous accretions, reflect and reinforce the structure of the community to which it is correlative. Trophic asymmetries constitute the kernel of the biotic community. It seems unjust, unfair. But that is how the economy of nature is organized (and has been for thousands of millions of years). The land ethic, thus, affirms as good, and strives to preserve, the very inequities in nature whose social counterparts in human communities are condemned as bad and would be eradicated by familiar social ethics, especially by the more recent Christian and secular egalitarian exemplars. A "right to life" for individual members is not consistent with the structure of the biotic community and hence is not mandated by the land ethic. This disparity between the land ethic and its more familiar social precedents contributes to the apparent devaluation of individual members of the biotic community and augments and reinforces the tendency of the land ethic, driven by the systemic vision of ecology, toward a more holistic or community-per-se orientation.

Of the few moral philosophers who have given the land ethic a moment's serious thought, most have regarded it with horror because of its emphasis on the good of the community and its deemphasis on the welfare of individual members of the community. Not only are other sentient creatures members of the biotic community and subordinate to its integrity, beauty, and stability; so are *we*. Thus, if it is not only morally permissible, from the point of view of the land ethic, but morally required, that members of certain species be abandoned to predation and other vicissitudes of wild life or even deliberately culled (as in the case of alert and sentient whitetail deer) for the sake of the integrity, stability, and beauty of the biotic community, how can we consistently exempt ourselves from a similar draconian regime? We too are only "plain members and citizens" of the biotic community. And our global population is growing unchecked. According to William Aiken, from the point of view of the land ethic, therefore, "massive human diebacks would be good. It is our duty to cause them. It is our species' duty, relative to the whole, to eliminate 90 percent of our numbers." Thus, according to Tom Regan, the land ethic is a clear case of "environmental fascism."[41]

Of course Leopold never intended the land ethic to have either inhumane or antihumanitarian implications or consequences. But whether he intended them or not, a logically consistent deduction from the theoretical premises of the land ethic might force such untoward conclusions. And given their magnitude and monstrosity, these derivations would constitute a *reductio ad absurdum* of the whole land ethic enterprise and entrench and reinforce our current human chauvinism and moral alienation from nature. If this is what membership in the biotic community entails, then all but the most radical misanthropes would surely want to opt out.

## XII

The land ethic, happily, implies neither inhumane nor inhuman consequences. That some philosophers think it must follows more from their own theoretical presuppositions than from the theoretical elements of the land ethic itself. Conventional modern ethical theory rests moral entitlement, as I earlier pointed out, on a criterion or qualification. If a candidate meets the criterion—rationality of sentiency are the most commonly posited—he, she, or it is entitled to equal moral standing with others who possess the same qualification in equal degree. Hence, reasoning in this philosophically orthodox way, and forcing Leopold's theory to conform: if human beings are, with other animals, plants, soils, and waters, equally members of the biotic community, and if community membership is the criterion of equal moral consideration, then not only do animals, plants, soils, and waters have equal (highly attenuated) "rights," but human beings are equally subject to the same subordination of individual welfare and rights in respect to the good of the community as a whole.

But the land ethic, as I have been at pains to point out, is heir to a line of moral analysis different from that institutionalized in contemporary moral philosophy. From the biosocial evolutionary analysis of ethics upon which Leopold builds the land ethic, it (the land ethic) neither replaces nor overrides previous accretions. Prior moral sensibilities and obligations attendant upon and correlative to prior strata of social involvement remain operative and preemptive.

Being citizens of the United States, or the United Kingdom, or the Soviet Union, or Venezuela, or some other nation-state, and therefore having national obligations and patriotic duties, does not mean that we are not also members of smaller communities or social groups—cities or townships, neighborhoods, and families—or that we are relieved of the peculiar moral responsibilities attendant upon and correlative to these memberships as well. Similarly, our recognition of the biotic community and our immersion in it does not imply that we do not also remain members of the human community—the "family of man" or "global village"—or that we are relieved of the attendant and correlative moral responsibilities of that membership, among them to respect universal human rights and uphold the principles of individual human worth and dignity. The biosocial development of morality does not grow in extent like an expanding balloon, leaving no trace of its previous boundaries, so much as like the circumference of a tree.[42] Each emergent, and larger, social unit is layered over the more primitive, and intimate, ones.

Moreover, as a general rule, the duties correlative to the inner social circles to which we belong eclipse those correlative to the rings farther from the heartwood when conflicts arise. Consider our moral revulsion when zealous ideological nationalists encourage children to turn their parents in to the authorities if their parents should dissent from the political or economic doctrines of the ruling party. A zealous environmentalist who advocated visiting war, famine, or pestilence on human populations (those existing somewhere else, of course) in the name of the integrity, beauty, and stability of the biotic community would be similarly perverse. Family obligations in general come before nationalistic duties and humanitarian obligations in general come before environmental duties. The land ethic, therefore, is not draconian or fascist. It does not cancel human morality. The land ethic may, however, as with any new accretion, demand choices which affect, in turn, the demands of the more interior social-ethical circles. Taxes and the military draft may conflict with family-level obligations. While the land ethic, certainly, does not cancel human morality, neither does it leave it unaffected.

Nor is the land ethic inhumane. Nonhuman fellow members of the biotic community have no "human rights," because they are not, by definition, members of the human community. As fellow members of the biotic community, however, they deserve respect.

How exactly to express or manifest respect, while at the same time abandoning our fellow members of the biotic community to their several fates or even actively consuming them for our own needs (and wants), or deliberately making them casualties of wildlife management for ecological integrity, is a difficult and delicate question.

Fortunately, American Indian and other traditional patterns of human-nature interaction provide rich and detailed models. Algonkian woodland peoples, for instance, represented animals, plants, birds, waters, and minerals as other-than-human persons engaged in reciprocal, mutually beneficial socioeconomic intercourse with human beings.[43] Tokens of payment, together with expressions of apology, were routinely offered to the beings whom it was necessary for these Indians to expolit. Care not to waste the usable parts and care in the disposal of unusable animal and plant remains were also an aspect of the respectful, albeit necessarily consumptive, Algonkian relationship with fellow members of the land community. As I have more fully argued elsewhere, the Algonkian portrayal of human-nature relationships is, indeed, although certainly different in specifics, identical in abstract form to that recommended by Leopold in the land ethic.[44]

## XIII

Ernest Partridge has turned the existence of an American Indian land ethic, however, against the historicity of the biosocial theoretical foundations of the land ethic:

> Anthropologists will find much to criticize in [Leopold's] account. ... The anthropologist will point out that in many primitive cultures, far greater moral concern may be given to animals or even to trees, rocks, and mountains, than are given to persons in other tribes.... Thus we find not an "extension of ethics," but a "leapfrogging" of ethics, over and beyond persons to natural beings and objects. Worse still for Leopold's view, a primitive culture's moral concern for nature often appears to "draw back" to a human centered perspective as that culture evolves toward a civilized condition.[45]

Actually, the apparent historical anomalies, which Partridge points out, confirm, rather than confute, Leopold's ethical sequence. At the tribal stage of human social evolution, a member of another tribe was a member of a separate and independent social organization, and hence of a separate and alien moral community; thus, "[human] persons in other tribes" were not extended moral consideration, just as the biosocial model predicts. However, at least among those tribal people whose world view I have studied in detail, the animals, trees, rocks, and mountains of a tribe's territory were portrayed as working members and trading partners of the local community. Totem representation of clan units within tribal communities facilitated this view. Groups of people were identified as cranes, bears, turtles, and so on; similarly, populations of deer, beaver, fox, etc., were clans of "people"—people who liked going about in outlandish get-ups. Frequent episodes in tribal mythologies of "metamorphosis"—the change from animal to human form and vice versa—further cemented the tribal integration of local nonhuman natural entities. It would be very interesting to know if the flora and fauna living in another tribe's territory would be regarded, like its human members, as beyond the moral pale.

Neither does the "'draw-back' to a human centered [ethical] perspective as [a] culture evolves toward a civilized condition," noticed by Partridge, undermine the biosocial theoretical foundations of the land ethic. Rather, the biosocial theoretical foundations of the land ethic elucidate this historical phenomenon as well. As a culture evolves toward civilization, it increasingly distances itself from the biotic community. "*Civil*ization" means "cityfication"—inhabitation of and participation in an artificial, humanized environment and a corresponding perception of isolation and alienation from nature. Nonhuman natural entities, thus, are divested of their status as members in good standing of the moral community as civilization develops. Today, two processes internal to civilization are bringing us to a recognition that our renunciation of our biotic citizenship was a mistaken self-deception. Evolutionary science and ecological science, which certainly are products of modern civilization now supplanting the anthropomorphic and anthropocentric myths of earlier civilized generations, have rediscovered our integration with the biotic community. And the negative feedback received from modern civilization's technological impact upon nature —pollution, biological impoverishment, and so forth—forcefully reminds us that mankind never really has, despite past assumptions to the contrary, existed apart from the environing biotic community.

## XIV

This reminder of our recent rediscovery of our biotic citizenship brings us face to face with the paradox posed by Peter Fritzell:[46] Either we are plain members and citizens of the biotic community, on a par with other creatures, or we are not. If we are, then we have no moral obligations to our fellow members or to the community per se because, as understood from a modern scientific perspective, nature and natural phenomena are amoral. Wolves and alligators do no wrong in killing and eating deer and dogs (respectively). Elephants cannot be blamed for bulldozing acacia trees and generally wreaking havoc in their natural habitats. If human beings are natural beings, then human behavior, however destructive, is natural behavior and is as blameless, from a natural point of view, as any other behavioral phenomenon exhibited by other natural beings. On the other hand, we are moral beings, the implication seems clear, precisely to the extent that we are civilized, that we have removed ourselves from nature. We are more than natural beings; we are metanatural—not to say, "supernatural"—beings. But then our moral community is limited to only those being who share our transcendence of nature, that is, to human beings (and perhaps to pets who have joined our civilized community as surrogate persons) and to the human community. Hence, have it either way—we are members of the biotic community or we are not—a land or environmental ethic is aborted by either choice.

But nature is *not* amoral. The tacit assumption that we are deliberating, choice-making ethical beings only to the extent that we are metanatural, civilized beings, generates this dilemma. The biosocial analysis of human moral behavior, in which the land ethic is grounded, is designed precisely to show that in fact intelligent moral behavior *is* natural behavior. Hence, we are moral beings not in spite of, but in accordance with, nature. To the extent that nature has produced at least one ethical species, *Homo sapiens,* nature is not amoral.

Alligators, wolves, and elephants are not subject to reciprocal inter-species duties or land ethical obligations themselves because they are incapable of conceiving and/or assuming them. Alligators, as mostly solitary, entrepreneurial reptiles, have no apparent moral sentiments or social instincts whatever. And while wolves and elephants certainly do have social instincts and at least protomoral sentiments, as their social behavior amply indicates, their conception or imagination of community appears to be less culturally plastic than ours and less amenable to cognitive information. Thus, while we might regard them as ethical beings, they are not able, as we are, to form the concept of a universal biotic community, and hence conceive an all-inclusive, holistic land ethic.

The paradox of the land ethic, elaborately noticed by Fritzell, may be cast more generally still in more conventional philosophical terms: Is the land ethic prudential or deontological? Is the land ethic, in other words, a matter of enlightened (collective, human) self-interest, or does it genuinely admit nonhuman natural entities and nature as a whole to true moral standing?

The conceptual foundations of the land ethic, as I have here set them out, and much of Leopold's hortatory rhetoric, would certainly indicate that the land ethic is deontological (or duty oriented) rather than prudential. In the section significantly titled 'The Ecological Conscience,' Leopold complains that the then-current conservation philosophy is inadequate because "it defines no right or wrong, assigns no obligation, calls for no sacrifice, implies no change in the current philosophy of values. In respect of land-use, it urges *only* enlightened self-interest" (pp. 207–8, emphasis added). Clearly, Leopold himself thinks that the land ethic goes beyond prudence. In this section he disparages mere "self-interest" two more times, and concludes that "obligations have no meaning without conscience, and the problem we face is the extension of the social conscience from people to land" (p. 209).

In the next section, 'Substitutes for a Land Ethic,' he mentions rights twice—the "biotic right" of birds to continuance and the absence of a right on the part of human special interest to exterminate predators.

Finally, the first sentences of 'The Outlook' read: "It is inconceivable to me that an ethical relation to land can exist without love, respect, and admiration for land, and a high regard for its value. By value, I of course mean something far broader than mere economic value; I mean value in the philosophical sense" (p. 223). By "value in the philosophical sense," Leopold can only mean what philosophers more technically call "intrinsic value" or "inherent worth."[47] Something that has intrinsic value or inherent worth is valuable in and of itself, not because of what it can do for us. "Obligation," "sacrifice," "a conscience," "respect," the ascription of rights, and intrinsic value—all of these are consistently opposed to self-interest and seem to indicate decisively that the land ethic is of the deontological type.

Some philosophers, however, have seen it differently. Scott Lehmann, for example, writes,

> Although Leopold claims for communities of plants and animals a "right to continued existence," his argument is homocentric, appealing to the human stake in preservation. Basically it is an argument from enlightened self-interest, where the self in question is not an individual human being but humanity—present and future—as a whole.[48]

Lehmann's claim has some merits, even though it flies in the face of Leopold's express commitments. Leopold does frequently lapse into the language of (collective, long-range, human) self-interest. Early on, for example, he remarks, "in human history, we have learned (I hope) that the conqueror role is eventually *self*-defeating" (p. 204, emphasis added). And later, of the 95 percent of Wisconsin species which cannot be "sold, fed, eaten, or otherwise put to economic use," Leopold reminds us that "these creatures are members of the biotic community, and if (as I believe) its stability depends on its integrity, they are entitled to continuance" (p. 210). The implication is clear: the economic 5 percent cannot survive if a significant portion of the uneconomic 95 percent are extirpated; nor may *we*, it goes without saying, survive without these "resources."

Leopold, in fact, seems to be consciously aware of this moral paradox. Consistent with the biosocial foundations of his theory, he expresses it in sociobiological terms:

> An ethic may be regarded as a mode of guidance for meeting ecological situations so new or intricate, or involving such deferred reactions, that the path of social expediency is not discernible to the average individual. Animal instincts are modes of guidance for the individual in meeting such situations. Ethics are possibly a kind of community instinct in-the-making. (p. 203)

From an objective, descriptive sociobiological point of view, ethics evolve because they contribute to the inclusive fitness of their carriers (or, more reductively still, to the multiplication of their carriers' genes);

they are expedient. However, the path to self-interest (or to the self-interest of the selfish gene) is not discernible to the participating individuals (nor, certainly, to their genes). Hence, ethics are grounded in instinctive feeling—love, sympathy, respect—not in self-conscious calculating intelligence. Somewhat like the paradox of hedonism—the notion that one cannot achieve happiness if one directly pursues happiness per se and not other things—one can only secure self-interest by putting the interests of others on a par with one's own (in this case long-range collective human self-interest and the interest of other forms of life and of the biotic community per se).

So, is the land ethic deontological or prudential, after all? It is both —self-consistently both—depending upon point of view. From the inside, from the lived, felt point of view of the community member with evolved moral sensibilities, it is deontological. It involves an affective-cognitive posture of genuine love, respect, admiration, obligation, self-sacrifice, conscience, duty, and the ascription of intrinsic value and biotic rights. From the outside, from the objective and analytic scientific point of view, it is prudential. "There is no other way for land to survive the impact of mechanized man," nor, therefore, for mechanized man to survive his own impact upon the land (p. viii).

# 6

## The Metaphysical Implications of Ecology

### I

The subject of this essay is the metaphysical implications of ecology. From an orthodox philosophical point of view, not only is value segregated from fact, but philosophy is substantively informed only by the universal and foundational sciences.[1] The idea, therefore, that ecology—a scientific newcomer and a science remote from the more fundamental natural sciences—might have *metaphysical implications* may appear, on the face of it, ridiculous. So here at the beginning let me enter a couple of apologetic caveats.

Although it is not a foundational science like physics or a universal science like astronomy, ecology has profoundly altered our understanding of the proximate terrestrial environment in which we live, move, and have our being. And by "implications" I do not mean to suggest that there exist logical relationships between ecological premises and metaphysical conclusions such that if the former are true the latter must also be true. "Imply," "implicate," and "implication" have a wider meaning evolved from the Latin root, *implicare*—to enfold, involve, or engage—which I wish to evoke. Ecology has made plain to us the fact that we are enfolded, involved, and engaged within the living, terrestrial environment—that is, implicated in and implied by it. (This proposition is itself among the metaphysical implications of ecology.) Therefore, ecology also necessarily alters profoundly our understanding of ourselves, severally, and of human nature, collectively. From this altered representation of environment, people (personally and collectively), and the relationships in the environment and between the environment and ourselves, we may *abstract* certain general conceptual notions. These abstractive distillates are the metaphysical implications of ecology to which I draw attention in this discussion.

Ecology and contemporary physics, interestingly, complement one another conceptually and converge toward the same metaphysical notions. Hence, the sciences at the apex of the hierarchy of the natural

101

sciences and those at the base, the "New Ecology" and the "New Physics" respectively, draw mutually consistent and mutually support-ing abstract pictures of nature in its most elementary and universal and in its most complex and local manifestations.[2] A consolidated metaphysical consensus thus appears to be emerging presently from twentieth-century science which may at last supplant the metaphys-ical consensus distilled from the scientific paradigm of the seventeenth century.

## II

To bring dramatically to light the metaphysical implications of ecology, let me begin with a foil: the metaphysical ideas just mentioned, implicated in modern classical science, including pre-ecological natural history. Modern classical science adopted and adapted an ontology first set out in Western thought by Leucippus and Democritus in the fifth century B.C.—atomic materialism.[3]

The classical "atom" is essentially a mathematical entity and its so-called primary qualities may be precisely and quantitatively ex-pressed as aspects or "modes" of geometrical space. An atom's solid mass was thus understood, mathematically, as a positive or "full" portion of negative or "empty" euclidean space—shape its plane limits in a three-dimensional continuum, size its cubic volume, and motion its linear translation from one location (point) to another.[4]

The void and the simple bodies (or atoms) it contains were conceived by Democritus to be uncreated and indestructible. The the-istic moderns, however, conceived space, time, and the atoms to have been uniquely created by God as the permanent theater and immut-able constituents of the universe.[5]

Composite bodies, the macroscopic things composed of atoms, however, routinely come and go. The "generation" and "corruption" (or "coming into being" and "passing away") of composite bodies was understood as the temporary association and dissociation of the atoms in the course of their ceaseless jostling and shuffling.[6]

Atomism, thus, is reductive. A composite body is ontologically reducible to its simple constituents. And the career of a composite body—its generation, growth, corruption, and disintegration—is reduc-ible to the local motion of its constituents.

And atomism, thus, is mechanical. All causal relations are reducible to the motion or translation from point to point of simple bodies or the composite bodies made up of them. The mysterious casual efficacy of fire, disease, light, or anything else is explicable, in the last analysis, as the motion, bump, and grind of the implacable particles. Putative casual relations which could not be so conceived—those postulated in astrology, magic, witchcraft, priestcraft, Newton's gravitational theory, the Faraday-Maxwell representation of magnetism, and so on—were either dismissed as superstitions and their existence denied or regarded as physical problems awaiting a mechanical solution.[7] Only a mechanical solution could be satisfactory, since only a mechanical solution implicated exclusively the fundamental ontology of atomic materialism.[8]

This material, reductive, particulate, aggregative, mechanical, geometric, and quantitative paradigm in physics governed thought in other areas of interest, for example in moral psychology and biology.

Although Democritus, Lucretius, and Hobbes were thoroughgoing materialists and attempted to treat mind in exactly the same mechanical terms as, say, fire, light, and heat, dualism as espoused by Pythagoras, Plato, and Descartes became more characteristic of the dominant psychology of modern classical science.[9]

Mind, nevertheless, was derivatively and analogously conceived by the dualists in atomistic terms—as a psychic monad. Each mind, in other words, was a discrete psychic substance insulated within an alien (to its own nature) material cladding.[10] The mind was passively bedazzled and deluded by the bodily senses, which were mechanically excited by the local "external" world. But minds were not otherwise informed by interaction with matter. That is, the rational structure of the human mind together with its passions and volitions was regarded as an independent given. By carefully sifting and sorting the raw, confused data afforded by sensation, disciplined rational minds could figure out the mechanical laws of the foreign material world and apply that knowledge to practical problem solving.

Given a monadic moral psychology, there are two fundamental options for ethics. As represented most clearly by Hobbes, ethics might consist in finding the most felicitous rules to harmonize the inertial appetites of individual egos (or social atoms).[11] Or a conceptual talisman to overcome the appetitive egoism of the discrete psychic monads might be posited. The concept of Reason functions as such a transcendental principle in Kant's ethic.[12]

In biology, an even more subtle conceptual atomism prevailed. To explain the existence of natural kinds or species had been a major burden of Plato's theory of Forms.[13] For each species or natural kind there was a corresponding eternal "Form" or "Idea." Individuals acquired their essences, their specific, discrete natures, by participation in the Forms. Thus lions were lions and differed from panthers because lions participated in the form Lion, and panthers in the form

Panther. And so for horses, cows, and all other living specimens: each acquired the specific characteristics it to one degree or another possessed through its association as token to type with a specific form.

Aristotle (whose relationship to subsequent Western biology is comparable to Pythagoras's[13] relationship to subsequent Western mathematics) of course rejected Plato's theory of independently existing forms. But he retained the more insidious Platonic doctrine of essences. According to Aristotle, a thing's essence was its definition, given in terms of a classificatory hierarchy.[14] The universals of this hierarchy (later modified and refined by Carl Linnaeus)—species, genus, family, order, class, phylum, and kingdom—were not real or actual; only individual organisms fully existed. Nevertheless, for Aristotle, a species acquires its peculiar characteristics not through interaction with other species, but through the place it occupies in a logically determined classificatory schematism.

Aristotle's teleological conception of nature introduced into biology a hierarchy of another sort. Some species were "lower," others "higher" on the scale of ends. Lower organisms existed for the sake of higher ones.[15] This habit of calling evolutionarily more venerable beings "lower organisms" persists today as an Aristotelian residue in modern biology much as the habit of referring to certain numbers as "square" or "cubic"' persists as a Pythagorean residue in modern mathematics. The former, however, seems somehow more than a quaint and harmless terminological legacy of classical antiquity; it seems to impute a distinct pecking order to nature.

In sum, then, the endemic Western picture of living nature prior to its transformation by ecology might be characterized (or caricatured) somewhat as follows. The terrestrial natural environment consists of a collection of bodies composed of molecular aggregates of atoms. A living natural body is in principle a very elaborate machine. That is, its generation, gestation, development, decay, and death can be exhaustively explained reductively and mechanically. Some of these natural machines are mysteriously inhabited by a conscious monad, a "ghost in the machine." Living natural bodies come in a wide variety of types or species, which are determined by a logico-conceptual order, and have, otherwise, no essential connection to one another. They are, as it were, loosed upon the landscape, each outfitted with its (literally God-given) Platonic-Aristotelian essence, to interact catch-as-catch-can.

Anthony Quinton has recently characterized (or caricatured) the modern classical world view similarly, but even more graphically. According to Quinton,

In that conception (the Newtonian) the world consists of an array of precisely demarcated individual things or substances, which preserve their identity through time, occupy definite positions in space, have their own essential natures independently of their relations to anything else, and fall into clearly distinct natural kinds. Such a world resembles a warehouse of automobile parts. Each item is standard in character, independent of all other items, in its own place, and ordinarily unchanging in its intrinsic nature.[16]

## III

Ecology was given its name in 1866 by Ernst Haeckel, but the concept of an economy of nature had been current in natural history since Linnaeus had devoted a treatise to it a century earlier.[17] Although the idea of an orderly economy of nature was an improvement over the Hobbesean picture of nature as a chaotic free-for-all, Linnaeus and his exponents explicitly represented it in mechanical terms. Living nature is, as it were, a mechanical Leviathan, a vast machine which is itself composed of machines. "Like a planet in its orbit or a gear in its box, each species exists to perform some function in the grand apparatus."[18] The grand apparatus and its functions, to which each species is fitted, were, like the component species, believed to be designed by God. So all natural relations and interactions remain albeit orderly, external.

The subsequent arcadian and romantic intellectual countercurrents to eighteenth-century rationalism and mechanism, however, gave the proto-ecological notion of a natural economy a more integrative and holistic cast. Ecology as it eventually emerged as a distinct subdiscipline of natural history was shaped by a complex of governing metaphors derived from these minority traditions. Natural relations among species were portrayed, for example by Gilbert White in the late eighteenth century, as a "harmony" and as in a felicitous "balance"— balance both in the physical sense of a dynamic equilibrium and in the distinctly aesthetic sense of a tension and resolution of opposites, as in beautiful painting, poetry, and music.[19]

In contrast to the designed and reductive mechanical Leviathan of Linnaeus, in the late nineteenth century John Burroughs posited an evolving and animated organic Leviathan, an idea later given theoretical definition and articulation by the dean of early-twentieth-century ecology, Frederick Clements.[20] Clements was a self-conscious philosophical holist with intellectual roots going back to Spencer, Goethe, Hegel, and Kant. He explicitly suggested that ecology was the study of the physiology of superorganisms.[21] From the point of view of the

Clementsean ecological organicism at the turn of the century, the whole Earth's living mantle might similarly be represented as a vast "comprehensive" organic being. Furthermore, each higher level of organization —from single cell to multicelled organism, from organism to local superorganism (or "ecosystem," in a terminology not yet invented in Clements's day), from ecosystem to biome and biome to biosphere—is "emergent"; thus the whole cannot be reduced to the sum of the parts.

The original Linnaean notion of an economy of nature was itself a metaphor which Charles Elton in the nineteen-twenties and thirties began to unpack to construct what probably has been ecology's most important theoretical model: Plant and animal associations might be studied as "biotic communities." Each species occupies a "trophic niche" in the biotic community which is, as it were, a "profession" in the economy of nature.[22] There are three great "guilds"—producers (the green plants), consumers, both first- and second-order (herbivorous and carnivorous animals respectively), and decomposers (fungi and bacteria). In biotic communities the myriad specialists in each great group are linked in "food chains" which when considered together constitute tangled "food webs." Certain common structures characterize all biotic communities, however different their component species and peculiar professions. For example, the producers must be many times more numerous than the consumers and prey many times more numerous than predators, nor may any two species share precisely the same ecological niche.

Oxford University ecologist Arthur Tansley coined the term "ecosystem" in 1935 deliberately to supplant the more metaphorical characterizations of biocenoses as "communities" of plants and animals or as "super-organismic" entities.[23] Tansley's ecosystem model of biotic processes was intended to bring ecology as a science out of a qualitative, descriptive stage, with anthropomorphic and mystic overtones, and transform it into a value-free, exact quantitative science. Hence, Tansley suggested that measurable "energy" contained in food coursed through the ecosystem and was at the foundation of its structure.

The scientific exemplar to which Tansley looked was physics. Of the so-called New Ecology, for which Tansley's ecosystem model was the critical ingredient, Donald Worster writes that "it owed nothing to any of its forebears in the history of science.... It was born of entirely different parentage: that is modern, thermodynamic physics, not biology."[24] Hence it is no wonder that the New Physics and the New Ecology should be conceptually complementary and convergent. Tansley's exemplar for a new paradigm in ecology was, it turns out, the new paradigm emerging in physics. The ecosystem model was expressly designed to be the field theory of modern biology.

However, as Worster emphatically points out, the quantitative, thermodynamic, biophysical model of nature which is the hallmark of the New Ecology was immediately turned to economic advantage as a powerful new weapon in mankind's age-old campaign to conquer nature. With the quantitative precision of which Tansley's energy-circuit model was capable, ecosystems could be made more "productive" and "efficient" so as to "yield" a higher caloric "crop." But just as the philosophical interpretation of the New Physics, the Copenhagen Interpretation and its variations and alternatives, is quite another thing from its economic and military applications—from television to laser weaponry—so the philosophical interpretation of the new ecology is quite another thing from its agronomic and managerial applications—from Ducks Unlimited to the green revolution. As Worster prophetically remarks, "Organicism has a way of gaining a foothold on even the most unpromising surface."[25]

## IV

At mid-century, ecologist and conservationist Aldo Leopold strove to erect a secular environmental ethic on evolutionary and ecological foundations.[26] In his land ethic one finds traces of Clements's organic image of nature, although Leopold himself earlier articulated the idea in terms borrowed from the Russian philosopher P. D. Ouspensky.[27] And certainly crucial to the conceptual foundations of the land ethic is Elton's community concept. However, when Leopold, in *A Sand County Almanac*, turns more deliberately to the construction of a "mental image" of the natural environment in relation to which he urges new ethical sensibilities, he sketches, in poetic terms, the physics-born ecosystem model. According to Leopold, "land," his shorthand term for the natural environment,

> is a fountain of energy flowing through a circuit of soils, plants, and animals. Food chains are the living channels conducting energy upward [scholium, to the apex of the trophic pyramid].... The velocity and character of the upward flow of energy depend on the complex structure of the plant and animal community.... Without this complexity normal circulation would presumably not occur.[28]

Ecologist Paul Shepard, a decade or so later, developed more consciously the metaphysical overtones of this field theory of living nature adumbrated by Leopold. According to Shepard, from the modern classical perspective

> nature is epitomized by living objects rather than the complex flow patterns of which objects are temporary formations.... The landscape [from the classical point of view] is a room-like collection of animated furniture.... But it should be noted that it is best describable in terms of events which constitute a field pattern.[29]

Shepard, thus, more abstractively than Leopold, suggested that an object-ontology is inappropriate to an ecological description of the natural environment. Living natural objects should be regarded as ontologically subordinate to "events," to "flow patterns" or "field patterns." As reflectively represented at mid-century from the point of view of a mature ecological science, the biological reality seems to be, at the very least, more fluid and integrally patterned and less substantive and discrete than it had been previously represented.

In the early seventies Yale University biophysicist Harold Morowitz still more deliberately and emphatically set out the field-ontology suggested by Leopold and Shepard as a more ecologically informed portrayal of the natural environment. According to Morowitz,

> viewed from the point of view of modern [ecology], each living thing is a dissipative structure, that is, it does not endure in and of itself but only as a result of the continual flow of energy in the system.... From this point of view, the reality of individuals is problematic because they do not exist per se but only as local perturbations in this universal energy flow.... An example might be instructive. Consider a vortex in a stream of flowing water. The vortex is a structure made of an ever-changing group of water molecules. It does not exist as an entity in the classical Western sense; it exists only because of the flow of water through the stream. If the flow ceases the vortex disappears. In the same sense the structures out of which the biological entities are made are transient, unstable entities with constantly changing molecules dependent on a constant flow of energy to maintain form and structure.[30]

Later in the same decade, Norwegian philosopher Arne Naess attempted to persuade the community of academic philosophers that ecology might have important and sweeping metaphysical implications. Naess entered a caveat similar to the one registered at the outset of this discussion, namely, that metaphysical conclusions "are not derived from ecology by logic or induction."[31] Rather, according to Naess, ecology "suggests" or "inspires" a "relational total field image [in which] organisms [are] knots in the biospherical net of intrinsic relations."[32] Naess called this metaphysical dimension of ecology "Deep Ecology," and the nebula of normative and public policy tendencies associated with it "the Deep Ecology movement."

Let me sum up and attempt to express more precisely the abstractive general concept of nature distilled from the New Ecology in the tradition of Leopold, Shepard, Morowitz, and Naess.

First, in the "organic" concept of nature implied by the New Ecology as in that implied by the New Physics, energy seems to be a more fundamental and primitive reality than are material objects or discrete entities—elementary particles and organisms respectively.[33] An individual organism, like an elementary particle is, as it were, a momentary configuration, a local perturbation, in an energy flux or field.

The metaphysical ecologists here quoted, however, if pressed, would seem hardly prepared to deny outright a primary reality to atomic and molecular matter per se in addition to energy and its flow. Organisms, though conduits of and configured by energy, remain composed of molecules—solid material substances. Rather, ecological interactions, primarily and especially trophic relationships, constitute a macrocosmic network or pattern through which solar energy, fixed by photosynthesis, is transferred from organism to organism until it is dissipated. Organisms are moments in this network, knots in this web of life.

However, if we combine quantum theory with ecology, as well as compare them, and resolve the erstwhile solid and immutable atoms of matter which compose the molecules, which in turn compose the cells, of organic bodies into the ephemeral, energetic quanta, then we may say quite literally and unambiguously that organisms are, in their entire structure—from subatomic microcosm to ecosystemic macrocosm—patterns, perturbations, or configurations of energy.

Deep-Ecology poet and philosopher Gary Snyder captured this vertical integration of metaphysical ideas in a poem:

Eating the living germs of grasses
   Eating the ova of large birds ...
Drawing on life of living
   *clustered points of light spun*
     *out of space*
hidden in the grape.[34]

In these lines the "clustered points of light spun out of space" apparently allude to the dynamic configurations of the microcosm, the patterns of energy in the subatomic world; and, obviously, eating grains, eggs, and fruit, unambiguously calls attention—especially by the persistent use of progressive verb forms ("eating," "drawing")—to the dynamic, patterned energy flux at the core of ecological relationships as conceived on the ecosystem model.

Second, the concept of nature emergent from the New Ecology, as that emergent from the New Physics, is holistic. It is impossible to conceive of organisms—if they are, as it were, knots in the web of life, or temporary formations or perturbations in complex flow patterns—apart from the field, the matrix of which they are modes. Contrary to the object-ontology of classical physics and biology in which it was possible to conceive of an entity in isolation from its milieu—hanging alone in the void or catalogued in a specimen museum—the conception of one thing in the New Physics and New Ecology necessarily involves the conception of others and so on, until the entire system is, in principle, implicated.

Naess points out another sense in which ecology implies a holistic conception of the organic world, the import of which only an academic philosopher would be likely to notice. He claims, in effect, that ecology revives the metaphysical doctrine of internal relations.[35] This suggestion, remarkably, had been advanced even earlier by comparative philosopher Eliot Deutsch who also connected it with the Vedantic concept of karma.[36]

The doctrine of internal relations is, of course, associated with nineteenth- and early-twentieth-century German and English Idealism—with the philosophies of Hegel, Fichte, Bradley, Royce, and Bosanquet. The basic idea is that a thing's essence is exhaustively determined by its relationships, that it cannot be conceived apart from its relationships with other things. Whatever the motives of the Idealists (coherency theories of truth, the omniscience and omnipresence of spirit, or whatever) and notwithstanding the inevitable entanglement by mid-century neo-scholastic, academic philosophers of the doctrine of internal relations with other concurrently fashionable topics (with "bare particulars," nominalism, the analytic-synthetic distinction, and so on), internal relations are straightforwardly implicated in ecology.

From the perspective of modern biology, species adapt to a niche in an ecosystem. Their actual relationships to other organisms (to predators, to prey, to parasites and disease organisms) and to physical and chemical conditions (to temperature, radiation, salinity, wind, soil and water pH) literally sculpt their outward forms, their metabolic, physiological, and reproductive processes, and even their psychological and mental capacities. A specimen is, in effect, a summation of its species' historical, adaptive relationship to the environment. This observation led Shepard to claim that "relationships of things are as real as the things."[37] Indeed, I would be inclined to go even further. To convey an anti-Aristotelian thought in an Aristotelian manner of speech one might say that from an ecological perspective, relations are "prior to" the things related, and the systemic wholes woven from these relations are prior to their component parts. Ecosystemic wholes are logically prior to their component species because the nature of the part is determined by its relationship to the whole. That is, more simply and concretely expressed, a species has the particular characteristics that it has because those characteristics result from its adaptation to a niche in an *ecosystem*.

It is necessary to add immediately however, that the holistic concept of nature implied, analogously, by the New Ecology and the New Physics at the macro and micro levels of organization is a holism of a different stripe from that associated with classical Hindu metaphysics. Eliot Deutsch and Fritjof Capra have each drawn this perhaps natural, but unfortunate, comparison. According to Capra, in the "Eastern world view" (which he seems to regard as a monolithic body of wisdom encompassing the independent indigenous traditions of thought from the Indian subcontinent to Japan) and in "modern [quantum] physics, all things are seen as interdependent and inseparable parts of this cosmic whole; as different manifestations of the same ultimate reality. The Eastern traditions constantly refer to this ultimate, indivisible reality which manifests itself in things....It is called *Brahman* in Hinduism...."[38] And according to Deutsch: "What does it mean to affirm continuity between man and the rest of life [as in ecology]? Vedanta would maintain that this means the recognition that fundamentally all life is one, that in essence everything is reality;...that *Brahman*, the oneness of reality, is the most fundamental ground of all existence."[39]

There is a crucial conceptual distinction, however, in the very different ways in which things are thought to be "one" in classical Indian thought, on the one hand, and in contemporary ecology and quantum theory, on the other. In classical Indian thought all things are one because all things are phenomenal and ultimately illusory manifestations or expressions of Brahman. The unity of things is thus substantive and essential and the experience of it homogeneous and oceanic. In both contemporary ecology and quantum theory at their respective levels of phenomena the oneness of nature is systemic and (internally) relational. No undifferentiated Being mysteriously "manifests" itself. Rather, nature is a *structured, differentiated* whole. The multiplicity of particles and of living organisms, at either level or organization, retain, ultimately, their peculiar, if ephemeral, characters and identities. But they are systemically integrated and mutually defining. The wholes revealed by ecology and quantum theory are unified, not blankly unitary; they are "one" as organisms are one, rather than "one" as an indivisible, homogeneous, quality-less substance is one.

V

Ecology has signal implications for moral psychology, which we may treat here for convenience as part of metaphysics. Since individual organisms, from an ecological point of view, are less discrete objects than modes of a continuous, albeit differentiated, whole, the distinction between self and other is blurred. Hence the central problem of modern classical moral philosophy as elegantly exposed by Kenneth Goodpaster in a recent discussion—the problem of either managing or overcoming egoism—is not solved by the moral psychology implicated in ecology so much as it is outflanked.[40]

Paul Shepard remarked that

> in one aspect the self is an arrangement of organs, feelings, and thoughts—a "me"—surrounded by a hard body boundary: skin, clothes, and insular habits.... The alternative [aspect] is a self as a center of organization, constantly drawing on and influencing the surroundings.... Ecological thinking... requires a kind of vision across boundaries. The epidermis of the skin is ecologically like a pond surface or a forest soil, not a shell so much as delicate interpenetration. It reveals the self ennobled and extended ... as part of the landscape and the ecosystem.[41]

Shepard went on to endorse a notion earlier crystallized by Alan Watts (whose inspiration came from oriental philosophies)—that "the world is your body."[42]

Environmental philosopher Holmes Rolston, III alluded to and extended Shepard's notion of the "relational self" implied by ecology. Meditating by the shores of a Rocky Mountain wilderness lake, Rolston asked,

> Does not my skin resemble this lake surface? Neither lake nor self has independent being.... Inlet waters have crossed this interface and are now embodied within me.... The waters of North Inlet are part of my circulatory system; and the more literally we take this truth the more nearly we understand it. I incarnate the solar energies that flow through this lake. No one is free-living.... *Bios* is intrinsically symbiosis.[43]

As one moves, in imagination, outwardly from the core of one's organism, it is impossible to find a clear demarcation between oneself and one's environment. The environing gases and fluids flow continuously in and out. The organisms outside (and inside!) one's osmotic envelope are continually, albeit selectively, transubstantiated into and through oneself. In the time-lapse cinematography of imagination one can see oneself arising from the earth, as it were, a pulsating structure in a vast sea of other patterns large and small—some of them mysteriously translating through oneself—finally to be transmuted oneself into the others. The world is, indeed, one's extended body and one's body is the precipitation, the focus of the world in a particular space-time locale.

This idea is very old, even in the West, expressed abstractly and philosophically by Heraclitus in the Greek tradition and concretely and poetically—with the phrase, "for dust thou art, and unto dust shalt thou return"—by the author(s) of Genesis-J. In the West, however, there still lingers the image of the substantive *nephcsh*, psyche, soul, or conscious mind—the more diaphanous and insubstantial its organic cladding is perceived to be, the more vulnerable and self-pitying. Paul Shepard, however, has pointed out that the relational concept of *self* extends to consciousness as well as organism, to mind as well as matter. According to Shepard,

> Internal complexity, as the mind of a primate, is an extension of natural complexity, measured by the variety of plants and animals and the variety of nerve cells—organic extensions of each other.
> The exuberance of kinds [is] the setting in which a good mind could evolve (to deal with a complex world).... The idea of natural complexity as a counterpart to human intricacy is essential to an ecology of man.[44]

In a subsequent discussion Shepard elaborated this insight.[45] The more primitive elements of animal consciousness—palpable hunger and thirst, fear and rage, pleasure and pain—are as clearly evolutionary adaptations to an ever more elaborate ecosystem as fur and feathers, toes and digits, eye and ear. The distinctive mark of human consciousness and the *materiel* of human reason are the systems of concepts embodied by human languages. Shepard has suggested that conceptual thought evolved as the taxonomical array of animals and plants was mapped by the emergent consciousness of primate hunter-gatherers. In a very direct way, therefore, human consciousness, including abstract rational thought, is an extension of the environment, just as the environment becomes fully actual, in the mind-body unity of the New Physics, only as it interacts with consciousness.[46]

Shepard has constructed on this basis an interesting argument for species conservation: If we simplify and impoverish the Earth's ecosystems, we shall risk rendering future generations of human beings mentally degenerate. Lacking a rich and complex natural environment to support a rich and complex intelligence—as correspondent, analogue, and stimulus—human intelligence may atrophy.

The relational view of *self*—both self as bodily organism and self as conscious, thinking thing—transforms egoism into environmentalism, to borrow Kenneth Goodpaster's felicitous phrase. As I have elsewhere pointed out, egoism has been regarded as axiologically privileged.[47] The intrinsic value of oneself is taken as a given. How to account for the value of "others"—human others and now nonhuman natural others— has been the principal problematic of nonegoistic ethics.[48]

However, if the world is one's body, and not only does one's consciousness image in its specific content the world around, but the very structure of one's psyche and rational faculties are formed through adaptive interaction with the ecological organization of nature, then one's self, both physically and psychologically, merges in a gradient from its central core outwardly into the environment. One cannot thus draw hard-and-fast boundaries between oneself, either physically or spiritually, and the environment.

For me this realization took concrete form as I stood, two decades and an ecological education later, on the banks of the Mississippi River where I had roamed as a boy. As I gazed at the brown silt-choked waters absorbing a black plume of industrial and municipal sewage from Memphis, and, as my eye tracked bits of some unknown beige froth floating continually down from Cincinnati, Louisville, or St. Louis, I experienced a palpable pain. It was not distinctly locable in any of my extremities, nor was it like a headache or nausea. Still, it was very real. I had no plans to swim in the river, no need to drink from it, no intention of buying real estate on its shores. My narrowly personal interests were not affected, and yet somehow I was personally injured. It occurred to me then, in a flash of self-discovery, that the river was a part of me. And I recalled a line from Leopold's *Sand County Almanac*— "One of the penalties of an ecological education is that one lives alone in a world of wounds."[49]

Australian conservationist John Seed, musing on his efforts on behalf of rain forest preservation in Queensland, has come to a similar conclusion:

> As the implications of evolution and ecology are internalized... there is an identification with all life....Alienation subsides.... "I am protecting the rain forest" develops to "I am part of the rain forest protecting myself. I am that part of the rain forest recently emerged into thinking."[50]

Ecology thus gives a new meaning as well as new substance to the phrase "enlightened self-interest."

# III

# A Non-anthropocentric Value Theory for Environmental Ethics

# 7

## Hume's *Is/Ought* Dichotomy and the Relation of Ecology to Leopold's Land Ethic

### I

The third part of Aldo Leopold's *A Sand County Almanac*, a work which has become the modern classic of environmental philosophy, is called "The Upshot." It seems to have been intended as a presentation in a conceptually more abstract and logically more systematic way of some implications of the ecological ideas which are concretely and poetically conveyed in parts one and two. The essay, "The Land Ethic," is the culmination of that third section, the upshot of the upshot, so to speak. The land ethic thus appears to have been supposed by its author to *follow from* the largely descriptive essays which illustrate ecological principles and which precede it. Indeed, just months before his death in 1948 Leopold wrote the foreword to this collection of essays in which he reveals his own sense of the relationship of the descriptive narratives to the prescriptive epilogue: "That land is a community is the basic concept of ecology, but that land is to be loved and respected is an extension of ethics. That land yields a cultural harvest is a fact long known but latterly often forgotten. These essays attempt to weld these three concepts."[1]

Upon reading these words academic philosophers may be inclined to read no further, for Leopold, the father of contemporary environmental ethics, here has blithely stepped across the barrier separating *is* from *ought,* that is, he has committed the naturalistic fallacy (as sometimes the transition from *is* to *ought* is mistakenly called); he has ventured to derive *value* from *fact* (or at least from a certain theoretical organization of facts). Environmental ethics, therefore, as a distinct ethical theory which provides direct moral standing for land (in Leopold's inclusive sense)—if stimulated and informed by the body of empirical information and theory of ecology—seems, in its original and most powerful expression, doomed to break up on the shoals of the *is/ought* dichotomy.

During the last decade, environmental ethics, which quite clearly has been inspired by ecology and the other environmental sciences, has come to the attention of the academic philosophical community. Not surprisingly, the is/ought dichotomy has haunted academic environmental ethics and threatens to be its Achilles' heel. In a seminal discussion, Holmes Rolston, III provides a clear statement of the fact/value problem as it applies to environmental ethics and explores a conceptual framework for its solution, which he calls "metaecology" (in which "description and evaluation to some extent arise together") and he develops this approach more fully in two subsequent articles.[2] Don E. Marietta, Jr., meanwhile, has addressed the same problem employing the conceptual tools of phenomenology in two papers, the first of which drew criticism and a reaffirmation of the recalcitrance of the is/ought dichotomy for environmental ethics from Tom Regan.[3] In this paper, I pursue a less creative and forward-looking approach than my colleagues, Rolston and Marietta; I wage, as it were, a rearguard historical action on their behalf, in case their arguments fall on deaf ears and the received opinion is dogmatically and uncritically reasserted by their opponents. Accordingly, I first locate both the is/ought dichotomy and the naturalistic fallacy in their respective historical contexts. The naturalistic fallacy is dismissed as an issue too parochial to be practically relevant to contemporary environmental ethics. I argue that the much more general problem of the transition from *is* to *ought* in practical moral reasoning actually has an easy solution within the ethical system of Hume, the first to pose the problem. Finally, I show that the conceptual foundations of the Leopold land ethic, the modern paradigm of environmental ethics provide, on Humean grounds, for a direct passage from the perceived facts that we are natural beings and that we belong to a biotic community to the principal values of the land ethic.

A resolution of the fact/value problem on Humean grounds is especially appropriate and important to the Leopold land ethic because the Leopold land ethic rests, ultimately, upon a Humean theoretical foundation. Leopold's conception of an ethic ("a limitation on freedom of action in the *struggle for existence*" and "a differentiation of *social from anti-social conduct*") and his understanding of the origin of ethics ("in the tendency of interdependent individuals or groups to *evolve* modes of cooperation") lies, quite clearly, squarely within the tradition of biological thought about ethics that began with Darwin and has been recently formalized by Edward O. Wilson.[4] What may not be obvious from reading Leopold is that Darwin's conception of ethics, in turn, owes a debt to Hume, who argues that ethical behavior depends upon and is motivated by "the moral sentiments."

As Anthony Flew has pointed out, Hume's ethics "might almost seem to demand an evolutionary background."[5] How else could Hume explain, what he claims to be a fact, that the moral sentiments are both natural and universal, that is, that they are fixed psychological characteristics of human nature?[6] Darwin's theory provides a very plausible explanation, namely, that the moral sentiments are fixed in human nature, like all other standard traits, by natural selection. On the other hand, no available analysis of morals other than Hume's would have been useful to Darwin. Natural history could not in principle brook a "divine will" or other supernatural account of ethics, and the standard philosophical account, so forcefully represented by Kant, that morality depends exclusively upon reason, from an evolutionary point of view, puts the cart before the horse. Reason appears to be the most advanced and delicate human faculty, one which cannot possibly be imagined as having evolved apart from an intensely social context, while society itself cannot be imagined as existing in the absence of moral restraints, that is, limitations on freedom of action in the struggle for existence.

The moral sentiments (as fellow-feeling, sympathy, benevolence, affection, generosity), Darwin argues, co-evolved with the evolution of protohuman societies. On the subject of "the all-important emotion of sympathy" (which, revealingly, is also all-important to Hume), Darwin writes:

> In however complex a manner this *feeling* may have originated, as it is one of high importance to all those animals which aid and defend one another, it will have been increased through natural selection; for those *communities*, which included the greatest number of sympathetic members, would flourish best, and rear the greatest number of offspring.[7]

There, in brief, is Darwin's explanation of the origin of ethics. They arise in association with the survival advantages of society or community and depend ultimately, as Hume so powerfully argued, not on reason alone, but upon passion, feeling, or sentiment. It is clear, moreover, from his language that Leopold follows Darwin's basic account of the origin and evolution of ethics and thus, through Darwin, is committed to an essentially Humean theory of the foundations of morals.

## II

The term *naturalistic fallacy* was introduced in 1903 by G. E. Moore in *Principia Ethica*.[8] It is not, properly speaking, another name for the is/ought logical lacuna, the putative fallacy, discovered by Hume, of stating a conclusion containing the copula *ought* derived from premises all connected by the copula *is*, although some writers have apparently supposed that it is.[9] Rather, what vexed Moore was the identification of goodness with some other quality. When Bentham, for example, says that only pleasure is good and only pain evil, he commits the naturalistic fallacy, as defined by Moore. Moore claimed that *good* is not some other "natural thing," like pleasure or intelligence; it is an irreducible "nonnatural quality" inhering in objects, and we somehow intuit its presence. The naturalistic fallacy as Moore defined it, thus, is not, logically speaking, a fallacy proper, since no argument or passage from premises to conclusion is involved. In its strict Moorean sense it is so specifically tied to Moore's ethics, to serve as a rubric to characterize all those theories at odds with his doctrine of nonnatural moral qualities, as to be of little moment, one way or the other. To accuse Leopold (or other environmental ethicists) of committing the naturalistic fallacy, in other words, amounts to little more than the accusation that they do not conform to Moore's beliefs about the nature of goodness—hardly a cause for alarm.

Hume's is/ought dichotomy, however, is much more general in scope and application, and is therefore a much more formidable problem for environmental ethics, as it is for any ethic whose conceptual foundations rest in part upon empirical and theoretical claims about the world as well as upon strictly valuative and deontic statements.

## III

Hume's famous observation respecting the unexplained and unjustified transition from *is* and *is not* to *ought not* in most "vulgar systems of morality" occurs at the end of book 3, part 1, section 1 of the *Treatise* as the coup de grace in a series of arguments all designed to prove that distinctions of good and evil, vice and virtue, are not "founded merely on the relations of objects nor . . . perceiv'd by reason." Such judgments, as, for example, that this action is good or that that is vicious, are founded, rather, upon *sentiment*, not reason, according to Hume. Good and evil are not, as we should say today, objective qualities; they are, in Hume's terms, neither "matters of fact" nor "real relations" among objects. We find them rather in our "own breast"; they are feelings of approbation or disapprobation, warm approval or repugnance, which spontaneously arise in us upon the contemplation of some action or object. If we should witness some act of willful murder, for example, the evil or vice is not a quality of the act as red is a quality of spilled blood; rather, "from the constitution of your nature you have a feeling or sentiment of blame from the contemplation of it."[10] The alleged evil of the action is, as it were, a projection of the quality of that subjective feeling which originates within us when we witness or imagine murder. And so similarly with other moral judgments, for example, that charity is good, that injustice is bad, and so on: feeling, not reason (in the sense of dispassionate observation), is their ultimate foundation.

From this brief account of the core concepts of Hume's moral theory, one might jump to the conclusion that Hume's ethics is both abjectly relativistic and abjectly skeptical. It is neither. The moral sentiments are both natural and universally distributed among human beings as I mentioned before. In other words, like physical features— the placement of the eyes in the head, two arms, two legs, an opposed thumb, and so forth—the moral sentiments are only slightly variable psychological features common to all people. Just as there are people, to be sure, who are physically freakish or maimed, so there may be people who, because of congenital defect or the vagaries of life, are lacking one, several, or all of the moral sentiments to one degree or another. Still, we can speak of normal and even correct moral judgments, the exceptions notwithstanding, just as we can speak of physical normality and even correct bodily proportions and conditions. Hume's ethical subjectivism, therefore, does not necessarily imply that right and wrong, good and evil, virtue and vice are, so to speak, existentially indeterminate, nor does his theory collapse into an emotive relativism.

Furthermore, according to Hume, cognition plays a significant and substantial role in moral action and judgment; in Hume's words, "reason in a strict and philosophical sense can have an influence on our conduct only after two ways: either when it excites a passion by informing us of the existence of something which is a proper object of it; or when it discovers the connexion of causes and effects, so as to afford us means of exerting any passion."[11] Both of these influences of reason on our conduct are especially relevant to the immediate problem with which this discussion began, the metaethical defensibility of the informative relationship of ecology and environmental science to environmental ethics.

First, let us take a simple example to illustrate the latter use of reason in a practical argument meeting Hume's precise and exacting criteria. (Our example involves only "self-love," not any of the "moral sentiments.") Suppose a parent says to her teenage daughter, "You *ought not* smoke cigarettes"; the teenager asks, "Why not?"; and the parent replies, "Because cigarette smoking *is* deleterious to health." If the daughter has taken a freshman course in philosophy, she might well triumphantly reply, "Hah, you have deduced an *ought* from an *is;* you have committed the naturalistic fallacy [a sophomoric misnomer]. Unless you can provide a metaethically more cogent argument, I shall continue to smoke cigarettes."

Reason (i.e., medical science) has rather recently discovered that cigarette smoking is indeed deleterious to health. It has discovered a previously unknown "connexion of causes and effects." This discovery "afford[s] us means of exerting...passion," namely the passion we normally all feel for our own good health and well-being. But precisely because this passion is so nearly universal in human nature, mention of it is ordinarily omitted from practical argument. And because it is not mentioned, we may experience what one writer recently has called, "the mystery of the passage from 'is' to 'ought.' "[12]

The mystery dissolves, on Hume's own grounds, when the missing premise referring to passion, feeling, or sentiment is explicitly included in the argument. Let our parent formulate her argument as follows: "(1) Cigarette smoking is deleterious to health. (2) Your health is something toward which as a matter of fact you have a positive attitude (as today we would say; a warm sentiment or passion, as Hume, more colorfully, would put it). (3) Therefore, you ought not smoke cigarettes." If Hume has not simply contradicted himself in granting to reason the role in practical deliberation of discovering "the connexion of causes and effects, so as to afford us means of exerting any passion," then this is a perfectly legitimate transition from *is*-statements to an *ought*-statement. It may not be a deduction, in the strictest logical sense, but it is a cogent practical argument, according to Hume's own criteria (which are in his judgment so "strict and philosophical").[13]

It may be worth noting in passing that Kant, an attentive reader of Hume, did, as a matter of fact, regard practical arguments like the one above as deductive. In Kantian terminology the conclusion, "you ought not to smoke" is a hypothetical imperative, more specifically, an imperative of prudence. And Kant tells us that "whoever wills the end [in our example, health], so far as reason has decisive influence on his action, wills also the indispensably necessary means to it [in our example, refraining from smoking cigarettes] that lie in his power. This proposition, in what concerns the will is *analytical*."[14]

Our smoking teenager may still have a rejoinder; she may deny (or at least discount) either premise (1) or (2). Following the example of the tobacco industry, a philosophical teenager might deny premise (1) and insist upon (an incidentally un-Humean) strict interpretation of cause and effect as necessary connection, not as mere correlation of events. Premise (2) might be "denied" in several ways. A reckless indifference to health might be insisted upon or, admitting a positive attitude toward health, other, conflicting passions may be confessed to be more intense and thus to motivate action, for example, a need for acceptance among a certain peer group, or an overwhelming desire for the immediate sensations that cigarette smoking produces. If either premise (1) or premise (2) is denied, our hapless parent has no further recourse to practical argument. If premise (1) is denied, the expert witness of a physiologist or philosopher of science might help, or if premise (2) is, psychological counseling could be prescribed.

## IV

Returning to the relationship of ecology and the environmental sciences to environmental ethics, it should now be obvious what sort of defense might be put up on behalf of Leopold and his more recent exponents, who are accused of attempting illicitly to reason out *ought*-statements from *is*-statements. Let us construct an environmental ethical argument having the same form as our simple paradigm, but involving a premise drawn from ecology and the environmental sciences, just as that of the paradigm involved a premise drawn from the medical sciences.

(1) The biological sciences including ecology have disclosed (a) that organic nature is systemically integrated, (b) that mankind is a non-privileged member of the organic continuum, and (c) that therefore environmental abuse threatens human life, health, and happiness. (2) We human beings share a common interest in human life, health, and happiness. (3) Therefore, we ought not violate the integrity and stability of the natural environment by loading it with hazardous wastes or by extirpating species, upon which its vital functions depend, or by any other insults or dislocations.

The conclusion of this argument, as that of our paradigm, may, of course, be avoided by denying or discounting either or both its premises. Theologians might, for example, deny (1b); Newtonian mechanists (1a). There is a recent and alarming tendency by industrialists, thoughtless consumers, and their political allies to follow one of the stratagems available to the smoking teenager in our simple sample argument respecting premise (2), for presently we all too often hear that although human life, health, and happiness for ourselves, in the future for our children, and so on, is something for which everyone has a positive sentiment, uninterrupted economic growth and profligate consumption, that is, maintenance of "the American way of life," is something for which we have a greater passion.[15] This is formally similar to the smoking teenager's rejoinder that she simply places greater priority on the immediate pleasures of cigarette smoking than upon future health and long life. More cynically still, we sometimes hear the rhetorical question, "What, after all, has posterity ever done for me?"

## V

So far, we have only defended the relevancy of ecology and the environmental sciences to an essentially prudential and utilitarian version of environmental ethics. There is a more radical and metaethically more challenging aspect of Leopold's land ethic. Indeed, the novel and interesting feature of Leopold's land ethic is the extension of direct moral standing, of moral considerability, or of primary moral status, to "soils, waters, plants, and animals."[18] This, as he himself insists, goes beyond "enlightened self-interest," that is, beyond prudence, even if we construe prudence in the most expansive sense possible to include our collective human well-being, for the present generation and for generations to come.[17] Furthermore, this novel biocentric ethic, which in a single stroke "changes the role of *Homo sapiens* from conqueror of the land-community to plain member and citizen of it [and] implies respect for his fellow-members and also respect for the community as such,"[18] is also represented as a shift of values which is supposed to *follow from* ecological enlightenment!

Ironically, Hume, usually regarded as the nemesis of any attempt to discover values in facts and, a fortiori, any proposal to change values upon the discovery of *new* facts, once more provides a classical, metaethical model which justifies Leopold's more radical claims. Let us recall again the first of the two ways, according to Hume, that reason can have an influence on our conduct, namely, "when it excites a passion by informing us of the existence of something which is a proper object of it."

According to Hume, for the purpose of moral analysis the passions may be divided into two classes, those concerning oneself and those extending to others, and the latter are no less motives to action than the former.[19] Moreover, human beings, Hume points out, are, as a matter of fact, thoroughly dependent upon society and there exists a certain sentiment which *naturally* resides in us for what he frequently calls the "publick interest," that is, for the commonweal or for the integrity of society per se.[20]

Now, a moralist may legitimately use reason to excite any of these passions in us and thus influence our actions. For example, opponents of abortion present medical evidence to show that a fetus only five months after conception has all the outward physical features, circulatory and nervous systems, and internal organs of a human being. They wish us to conclude that the fetus is a proper object of those of our moral sympathies which are naturally excited by human beings, especially by human infants.

Leopold makes use of an analgous ploy in the shack sketches of *A Sand County Almanac* when he represents other animals anthropomorphically: amorous woodcocks sky dancing, mouse engineers fretting, bird dogs patiently educating their smell-deficient masters in the fine art of olfactory discrimination, and so forth. Leopold's anthropomorphism is always restrained by and confined to the ethological facts of the animal behavior he describes. The mouse engineer is not equipped with a transit, nor does the woodcock present his lady with an engagement ring. Unlike Kenneth Grahame in *Wind in the Willows,* Leopold does not dress his animals in morning coats and sit them at table for tea and biscuits. Nonetheless, Leopold tries to excite our sympathy and fellow-feeling by portraying animal behavior as in many ways similar to our own and as motivated by similar psychological experiences.

The land ethic depends in large measure upon this logically quite legitimate influence of science on our human psychological responses. As Leopold directly says:

> It is a century now since Darwin gave us the first glimpse of the origin of species. We know now what was unknown to all the preceding caravan of generations: that men are only fellow-voyagers with other creatures in the odyssey of evolution. This new *knowledge* should have given us by this time a *sense of kinship* [i.e., it should have excited our sentiment of sympathy or fellow-feeling] *with fellow-creatures;* a wish to live and let live; a sense of wonder over the magnitude and duration of the biotic enterprise.[21]

To expose its Humean legitimacy this argument may be schematically set out as follows: (1) we (i.e., all psychologically normal people) are endowed with certain moral sentiments (sympathy, concern, respect, and so on) for our fellows, especially for our kin; (2) modern biology treats *Homo sapiens* (a) as, like all other living species, a product of the process of organic evolution; and hence, (b) people are literally kin (because of common ancestry) to all other contemporary forms of life; (3) therefore, if so enlightened, we should feel and thus behave (I here assume as I have throughout Hume's interpretively undisputed general theory of action) toward other living things in ways similar to the way we feel and thus behave toward our human kin.[22]

Ignoring the more collective or holistic object of the feeling of wonder—the whole biotic enterprise, its magnitude and duration—to which Leopold refers in his informal derivation of the moral implications of the theory of evolution, we are led beyond humanism and animal liberationism to what I have elsewhere labeled "the reverence-for-life ethic."[23] But we have not yet reached "soils and waters."

## VI

The Leopold land ethic per se rests, more formally, upon the ecological concept of a biotic community.[24] Ecology, Leopold points out, represents living nature as a biotic community, that is, as a *society* of plants, animals, minerals, fluids, and gases. This is a genuinely novel conception of nature. Prior to the emergence of the science of ecology, when natural history was largely a matter of taxonomy, nature was perceived more as a mere collection of objects, like a room full of furniture, the parts of which were incidentally and externally related. Natural things, thus, had either an indifferent value, a positive utilitarian resource value, or a negative value (as pests, weeds, vermin, and so on). Ecology has changed all this. It has brought into being a new natural paradigm. The natural world is now perceived as a living whole, "one humming community." The myriad species, previously conceived as haphazardly scattered upon an inert landscape, relating catch-as-catch-can, are now conceived as intimately conjoined, specifically adapted to one another, to types of soil and parameters of climate. Each species has a role in the economy of nature, a niche or, as it were, a profession. We human beings exist within this natural or biotic community; certainly we cannot exist outside it, on the moon or on Mars or indeed anywhere else except on Earth.

Now, as Hume observed, not only have we sympathy for our fellows, we also are naturally endowed with a sentiment, the proper object of which is society itself. Ecology and the environmental sciences thus inform us of the existence of something which is a proper object of one of our most fundamental moral passions. The biotic community is a proper object of that passion which is actuated by the contemplation of the complexity, diversity, integrity, and stability of the community to which we belong. Ecology, thus, has transformed the value of nature as a whole just as evolutionary biology has transformed the value of the components of nature severally. Leopold sums up his land ethic with the following moral precept: "A thing is right when it tends to preserve the integrity, stability, and beauty of the biotic community. It is wrong when it tends otherwise."[25]

This precept is derived from ecology and the environmental sciences. The derivation of this conclusion, in much the same way as that concerning cigarette smoking, falls within the strict confines of Hume's metaethics. Schematically arranged in a permutation of our familiar format, Leopold urges upon us the conclusion, (3) we ought to "preserve the integrity, stability, and beauty of the biotic community." Why ought we? Because (1) we all generally have a positive attitude toward the community or society to which we belong; and (2) science has now discovered that the natural environment is a community or society to which we belong, no less than to the human global village. Like the conclusion, "one ought not smoke cigarettes," it infers *ought* from *is* and derives value from fact (actually from a theoretical arrangement of natural facts, on the one hand, and from certain psychological facts, on the other).

If Hume's analysis is essentially correct, ecology and the environmental sciences can thus directly change our values: what we value, not how we value. They do not, in other words, change our inherited capacity for moral discrimination and response, nor do they change the specific profile of our human moral sentiments of passions (these change, if they change at all, only through an evolutionary process, that is, through random variation, natural selection, and so forth).[26] Rather, ecology changes our values by changing our concepts of the world and of ourselves in relation to the world. It reveals new relations among objects which, once revealed, stir our ancient centers of moral feeling.

# 8

## On the Intrinsic Value of
## Nonhuman Species

### The "Facts" and the Values

At present the earth is in the throes of an episode of biotic impoverishment of, perhaps, unprecedented magnitude.[1] The current rate of species extinction is the subject of controversy, but all parties agree that it is alarmingly great, and accelerating.[2] From 1600 to 1900 the average rate of species extinction was roughly one every four years, from 1900 to the present one per year;[3] and, according to Norman Myers, "if present average patterns of exploitation persist," the rate of extinction during the last quarter of the twentieth century may reach something over 100 species per day![4] It is conceivable that by the end of the century one million or more species could become extinct.[5] Already gone are, in the words of Alfred Russel Wallace, "the hugest, and fiercest, and strangest forms."[6] Next to go will be myraid species of plants and invertebrates.

Well, so what? Why should we care? Aren't more than 90 percent of the species ever to have existed on earth now extinct?[7] Isn't species extinction, after all, a natural process?

Undoubtedly, species extinction is natural, in the sense that all natural phenomena are natural. (Certainly it is not supernatural.) Species extinction, when compensated by speciation, moreover, is normal as well as natural. But massive, abrupt species extinction and consequent biological impoverishment are *not* normal. The fossil record indicates that several discernible mass extinction events occurred in the geologic past, but it also indicates that the rate of "background" or routine extinctions has declined with time and, correspondingly, that biological diversity has increased with time.[8] On the average, speciation has outpaced extinction. The earth's evolutionary process tends toward greater biological diversity (and I do not mean to suggest here anything teleological), although it has been interrupted by widely spaced setbacks.

To know that massive species extinction is abnormal, albeit natural, and that the tendency of organic evolution is toward greater biological diversity, however, does not settle the question of value. Why should one species be concerned about the threat of destruction it poses to others? More to the point, why should we, *Homo sapiens*, preserve and nurture those species yet surviving?

Many cogent arguments for species preservation of a kind vulgarly called "utilitarian" have recently appeared.[9] Any argument for species preservation which is addressed to human welfare or human happiness (whether material or spiritual) is essentially utilitarian in the received sense of the term.[10] There are, in general, two kinds of value: (1) intrinsic value and (2) instrumental value. A utilitarian or homocentric argument for species preservation either explicitly or implicitly assumes that human beings (or, more abstractly, human welfare or happiness) are intrinsically valuable and that all other things, including other forms of life, are valuable only as means or instruments which may serve human beings (or facilitate human welfare or happiness).

One often finds, however, lurking beneath a recitation of the benefits to man provided by other species severally and the existing biotic complement of earth collectively, a scarcely concealed nonutilitarian substratum of value. George Woodwell, for example, wistfully remarks that "one might dream that on the only green planet we know, life would have a special value of its own." But, since such a value is not universally acknowledged, he and his colleague Howard Irwin agree that it is necessary to argue for species preservation in terms "understandable and usable in politics," and which "the public can easily understand and accept," that is, utilitarian terms.[11] The utilitarian arguments, in other words, seem often to be a way of selling the public on policies that are felt to be somehow right independently of present and future human well-being. One suspects that for Woodwell, Irwin, and many other ardent advocates of species preservation the conventional utilitarian arguments are but a subterfuge and that their deeper concerns emanate from other ideals and values.[12] Many distinguished conservationists, indeed, have openly and boldly declared that other species have a right to exist or conversely that we, *Homo sapiens*, have no right to cause their extinction.[13]

While the utilitarian case for species preservation has been fully and persuasively articulated, the nonutilitarian case has been neglected. Upon consideration of the philosophical problem of providing a nonutilitarian case for species preservation Alastair Gunn has recently even expressed despair: "It seems impossible to provide *reasons* for valuing natural kinds. It seems to me that the world would be a worse place if we were to lose the tiger, the bald eagle, or the various species of whale, but I do not know how to justify this view to someone who disagrees."[14] In the absence of well-considered reasons, it is simply asserted that we *Homo sapiens* have "moral obligations" in regard to other species or that other species have a "right to exist" or that we have "no right to render them extinct" and left at that. In this essay I try to provide the missing discussion of the "rights" (the intrinsic value) of other species. First, I critically explore the concept of "species rights." I then turn to my principal task: a discussion of several distinct axiologies which may provide intrinsic value for nonhuman forms of life. While arguments for species preservation based upon the aesthetic value of other species may sometimes seem genuinely disinterested or biocentric, they are, nevertheless, readily reducible to a homocentric or utilitarian form: other species, in the final analysis, are valuable as aesthetic resources for the aesthetic enjoyment they afford (some) people.[15] Appeals for species preservation based upon the alleged rights of other species are more resistant to reduction.

An analysis of the concept of rights, sufficient for the needs of this discussion, is provided in the next section. There I argue that the assertion of rights on behalf of species, taken literally, is incoherent and thus that the persistent popular call for "species rights" is essentially symbolic. What it symbolizes, that is, what it imprecisely but dramatically expresses, I suggest, is the widely shared intuition that nonhuman species possess intrinsic value. Since this concept, the concept of "intrinsic value," is, though traditional, somewhat technical and absolutely central to the main body of this discussion, it should, perhaps, be explicitly defined here at the outset.

Something is intrinsically valuable if it is valuable *in* and *for* itself—if its value is not derived from its utility, but is independent of any use or function it may have in relation to something or someone else. In classical philosophical terminology, an intrinsically valuable entity is said to be an "end-in-itself," not just a "means" to another's ends.

Most systems of modern ethics, both formal philosophical systems (e.g., Kant's deontology), and less formal popular system (e.g., the Christian ethic), take it for granted that human beings are intrinsically valuable, that, in other words, each human being is valuable in and for himself or herself independently of any contribution he or she may make to the welfare of another person or to society collectively. We may not discard or destroy worn-out, broken, or imperfectly made human beings as we might tools in similar condition because human beings are, it is almost universally supposed, intrinsically—not, like tools or "resources," merely instrumentally—valuable.

Accounts of intrinsic value in the Western philosophical tradition have varied considerably. Plato, who did not share the modern dogma that human beings are paradigmatic cases of intrinsically valuable entities, posited a "form," the Good, as the ultimate source of intrinsic value for intrinsically valuable entities. I shall have occasion in a subsequent section of this chapter to explain Plato's understanding of the Good, that is, of intrinsic value, more fully, and apply it to my central theme, the problematic intrinsic value of nonhuman species. Aristotle, somewhat less abstractly and elusively than Plato, concluded that happiness is the only intrinsically valuable thing, among other reasons because, he thought, happiness is the only thing pursued for the sake of itself. Kant, to whom I also refer more fully below, rested the intrinsic value of persons (human beings) on our capacity to reason. G. E. Moore, whose account is not outlined here and applied to the problem of the value of species because in the final analysis it appeals to mute intuition, thought that intrinsic value was a primitive non-natural property of objects as the color red is a primitive natural property. One either perceived it, he thought, or one did not. Such a theory as Moore's leaves no room for rational discussion of controversial cases. I may perceive the intrinsic value of species and you may not. Since intrinsic value, so construed, is a primitive non-natural property, I cannot explain why species are intrinsically valuable; I can only accuse you of a kind of moral insensitivity. Moore's theory reduces moral debate to question-begging and/or brow-beating.

A fundamental doctrine of modern science remains a formidable obstacle, however, to all the heroic attempts of philosophers to establish the existence, and adequately explain the nature, of intrinsic value, the value of something in and for itself. The objective physical world is sharply distinguished from subjective consciousness in the metaphysical posture of modern science as originally formulated by Descartes. Thought, feeling, sensation, and value have ever since been, from the point of view of scientific naturalism, regarded as confined to the subjective realm of consciousness. The objective, physical world is therefore value-free from a scientific point of view.

Quantum theory, relativity, and the other revolutionary developments of postmodern science are said to have invalidated the Cartesian distinction between the subjective and the objective domains, and hence to promise profound consequences not only for epistemology and ontology, but for value theory as well.[16] The axiological consequences of postmodern science, however, remain at this point programmatic; they have not been worked out in any detail, and seem, in any case, remote and metaphorical. Further, in the structure of science itself, quantum theory has little direct relationship to or influence on biology. Hence, at the level of organization with which we are concerned, the macroscopic world of terrestrial life and the value of its component species, the classical attitude that nature is value-neutral remains a virtually unchallenged dogma of the scientific world view. From this perspective, the attribution of intrinsic value to species, as to anything else under the sun, is doomed at the outset to failure.

On the other hand, many people, including some scientists, persist intuitively to feel that nonhuman species are valuable in and for themselves, quite apart from their usefulness to us as resources, either material or spiritual, or as providers of (human) life-supporting services. In the discussion which follows I explore several possible and preferred grounds for this very genuine and sincere ethical intuition.

The classical scientific world view is not, after all, the only world view represented in Western civilization today. The intrinsic value of species may be quite straightforwardly defended in terms of some elements of the prescientific, but still well-represented, Judeo-Christian world view. In the last section of this essay, I attempt to find a compromise, recommending a theory of "intrinsic value" which at once respects the institutionalized cleavage between object and subject, fact and value of the scientific world view, and yet does justice to the intuition that some natural "entities," nonhuman species among them, are more than merely instrumentally valuable. In the process, the concept of intrinsic value is transformed, or more precisely, truncated.

I concede that, from the point of view of scientific naturalism, the *source* of all value is human consciousness, but it by no means follows that the *locus* of all value is consciousness itself or a mode of consciousness like reason, pleasure, or knowledge. In other words, something may be valuable only because someone values it, but it may also be valued for itself, not for the sake of any subjective experience (pleasure, knowledge, aesthetic satisfaction, and so forth) it may afford the valuer. Value may be subjective and affective, but it is intentional, not self-referential. For example, a newborn infant is valuable to its parents for its own sake as well as for the joy or any other experience it may afford them. In and of itself an infant child is as value-neutral as a stone or a hydrogen atom, considered in strict accordance with the subject-object/fact-value dichotomy of modern science. Yet we still may wish to say that a newborn infant is "intrinsically valuable" (even though its value depends, in the last analysis, on human consciousness) in order to distinguish the *noninstrumental* value it has for its parents, relatives, and the human community generally from its actual or potential instrumental value—the pleasure it gives its parents, the pride it affords its relatives, the contribution it may make to society, and so forth. In so doing, however, "intrinsic value" retains only half its traditional meaning. An intrinsically valuable thing on this reading is valuable *for* its own sake, *for* itself, but it is not valuable in itself, that is, completely independently of any consciousness, since no value can, in principle, from the point of view of classical normal science, be altogether independent of a valuing consciousness. Nonhuman species, I argue, may possess intrinsic value in this truncated sense, which is consistent with the world view of scientific naturalism. Indeed, my suggestion is that the world view of modern science not only allows for the intrinsic value of nonhuman species in this limited sense, but its cosmological, evolutionary, and ecological perspectives actually foster such value.

## "Species Rights" or Specious Rights?

There is, I think, a certain aura of mystery surrounding so-called natural or moral rights (as opposed to civil or legal rights which may be defined in a positive or operational way).[17] Because it is a noun, "right" seems to be the name of an entity of some sort. A person possesses shoes, teeth, kidneys, feelings, thoughts, and certain inalienable natural rights. Feelings and thoughts may not be entities on a par with kidneys, teeth, and shoes, but they are at least palpable states of a human organism. Rights are not even entities of this tenuous sort. The term "rights" is, rather, an expressive locution masquerading as a substantive.[18] Of course, that is a big part of its talismanic power.

In this connection it is instructive to note that the concept of a moral right is both modern and Western. Plato and Aristotle never so much as mention rights in their ethical and political philosophies. The Bible contains no myth, allegory, sermon, or homily on rights. Oriental religious philosophies contain little that can be interpreted as pertaining to rights. Indeed, there appear to be no clear instances of the systematic assertion and theoretical defense of moral rights before the seventeenth century. If rights were real natural entities associated with us from birth, it is surprising that they were not sooner and more universally noticed.

Talk about the "rights" of species to a share of life seems clearly to be an extension of this relatively recent tradition of Western ethical discourse about natural or moral rights. Having exorcised the ghostly presence of some occult entity that the substantive term "rights" conjures, I suggest that a fundamental part of its function in popular discourse is to assert "standing" for someone (or something) in the moral community, that is, status as an end rather than a mere means to be used for another's betterment. If this minimalistic interpretation is correct, then the argument that we ought not to cause the extinction of other species because they have a right to exist not only resists reduction to a utilitarian form; it avows that whatever instrumental value species may (or may not) have, they, no less than we, have intrinsic value too.[19]

It is understandable but regrettable that the moral intuition that nonhuman species have intrinsic as well as instrumental value is popularly expressed in terms of rights, "species rights." It is understandable because talk of rights has become the usual and preferred way to express moral considerability; but it is regrettable because the concept of species rights taken at face value seems to be philosophical nonsense. The "grammar" of the term "rights" appears to require that those possessing them be, if not persons, at least localizable things of some sort. But the term "species" traditionally designates a class or kind. A class, by definition, is not an individual or localizable thing. How then could it possibly have rights? The proposition itself seems, upon its face, conceptually odd if not logically contradictory.

There are several ways of circumventing this difficulty, but none of them is satisfactory. One would be to follow Plato and hypostatize classes. It would then be logically possible to endow species with rights, although to do so would be pointless since according to the same ontological theory species are eternal forms and could not therefore be threatened or endangered.

One could argue that talk about "species rights" is just a loose and imprecise way of talking about the putative rights of individual nonhuman organisms. Analogously with "gay rights" or "minority rights," which we understand to devolve upon members of certain classes, "species rights" could be construed to refer not to species per se but to specimens. Such a reduction from type to token, however, would miss the point. Those who claim that nonhuman species have a right to exist are concerned with species preservation, not necessarily with animal and/or plant welfare, an entirely separate issue. It is logically consistent to hold that species have intrinsic value, but that specimens of some species do not. Indeed, I am inclined to think that for some ardent species preservationists, species have intrinsic value while specimens have only instrumental value—as means to the preservation of species. An individual whooping crane, for example, is no more or less valuable than a sandhill crane qua individual, but because a fertile whooping crane carries a significant fraction of the genetic material of her species, her life is a precious instrument for the salvation of her kind. If whooping cranes are ever rescued from the brink, specimens may even be routinely "culled" from the "herd" to improve the "stock."

Finally, one may adopt a nontraditional interpretation of the term "species." David Hull has argued, for example, that the traditional interpretation of "species" as a class designator is theoretically useless in

evolutionary biology. In his view, species are "superorganismic entities" or "historical entities," localizable (as classes or kinds are not) in
space, however diffusely, and in time, however protractedly.[20] Although paradigmatic holders of rights are individual persons, it is not
at all unusual or conceptually odd to ascribe rights to "superorganismic
entities"—corporations, for example. Nations, to take another example,
have certain rights which are not the same as the sum of the rights of
their individual citizens. A nation's right to sovereignty is hardly the
sum of the respective rights of its several citizens to sovereignty (whatever that may mean). "Species rights" might be understood, in short,
by analogy with "national rights." This is the most attractive way to
reify the reference of the term "species" so that the phrase "species
rights," taken at face value, is at least intelligible. However, Hull's
proposed reference for the term "species" has not been universally
accepted among philosophers of science.[21] In any case, the assertion of
species rights is primarily symbolic; it seems to be less a literal assertion
of rights than an assertion in familiar, strong moral terms of the intrinsic
value of nonhuman species.

Species rights is indeed a specious notion. It would be better if the
notion simply went away. But of course it won't, because it expresses in
a particularly current and forceful manner of speech a deeply felt and
widely shared intuition that species are intrinsically valuable.

Of course, this analysis of certain claims being made on behalf of
nonhuman forms of life takes us, so to speak, out of the frying pan into
the fire. "Intrinsic value" is no less mysterious a notion than "natural
rights." Indeed it is frankly metaphysical. But that is, in fact, its virtue.
We do not require a more liberal theory of rights; we need to discover,
rather, metaphysical foundations for the intrinsic value of other species
which the assertion of rights on their behalf expresses. What are the
ethical systems and, more generally, the world views in which claims of
the intrinsic value of nonhuman species are embedded? I next sketch
several alternative metaphysics of morals in which the intrinsic value
of other species may be grounded.[22]


## J-Theism

In a deservedly famous discussion of the relative merits of utilitarian and nonutilitarian arguments for species preservation, David
Ehrenfeld places the "non-economic [i.e., intrinsic] value" and "unim-
peachable right to continued existence" of ecosystems and species in a
religious context.[23] Ehrenfeld invokes the Judeo-Christian religious
belief system (to which the concept of natural rights has been grafted

since the seventeenth century) as a supporting matrix of ideas for "species rights." He suggests we call it the " 'Noah Principle' after the person who was one of the first to put it into practice."[24]

At first glance the Judeo-Christian world view would seem inhospitable to the suggestion that nonhuman species are intrinsically valuable. "Academic" Christian theology, from Origen and Augustine to Bultmann and Teilhard, has been consistently hostile to the idea that human beings have any duties directly to individual animals and plants (to say nothing of species), precisely because animals and plants lack the requisite qualifications (an immortal soul, the *imago Dei*, or whatever) for membership in the moral community. Orthodox Christian theology, historically, lines up overwhelmingly against the notion that nonhuman creatures considered individually or collectively have any sort of value other than instrumental value or any other role in creation other than to serve man.[25]

Lynn White, Jr., in his celebrated environmentalist critique of the Judeo-Christian world view, traces this attitude to those verses in Genesis (1:26-30) which set man apart from the rest of creation and appear to deliver the creation into his hands.[26] White emphatically declares, indeed, that "Christianity is the most anthropocentric religion the world has seen."[27]

There is, however, a countercurrent of thought powerfully and discernibly running in the text of Genesis itself, however little representation it may have enjoyed in subsequent theology and popular Christianity. Within the general outlines of the traditional scriptural world view, nonhuman species may have intrinsic value because they are parts of God's creation and God has conferred intrinsic value upon them, either by creating them or by a secondary fiat.[28]

The God of the Judeo-Christian tradition is transcendent, not immanent. The hypothesis of such a God therefore permits us to conceive of intrinsic value as determined objectively, that is, from some point of reference outside human consciousness. From God's point of view, we may imagine, the creation as a whole and all its parts are "good." Everything may not seem good from a subjective human perspective—poison ivy, mosquitoes, rattlesnakes—but they are all "God's creatures" and therefore good in His eyes.

It was upon just this theological-metaphysical ground that John Muir argued for "species rights." Notice how closely Muir's assertion of a natural right to existence for a vermin species is followed by appeal to God as a more objective axiological reference point: "Again and again, in season and out of season, the question comes up, 'what are rattlesnakes good for?' as if nothing that does not rightly make for the benefit of man had any *right to exist*; as if our ways were *God's ways*."[29]

Muir repeatedly presses this theocentric orientation. All creatures, he urges, "are part of God's family, unfallen, undepraved, and cared for with the same species of tenderness and love as is bestowed on angels in heaven or saints on earth."[30]

How can we square Muir's and Ehrenfeld's interpretation of the axiology of Scripture with White's? A close reading of Genesis, in fact, discloses two different and even contradictory messages respecting the appropriate place and role of people in relation to the rest of creation. This should not be surprising in view of the modern discovery that Genesis as we have received it is woven together from three main narrative strands (designated as J, E, and P) all of different provenance.[31] J, the Yahwist strand, is by scholarly consensus the oldest, dating from the ninth century B.C., and P, the Priestly narrative, the most recent, composed in the fifth century B.C.[32]

The Priestly version of Creation (Genesis 1-2:4), in comparison with the Yahwist version, presents an orderly, rational "quasi-scientific" account of the "evolution" of the cosmos. When reduced to its abstract moments—a primal unity (void, waters), separation of opposites (light/darkness, above/beneath), and serial production of living beings (plants, animals, people)—it is in form identical with the general outline of creation in fifth-century Ionian Greek natural philosophy. And like its contemporary Greek counterpart, the natural philosophy of the P strand of Genesis exhibits a distinct tendency toward humanism: man is created in the image of God and given dominion over the rest of creation and charged to subdue it.[33]

In the Yahwist creation myth (Genesis 2:4-4:26), the less "scientific" sequence of creation goes: man, then plants, then animals—and man's role is decidedly different. Adam is charged not to subdue and have dominion over the creation, but to "dress the garden and keep it" (Genesis 2:15). If he is not, in Aldo Leopold's terms, "a plain member and citizen" of Eden, neither is he its conqueror or master. Rather, Adam's role is to be custodian or steward of the creation.

Genesis-J thus seems quite clearly to imply that God cares for the creation as a whole (as "one great unit" in Muir's words) and for its several parts equally. The mastery of *Homo sapiens* over other species, the J narrative appears to assert, is a sign of the fallen and cursed condition of *Homo sapiens*, not of a privilege ordained by God. The assumption by humans of a self-centered or homocentric value orientation, indeed, seems radically to have unsettled the balance and order of the creation. Some animals and plants were enslaved (i.e., domesticated), those for which people could find no use were declared worthless, and those which confounded human purposes or made human life less comfortable or secure were declared pests and vermin and were put on an agenda for extermination.

There follows immediately the story of the destructive flood and of Noah, the original species conservator, for whom Ehrenfeld names his principle of "species rights."

Intrinsic value for nonhuman species based upon Ehrenfeld's Noah Principle and the metaphysic of Genesis-J would devolve upon species per se, not specimens. Individual beings come and go, each after its kind, while the created forms, species, persist. The destruction of species, though not of individuals, therefore, would be a denial of divine fiat by man. After all, Noah, following God's orders, did not attempt to save every individual living thing he could; rather he took specimens aboard the ark in male-female pairs so as to preserve their species. From this stock the creation could be restored, complete and intact. As the modern descendants of Noah, we ought, presumably, also to be more concerned with preserving species, with the value of species per se, and less with specimens and with individual nonhuman rights.

## Holistic Rationalism

In the theistic moral metaphysic outlined in the previous section, God is the sole legitimate arbiter of value. It is not clear, however, how God goes about determining the value of nonhuman natural entities. On the one hand, it seems absurd to suppose that God has self-interests of any kind and, like man, determines value in relation to them, or that He is in need or want of anything or could be benefited or harmed in any way. God, we must suppose, is not injured so much as defied when His creation is altered or parts of it (species) are destroyed. It seems equally absurd, on the other hand, to suppose that God is arbitrary, that He simply and whimsically values the smallpox virus, the tsetse fly, and all the other forms of life that people, for the most part, find life-threatening, annoying, loathsome, or inconvenient. God must have followed some axiological principle(s) in deciding what to create and thus to confer value upon.

This line of thought, pursued far enough, separates value, classically called "the Good," from God. God Himself, from this perspective, is no longer the primary axiological reference point, since God now is thought to be determined or at least persuaded by some impersonal axiological principle, the Good.

The Good was classically conceived to be something "objective," that is, independent of both divine and human interests, preferences, or desires. The intrinsic value of nonhuman species could thus conceivably be grounded in an objective, impersonal principle of value as the primary axiological reference point.

One philosophical tradition, perhaps going all the way back to Plato, locates value or goodness in certain formal characteristics of systems or organized wholes. On the nature of the Good Plato was more suggestive than explicit. Recent Platonic scholarship inclines to the view that by "the Good" Plato meant a formal principle of order of the highest degree of generality, and by "order" meant formal logico-mathematical design.[34] A good house or ship is one that is well ordered, that is, its parts are measured, proportioned, and fitted together according to a rational design; the goodness of body (health), of soul (virtue), of society (justice), and of the cosmos as a whole—literally, the world-order—is similarly defined.[35]

In the early modern period Leibniz more clearly or at least more explicitly defined what he took to be the objective, impersonal principle of value. Musing on why God chose just this world to create, Leibniz concludes that this one must be the best of all possible worlds. The enormous quantity of vice, pestilence, and calamity in the actual world makes this an outrageous statement from a homocentric point of view. It provoked Voltaire, indeed, to write *Candide* to illustrate the opposite thesis. But Voltaire's satire was beside the point, since by "best" Leibniz meant logico-mathematical elegance, not the absence of human frustration and suffering. According to Leibniz the Good that God had in view when choosing among possible worlds was "the greatest possible variety, together with the greatest order that may be; that is to say, ... the greatest possible perfection."[36] Leibniz says that "God, however, has chosen the most perfect [world], that is to say the one which is at the same time the simplest in hypotheses and the richest in phenomena."[37]

Similarly, in contemporary conservation literature one sometimes finds biological diversity and/or complexity posited as a good in itself.[38] The most well-known application to ecological conservation of the general theory that the formal properties of natural systems—order, parsimony, harmony, complexity, and variety—are objective intrinsic values is the summary maxim of Aldo Leopold's land ethic: "A thing is right when it tends to preserve the integrity, stability and beauty of the biotic community. It is wrong when it tends otherwise."[39]

Leopold makes no deliberate effort specifically to explain or defend his cardinal moral precept. A philosophical development of his ideas has recently been attempted by Peter Miller. Miller quite correctly points out that "most modern theories of ... value, and indeed many classical ones, are psychologically [i.e., subjectively] based. They differ from one another just in the psychological phenomena they select as values."[40] Miller attempts to go beyond the orbit of all such subjective, homocentric theories by positing "richness" as an irreducible, objective, intrinsic value. While Miller very fully characterizes or describes "richness" ("the richness of natural systems [consists of] their inner and outer profusion, unity," and so forth), he does not adequately explain why richness should be valued for its own sake, or, more concretely, why a diverse, complex, and stable biota is intrinsically better than a simple, impoverished, or unstable one. The value of "richness" is certainly explicable instrumentally: a biologically rich world is more satisfying and more secure than an impoverished world, but these are clearly homocentric concerns.

The nonhomocentric explanation of the goodness of order and variety which eludes Miller depends, in Leibniz's account as mentioned above, upon the hypothesis of God, certain assumptions about God's psychology, and the principle of sufficient reason.[41] God, as Leibniz forthrightly declares, has the tastes of a classical or early modern mathematician and natural philosopher.[42] Being infinitely rational, God prefers a logico-mathematically elegant world to one that is inelegantly designed. However, in the course of this Leibnizian explanation of the goodness of "richness," the alleged objective value of richness is reduced to a subjective preference—God's preference, to be sure, not ours, and a constitutional preference, not an arbitrary one, but a subjective preference nonetheless.

In any case, a persistent strain of Western axiological thought with the best philosophical pedigree posits an objective, impersonal Good and, further, characterizes or describes the Good in terms of formal elegance or logico-mathematical perfection: maximum economy of premises, axioms, or fundamental laws; maximum variety or diversity of implications or resulting phenomena; and consistency, order, or "harmony." Historically the universe has been found to exemplify these characteristics and thus to be objectively and impersonally good, even though from a subjective, homocentric standpoint it contains many "evils" which cause much human suffering. More recently the "biosphere" or global "ecosystem" has been found to exemplify similar characteristics and thus felt to be "good in itself," even though it may not be altogether accommodating to human interests.

Earth's biosphere is indeed an elegant system. The basic biological "laws" from which all its diversity and complexity result are wonderfully parsimonious. And while the relationships among species are many, intricate, and sometimes quite amazing, it seems they are comprehensible in terms of a relatively few basic chemical, physical, and perhaps topological processes.

From the rationalistic perspective, the system itself (the biosphere as a whole and/or its several biomes and integrated ecosystems) is valuable per se or at least exemplifies or embodies the Good. Therefore, from this perspective, species taken separately are not intrinsically valuable. However, since the intrinsically valuable biosphere is not some mystical or transcendental whole, but a systemic whole (i.e., a whole by virtue of the functional integration of its parts), its integrity, complexity, stability, variety, in a word, its inherently good or intrinsically valuable richness depends, obviously, on the continued existence of its component parts, that is, its full complement of species. From the rationalist perspective, therefore, the preservation of species, as the sine qua non of the preservation of biotic diversity, ought to be pursued quite apart from the instrumental value preservation may have in relation to human interests.

Or at least so it would seem. However, if one defends one's intuition that biological impoverishment is objectively wrong by positing organic richness as objectively good, one might well be accused of temporal parochialism and a very subtle form of human arrogance. Considering our time as but an infinitesimal moment of the three-and-one-half-billion-year tenure of life on planet earth (let alone the possibility that earth may be but one of many planets to possess a biota), man's tendency to destroy other species might be viewed quite disinterestedly as a transitional stage in the earth's evolutionary odyssey. The Age of Reptiles came to a close in due course (for whatever reason) to be followed by the Age of Mammals. A holistic rationalist could not regret the massive die-off of the late Cretaceous because it made possible our yet richer mammal-populated world. The Age of Mammals may likewise end. But the "laws" of organic evolution and of ecology (if any there be) will remain operative. Nonhuman life would go on even after a nuclear holocaust. In time speciation would occur and species would radiate anew. Future "intelligent" forms of life may even feel grateful, if not to us then to their God (or the Good), for making their world possible. The new Age (of Insects, perhaps) would eventually be just as diverse, orderly, harmonious, and stable and thus no less good than our current ecosystem with its present complement of species.

With friends like the holistic rationalists, species preservation needs no enemies.

## Conativism

In sharp contrast to the objective, holistic orientation of moral thought in the ancient and early modern period, Western moral thought since the Enlightenment has been singularly narcissistic. Kenneth Goodpaster has argued that the "impotence" of modern

Western ethics in the face of contemporary environmental problems is due to the fact that the two main modern schools of moral philosophy, deontological and utilitarian, assume egoism as an unquestioned given and then generalize to a larger set of intrinsically valuable "others."[43] The process of generalization begins by identifying an essential *psychological* characteristic that makes oneself, in one's own eyes, intrinsically valuable. According to Kant, founder of the deontological school, the characteristic is reason or rationality, and according to Bentham, founder of the utilitarian school, it is sentiency or the capacity to experience pleasure and pain. Egoism is then transcended by discovering the same characteristic in a select class of beings outside oneself.[44] It is revealing that both Kant and Mill, Bentham's protégé, invoke the Christian Golden Rule—love thy neighbor *as thyself*—as the perfect summary statement of their moral philosophies.

Kant's moral metaphysic limits intrinsic value to rational beings. Therefore, Kant's moral metaphysic is unsupportive of intrinsic value for nonhuman beings, either individually or collectively as species. Kant, indeed, directly stated that nonhuman living beings were of instrumental value only.[45]

Bentham's axiology is more inclusive than Kant's and is, in fact, the metaphysical foundation of the contemporary animal liberation / animal rights movement. Bentham himself recognized that the pleasure and pain of sentient animals must be taken into consideration no less than that of human beings,[46] but until very recently mainstream utilitarianism limited moral consideration to human welfare only. The contemporary animal liberation / animal rights philosophy gains much of its persuasive force from simply insisting that utilitarianism be put into practice in a logically consistent and intellectually honest way.

The core moral metaphysic of utilitarianism and of the animal liberation / animal rights movement is inadequate, however, to address massive species extinction.[47] In fact, it could under a certain extreme interpretation make matters worse. First, animal liberation excludes plants from moral consideration, shifting the burden of support for the rights-holding human-animal community onto plant species. Second, animal liberation / animal rights provides no philosophical basis for concern for species qua species, as Peter Singer, a leading animal liberation theorist, openly admits.[48] Animal liberation is concerned with the psychological well-being of individual animals, domestic no less than wild; its aim is to reduce individual animal suffering. A species qua species cannot experience pleasure or pain and thus upon Benthamic principles is entitled to no moral consideration. Since wild animals often suffer considerably in their natural habitats from extremes of cold, drought, starvation, disease, and predation, the animal liberationists' program of reducing individual animal suffering might achieve a "final solution" by the deliberate, painless extinction of all sentient nonhuman animal species.[49] Or perhaps, as Mark Sagoff once remarked, from the point of view of animal liberation, the best thing for wild animals would be relocation in zoos, where they could be cared for and protected from the suffering inflicted on them by the elements and by one another.[50]

While Bentham's utilitarian moral metaphysic is more inclusive than Kant's, it proves to be useless as a foundation for the intrinsic value of nonhuman species. However, certain historical modifications of Kant's deontological ethic, surprisingly, may be of some service in building a nonhomocentric case for species preservation.

The neo-Kantian Voluntarist ethical tradition which begins with Schopenhauer substitutes conation (the "will-to-live") for reason as the essence of the self.[51] Conation or the "will-to-live," of course, is far more universal than reason, and at the very least resides in every living thing. (Schopenhauer thought that it also was the "kernel" of everything right down to elemental matter—of which inertia and gravity were the striving—but more recent theorists in the conativist or Voluntarist tradition are not so generous.) Generalizing from conation as the essence of self, it follows that all beings which are "manifestations" of the "will-to-live," that is, at the very least all living things, have intrinsic value.

Among recent exponents of conativism, Albert Schweitzer's reverence-for-life ethic exhibits the clearest traces of Schopenhauer's influence together with an explicit illustration of the modern method of generalizing from egoism to altruism.[52] Those Anglo-American moral philosophers who base moral standing (and sometimes rights) upon "interests" construed in the broadest sense are also, though they are usually not so identified, Voluntarist fellow travelers. The term "interest" is, of course, ambiguous. Setting aside nonpsychological, nondispositional senses (e.g., the financial sense), "interest" has been construed in three principal ways. One may have an interest in the sense of having one's attention engaged. This may be called the cognitive sense of "interest." If having interests means having one's attention engaged and the capacity for having interests is the criterion of intrinsic value, then only those human beings and the higher vertebrates with cognitive capacities are intrinsically valuable.[53] The capacity for having interests has been somewhat more broadly construed by animal liberationists in terms of sentiency, the capacity for experiencing pleasure and pain.[54] This may be called the *hedonic* sense of "interest." Joel Feinberg has construed "interests" in a sense broader still to mean a *conative* capacity:

> A mere thing, however valuable to others, has no good of its own. The explanation of that fact, I suspect, is that mere things have no conative life; neither conscious wishes, desires and hopes; nor urges and impulses; nor unconscious drives, aims, goals; nor latent tendencies, directions of growth, and natural fulfillments. Interests must be compounded somehow out of conations.[55]

Though Feinberg himself does not appear to appreciate the consequence, under this view of "interests" plants as well as animals may have interests and thus intrinsic value, because, though plants may not have "conscious wishes, desires, and hopes," they have "tendencies, directions of growth, and natural fulfillments." Goodpaster explicitly draws the implication, from Feinberg's discussion of interests, that plants, too, are in Goodpaster's terminology "morally considerable."[56] On this basis, Goodpaster defends a "life principle" of moral considerability which includes all living things.

The Schopenhauer-Schweitzer reverence-for-life ethic and the Feinberg-Goodpaster life principle ethic avoid some of the untoward characteristics of the Benthamic animal liberation moral metaphysic as applied to the question of species extinction. Clearly plants are included within the moral community as well as animals. And since the essential capacity identified as the criterion of moral considerability is conativity, not sentiency a thrusting, striving, driving, developmental tendency or direction (whether conscious or unconscious)— the life principle and reverence-for-life ethics do not have the effete and prophylactic connotations of the animal liberation / animal rights hedonic ethic. They suggest, to me at any rate, that living things should be left alone to fulfill their natural urges, drives, and developmental and reproductive sequences, or to struggle, fight, and die in the attempt rather than be coddled, sheltered, protected, anesthetized, or otherwise "saved." One's cardinal duty is not to interfere, to live and let live.

Species per se, however, are no more conative than they are sentient or rational, hence species per se are not intrinsically valuable from this point of view. Species qua species may however be the incidental beneficiaries of an ethic directed toward the preservation of individual living beings since the reverence-for-life and life principle ethics would surely imply a far less callous, mindlessly destructive approach to the biota than that which currently prevails.

Indeed, one of the principal problems with the conation-based moral metaphysic is that, if rigorously practiced, it would seem to require a restraint so severe that it would lead if not to suicide by starvation, at best to a life intolerably fettered. Schopenhauer, always intellectually honest, was prepared to accept these practical conse-

quences. His more recent exponents recognize them as practical consequences, but treat them as a problem to be somehow overcome. As
Schweitzer remarks, "It remains a painful enigma how I am to live by
the rule of reverence for life in a world ruled by creative will which is at
the same time destructive will"; and Goodpaster remarks, "the clearest
and most decisive refutation of the principle of respect for life is that
one cannot *live* according to it.... we must eat, experiment to gain
knowledge, protect ourselves from predation (macroscopic and micro-
scopic).... to take seriously the criterion of considerability being
defended, all these things must be seen as somehow morally wrong."[57]

Goodpaster addresses this problem by means of a formal distinction which is, despite his claim to the contrary, largely vacuous. Since
we are subject to certain "thresholds of moral sensitivity," ideally we
may acknowledge the "rights" of all living things to exist, but practically we may be unable to live on such terms. Such ideals are "regu-
lative," not "operative"[58] We are thus left paying lip service to an
impractical ideal while day-to-day life goes on pretty much business as
usual.

Schweitzer hints at a decision procedure which might put some
teeth in the reverence-for-life ethical ideal: "Whenever I injure life of
any kind, I must be quite clear as to whether this is necessary or not. I
ought never to pass the limits of the unavoidable, even in apparently
insignificant cases."[59] But the rule "never to pass the limits of the unavoidable" is very vague and indeterminate. The destruction of critical
habitat for an endangered species may be judged "unavoidable" by a
consortium intent on developing its "resources" at a reasonable profit.
The extinction of several species of great whales may be "unavoidable"
if the whaling industry is to recover its capital investment. More explicit
criteria are needed if a moral theory according intrinsic value to all
living things is to be at once "operative" (in Goodpaster's sense) and
practical or livable.[60]

If our society were to acknowledge and institutionalize a reverence-
for-life or life principle ethic to the same extent that it has acknowledged and institutionalized an ethic based upon justice and human
equality, things would be as different from what they are today for
nonhuman forms of life as contemporary human life (in most democratic societies at least) is from the oppressive conditions of the
imperial and feudal past. Still, there is no logical link as far as I can see
between a concern for the intrinsic value of *individual* plants and
animals and a concern for *species* preservation. To be sure, a species
survives only if its representative specimens are allowed to survive
and to reproduce successfully. However, according to the conative
theory of intrinsic value, individual living things are in principle of

equal value, while species preservationists set a much higher value, for example, on an individual furbish lousewort (a "mere" plant, but a precious custodian of unique genetic material) than on a individual whitetailed deer, a commonplace mammal. A life-respecting society might significantly slow the rate of species extinction, but species preservation would be, nevertheless, an *incidental* consequence, a side effect. This is, however, the best that the prevailing structure of modern moral philosophy can do.[61]

## Bio-Empathy

There remains a modern moral metaphysic which has been largely ignored or dismissed by the philosophical community, but which has survived largely in biological discussions of moral or moral-like phenomena. Hume's grounding of morality in feeling or emotion has been the basis for several recent attempts to explain the intrinsic value of other species. According to Hume, one may have a strong emotional attachment to one's own interests, but such an attachment is entirely contingent. It is possible, indeed, that one may also have strong feelings for the interests of other beings.[62] Sometimes these overcome the self-regarding passions and issue in behavior which we praise as heroic, noble, or saintly (or condemn as foolhardy or daft).

Hume's famous sharp distinction between fact and value, his is/ought dichotomy, has made his moral metaphysic more appealing and useful to scientists interested in moral phenomena than any other philosophical analysis of ethics, since in science nature is conceived to be an objective and, more to the point so far as our interests are concerned, value-free system. From the scientific point of view, nature throughout, from atoms to galaxies, is an orderly, objective, axiologically neutral domain. Value is, as it were, projected onto natural objects or events by the subjective feelings of observers. If all consciousness were annihilated at a stroke, there would be no good and evil, no beauty and ugliness, no right and wrong; only impassive phenomena would remain. Accordingly, it has been characteristic of evolutionary biological thought about moral phenomena to follow Hume (whether deliberately or not) and treat moral valuation and behavior as both subjective and affective.

One of the more conspicuous problems for an evolutionary biological account of animal behavior is this: How is it possible to account for the existence of something like morality or ethics among human beings and their prehuman ancestors in a manner consistent with evolutionary theory? One would suppose, given the struggle for existence, that hostile, aggressive traits would be of great advantage to individuals in competition with one another for limited resources and that therefore such traits would be represented in ever-increasing magnitude in future generations. As time goes on we should see less inclination toward "moral" behavior, rather than, as the history of civilization seems to indicate (though cynics might well contest this point), more. At this late date, in any case, all human beings, indeed all animals, should be thoroughly rapacious and utterly merciless. Kindness, pity, generosity, benevolence, justice, and similar dispositions should have been nipped in the bud as soon as they appeared, winnowed by the remorseless and impersonal principle of natural selection.

Charles Darwin himself tackled this problem in *The Descent of Man*.[63] He begins with the observation that for many species, and especially mammals, prolonged parental care is necessary to ensure reproductive success. Such care is motivated by a certain strong emotion which adult mammals (in some species perhaps only the females) experience toward their offspring—parental love. Selection for this capacity would affect a species' psychological profile since it would strongly contribute to inclusive fitness (not necessarily prolonged individual survival, so much as reproductive success).

Once established, Darwin argued, the "parental and filial affections" permitted the formation of small social units originally consisting, presumably, of parent(s) and offspring. The survival advantages to the individual of membership in a protective social unit like a family group are obvious and would tend to conserve slight variations of the parent-child emotional bond, such as affection for other kin—siblings, uncles, aunts, cousins, and so on. Those individuals in whom these affections were strongest would form the most closely knit family and clan bonds. Now, these and similar "social sentiments" or "social instincts," such as "the all-important emotion of sympathy," Darwin reasoned, "will have been increased through natural selection; for those communities which included the greatest number of the most sympathetic members would flourish best, and rear the greatest number of offspring."[64]

As family group competes with family group, ironically, the same principles which at first would seem to lead to greater intolerance and rapacity lead instead to increased affection, kindness, and sympathy, for now the struggle for limited resources is understood to be pursued collectively, and groups with "the greatest number of the most sympathetic members" may be supposed to out-compete those whose members are quarrelsome and disagreeable. "No tribe," Darwin tells us, "could hold together if murder, robbery, treachery, etc., were common; consequently, such crimes within the limits of the same tribe 'are branded with everlasting infamy'; but excite no such sentiment beyond these limits."[65] Indeed, beyond these limits, it remains biologically important for the passions of aggression, rage, and bloodlust to come into play.

Not only was there selective pressure for more intense sympathy and affection within group boundaries, there was selective pressure for more widely cast social sentiments, since in competition among the most internally peaceable and cooperative groups the larger will win out. "As man advances in civilization, and small tribes are united into larger communities, the simplest reason would tell each individual that he ought to extend his social instincts and sympathies to all the members of the same nation though personally unknown to him [and unrelated to him genetically]."[66]

Unlike both the (Benthamic) utilitarian and (Kantian) deontological schools of modern moral philosophy, the Humean-Darwinian natural history of morals does not regard egoism as the only genuine and self-explanatory value. Selfishness and altruism are equally primitive and both are explained by natural selection. Self-assertion and aggressiveness are necessary for survival to reproductive age and to reproductive success, but so are caring, cooperativeness, and love.

Darwin's account of the origin and evolution of morals obviously involves the current biological anathema of "group selection," that is, natural selection operating with respect to groups rather than to individual phenotypes who are the immediate carriers of their genes.[67] A more rigorous theoretical account of social-moral phenomena has recently been provided by social evolutionary theorists.[68] Darwin's classical account, however, is an indispensable ingredient in the theoretical structure of Aldo Leopold's land ethic (which contains a plea for the "biotic right" of other species to exist), and it is the basis for Paul and Anne Ehrlich's argument for the "rights" of species to exist, as well.

Leopold's biological description of an ethic as "a limitation on freedom of action in the struggle for existence"[69] at once locates ethics in a Darwinian context and suggests the evolutionary paradox presented by ethical phenomena. His resolution of the paradox is Darwin's in a nutshell. An ethic, according to Leopold, "has its origin in the tendency of interdependent individuals or groups to evolve modes of cooperation."[70] Leopold, following Darwin, believes that growth in the extent and complexity of human ethics, what he calls the "ethical sequence," has paralleled and facilitated growth in the extent and complexity of human societies. Leopold envisions the land ethic as the next "step" in this pattern of social-ethical expansion. Social evolution has recently achieved a worldwide human society, and ethically we have achieved, corresponding to this social condition, the ideal of universal "human rights." Ecology, Leopold points out, represents the relationship of human and nonhuman organisms in the natural environment by means of a "community concept." Were this ecological idea of a "biotic community" to become widely current, Leopold foresees the emergence, correlatively, of a "land ethic" or "ecological conscience."

Many biologists have come to see the world through a prism of evolutionary and ecological theory. Moreover, as scientists they participate in a more general "Copernican" world view. The earth is perceived as a very small, lush, blue-green island in a vast desert sea of space. Biotas may exist on other planets, but these would be genuinely "foreign," "alien," in comparison to which earth's organisms are all literally kin. If Darwin is correct that the perception of another being as a family and/or community member triggers in us certain instinctive emotional responses, and if all the denizens of the "small planet" earth are so perceived, then something like Leopold's land ethic may become an operative ideal for future civilization.

These conceptual elements are all present in abbreviated form in Paul and Anne Ehrlich's impassioned appeal for "species rights": "Our fellow passengers on Spaceship Earth, who are quite possibly our only living companions in the entire universe, *have a right to exist.*"[71] The phrases "Spaceship Earth" and the "entire universe" evoke the Copernican perspective and "fellow passengers" and "living companions" evoke the evolutionary-ecological world view.

The Ehrlichs go on to provide a more extended rationale for "species rights," and though they do not mention Darwin by name, their understanding of the origin and evolution of morals is step-for-step Darwin's own, and their projection of future moral evolution to include other species recapitulates the next step in the "ethical sequence" of Leopold's land ethic:

> Along with other ecologists, we feel that the extension of the notion of "rights" to other creatures ... is a natural and necessary extension of the cultural evolution of *Homo sapiens*.... From an original concern only with the family or immediate group there has been a steady trend toward enlarging the circle toward which ethical behavior is expected. First the entire tribe was included, then the city-state, and more recently the nation. In this century concern has been extended in many groups to encompass all of humanity.... In the last hundred years, the ranks of those in the United States and Europe advocating compassion for, and unity with, the rest of the natural world have swollen considerably.[72]

Moral metaphysics "from the side of natural history," as represented by Hume, Darwin, Leopold, and the Ehrlichs, differs at several key points from moral metaphysics from the side of philosophy. I have already pointed out that in the biological tradition egoism is not the only irreducible, primitive value. Affection and sympathy, the "moral sentiments," are on equal footing with "self-love." Further, there is no preoccupation with psychological states as intrinsically valuable in and of themselves—no special concern with pleasure and pain, reason and knowledge, interests, or a hierarchy of beings determined by psychological complexity. The importance of this difference and the next cannot be stressed enough. The value of organisms is not gauged by how they feel, nor by how they make humans feel, although their value ultimately depends upon certain "intentional" mammalian affections. And, while the two mainstream modern philosophical accounts and the natural history account of morality can provide for the intrinsic value of individual nonhuman organisms, the philosophical accounts grant moral standing to individuals only, while the natural history account makes possible moral status for wholes. Hume, for example, recognizes a distinct sentiment which naturally resides in human beings for the "publick interest."[73] Darwin recognizes affection not only for "fellows" but for "family" and "tribe," that is, in general, for "the good or welfare of the community."[74] Leopold says that his land ethic would require of *Homo sapiens* "respect for the [biotic] community as such."[75] The Ehrlichs talk about species qua species, as well.

Thus I think we have found, at last, an axiology which faithfully articulates and adequately grounds the moral intuition that nonhuman species have "intrinsic value." They may not be valuable *in* themselves, but they may certainly be valued *for* themselves. According to this expanded Humean account, value is, to be sure, humanly conferred, but not necessarily homocentric. We certainly experience strong self-oriented feelings and appraise other things in reference to our human interests. But we experience certain distinct disinterested affections as well. We can foster, for example, the welfare of our own kin at considerable cost or even sacrifice to ourselves. We are capable of a disinterested sympathy and selfless charity to persons unrelated and unknown to us. According to Hume, the "intrinsic value" we attribute to all human beings is a projection or objectification of this "sentiment of humanity."

The philosophical and popular disagreement about which beings are intrinsically valuable, though all value is itself affective, is, according to this theory, a matter of cognitive rather than affective differences. The human capacity for the moral sentiments upon which intrinsic value depends is fairly uniform (because this capacity is a genetically fixed psychological characteristic like sexual appetite) and roughly equally distributed throughout the human population. To whom or to what these affections are directed, however, is an open matter, a matter of cognitive representation—of "nurture," not "nature." A person whose social and intellectual horizons are more or less narrow regards only a more or less limited set of persons and a more or less local social whole to be intrinsically valuable. To perceive nonhuman species as intrinsically valuable involves, thus, not only the moral sentiments, but an expansive cognitive representation of nature.

The Humean/Darwinian bio-empathetic moral metaphysic, based upon naturally selected moral sentiments, provides a theory according to which species qua species may have "intrinsic value." That is, they may be valued for themselves. Because the theory is humanly grounded, though not humanly centered, it does not impel us toward some detached and impersonal axiological reference point and thus submerge the value of the present ecosystem in a temporally and spatially infinite cosmos, as Holistic Rationalism does. Our social affections are extended to our fellow members and to the social whole of which we are part. The tribesmen who stand helplessly by and witness the "extinction" of their culture, as so many nineteenth-century American Indians unfortunately had to do, take little comfort in knowing that another cultural order will replace their own. Similarly, this is the biotic community of which we are a part, these are our companions in the odyssey of evolution, and it is to them, not to any future complement, that our loyalties properly extend.

Hume's grounding of morality in feeling or emotion has usually been regarded by the philosophical community as leading inevitably to an irresponsible ethical relativism.[76] If good and evil, right and wrong, are, like beauty and ugliness, in the eye of the beholder, then there can be no moral truths. We could no more reject as mistaken the opinion that matricide, say, is good, than the opinion that Picasso's Cubist paintings are ugly.

While Hume's theory of morality is certainly an emotive theory, it does not necessarily collapse into emotive relativism. Hume provides for a functional equivalent of objective moral truths by what may be called a "consensus of feeling." The human psychological profile in certain crucial respects is standardized, fixed. Unlike aesthetic judgments, which notoriously vary widely from culture to culture and within the same culture from person to person, moral judgments (allowing for certain peripheral divergences) are both culturally and individually invariant. Christian cultures may regard polygamy with horror, while Muslim cultures may approve it. Still, all cultures abominate murder, theft, treachery, dishonesty, and the other cardinal vices. Certainly individuals differ in the degree to which they are endowed with the moral sentiments. Still, just as we can speak of certain normal physical proportions and conditions among human beings while allowing for all sorts of variations, so we can speak of a certain normal human affective profile while allowing for all sorts of variations. Some people are tall, others are short, and both the tall and the short are normal. Then there are giants and midgets. Similarly, some people are overflowing with moral sentiments while others experience tham far less intensely and are more possessed by self-love. Depraved criminals, for example, exceed the limits of normality. They are the psychological equivalent of the physically freakish. Their emotional responses are not untrue, but by the human consensus of feeling they are "wrong," morally, if not epistemically.

For Hume the "universality" of human moral dispositions was an ad hoc fact. Darwin completed Hume's theory by explaining how such a standardization came about. Like the complex of normal human physical characteristics, normal human psychological characteristics, including the moral sentiments, were fixed by natural (and perhaps by sexual) selection.

Still, it may seem defeating to say that the nonutilitarian value of other forms of life is ultimately emotional, that it rests upon feeling, that species are valuable and we ought to save them simply because we have an affection for them. This would be defeating if there were some viable alternative and if emotivism implied moral relativism. But according to the Humean-Darwinian axiology, the only tenable axiology from the general perspective of traditional normal science, all value is affective. The intrinsic value we attribute to individual human beings and to humanity expresses only our feelings for co-members of our global village and for our human community. I therefore remain convinced that the Humean-Darwinian moral metaphysic is, intellectually, the most coherent and defensible axiology and, practically, the most convincing basis for an environmental ethic which includes intrinsic value for nonhuman species.

## Conclusion

In the foregoing discussion I have stressed the importance of the question, "Why try to preserve threatened and endangered species?" There are good "utilitarian" or "homocentric" reasons for preserving all or almost all existing species. Other species contribute to human well-being as performers of vital services, as resources, and as functional components in the global (human) life-support system, "Spaceship Earth." Frequently one also finds a distinctly nonutilitarian or nonhomocentric argument for species preservation, namely, that we have a moral obligation not to extirpate species or, more commonly, that other species, no less than we, have a right to exist, a right to a share of life on the planet. The nonutilitarian or nonhomocentric ethical argument for species preservation is said (by some at least) to be the most compelling reason for species preservation, but, paradoxically, it has been the least well articulated. Accordingly, my primary goal has been to explore and evaluate possible conceptual bases of the nonutilitarian or nonhomocentric argument for species preservation, and, more particularly, to analyze and evaluate the assertion of rights on behalf of species.

The concept of "species rights" is not without its problems. Because of its conceptual difficulties, from a philosophical point of view it would be better abandoned altogether. But philosophers have little influence on the vagaries of popular usage. The assertion of "species rights," upon analysis, appears to be the modern way to express what philosophers call "intrinsic value" on behalf of nonhuman species. Thus, the question, "Do nonhuman species have a right to exist?" transposes to the question, "Do nonhuman species have intrinsic value?" There are several distinct moral metaphysics which might yield a positive answer to this question: J-Theism, Rational Holism, Conativism, and Bio-empathy.

Of these distinct types of moral theory, J-Theism and bio-empathy appear to me to provide most effectively for the intrinsic value of other species. Each has wide appeal to different and complementary segments of the public, and each is relatively simple and straightforward.

Conativism most accords with prevailing biases in philosophical ethics, but because of its intractably "atomic" or "individualistic" ontology it can provide at best only incidentally for moral concern about vanishing species. Holistic Rationalism has some contemporary popular appeal and some contemporary philosophical representation, but it is more plausible in an ancient and early modern creationist context of thought. As a value theory it is so general, abstract, and impersonal that pressed to its logical extremes it might ill serve the cause of species preservation.

Only J-Theism unequivocally provides for objective intrinsic value for existing nonhuman species. The cognitive complex with which J-Theism is associated, the Judeo-Christian world view, is culturally well established and familiar. The greatest cultural competitor of the Judeo-Christian world view is scientific naturalism, with which the Bio-empathic axiology is conceptually and historically associated. Those unpersuaded by J-Theism because of Judeo-Christianity's conflict with scientific naturalism are likely, therefore, to be persuaded by Bio-empathy.

So, if the Western world's two main cultural belief systems, Judeo-

Christianity and scientific naturalism, both provide for the intrinsic value of other species, why does the notion that nonhuman species have intrinsic value seem so foreign and why does it attract so much skepticism, opposition, and ridicule? Unfortunately for our nonhuman companions on the planet, the Judeo-Christian world view also harbors an axiology contradictory to J-Theism, namely P-Theism. P-Theism's moral metaphysic permits, if it does not require, the interpretation that human beings are morally privileged. In the P version of Genesis, human privilege is supported by the doctrine that God created human beings in His own image and favored them in His creation as rightfully holding "dominion" over nature. "Dominion" could be taken in several senses, one of which might imply a steward role for man in relation to nature, but it has more usually been taken to imply mastery. The dogged insistence by many people that other forms of life have only instrumental value is probably traceable to this strain of thought in the Judeo-Christian tradition. Resistance to the notion of intrinsic value for other species in the scientific community, on the other hand, may be the result of residual acceptance of Judeo-Christian human chauvinism or may stem from the mistaken belief that since values, from a scientific point of view, are not wholly objective, they are therefore necessarily selfish, somehow unreal, or otherwise vacuous.

# 9

## Intrinsic Value, Quantum Theory, and Environmental Ethics

In a programmatic paper published in 1973 Richard Routley dramatically delineated, but did not attempt to solve, the central theoretical problem for any future environmental ethics.[1] What Routley called "dominant Western ethical traditions," or what might better be labeled "normal Western ethics," provide, he claimed in effect, only instrumental, not intrinsic, value for nonhuman natural entities and nature as a whole. Routley informally or intuitively demonstrated the universal assumption of an axiology in which only people are intrinsically valuable in normal Western ethics by appeal to his "last man" or "last people" thought experiment. Actions wantonly destructive of the natural environment undertaken by the last people or *in extremus* last person could not, in the context of normal moral theory, be morally censurable since, by hypothesis, no other people (future generations, in the former case, contemporaries in the latter) would be adversely affected by them. Hence, from the point of view of normal Western ethics, the last people or the last person would do nothing *morally* wrong, for example, by systematically extirpating species. Routley, thus, suggested that a genuinely *environmental* ethic would be both "new" and involve as a central or "core" feature an axiology that vested intrinsic value in nature.

More recently, Tom Regan reiterated the centrality of the axiological problem for environmental ethics: "The development of what can properly be called an environmental ethic requires that we postulate inherent value in nature."[2] Otherwise, according to Regan, a putative environmental ethic would collapse into a "management ethic," an ethic for the "use of the environment," not an ethic the beneficiary of which is the environment per se. In his discussion Regan defines *inherent value* in the strongest possible terms and then expresses doubts that a "rationally coherent" theory of inherent value in nature is philosophically attainable. According to Regan, inherent value must be either a property of an inherently valuable natural entity or be grounded in its actual properties, and it must be objective and *independent of any valuing consciousness.* Regan thus insists that any theory of inherent value in nature must be limited in effect to some version of naturalism or its objectivist alternative, non-naturalism.

Classical naturalistic axiologies ground the inherent value of some beings, very often only human beings, in properties like reason, self-consciousness, and moral autonomy. More liberal or inclusive theories associate intrinsic value with sentiency or consciousness, life or the will to live, organization or, more recently, "richness."

The nemesis of any naturalistic theory of inherent or intrinsic value, however, is, of course, G. E. Moore's naturalistic fallacy. Regan tacitly invokes the naturalistic fallacy in criticizing Kenneth Goodpaster's proposal for a non-anthropocentric axiology for environmental ethics. Goodpaster argued that life is intrinsically valuable and thus that all living moral beings should be granted moral considerability.[3] But according to Regan, "Limiting the class of beings which have inherent value to the class of living beings seems to be an arbitrary decision...."[4] Of course, the same could be said with equal force and finality of any actual objective property or set of properties proposed to be the ground of intrinsic value. It seems arbitrary to say, following Kant, that only rational beings are intrinsically valuable because reason is objectively good, or following Bentham, that only sentient beings are intrinsically valuable because pleasure is objectively good, or following Plato and Leibniz, that only ordered things are intrinsically valuable because order is objectively good, and so on. A sincere skeptic is always entitled to ask why reason, pleasure, order, or whatever *is* good and/or why rational, sentient, organized, etc., beings should therefore be intrinsically valuable. In the end, all a naturalistic advocate can do is to commend a property to our evaluative faculty of judgment or evaluative sensibilities. Peter Miller's recent attempt to provide a naturalistic theory of value for environmental ethics is painfully illustrative of the bankruptcy of a naturalistic approach.[5] According to Miller, "richness" is the property which makes people, other organisms, exosystems, and nature as a whole intrinsically valuable. Miller very fully and enthusiastically characterizes or describes "richness," but he does not adequately explain why richness, apart from some subjective judgment or conscious preference, is per se the ground of intrinsic value in nature.

The bankruptcy of the naturalistic approach to a fitting axiology for environmental ethics is, I wish to emphasize, quite general. The problem is not with the metaethically revolutionary axiological goal, which is to provide intrinsic value for nonhuman natural entities, nor with the sincerity and industry of revolutionary naturalistic theorists like Goodpaster and Miller, but with the general theoretical approach itself. Normal naturalistic axiologies which provide intrinsic value only for human beings are no less suspect than Goodpaster's or Miller's more inclusive naturalistic axiologies; they are only more familiar and self-serving. In isolation from all valuational consciousness, it seems no less quixotic to claim that reason is good and that rational beings are intrinsically valuable or that pleasure is good and sentient beings are intrinsically valuable than to claim that life is good and living things are intrinsically valuable or that richness is good and that rich ecosystems are intrinsically valuable.

If intrinsic value cannot be logically equated with some objective natural property or set of properties of an entity independently of any reference to a subjective or conscious preference for that property or set of properties, the only way to rescue the objectivity and independence of intrinsic value is desperately metaphysical: One may say that goodness or intrinsic value is a primitive or irreducible objective *non-natural* property of some entities. Natural properties of objects may be recognized or discovered empirically or by reasoning based upon experience. We know, for example, that an entity is rectangular by immediate experience and that it is radioactive by inference from other immediate experiences (like Geiger-counter reports). The non-natural objective property of inherent goodness or intrinsic value, however, cannot by definition (that is the force of saying it is a non-natural property) be empirically apprehended or inferred from ordinary sensory experience. It can only be known or discovered, thus, by some mystical faculty. If such a capacity for moral intuition were generally distributed in everyone alike, there would be as little controversy about the intrinsic value of sperm whales as there is about the color of the sky. Since the intrinsic value of various things is far from a settled matter, the intuitive faculty for its apprehension must be either vested in only a few gifted moral seers or, though generally distributed, wildly variable from individual to individual, such that what appears intrinsically valuable to one does not to another. In either case, the hope of moral persuasion based upon rational discussion is aborted. One can only say I (or the moral adept to whom I defer) "see" the intrinsic value of X and if you don't, you are morally blind. We are thus left with undefended, entrenched opinions philosophically tricked out as intuitions of irreducible, non-natural moral properties.

Facing up to these apparently insurmountable logical impediments to axiological objectivism, I have attempted, in the two previous essays, to elaborate a less ambitious, but also less problematic, subjectivist approach to the problem of an appropriate axiology for environmental ethics based upon and inspired by the land ethic of Aldo

Leopold. Working backward historically, I have traced the axiological kernel of the land ethic through Darwin (whose thought about the nature and origin of ethics manifestly influenced Leopold) back to Hume (whose analysis of ethics Leopold may or may not have known or consciously considered, but which certainly, in turn, directly informed Darwin). If my historical reading is correct, the seminal paradigm for contemporary environmental ethics, the Leopold land ethic, rests upon Humean axiological foundations.

According to Hume, moral value, like aesthetic value, is in the eye of the beholder. Good and evil, like beauty and ugliness, rest in the final analysis upon feelings or sentiments which are, as it were, projected onto objects, persons, or actions and affectively "color" them. "You never can find it," Hume wrote of the vice or evil of willful murder, "till you turn your reflexion into your own breast, and find a sentiment of disapprobation, which arises in you, towards this action":

> Here is a matter of fact; but 'tis the object of feeling, not of reason. It lies in yourself, not in the object. So that when you pronounce any action or character to be vicious, you mean nothing, but that from the constitution of your nature you have a feeling or sentiment of blame from the contemplation of it.[6]

If the integrity of environmental ethics turns on the development of a theory of value which provides *intrinsic* or *inherent* value for non-human natural entities and nature as a whole as Routley and Regan have variously insisted, then a naked, unadorned subjectivism like Hume's, however honest, simple, and straightforward, seems hardly a promising point of departure. The words *inherent* and *intrinsic* mean respectively "the essential character of something" or "belonging to the essential nature or constitution of a thing."[7] Thus, the very sense of the hypothesis that inherent or intrinsic value in nature seems to be that value *inheres* in natural objects as an intrinsic characteristic, that is, as part of the constitution of things. To assert that something is inherently or intrinsically valuable seems, indeed, to entail that its value is objective. Hence, if values are, as Hume has claimed, really referred or projected feelings or sentiments which originate with and depend upon a valuing subject and do not really belong at all to valuable objects, then there simply is no inherent or intrinsic value in nature and the cause is lost before the campaign gets fairly underway.

As I have been at pains to point out, however, a crucially important distinction may be overlooked in such a hasty rejection of axiological subjectivism as an approach to the central theoretical problem of environmental ethics—the construction of a coherent and persuasive theory of intrinsic or inherent value in nature. Intrinsic or inherent value in nature in the strict, objective sense of the terms must by definition be abandoned if one assumes a Humean subjectivist axiology. Nevertheless, in an important sense, consistently with this axiology, persons certainly and other natural beings may be valued *for themselves* as well as for the utility they afford those who value them.

To take a concrete example, consider a newborn infant. Let us assume, for the sake of clarity and simplicity, that the infant yet lacks self-consciousness and hence does not value itself and that there is no God who superordinately values it. According to Hume's classical subjectivist axiology, then, the value of the newborn infant of our example is wholly conferred upon it by its parents, other relatives, the family dog, family friends, and perhaps impersonally and anonymously by some unrelated and unacquainted members of society.

To be sure, part of the value of the newborn infant is merely instrumental. At a crass material or economic level it is valuable as a "human resource" to society because one day it will fill an empty chair in a schoolroom, perhaps serve in the armed forces, or maybe even discover a cure for cancer. To its parents who may economically value it as, say, a future helping hand on the family farm, it is also a "little bundle of joy," that is, it is the occasion of valued psycho-spiritual experiences *for them*. But if the parents of the infant of our example are like my parents and, as a parent myself, like me, and like most of the parents of my acquaintance, the foregoing account of the value of the hypothetical newborn leaves something out. Almost certainly its parents, and most probably its other relatives, family friends, and benignly disposed strangers value it *for itself*, above and beyond either its material-economic or psycho-spiritual utility. Assuming axiological subjectivism, it lacks in principle intrinsic value objectively construed, since all value, according to axiological subjectivism, is subjective. But it "has"—that is, there is conferred or projected upon it, by those who value it for its own sake—*something more* than instrumental value, since it is valued for itself as well as for the joy or other utility it affords them.

Let me seize upon the confusing accident that two terms, *inherent* and *intrinsic*, with virtually identical lexical definitions have been promiscuously employed by philosophers to discriminate the value of something in and for itself from the instrumental value it has in and for others, and stipulatively distinguish between them. Let something be said to possess *intrinsic* value, on the one hand, if its value is objective and independent of all valuing consciousness. On the other, let something be said to possess *inherent* value, if (while its value is not independent of all valuing consciousness) it is valued for itself and not only and merely because it serves as a means to satisfy the desires, further the interests, or occasion the preferred experiences of the valuers. Hume's classical subjectivist axiology theoretically provides in general for both instrumental and inherent value, so defined, but not for intrinsic value.[8]

According to Hume, in addition to the several passions gathered under the head of *self-love* there are the social sentiments and the sentiment of morality which have other beings than oneself as their direct objects. Hence, though all value may be of subjective provenance, it is not the case, upon Hume's account, either (1) that only valuing subjects and/or (2) that only the feelings of valuing subjects are valuable.[9] Valuing subjects for the most part do value themselves, but they may, and very often do, value other things equally with or even more highly than themselves. And while valuing certain of their own feelings, joy, for example, the valuing feelings per se are not self-referential; they are not themselves the objects of value. The moral sentiment, the social sentiments, and the sentiments of self-love are intentional and never themselves their own objects except perhaps in derivative and paradoxical cases, as when we say that someone is in love with love. Normally to love something, including oneself, is not to love love, rather the grammar of an intentional feeling like love requires in its normal paradigm instances an object other than itself.

Hume's subjectivist axiology is entirely adequate for environmental ethics proper because it provides a very genuine and vivid distinction between instrumental and inherent value. Darwin provided Hume's subjective and affective axiology with an evolutionary explanation and a kind of genotypic fixity. And Leopold later employed Darwin's development of Hume's axiology to establish inherent value in nature.

In the previously quoted remark from the *Treatise,* Hume suggests that the values you project onto objects are not arbitrary, but arise spontaneously in you because of the "constitution of your nature." The affective constitution of human nature, Darwin plausibly argued, is standardized by natural selection. *Homo sapiens* is an intensely social species and so certain sentiments were naturally selected in a social environment which permitted and facilitated growth in the size and complexity of society. The social sentiments, however, though fixed by natural selection, are open-ended. There is more than just a little room for the cultural determination of their objects. Thus, just what is of value, either instrumentally or inherently is partly determined by what Hume called "reason," but what might be better called "cultural representation." Aldo Leopold masterfully played upon our open social and moral sentiments by representing plants and animals, soils and waters as "fellow members" of our maximally expanded "biotic community." Hence, to those who are ecologically well-informed, nonhuman natural entities are inherently valuable—as putative members of one extended family or society. And nature as a whole is inherently valuable—as the one great family or society to which we belong as members or citizens.

Thus, for those who participate in the expansive evolutionary and ecological representation of nature, the blue whale, the Bridger wilderness, and other natural entities may, therefore, be said in a quite definite, straightforward sense to own inherent value, that is, to be valued *for themselves*, quite independently from the satisfying aesthetic, religious, or epistemic experiences they may occasion in nature aesthetes, nature worshipers, or natural scientists. Upon this account of inherent value, environmental ethics does not collapse (as Regan rightly points out that it would without some coherent account of inherent value in nature) into a management ethic, an ethic for the use of the environment, as opposed to an ethic of the environment. Environmental policy decisions, because they may thus be based upon a genuine environmental ethic, may thus be rescued from reduction to cost-benefit analyses in which valued natural aesthetic, religious, and epistemic experiences are shadow priced and weighed against the usually overwhelming material and economic benefits of development and exploitation. Upon this account of inherent value, Routley's last people or even last man would indeed do wrong to wantonly destroy an ecosystem or a species. At least it would be as wrong for the last man to destroy an ecosystem or a species upon the Hume-Darwin-Leopold subjectivist axiology as it would be for the last man to wantonly murder the newborn infant of the late last woman. The last man may not value for themselves the orphaned infant, the ecosystem, or the species in question, but since the last woman did, or indeed, since now we do, it is possible for her and us to imagine the murder and mayhem of the depraved and boorish last man (as now we may justifiably call him) and forejudge them to be wrong because they are destructive of inherently valuable things, that is, things we mothers and environmentalists value for the sake of themselves, independently of what they do for us.

In the literature of normal metaethics the line on subjectivism is that it necessarily degenerates into a morally intolerable radical relativism.[10] If value originates in subjects and is projected onto objects, then the same object may be differently valued by different subjects. Thus, while willful murder may appall and disgust you and me so that we color it evil, it may fascinate and delight an insane criminal who may thus color it good. Our condemnation of murder as evil cannot be more true than the criminal's commendation of it as good, since there is no fact to which these conflicting value judgments can be compared to see which *corresponds*. Hence, universal value judgments cannot be supported by subjectivism and the imposition of "our" moral values on so-called "criminals" appears to be altogether arbitrary and rationally indefensible.

That this putative necessary association between subjectivism and radical moral relativism has held sway in the literature of normal meta-ethics is, I suspect, because of the nearly universal inattention of philosophers to what E. O. Wilson has called the "biologization of ethics" which began with Darwin and has very lately been put on a much more rigorous footing by Wilson and other sociobiologists.[11] There may be no "truth" or "falsity" to value judgments, since there are no objective or intrinsic values to which value judgments may or may not correspond. However, there does exist a functional equivalent in what I have elsewhere called a "consensus of feeling."[12] Human feelings, like human fingers, human ears, and human teeth, though both individually variable and open to information by cultural manipulation, have been standardized by natural selection. There are, of course, occasional psychological sports of nature whose feelings are deranged just as there are physical sports whose bodies are deformed. Hence, radically eccentric value judgments may be said to be abnormal or even incorrect in the same sense that we might say that someone's radically curved spine is abnormal or incorrect.

While the alleged arbitrariness of value judgments as they are represented by subjectivism has thus been obviated by the compelling biological account of the standardization through natural selection of the moral sentiments and social instincts, Holmes Rolston, III has also pointed out, symmetrically, that there are, after all, on the side of the object, characteristics which are naturally fit to be valued. In a paper published in 1981 Rolston seemed somewhat reluctantly to concede that values "are only in the human response to the world . . . only in people."[13] Yet, he quite correctly points out that even though "we may not want to say that the valuing of nature is a descriptive registering of properties, . . . neither do we value nature altogether oblivious of its descriptions. We make something a target merely by aiming at it. But our interest in apples is not so arbitrary. It depends in part on something which is found there."[14] Rolston then goes on to provide a ten-category taxonomy of "values in nature," that is, the sorts of general characteristics actually present in nature which people appropriately find valuable. On the subjective side, the moral sentiments, albeit individually variable and certainly open to information by cultural representation, are fixed by natural selection, according to Wilson et al., and on the objective side, the actual properties of objects may or may not be fit to value, according to Rolston. Thus, value in nature, though subjective, is not radically relative, although, of course, it may be, as actually we find it to be, culturally relative.

## II

That Leopold rested his land ethic upon Humean axiological foundations was not historically accidental or philosophically whimsical. Leopold was a professionally trained forester and served in the U.S. Forest Service. He later became a self-educated ecologist and inaugurated and professed "game management" (now less tendentiously called "wildlife ecology") at the University of Wisconsin. Although he shed many of the utilitarian values bequeathed to American forestry by Gifford Pinchot, Leopold never abandoned a general, normal scientific outlook or world view. The land ethic itself is, indeed, thoroughly embedded in and logically integrated with classical scientific naturalism, as Leopold explicitly avers in the foreword to *A Sand County Almanac*. Now it is a well-known dogma of classical scientific naturalism that nature, in the broadest sense of the word, from atoms to galaxies and from elemental matter to the most complex life forms is value free, axiologically neutral. In formulating the land ethic, an objectivist axiology was, therefore, simply not a scientifically respectable option open to Leopold.

One of the cornerstones constituting the metaphysical foundations of classical modern science is the firm distinction, first clearly drawn by Descartes, between object and subject, between the *res extensa* and the *res cogitans*. The famous distinction of Hume between fact and value and Hume's development of a subjectivist axiology may be historically interpreted as an application or extension to ethics of Descartes' more general metaphysical and epistemic distinction. Logically interpreted, the object-subject dichotomy is a more general conceptual distinction to which the fact-value dichotomy is ancillary. Axiological subjectivism, indeed, may be clearly formulated only if the objective and subjective realms, the *res extensa* and the *res cogitans*, are clearly distinguished. How could it be meaningful to claim that values are not objective, that they are, rather, projected affections, feelings, or sentiments ultimately originating in valuing subjects, if subjects and objects are not clearly separate and distinct?

I am indebted to Peter Miller for pointing out to me that since revolutionary developments in twentieth-century science, especially in quantum theory, have forced the abandonment of the simple, sharp distinction between object and subject (between the *res extensa* and *res cogitans*), the ancillary simple, sharp distinction between fact and value (between intrinsically value-free objects and intentionally valuing subjects) is no longer tenable.[15] Hence, although Hume's classical subjectivist axiology, evolutionarily explained by Darwin, and ecologically informed by Leopold, provides for inherent value in nature and thus a serviceable axiology for a properly environmental ethic, it is not consistent with a contemporary or post-revolutionary scientific world view. Moreover, as Warwick Fox has recently argued, ecology and certain interpretations of quantum theory provide "structurally similar" or analogous representations of terrestrial organic nature and cosmic micro-physical nature, respectively.[16] The essentially Humean axiological foundation of Leopold's land ethic is actually, therefore, an insidious theoretical legacy of classical mechanics in a larger fabric of ideas which has succeeded and indeed transcended mechanism. Though consistent with Leopold's prerevolutionary scientific naturalism, Hume's subjectivist axiology betrays the deeper intuitions of Leopold's essentially ecological and organic vision of reality.

A fully consistent contemporary environmental ethic thus requires a theory of the noninstrumental value of nature which is neither subjectivist nor objectivist. It requires a wholly new axiology which does not rest, either explicitly or implicity, upon Descartes' obsolete bifurcation. Perhaps quantum theory may serve as a constructive paradigm for a value theory for an ecologically informed environmental ethic, as well as an occasion for the deconstruction of the classical Cartesian metaphysical paradigm and its Humean axiological interpretation. To put this thought in the interrogative, if quantum theory negates the object-subject, fact-value dichotomies, what more positively might it imply for the ontology of natural values?

Although I have so far represented the insight that quantum theory negates the object-subject, fact-value dichotomies to which modern value theory had dutifully conformed as original with Miller and unheralded until this moment, the idea has been broached in the previously published literature of environmental ethics. In 1979 Don Marrietta provocatively remarked that the "notion of brute, theory-free facts is an obsolete concept, no longer useful in science or the philosophy of science. Both factual and valuational observations of the world are constituted together by consciousness."[17] In 1980 Richard and Val Routley, though making no allusion to quantum theory, attempted to articulate an elaborate theory of value in nature for environmental ethics based on philosophically fashionable cross-world semantics. The Routleys suggested that we "call the resulting account, which is neither objective, nor ... subjective, *nonjective*," a term which, they admit, "is ugly, but memorable."[18] And in 1982 Holmes Rolston, III seemed to repudiate his earlier, less than wholehearted, alliance with subjectivism as the only scientifically respectable axiology and attempted "to defend all the objectivity I can for natural value."[19] In the course of his dazzling acrobatic effort to tease all the objectivity he could out of natural science for natural value, Rolston, more fully than Marrietta, discussed the implications of revolutionary science—quantum theory (and relativity as well)—for axiology. Rolston, in my judgment, put virtually all the pieces in place for a constructive value theory consistent with the new metaphysical foundations forced upon scientific naturalism by quantum theory, but he backed off at that point from doing so and turned instead to the biological sciences for the conceptual foundations for his enterprise. While Rolston's defense of objectivity for natural values, ably utilizing the conceptual resources of the sciences of the "middle-level" world, is a philosophical tour de force and is very rewarding to read, the bottom line appears to me to be that as long as the metaphysical dichotomy of classical modern normal science between subject and object remains an unchallenged background assumption, the axiological dichotomy of modern normal ethics between value and fact will remain intractable.

Rolston's stated reason for turning aside from a more fully developed, vigorously prosecuted axiological program informed by the metaphysical implications of quantum theory is his surprising conclusion that *as a result* of relativity and quantum theory "the subjectivists have won all the chips," that "subjectivity has eaten up everything."[20] The appropriate and usual conclusion is not this one—that the subjectivists have emerged victorious—it is rather that since the distinction between subject and object is untenable, then the sorting of experience into one or the other category is nonsensical. Subjectivists haven't won all the chips; they have simply been dealt out of the game. The factoring of experience into either exclusively subjective or objective components will be as otiose for future philosophers as the factoring of properties into the categories of essential and accidental has been for modern philosophers.

The fate of Descartes's apparently innocent and natural distinction between the *res cogitans* and *res extensa,* between subject and object, was sealed when Max Planck discovered that energy was quantized and that there was in nature a least quantum of energy, Planck's constant, $h$.[21] At the meso- and macrolevels of phenomena, that is, at the levels of billiard balls, planets, and stars to which the investigations of early modern physics were largely confined, the illusion of a wholly passive, non-participating observer could be maintained. As more and more sophisticated experimental techniques permitted investigation into smaller and smaller levels of phenomena, it became increasingly evident that to make an observation energy must be exchanged between the object of observation and the observer. That energy is, among other things, information, and information energy, physicalizes knowledge and consciousness. The *res cogitans* collapses, thus, into the *res extensa*. The physicalization of our knowledge of nature at the very least might have revived with renewed intensity Descartes's most recalcitrant unsolved metaphysical problem, the problem of the causal interaction between the *res extensa* and the *res cogitans*. As long as the informative exchange of energy is imagined to run only in a one-way direction from object to subject, discussion of the metaphysical assumptions of classical normal science, however problematical, might remain merely "philosophical" and positive normal science could pursue its programs and leave such problems to the metaphysicists.

However, if the object of observation is so small as to be of an order of magnitude (please remember here Einstein's equivalency of mass and energy) comparable to Planck's constant, then in interacting with the sensory extensions, the experimental apparatus, of the observing subject, the object will necessarily be appreciably affected and the observing subject's knowldege of it thus necessarily rendered appreciably "uncertain." Now, because it is impermissible in positive normal science to posit the actual existence of things that cannot in principle be empirically observed, this unavoidable uncertainty has untoward ontological as well as epistemological implications.

The most well-known illustration of the ontological implications of the uncertainty principle, on the side of the erstwhile independently existing object, concerns the properties of velocity and location of leptons (of which the electron is the most familiar species). One or the other, but not both properties may be known definitely, or both may be known approximately. Hence, an electron cannot therefore be said to actually have a definite position and a definite velocity! Its actual properties are, thus, to some degree chosen for it by the observer, since the observer may choose to know its position definitely or its velocity definitely or a little of both. Its reality is thus in some sense constituted by the observer. It is in this sense, primarily, that object and subject cannot be clearly dissociated in the new physics as they were in the old.

Rolston pointed out in his paper on environmental value theory published in 1982 that the tripartite distinction developed by Locke, a self-styled underlaborer to the great Newton, to categorize experienced properties had been modified and extended by Samuel Alexander in 1933 to value properties.[22] According to Locke, an object's primary or wholly objective properties are its mass, its location, velocity, and so on. Its so-called secondary qualities are its color, flavor, odor, and so on which depend for their realization upon the effect of the primary qualities on consciousness. Locke also introduced the concept of tertiary qualities by which he meant the causal efficacies of objects to affect other objects as fire melts wax. As this third species of Lockean quality lapsed into philosophical disuse, Alexander refitted it to mean an object's value properties. Thus, in Alexander's system, an object's state of motion was among its primary qualities, its flavor among its secondary qualities, and its beauty among its tertiary qualities.

The new physics, in effect, collapses the distinction between primary and secondary qualities. Location and velocity are potential properties of an electron variously actualized in various experimental situations as color and flavor are potential properties of an apple awaiting the eye and tongue (and all the neural apparatus that goes with eyes and tongues) of a conscious being for their realization. Wilson and his colleagues have convincingly argued that our receptivity to value is every bit as much a part of our adaptive vertebrate biology as the capacity to see and taste, and Rolston has convincingly argued that an object's value is every bit as much dependent on the object's properties as on the valuing subject's psychological constitution. Hence, Alexander's tertiary qualities, like classical normal science's primary qualities, also gravitate toward the model of the secondary qualities. *All* properties, should be conceived as the classical secondary qualities were supposed to be, not dichotomous, existing actually either on the side of the object or on the side of the subject, but potential and dipolar requiring for their realization the interaction between erstwhile subjects and erstwhile objects. To borrow a metaphor from Plato, actual reality in its quantitative, qualitative, and valuational manifestations is the issue, the progeny of a marriage, not of Heaven and Earth or form and matter, but of two complementary potentialities: receptive but active consciousness and an exciting but excitable physical plenum. Mass and motion, color and flavor, good and evil, beauty and ugliness, all alike, are equally potentialities which are actualized in relationship to us or to other similarly constituted organisms.

Let me now return directly to the problem with which this discussion began, the most critical and most recalcitrant theoretical problem of environmental ethics, the problem of intrinsic value in nature. From the perspective of the emerging world view of contemporary revolutionary science, we may certainly not assert that value in nature is intrinsic, that is, ontologically objective and independent of consciousness. However, that is to concede nothing of consequence, since *no* properties in nature are strictly intrinsic, that is, ontologically objective and independent of consciousness. Borrowing now from the vocabulary of quantum theory, we may assert, rather, that values are virtual. Virtual value is an ontological category encompassing all values. Within its purview fall the entire spectrum of instrumental and inherent values as previously defined. In other words, nature affords a range of potential value; some things are potentially instrumentally valuable, that is, valued for their utility, as either economic-material resources or psycho-spiritual resources; and some things (sometimes but not always the same things) are inherently valuable, that is, are in themselves potentially valuable for their own sakes.

The difference between this account of inherent value and the account of axiological subjectivism is less practical than theoretical. On both accounts, practically speaking, nature may be valued for its own sake. According to axiological subjectivism, inherent value is an intentional affection originating in consciousness and projected onto objectively value-free nature, while according to my suggested quantum theoretical axiology, inherent value is a virtual value in nature actualized upon interaction with consciousness. The advantage of the quantum theoretical axiology lies in the fact that it renders an account of value which puts values on an ontological par with other properties, including culturally revered quantitative properties. In Rolston's words therefore, "there is just as little or as much reason to think that physics is objective as that value theory is."[23] Physics and ethics are, in other words, equally descriptive of nature.

## III

The foregoing account of the implications of quantum theory for the ontology of values is intended to be as conservatively and uncontroversially stated as possible. It relies only upon the most salient, well-established, and central features of the new physics, Planck's constant and Heisenberg's uncertainty principle. It assumes no speculative interpretation of the new physics unless one wishes to insist that the essentially Aristotelian ontological notions of potentiality and actuality as applied in the Copenhagen Interpretation of quantum theory to natural properties constitute by themselves a speculative interpretation of quantum theory.[24]

There is another approach to an axiology for environmental ethics which does assume a more speculative interpretation of quantum theory and does go beyond the standard, minimalistic Copenhagen Interpretation. This alternative approach to an axiology for environmental ethics, albeit more speculative and therefore more controversial, is more conceptually resonant with the representation of middle-sized living nature in ecology.

In his celebrated popular exposition of the metaphysical implications of the new physics, Fritjof Capra writes:

A careful analysis of the process of observation in atomic physics has shown that subatomic particles have no meaning as isolated entities, but can only be understood as interconnections between the preparation of an experiment and the subsequent measurement. Quantum theory thus reveals a basic oneness in the universe. It shows that we cannot decompose the world into independently existing smallest units. As we penetrate into matter nature does not show us any isolated "basic building blocks," but rather appears as a complicated web of relations between the various parts of the whole. These relations always include the observer in an essential way. The human observer constitutes the final link in the chain of observational processes, and the properties of any atomic object can only be understood in terms of the object's interaction with the observer. This means that the classical ideal of an objective description of nature is no longer valid. The Cartesian partition between the I and the world, between the observer and the observed, cannot be made when dealing with atomic matter. In atomic physics we can never speak about nature without, at the same time, speaking about ourselves.[25]

Capra here confirms much of what I have less eloquently and authoritatively set out respecting the implications of quantum theory for the Cartesian subject-object dichotomy in relation to which the Humean fact-value dichotomy is logically and historically ancillary. But he goes further. "A basic oneness in the universe" is also implied which "include[s] the observer [the 'I'] in an essential way." It is this unity, holism, and integration of self and world suggested by quantum theory to which Fox refers when he claims that ecology and the new physics each provide at different levels a similar structure of reality.

Compare Paul Shepard's equally celebrated, eloquent and authoritative characterization of the metaphysical implications of ecology with Capra's just quoted characterization of the metaphysical implications of quantum theory:

Ecological thinking ... requires a kind of vision across boundaries. The epidermis of the skin is ecologically like a pond surface or a forest soil, not a shell so much as a delicate interpenetration. It reveals the self ennobled and extended rather than threatened ... because the beauty and complexity of nature are continuous with ourselves. ... The ... self [is] a center of organization, constantly drawing on and influencing the surroundings, whose skin and behavior are soft zones contacting the world instead of excluding it.[26]

Shepard's comments on "ecological thinking" clearly convey the same general metaphysical concepts as Capra's on the thinking of atomic physics: nature is unified and we, erstwhile monadic individuals, are, actually, continuous with it.

The holistic quantum theoretical world view and the holistic ecological world view as portrayed by Capra and Shepard, respectively, both centrally involve a doctrine of real, internal relations. Therein lies their structural similarity. Capra declares that nature is "a complicated *web of relations* between the various parts of the whole," (emphasis added). Shepard subsequently declares that "relationships of things are as real as the things." [27] Real relations are the glue which binds the relata, the things or entities, of organic and microphysical nature, respectively, into a united whole. Relations, moreover, are, in both sciences, not only real, but ontologically prior to the relata: At both the organic and microphysical levels of nature, things (organisms and subatomic particles respectively) are what they are because of their relations with other things—in quantum theory with other physical states and with the experimental process itself and in ecology with the physical, chemical, and climatic regimes of their niches. Shepard, driving home this point, applies the doctrine of prior, real, internal relations not only to the human soma, but, as in quantum theory, to the human psyche itself: "The mind of a primate," he suggests, "is an extension of natural complexity, ... the variety of plants and animals and the variety of nerve cells [are] organic extensions of each other."[28] Nature is a unity, a whole, and the self, the "I" (mentally as well as physically construed), is not only continuous with it, but constituted by it. Nature and I are conceptually as well as metaphysically integrated.

Paul Shepard, accordingly, endorses Alan Watts's memorable summary of ecology's implications for the relationship of self and world, namely, that "the world is your body."[29] The conventional separation between self and world, Watts suggested, cannot withstand the reflective implications of contemporary science, both physical and ecological.

If these more speculatively analogous or structurally similar metaphysical interpretations of ecology and quantum theory are warranted, they bear directly on the central axiological problem of environmental ethics. Kenneth Goodpaster has forcefully argued that in modern normal ethics axiological egoism has not been thought to require justification.[30] The intrinsic value of oneself has for some reason been taken for granted; how to theoretically account for the intrinsic value of "others," rather, has been regarded as problematic. I have pointed out, in a recent discussion, that Goodpaster was wrong to have included Hume, who regarded the other-oriented sentiments as equally primitive with self-love;[31] nevertheless, I am convinced that Goodpaster is correct to claim that in the two major modern traditions stemming from Kant and Bentham, but not Hume, egoism *is* regarded as primitive and moral considerability is reached by the process of generalization that he (Goodpaster) describes. The Routleys have argued that "some values at least must be intrinsic,...some values are irreducible," on the grounds, apparently, that the existence of instrumentally valuable things (means) logically entails the existence of intrinsically valuable beings (ends).[32] The Routleys would not necessarily agree that in every system the ego is intrinsically valuable, but the claim that the ego is intrinsically valuable seems to have been treated very often as a privileged immediate datum of awareness, like the claim that I have a headache. Not a few modern and contemporary moral theorists have even equated self-interestedness with rationality, such that to act rationally is to act in ways that are self-serving.[33] The implication is that altruistic behavior is in some sense irrational or that, at the very least, its rationality is problematic and in need of justification.

Now *if* we assume, (a) with Shepard and Capra that nature is one and continuous with the self, and (b) with the bulk of modern moral theory that egoism is axiologically given and that self-interested behavior has a prima facie claim to be at the same time rational behavior, then the central axiological problem of environmental ethics, the problem of intrinsic value in nature may be directly and simply solved. If quantum theory and ecology both imply in structurally similar ways in both the physical and organic domains of nature the continuity of self and nature, and *if* the self is intrinsically valuable, then nature is intrinsically valuable. *If* it is rational for me to act in my own interest, and I and nature are one, then it is rational for me to act in the best interest of nature.

Borrowing once more from the terminology of quantum theory, let us call this integral self-world value precept of an environmental ethic informed by the mutually reinforcing holistic metaphysical interpretations of quantum theory and ecology, the principle of axiological complementarity. It should now be clear how as one contemplates the destruction of biomes and the consequent loss of perhaps hundreds of thousands of species that the palpable disvalue of the prospect is at once personal, but transcends the conventional limits of proprietary personal concern. I personally feel a very real loss of value to myself as I reflect upon the progressive destruction of the natural environment. But this palpable diminution of value to me cannot be plausibly reduced to deprivation of my monadic aesthetic, epistemic, or religious experience or to a threat to my monadic material well-being. The injury to me of environmental destruction transcends the secondary, indirect injury to the conventional, constricted ego encapsulated in this bag of skin and all the functioning organs it contains. Rather, the injury to me of environmental destruction is primarily and directly to my extended self, to the larger body and soul with which "I" (in the conventional narrow and constricted sense) am continuous. Aldo Leopold captured this ecological idea, as so many others in his inimitable epigrammatic style: "One of the penalties of an ecological education is that one lives alone in a world of wounds."[34]

Frustrated by the anemic results of the reduction of environmental values to the desires, interests, or preferences of environmentalists, environmentalists have correctly insisted upon the intrinsic value of nonhuman natural entities and nature as a whole, but hopelessly supposed that such objective intrinsic value could be persuasively established independently of self. The principle of axiological complementarity posits an essential unity between self and world and establishes the problematic intrinsic value of nature in relation to the axiologically privileged intrinsic value of self. Since nature is the self fully extended and diffused, and the self, complementarily, is nature concentrated and focused in one of the intersections, the "knots," of the web of life or in the trajectory of one of the world lines in the four dimensional space-time continuum, nature is intrinsically valuable, *to the extent* that the self is intrinsically valuable.

# IV

## American Indian
## Environmental Ethics

# 10

## Traditional American Indian and Western European Attitudes Toward Nature: An Overview

### I

In this paper I sketch (in broadest outline) the picture of nature endemic to two very different intellectual traditions: the familiar, globally dominant Western European civilization, on the one hand, and the presently beleaguered tribal cultures of the American Indians, on the other. I argue that the world view typical of American Indian peoples has included and supported an environmental ethic, while that of Europeans has encouraged human alienation from the natural environment and an exploitative practical relationship with it. I thus represent a romantic point of view; I argue that the North American "savages" were indeed more noble than "civilized" Europeans, at least in their outlook toward nature.

I do not enter into this discussion unaware of the difficulties and limitations which present themselves at the very outset. In the first place, there is no *one* thing that can be called *the* American Indian belief system. The aboriginal peoples of the North American continent lived in environments quite different from one another and had culturally adapted to these environments in quite different ways. For each tribe there were a cycle of myths and a set of ceremonies, and from these materials one might abstract *for each* a particular view of nature. However, recognition of the diversity and variety of American Indian cultures should not obscure a complementary unity to be found among them. Despite great internal differences there were common characteristics which culturally united American Indian peoples. Joseph Epes Brown claims that

> this common binding thread is found in beliefs and attitudes held by the people in the quality of their relationships to the natural environment. All American Indian peoples possessed what has been called a

metaphysic of nature; and manifest a reverence for the myriad forms and forces of the natural world specific to their immediate environment; and for all, their rich complexes of rites and ceremonies are expressed in terms which have reference to or utilize the forms of the natural world.[1]

Writing from a self-declared antiromantic perspective, Calvin Martin has more recently confirmed Brown's conjecture:

> What we are dealing with are two issues: the ideology of Indian land-use and the practical results of that ideology. Actually, there was a great diversity of ideologies, reflecting distinct cultural and ecological contexts. It is thus more than a little artificial to identify a single, monolithic ideology, as though all Native Americans were traditionally inspired by a universal ethos. Still, there were certain elements which many if not all these ideologies seemed to share, the most outstanding being a genuine respect for the welfare of other life-forms.[2]

A second obvious difficulty bedeviling any discussion of American Indian views of nature is our limited ability accurately to reconstruct the abstract culture of New World peoples prior to their contact with (and influence from) Europeans. Documentary records of pre-contact Indian thought simply do not exist. American Indian metaphysics was embedded in oral traditions. Left alone, an oral culture may be very tenacious and persistent. If radically stressed, it may prove to be very fragile and liable to total extinction. Hence, *contemporary* accounts by contemporary American Indians of *traditional* American Indian philosophy are vulnerable to the charge of inauthenticity, since for several generations American Indian cultures, cultures preserved in the living memory of their members, have been both ubiquitously and violently disturbed by transplanted European civilization.

We ought, therefore, perhaps to rely where possible upon the earliest written observations of Europeans concerning American Indian belief. The accounts of the North American "savages" by sixteenth-, seventeenth-, and eighteenth-century Europeans, however, are invariably distorted by ethnocentrism, which to the cosmopolitan twentieth-century student appears so hopelessly abject as to be more entertaining than illuminating. The written observations of Europeans who first encountered American Indian cultures provide rather an instructive record of the implicit European metaphysic. Since Indians were not loyal to the Christian religion, it was assumed that they had to be mindfully servants of Satan, and that the spirits about which they talked and the powers which their shamans attempted to direct had to be so many demons from hell. Concerning the Feast of the Dead among the Huron, Brebeuf wrote in 1636 that "nothing has ever better pictured for me the confusion among the damned."[3] His account, incidentally, is very informative and detailed concerning the physical requirements and artifacts of this ceremony, but the rigidity of his own system of belief makes it impossible for him to enter sympathetically that of the Huron.

Reconstructing the traditional Indian attitude toward nature is, therefore, to some extent a speculative matter. On the other hand, we must not abandon the inquiry as utterly hopeless. Post-contact American Indians do tell of their traditions and their conceptual heritage. Among the best of these nostalgic memoirs is Neihardt's classic, *Black Elk Speaks*, one of the most important and authentic resources available for the reconstruction of an American Indian attitude toward nature. The explorers', missionaries', and fur traders' accounts of woodland Indian attitudes are also useful, despite their ethnocentrism, since we may correct for the distortion of their biases and prejudices. Using these two sorts of sources, first-contact European records and transcribed personal recollections of tribal beliefs by spiritually favored Indians, plus disciplined and methodical modern ethnographic reports, we may achieve a fairly reliable reconstruction of traditional Indian attitudes toward nature.

## II

On the European side of the ledger, at first glance, an analogous pluralism appears to confound any generalizations. How different are the lands, the languages, the lifestyles of, say, the Swedes and the Spanish, or the Slavic and Gaelic peoples. If anything, Europeans appear to be a more ethnically diverse, motley collection of folks than Indians. Europeans, however, have enjoyed a collective intellectual *history* which the Indians, for better or worse, have not. Moreover, for many centuries a common learned language was shared by scholars of every civilized European country. This alone constitutes an enormously unifying force. The intellectual history of Europe has been, to be sure, dialectical and disputatious, but the pendulum of opinion has swung between well-defined limits, and certain universally accepted assumptions have prevailed.

As the European style of thought was set by the Greeks of classical antiquity, I begin with them. I treat modern science, that is, modern European natural philosophy, as a continuation and extrapolation of certain concepts originating with the fifth- and fourth-century-B.C. Greeks. Greek ideas about nature were remarkably rich and varied, but only some of these ideas, for historical reasons which cannot be explored in this discussion, inspired and informed modern natural philosophy. They became institutionalized in the modern Western world view. It is upon them, accordingly, that I especially focus.

Mythopoeic Greek cosmology had curious affinities with some of the central cosmological concepts of the American Indians. Sky and Earth (Uranus and Gaia) are represented by Hesiod in the *Theogony* as male and female parents (Father and Mother) of the first generation of gods and either directly or indirectly of all natural beings. Some Ionian Greeks in the city of Miletus apparently became disenchanted with traditional Greek mythology and embarked upon speculations of their own. Everything, they said, is water or air. Things change because of the struggle of the Hot with the Cold and the Wet with the Dry. The implicit question—what is the nature of that out of which all things come and into which all things are resolved?—proved to be both fascinating and fruitful. After about one hundred and fifty years of uninterrupted controversy, Leucippus and Democritus, with characteristic Ionian simplicity and force, brought this line of thought to a brilliant culmination in the atomic theory of matter. The atom was conceived by them to be an indestructible and internally changeless particle, "so small as to escape sensation." There are infinitely many of these. They have substance, that is they are solid or "full," and possess shape and relative size. All other qualities of things normally disclosed by perception exist, according to Democritus, only by "convention," not by "nature." In the terms of later philosophical jargon, characteristics of things such as flavor, odor, color, and sound were regarded as *secondary* qualities, the subjective effects of the primary qualities on the sensory patient. Complementary to the concept of the atom is the concept of the void—free, homogeneous, isotropic space. The atoms move haphazardly about in this space. Macroscopic objects are assemblages of atoms; they are wholes exactly equal to the sum of their parts. These undergo generation and destruction, which were conceived as the association and dissociation of the atomic parts. The atomists claimed to reduce all the phenomena of nature to this simple dichotomy: the "full" and the "empty," "thing" and "no-thing," the atom and space.

Thomas Kuhn succinctly comments that "early in the seventeenth century atomism experienced an immense revival. . . . Atomism was firmly merged with Copernicanism as a fundamental tenet of the 'new philosophy' which directed the scientific imagination."[4] The consolidated Newtonian world view included as one of its cornerstones the atomists' concept of free space, thinly occupied by moving particles or "corpuscles," as the early moderns called them. It was one of Newton's greatest achievements to supply a quantitative model of the regular motion of the putative material particles. These famous "laws of motion" made it possible to represent phenomena not only materially, but also mechanically.

That the *order* of nature can be successfully disclosed only by means of a quantitative description, a rational account in the most literal sense of that word, is itself, of course, an ideal which originated in sixth-century-B.C. Greece with Pythagoras. Pythagoras's insight had such tremendous scientific potential that it led Plato to eulogize it as Promethean, a veritable theft from the gods of the key to the secrets of the cosmos. It was cultivated and developed by the subsequent Pythagorean school and by Plato himself in the *Timaeus*, a work which enjoyed enormous popularity during the Renaissance. Modern philosophy of nature might be oversimply, but nonetheless not incorrectly, portrayed as a merger of the Pythagorean intuition that the structure of the world order is determined according to ratio, to quantitative proportions, and the Democritean ontology of void space (so very amenable to geometrical analysis) and material particles. The intellectual elegance and predictive power of the Newtonian natural philosophy resulted, as Kuhn suggests, in it becoming virtually institutionalized in the nascent European scientific community. Its actual and potential application to practical matters, to problems of engineering and tinkering, also made it a popular, working picture of nature, gladly and roundly embraced by all Europeans participating in enlightenment.

Paul Santmire characterized the modern European attitude toward nature as it took root in the American soil in the nineteenth century as follows:

> Nature is analogous to a machine; or in the more popular version nature *is* a machine. Nature is composed of hard, irreducible particles which have neither color nor smell nor taste. . . . Beauty and value in nature are in the eye of the beholder. Nature is the dead *res extensa*, perceived by the mind, which observes nature from a position of objective detachment. Nature in itself is basically a self-sufficient, self-enclosed complex of merely physical forces acting on colorless, tasteless, and odorless particles of hard, dead matter. That is the mechanical view of nature as it was popularly accepted in the circles of the educated [white Americans] in the nineteenth century.[5]

Santmire's comments bring to our attention a complementary feature of the European world view of particular interest to our overall discussion. If no qualms were felt about picturing rivers and mountains, trees, and (among the legions of Cartesians) even animals as inert, material, mechanical "objects," the line was drawn at the human mind. Democritus and later Hobbes had attempted a thoroughgoing and self-consistent materialism, but this intrusion of matter into the very soul of man did not catch on—everything else, maybe, but not the human ego.

The conception of the soul as not only separate and distinct from the body, but as essentially alien to it (i.e., of an entirely different, antagonistic nature) was also first introduced into Western thought by Pythagoras. Pythagoras conceived the soul to be a fallen divinity, incarcerated in the physical world as retribution for some unspecified sin. The goal in life for the Pythagoreans was to earn the release of the soul from the physical world upon death and to reunite the soul with its proper (divine) companions. The Pythagoreans accomplished this by several methods: asceticism, ritual purification, and intellectual exercise, particularly in mathematics. This led Plato, who was more than passingly influenced by Pythagoras, to (half-) joke in the *Phaedo* that philosophy is the study of death, an exercise in the disentanglement of the soul from the body. The Pythagoreans and Plato indeed inverted the concepts of life and death. In the *Cratylus,* for example, Plato alleges that the word *body (sôma)* was derived from *tomb (sêma)*. The body is thus the tomb of the soul as well as its place of imprisonment.

The Pythagorean-Platonic concept of the soul as immortal and otherworldly, essentially foreign to the hostile physical world, has profoundly influenced the European attitude toward nature. It was not only revived in a particularly extreme form by Descartes in the seventeenth century, it became popularized much earlier in Pauline Christianity. The essential self, the part of a person by means of which he or she perceives and thinks, and in which resides virtue or vice, is not of this world and has more in common with god(s) than with nature. If the natural world is the place of trial and temptation for the soul, if the body is the prison and the tomb of the soul, then nature must be despised as the source of all misery and corruption, a place of fear and loathing: "a joyless place where murder and vengeance dwell, and swarms of other fates—wasting diseases, putrefactions, and fluxes— roam in darkness over the meadow of doom."[6]

So what attitude to nature does modern classical European natural philosophy convey? In sum, nature is an inert, material, and mechanical continuum exhaustively described by means of the arid formulae of pure mathematics. In relation to nature the human person is a lonely exile sojourning in a strange and hostile world, alien not only to his physical environment, but to his own body, both of which he is encouraged to fear and attempt to conquer. Add to this Cartesian picture the Judaic themes forthrightly set out in Genesis (which Lynn White, Jr., Ian McHarg, and others have so thoroughly criticized—themes of dominion of man over nature, of its subjugation and domestication, of the *imago Dei,* and so on) and we have a very volatile mixture of ingredients set to explode in an all-out war on nature, a war which in the twentieth century has very nearly been won. To victors, of course, belong the spoils!

This world view might have been ameliorated by Greek biological theory beginning with Plato and reaching fruition with Aristotle, but unfortunately it too proved to be atomistic and ecologically blind. Plato accounted for the existence of kinds of individuals, that is, species, by means of his theory of ideas. Each individual or specimen "participated," according to Plato, in a certain essence or form and it derived its specific characteristics from the form in which it participated. The impression of the natural world conveyed by the theory of ideas is that the various species are determined by the static logical-mathematical order of the formal domain and then the individual organisms, each with its preordained essence, are loosed into the physical arena to interact clumsily, catch-as-catch-can. Nature is thus perceived, like a room full of furniture, as a collection, a mere aggregate of individuals of various types, relating to one another in an accidental and altogether external fashion. This picture of the world is an atomism of a most subtle and insidious sort. It breaks a highly integrated functional system into separate, discrete, and functionally unrelated sets of particulars. Pragmatically, approaching the world through this model—which we might call "conceptual" in contradistinction to "material" atomism —it is possible radically to rearrange parts of the landscape without the least concern for upsetting its functional integrity and organic unity. Certain species may be replaced by others (for example, grain by wildflowers in prairie biomes) or removed altogether (for example, predator extermination) without consequence, theoretically, for the function of the whole.

Aristotle recoiled, of course, from the otherworldliness of Plato's philosophy, both from his theory of the soul and from his theory of ideas. Aristotle, moreover, was a sensitive empirical biologist and did almost as much to advance biology as a science as Pythagoras did for mathematics and harmonics. Aristotle's subsequent influence on biological thought has been immense. Biology today still bears the personal stamp of his genius, especially in the system of classification (as modified and refined by Linnaeus) of organisms according to species, genus, family, order, class, phylum, and kingdom. This hierarchy of universals was not real or actual, according to Aristotle (to his everlasting credit); only individual organisms fully existed. However, Aristotle's taxonomical hierarchy (in isolation from evolutionary and ecological theory) resulted in a view of living nature which was, if that is possible, more ecologically blind than Plato's. Relations among things again are, in Aristotle's biological theory, accidental and inessential. A thing's essence is determined by its logical relations within the taxonomical schema rather than, as in ecological theory, by its working relations with other things in its environment—its trophic niche, its thermal and chemical requirements, and so on. As Aldo Leopold expressed this point with characteristic bluntness: "The species of a layer [in the biotic pyramid] are alike not in where they came from or in what they look like, but rather in what they eat."[7] Evolutionary and ecological theory suggest, metaphysically, that the essences of things, the specific characteristics of species, are a function of their relations with other things. To convey a very un-Aristotelian thought in an Aristotelian manner of speech, relations are "prior to" the things related, and systemic wholes are "prior to" their component parts. A taxonomical view of the biotic world untransformed by evolutionary and ecological theory has the same ecologically misrepresentative feature as Plato's theory of forms: nature is seen as an aggregate of individuals, divided into various types, which have no functional connection with one another. And the *practical* consequences are the same. The biotic mantle may be dealt with in a heavy-handed fashion, rearranged to suit one's fancy without danger of dysfunctions. If anything, Aristotle's taxonomical representation of nature has had a more insidious influence upon the Western mind than Plato's real universals, since the latter could be dismissed, as often they were, as abstracted Olympians in a charming and noble philosophical romance, while metaphysical taxonomy went unchallenged as "empirical" and "scientific."

We should also not forget another Aristotelian legacy, the natural *hierarchy*, according to which the world is arranged into "lower" and "higher" forms. Aristotle's teleology required that the lower forms exist for the sake of the higher forms. Since human beings are placed at the top of the pyramid, everything else exists for the sake of them. The practical tendencies of this idea are too obvious to require further elaboration.

### III

The late John Fire Lame Deer, a reflective Sioux Indian, comments, straight to the point, in his biographical and philosophical narrative, *Lame Deer: Seeker of Visions,* that although the whites (i.e., members of the European cultural tradition) imagine earth, rocks, water, and wind to be dead, they nevertheless "are very much alive."[8] In the previous section I tried to explain in what sense nature, as the *res extensa,* is conceived as "dead" in the mainstream of European natural thought. To say that rocks and rivers are dead is perhaps misleading since what is now dead once was alive. Rather in the usual European view of things such objects are considered inert. But what does Lame Deer mean when he says that they are "very much alive"?

He doesn't explain this provocative assertion as discursively as one might wish, but he provides examples, dozens of examples, of what he calls the "power" in various natural entities. According to Lame Deer, "Every man needs a stone. . . . You ask stones for aid to find things which are lost or missing. Stones can give warning of an enemy, of approaching misfortune."[9] Butterflies, coyotes, grasshoppers, eagles, owls, deer, especially elk and bear all talk and possess and convey power. "You have to listen to all these creatures, listen with your mind. They have secrets to tell."[10]

It would seem that for Lame Deer the "aliveness" of natural entities (including stones which to most Europeans are merely "material objects" and epitomize lifelessness) means that they have a share in the same consciousness that we human beings enjoy. Granted, animals and plants (if not stones and rivers) are recognized to be "alive" by conventional European conceptualization, but they lack awareness in a mode and degree comparable to human awareness. Among the Cartesians, as I mentioned earlier, even animal behavior was regarded as altogether automatic, resembling in every way the behavior of a machine. A somewhat more liberal and enlightened view allows that animals have a dim sort of consciousness, but get around largely by "instinct," a concept altogether lacking a clear definition and one very nearly as obscure as the notorious occult qualities (the "soporific virtues," and so on) of the Schoolmen. Of course, plants are regarded as, although alive, totally lacking in sentience. In any case, we hear that only human beings possess *self*-consciousness, that is, are aware that they are aware and can thus distinguish between themselves and everything else!

Every sophomore student of philosophy has learned, or should have, that solipsism is an impregnable philosophical position, and corollary to that, that every characterization of other minds—human as well as nonhuman—is a matter of conjecture. The Indian attitude, as represented by Lame Deer, apparently was based upon the consideration that since human beings have a physical body *and* an associated consciousness (conceptually hypostatized or reified as "spirit"), all other bodily things, animals, plants, and, yes, even stones, were also similar in this respect. Indeed, this strikes me as an eminently reasonable assumption. I can no more directly perceive another human being's consciousness than I can that of an animal or plant. I *assume* that another human being is conscious since he or she is perceptibly very like me (in other respects) and I am conscious. To anyone not hopelessly prejudiced by the metaphysical apartheid policy of Christianity and Western thought generally, human beings closely resemble in anatomy, physiology, and behavior other forms of life. The variety of organic forms themselves are clearly closely related, and the organic world, in turn, is continuous with the whole of nature. Virtually all things might be supposed, without the least strain upon credence, like ourselves, to be "alive," that is, conscious, aware, or possessed of spirit.

Lame Deer offers a brief, but most revealing and suggestive, metaphysical explanation:

> Nothing is so small and unimportant but it has a spirit given it by Wakan Tanka. Tunkan is what you might call a stone god, but he is also a part of the Great Spirit. The gods are separate beings, but they are all united in Wakan Tanka. It is hard to understand—something like the Holy Trinity. You can't explain it except by going back to the "circles within circles" idea, the spirit splitting itself up into stones, trees, tiny insects even, making them all *wakan* by his ever-presence. And in turn all these myriad of things which makes up the universe flowing back to their source, united in one Grandfather Spirit.[11]

This Lakota panentheism presents a conception of the world which is, to be sure, dualistic, but it is important to emphasize that, unlike the Pythagorean-Platonic-Cartesian tradition, it is not an *antagonistic* dualism in which body and spirit are conceived in contrary terms and pitted against one another in a moral struggle. Further, and most importantly for my subsequent remarks, the pervasiveness of spirit in nature, a spirit *in everything* which is a splinter of the Great Spirit, facilitates a perception of the human and natural realms as unified and akin.

Consider, complementary to this pan-psychism, the basics of Siouan cosmogony. Black Elk rhetorically asks, "Is not the sky a father and the earth a mother, and are not all living things with feet or wings or roots their children?"[12] Accordingly, Black Elk prays, "Give me the strength to walk the soft earth, a relative to all that is!"[13] He speaks of the great natural kingdom as, simply, "green things," "the wings of the air," "the four-leggeds," and "the two-legged."[14] Not only does everything have a spirit, in the last analysis all things are related together as members of one universal family, born of one father, the sky, the Great Spirit, and one mother, the Earth herself.

More is popularly known about the Sioux metaphysical vision than about those of most other American Indian peoples. The concept of the Great Spirit and of the Earth Mother and the family-like relatedness of all creatures seems, however, to have been very nearly a universal American Indian idea, and likewise the concept of a spiritual dimension or aspect to all natural things. N. Scott Momaday remarked, "'The earth is our mother. The sky is our father.' This concept of nature, which is at the center of the Native American world view, is familiar to us all. But it may well be that we do not understand entirely what the concept is in its ethical and philosophical implications."[15] And Ruth Underhill has written that "for the old time Indian, the world did not consist of inanimate materials. . . . It was alive, and everything in it could help or harm him."[16]

Concerning the Ojibwa Indians, who speak an Algonkian language and at the time of first contact maintained only hostile relations with the Sioux, Diamond Jenness reports:

> Thus, then, the Parry Island Ojibwa interprets his own being; and exactly the same interpretation he applies to everything around him. Not only men, but animals, trees, even rocks and water are tripartite, possessing bodies, souls, and shadows. They all have a life like the life in human beings, even if they have all been gifted with different powers and attributes. Consider the animals which most closely resemble human beings; they see and hear as we do, and clearly they reason about what they observe. The tree must have a life somewhat like our own, although it lacks the power of locomotion. . . . Water runs, it too must possess life, it too must have a soul and a shadow. Then observe how certain minerals cause the neighboring rocks to decompose and become loose and friable; evidently rocks too have power, and power means life, and life involves a soul and a shadow. All things then have souls and shadows. And all things die. But their souls are reincarnated again, and what were dead return to life.[17]

Irving Hallowell has noted an especially significant consequence of the pan-spiritualism among the Ojibwa: "Not only animate properties," he writes, "but even 'person' attributes may be projected upon objects which to us clearly belong to a physical inanimate category."[18] Central to the concept of *person* is the possibility of entering into social relations. Nonhuman persons may be spoken with, may be honored or insulted, may become allies or adversaries, no less than human persons.

The French fur traders and missionaries of the seventeenth century in the Great Lakes region were singularly impressed by the devotion to dreams of the savages with whom they lived. In 1648, Ragueneau speaking of the Huron, according to Kinietz, first suggested that dreams were "the language of the souls."[19] This expression lacks precision, but I think it goes very much to the core of the phenomenon. Through dreams, and most dramatically through visions, one came into direct contact with the spirits of both human and nonhuman persons, as it were, naked of bodily vestments. In words somewhat reminiscent of Ragueneau's, Hallowell comments, "It is in dreams that the individual comes into direct communication with the *atiso'kanak*, the powerful 'persons' of the other-than-human class."[20] Given the animistic or pan-spiritualistic world view of the Indians, acute sensitivity and pragmatic response to dreaming makes perfectly good sense.

Dreams and waking experiences are sharply discriminated, but the theater of action disclosed in dreams and visions is continuous with and often the same as the ordinary world. In contrast to the psychologized contemporary Western view in which dreams are images of sorts (like afterimages) existing only "in the mind," the American Indian while dreaming experiences reality, often the same reality as in waking experience, in another form of consciousness, as it were, by means of another sensory modality.

As one lies asleep and experiences people and other animals, places, and so on, it is natural to suppose that one's spirit becomes temporarily dissociated from the body and moves about encountering other spirits. Or, as Hallowell says, "when a human being is asleep and dreaming his *otcatcakwin* (vital part, soul), which is the core of the self, may become detached from the body (*miyo*). Viewed by another human being, a person's body may be easily located and observed in space. But his vital part may be somewhere else."[21] Dreaming indeed may be one element in the art of American Indian sorcery ("bear walking" among the Ojibwa). If the state of consciousness in dreams may be seized and controlled, and the phenomenal content of dreams volitionally directed, then the sorcerer may go where he wishes to spy upon his enemies or perhaps affect them in some malevolent way. It follows that dreams should have a higher degree of "truth" than ordinary waking experiences, since in the dream experience the person and everyone he meets is present in spirit, in essential self. This, notice, is precisely contrary to the European assumption that dreams are "false" or illusory and altogether private or subjective. For instance, in the Second Meditation, Descartes, casting around for an example fo the highest absurdity, says that it is "as though I were to say 'I am awake now, and discern some truth; but I do not see it clearly enough; so I will set about going to sleep, so that my dreams may give me a truer and clearer picture of the fact.'" Yet this, in all seriousness, is precisely what the Indian does. The following episode from Hallowell's discussion may serve as illustration. A boy claimed that during a thunderstorm he saw a thunderbird. His elders were skeptical, since to see a thunderbird in such fashion, that is, with the waking eye, was almost unheard of. He was believed, however, when a man who had dreamed of the thunderbird was consulted and the boy's description was *"verified!"*[22]

The Ojibwa, the Sioux and, if we may safely generalize, most American Indians, lived in a world which was peopled not only by human persons, but by persons and personalities associated with all natural phenomena. In one's practical dealings in such a world it is necessary to one's well-being and that of one's family and tribe to maintain good social relations not only with proximate human persons, one's immediate tribal neighbors, but also with the nonhuman persons abounding in the immediate environment. For example, Hallowell reports that among the Ojibwa "when bears were sought out in their dens in the spring they were addressed, asked to come out so that they could be killed, and an apology was offered to them."[23]

In characterizing the American Indian attitude toward nature with an eye to its eventual comparison with ecological attitudes and conservation values and precepts I have tried to limit the discussion to concepts so fundamental and pervasive as to be capable of generalization. In sum, I have claimed that the typical traditional American Indian attitude was to regard all features of the environment as enspirited. These entities possessed a consciousness, reason, and volition no less intense and complete than a human being's. The Earth itself, the sky, the winds, rocks, streams, trees, insects, birds, and all other animals therefore had personalities and were thus as fully persons as other human beings. In dreams and visions the spirits of things were directly encountered and could become powerful allies to the dreamer or visionary. We may therefore say that the Indian's social circle, his community, included all the nonhuman natural entities in his locale as well as his fellow clansmen and tribesmen.

Now a most significant conceptual connection obtains in all cultures between the concept of a person, on the one hand, and certain behavioral restraints, on the other. Toward persons it is necessary, whether for genuinely ethical or purely prudential reasons, to act in a careful and circumspect manner. Among the Ojibwa, for example, according to Hallowell, "a moral distinction is drawn between the kind of conduct demanded by the primary necessities of securing a livelihood, or defending oneself against aggression, and unnecessary acts of cruelty. The moral values implied document the consistency of the principle of *mutual obligations* which is inherent in all interactions with 'persons' throughout the Ojibwa world."[24]

The implicit overall metaphysic of American Indian cultures locates human beings in a larger *social*, as well as physical, environment. People belong not only to a human community, but to a community of all nature as well. Existence in this larger society, just as existence in a family and tribal context, places people in an environment in which reciprocal responsibilities and mutual obligations are taken for granted and assumed without question or reflection. Moreover, a person's basic cosmological representations in moments of meditation or cosmic reflection place him or her in a world all parts of which are united through ties of kinship. All creatures, be they elemental, green, finned, winged, or legged, are children of one father and one mother. One blood flows through all; one spirit has divided itself and enlivened all things with a consciousness that is essentially the same. The world around, though immense and overwhelmingly diversified and complex, is bound together through bonds of kinship, mutuality, and reciprocity. It is a world in which a person might feel at home, a relative to all that is, comfortable and secure, as one feels as a child in the midst of a large family. As Brown reports:

> But very early in life the child began to realize that wisdom was all about and everywhere and that there were many things to know. There was no such thing as emptiness in the world. Even in the sky there were no vacant places. Everywhere there was life, visible and invisible, and every object gave us great interest to life. Even without human companionship one was never alone. The world teemed with life and wisdom, there was no complete solitude for the Lakota (Luther Standing Bear).[25]

## IV

I turn now to the claim made at the beginning of this discussion, namely, that in its practical consequences the American Indian view of nature is on the whole more productive of a cooperative symbiosis of people with their environment than is the view of nature predominant in the Western European tradition.

Respecting the latter, Ian McHarg writes that "it requires little effort to mobilize a sweeping indictment of the physical environment which is [Western] man's creation [and] it takes little more to identify the source of the value system which is the culprit."[26] According to McHarg, the culprit is "the Judeo-Christian-Humanist view which is so unknowing of nature and of man, which has bred and sustained his simple-minded anthropocentrism."[27]

Popular ecologists and environmentalists (perhaps most notably Rachel Carson and Barry Commoner, along with McHarg and Lynn White, Jr.) have with almost loving attention recited a litany of environmental ills, spoken of "chlorinated hydrocarbons," "phosphate detergents," "nuclear tinkering," and "the gratified bulldozer" in language once reserved for detailing the precincts of hell and abominating its seductive Prince. Given the frequency with which we are reminded of the symptoms of strain in the global biosphere and the apocalyptic rhetoric in which they are usually cast I may be excused if I omit this particular step from the present argument. Let us stipulate that modern technological civilization (European in its origins) has been neither restrained nor especially delicate in manipulating the natural world.

With somewhat more humor than other advocates of environmental reform, Aldo Leopold characterized the modern Western approach to nature thus: "By and large our present problem is one of attitudes and implements. We are remodeling the Alhambra with a steam shovel, and we are proud of our yardage. We shall hardly relinquish the shovel, which after all has many good points, but we are in need of gentler and more objective criteria for its successful use."[28] So far as the historical roots of the environmental crisis are concerned, I have here suggested that the much maligned attitudes arising out of the Judeo-Christian tradition have not been so potent a force in the work of remodeling as the tradition of Western natural philosophy originating among the ancient Greeks and consolidated in modern scientific thought. At least the latter has been as formative of the cultural milieu, one artifact of which is the steam shovel itself, as the former; and together, mixed and blended, so to speak, they create a mentality in which unrestrained environmental exploitation and degradation could almost be predicted in advance.

It seems obvious (especially to philosophers and historians of ideas) that attitudes and values *do* directly "determine" behavior by setting goals (e.g., to subdue the Earth, to have dominion) and, through a conceptual representation of the world, by providing means (e.g., mechanics and other applied sciences). Skepticism regarding this assumption, however, has been forthcoming. Yi-Fu Tuan says in "Discrepancies between Environmental Attitude and Behavior: Examples from Europe and China":

> We may *believe* that a world-view which puts nature in subservience to man will lead to the exploitation of nature by man; and one that regards man as simply a component in nature will entail a modest view of his rights and capabilities, and so lead to the establishment of a harmonious relationship between man and his natural environment. But is this correct?[29]

Yi-Fu Tuan thinks not. The evidence from Chinese experience which he cites, however, is ambiguous. Concerning European experience, he marshals examples and cases in point of large-scale transformations, imposed, with serious ecological consequences, upon the Mediterranean environment by the Greeks and Romans. They were, of course, nominally pagans. He concludes this part of his discussion with the remark that "against this background of the vast transformations of nature in the pagan world, the inroads made in the early centuries of the Christian era were relatively modest."[30] I believe, nevertheless, that my discussion in part two of this essay has explained the environmental impact of Greek and Roman civilization consistently with the general thesis that world view substantially affects behavior! Among the Chinese before Westernization, the facts which Yi-Fu Tuan presents indicate as many congruences as discrepancies between the traditional Taoist and Buddhist attitude toward nature and Chinese environmental behavior.

A simple deterministic model will not suffice with respect to the question, do cultural attitudes and values really affect the collective behavior of a culture? On the one hand, it seems incredible to think that *all* our conceptualizations, our representations of the nature of nature, are, as it were, mere entertainment, some sort of epiphenomena of the mind, while our actions proceed in some blind way from instinctive or genetically programmed sources. After all, our picture of nature defines our theater of action. It defines both the possibilities and the limitations which circumscribe human endeavor. On the other hand, the facts of history and everyday experience do not support any simple cause-and-effect relationship between a given conceptual and valuational set and what people do. My own view is that it is basic to human nature to both consume and modify the natural environment. Representations of the order of nature and the proper relationship of people to that order may have either a tempering, restraining effect on manipulative and exploitative tendencies or they may have an accelerating, exacerbating effect. They also give form and direction to these inherently human drives and thus provide different cultures with their distinctive styles of doing things. It appears to me, further, that in the case of the predominant European mentality, shaped both by the Judeo-Christian and Greco-Roman images of nature and man, the effect was to accelerate the inherent human disposition to consume and modify surroundings. A kind of "take-off" or (to mix metaphors) "quantum leap" occurred, and Western European civilization was propelled for better or worse into its industrial, technological stage with a proportional increase in ecological and environmental distress. The decisive ingredient, the sine qua non, may have been the particulars of the European world view.

If the predominant traditional Chinese view of nature and man has been characterized by Yi-Fu Tuan as "quiescent" and "adaptive," the American Indian view of the world has been characterized as in essence "ecological," for example, by Stewart Udall, in *The Quiet Crisis*. In "First Americans, First Ecologists" Udall nostalgically invokes the memory of Thoreau and attributes to his ghost the opinion that "the Indians were, in truth, the pioneer ecologists of this country."[31] To assert without qualification that the American Indians were ecologists is, to say the least, overly bold. Ecology is a part of biology, just as organic chemistry is part of chemistry. It is a methodic and quantitative study of organisms in a contextual, functional relationship to conditions of their several ranges and habitats. Udall, of course, disclaims that he means to suggest that Indians were scientists. One might prefer to say that American Indians intuitively acquired an essentially ecological outlook, perspective, or habit of mind. That would be roughly to say that Indians viewed nature as a matrix of mutually dependent functional components integrated systemically into an organic whole. It would suggest a kind of global or holistic viewpoint; it would also imply an acute sensitivity to the complex factors influencing the life cycles of living things.

To attribute to American Indians, on the one hand, a highly abstract conceptual schematism and, on the other, a disinterested, systematic, disciplined, and meticulous observation of minutiae is to press the romantic interpretation of American Indian thought much too far. Much of the material which I have already cited *does* indicate that both woodland and plains Indians were careful students of their natural surroundings. Knowledge of animals and their ways, particularly those of utilitarian value, and knowledge of plants, especially edible and medicinal ones, is a well-known and much-respected dimension of traditional Indian cultures. The American Indian pharmacopoeia alone certainly testifies to Indian botanical acumen. My impression, nonetheless, is that the typically Indian representation of nature is more animistic and symbolic than mechanical and functional. The "rules" governing hunting and fishing seem more cast in the direction of achieving the correct etiquette toward game species than *consciously* achieving maximum sustained yield of protein "resources." Medicinal plants were sought as much for their magical, symbolic, and representational virtues as for their chemical effects. Of course, in the case of hunting and fishing, proper manners *are* behavioral restraints and, more often than not, the outcome of their being followed—of correct social forms in respect to bear, beaver, and so on, being observed—was to limit exploitation and therefore, incidentally, to achieve sustained yield.

To suggest that the Indians were intuitive (or natural or pioneer or even primitive) ecologists, in other words, strikes me as being very much like saying that Indian healers, like Black Elk, were intuitive (etc.)

physicians. Indian medicine was not at an earlier stage of development than European medicine, as if moving along the same path some distance behind. It followed a different path altogether. As Black Elk explains, "It is from understanding that power comes; and the power in the [curing] ceremony was in understanding what it meant; for nothing can live well except in a manner that is suited to the way the sacred Power of the World lives and moves."[32] The power that Black Elk employed was, *in his view,* ceremonial and symbolic.

The general American Indian world view (at least the one central part of it to which I have called attention) deflected the inertia of day-to-day, year-to-year subsistence in a way that resulted, on the average, in conservation. Conservation of resources may have been, but probably was not, a consciously posited goal, neither a personal ideal nor a tribal policy. Deliberate conservation would indeed, ironically, appear to be inconsistent with the spiritual and personal attributes which the Indians regarded as belonging to nature and natural things, since these are represented by most conservationists in the predominant Pinchot tradition as only commodities, subject to scarcity, and therefore in need of prudent "development" and "management." The American Indian posture toward nature was, I suggest, neither ecological nor conservative in the modern scientific sense so much as it was moral or ethical. Animals, plants, and minerals were treated as persons, and conceived to be coequal members of a natural social order.

My cautious claim that American Indians were neither deliberate conservationists nor ecologists in the conventional sense of these terms, but manifested rather a distinctly ethical attitude toward nature and the myriad variety of natural entities, is based upon the following basic points. The American Indians, on the whole, viewed the natural world as enspirited. Natural beings therefore felt, perceived, deliberated, and responded voluntarily as persons. Persons are members of a social order (i.e., part of the operational concept of *person* is the capacity for social interaction). Social interaction is limited by (culturally variable) behavioral restraints, rules of conduct, which we call, in sum, good manners, morals, and ethics. The American Indians therefore, in Aldo Leopold's turn of phrase, lived in accordance with a "land ethic." This view is also maintained by Scott Momaday: "Very old in the Native American world view is the conviction that the earth is vital, that there is a spiritual dimension to it, a dimension in which man rightly exists. It follows logically that there are ethical imperatives in this matter."[33]

To point to examples of wastage—buffaloes rotting on the plains under high cliffs or beaver all-but-trapped-out during the fur trade— which are supposed to deliver the coup de grace to all romantic illusions of the American Indian's reverence for nature is very much like pointing to examples of murder and war in European history and concluding therefrom that Europeans were altogether without a humanistic ethic of any sort.[34] What is lacking is a useful understanding of the function of ethics in human affairs. Ethics bear, as philosophers point out, a normative relation to behavior; they do not describe how people actually behave, but rather set out how people ought to behave. Therefore, people are free either to act in accordance with a given ethic or not. The fact that on some occasions some do not scarcely proves that ethics are not on the whole influential and effective behavioral restraints. The familiar Christian ethic has exerted a decisive influence within European civilization; it has inspired noble and even heroic deeds both of individuals and of whole societies. The documented influence of the Christian ethic is not in the least diminished by monstrous crimes on the part of individuals. Nor do shameful episodes of national depravity, like the Spanish Inquisition, and genocide, as in Nazi Germany, refute the assertion that a humanistic ethic has palpably affected behavior among members of the European civilization and substantially shaped the character of that civilization itself. By parity of reasoning, examples of occasional destruction of nature on the pre-Columbian American continent and even the extirpation of species, especially during periods of enormous cultural stress, as in the fur-trade era, do not, by themselves, refute the assertion that the American Indian lived not only by a tribal ethic but by a land ethic as well, the overall and usual effect of which was to establish a greater harmony between Indians and their environment than that enjoyed by their European successors.

## V

This conclusion would not, perhaps, require further elaboration or defense had it not recently been specifically denied by two authors, Calvin Martin and Tom Regan. In this brief polemical epilogue, I therefore undertake to defend it against their criticisms. Martin writes:

> Land-use was therefore not so much a moral issue for the Indian as technique animated by spiritual-social obligations and understandings. . . . There is nothing here to suggest morality; certainly there is nothing to suggest the presumptuous, condescending extension of ethics from man-to-man to man-to-land, as the Leopoldian land ethic implies. When Indians referred to other animal species as "people"— just a different sort of person from man—they were not being quaint. Nature was a community of such "people"—"people" for whom man had a great deal of genuine regard and with whom he had a contractual relationship to protect one another's interests and fulfill mutual

needs. Man and Nature, in short, were joined by compact—not by ethical ties—a compact predicated on mutual esteem. This was the essence of the traditional Indian-land relationship.[35]

As we see, Martin denies point-blank the major conclusion reached in the previous discussion: that the American Indian world view in its general and common characteristics incorporated an environmental ethos or fostered an ethical attitude toward land and the plants and animals belonging to the land community. But his statement is very puzzling when we analyze it closely and compare it further with some of the things he says immediately before it, for example, that one shared aspect of traditional American Indian world views was "*a genuine respect* for the welfare of other life forms;" that aboriginal man "felt a *genuine kinship* and often *affection* for wildlife and plant-life;" and that wildlife "were revered and propitiated not only out of fear that their favors might be withheld, although there was some sense of that, but also because they were felt to be *inherently deserving of such regard.*"[36]

What more do we mean by *morality* or ethics, one wonders, than a sense of respect, kinship, affection, regard, and esteem? At the risk of sounding trite, I suggest that it may be merely a semantical difference that is involved here. I have called these American Indian attitudes toward wildlife and plant life, mountains and rivers, sky and earth, "moral" or "ethical" attitudes, while Martin apparently wishes to hold the terms *moral* and *ethical* in reserve (though for what he does not say). He does say, "Ethics were involved only when either party broke regulations, if even then"; but he does not explain this cryptic remark or what precisely he means here by *ethics*.[37] My view of what counts as an ethical attitude is more Humean, I suppose, while Martin's is, perhaps, more Kantian. Following Hume, I am willing to label behavior toward nature "ethical" or "moral" which is motivated by esteem, respect, regard, kinship, affection, and sympathy; Kant, on the other hand, regarded all behavior motivated by "mere inclination" (i.e., sentiment or feeling), however unselfish, as lacking genuine moral worth. For Kant, to be counted as ethical an action must be inspired solely by unsentimental duty toward some abstract precept, some categorical imperative, issued by pure reason unsullied by any empirical content. Perhaps this exalted Kantian standard for ethical behavior lies behind Martin's disclaimer. But only by some special and highly technical definition of ethics, such as Kant's, can Martin's discussion be rescued from the allegation that it is plainly incoherent, indeed, that it is blatantly self-contradictory.

That issue having been, if not settled, at least clarified, let us consider another of Martin's disavowals, namely, that, more specifically, the overall traditional American Indian attitude toward nature was not akin to Aldo Leopold's land ethic. In this case, the evidence which Martin himself has so masterfully assembled and presented earlier in his book plainly contradicts this negative claim and I can see no way to rescue his discussion from self-contradiction by semantical distinctions or by any other interpretive concessions.

For purposes of illustrating the similarity of his impression of Indian attitudes toward nature and the attitudes toward nature recommended by Leopold's land ethic, consider the following sample from Martin's very full account:

> Nature, as conceived by the traditional Ojibwa, was a congeries of societies: every animal, fish and plant species functioned in a society that was parallel in all respects to mankind's. . . .[38]

> As we extend these ideas further, we come to realize that the key to understanding the Indian's role within Nature lies within the notion of mutual obligation: man and nature both had to adhere to a pre-scribed behavior toward one another. . . .[39]

> "According to Cree ideology . . . hunting rests on a kind of social relationship between men and animals. Throughout the cycle of hunt-ing rites men emphasize their respect by means of symbolic expres-sions of their subordination to animals. . . ."[40]

To see just how similar the precepts of Leopold's land ethic are to American Indian attitudes, we need only take a closer look at the foun-dations of the Leopold land ethic. First, the primary feature of the land ethic is the representation of nature as a congeries of societies and of human-nonhuman relationships as essentially social: "The land ethic simply enlarges the boundary of the community to include soils, waters, plants, and animals, or collectively: the land."[41] Second, it is social membership to which ethics and ethical attitudes are correlative: "All ethics so far evolved rest upon a single premise: that the individual is a member of a community of interdependent parts."[42] Third, Leopold takes a more Humean than Kantian approach to the concept of ethics and morality: "It is inconceivable to me," he writes, "that an ethical relation to land can exist without love, respect, and admiration for land and a high regard for its value."[43] As we see, according to the recon-struction that Martin himself so ably and persuasively presents (though he later unaccountably denies it), the traditional American Indian attitude toward nature was in its shared and general assumptions so similar to the essential notions of Leopold's land ethic as to be basically identical with it.

Martin does not explain why he finds Leopold's land ethic "pre-

sumptuous" and "condescending," nor shall I speculate on his reason
for these epithets. I find Leopold's land ethic to be, if anything, the
opposite of presumptuous and condescending. For the sake of comparison, there is a very different sort of "environment ethic," the so-called
animal liberation or animal rights ethic, that is based upon an arbitrary
condition, "sentience," for moral considerability which all human
beings paradigmatically exhibit; with moral standing then extended to
higher "lower animals" on the grounds that they too manifest the same
quality.[44] This humane ethic does seem to me to be condescending and
presumptuous. In Leopold's land ethic, the *summum bonum* resides in
the biotic community and moral value or moral standing devolves upon
plants, animals, people, and even soils and waters by virtue of their
membership in this (vastly) larger-than-human society.[45] As Leopold
rather bluntly puts it, "A land ethic changes the role of *Homo sapiens*
from conqueror of the land-community to plain member and citizen of
it."[46] The privileged position of human beings in the natural order is
thus, in the Leopold land ethic, done away with in a single bold stroke.
How can this be either presumptuous or condescending?

There is another unjustifiably skeptical remark which Calvin
Martin makes as his parting shot at the neoromantic environmentalist
view of Indians. He says that

> even if we absolve him of his ambiguous culpability in certain epi-
> sodes of despoliation, invoking instead *his pristine sentiments toward*
> *Nature* [once more, are these not the very soul of an ethical attitude?],
> the Indian still remains a misfit guru. . . . The Indian's was a pro-
> foundly different cosmic vision when it came to interpreting Nature
> —a vision Western man would never adjust to. There can therefore be
> no salvation in the Indian's traditional conception of Nature for the
> troubled environmentalist.[47]

This statement, though brief and scarcely defended, has had wide
influence. For example, one reviewer for a distinguished journal devoted to scholarship on American Indians, though thoroughly critical
of Martin's ethno-historical methods and his controversial hypothesis
of an Indian-animal war, assumes without question or criticism that
"his epilogue disparages effectively contemporary views about the
'ecological' Indian."[48]

After having so sharply contrasted the traditional Western European attitude toward nature with the traditional American Indian,
perhaps I should wholeheartedly agree with Martin on this particular,
especially as the basis of his claim goes back to cultural roots or fundamentals. Indeed, it is precisely because Western culture is grounded,
according to Martin, in the Judeo-Christian tradition that "even if he

[the Indian] were capable of leading us we could not follow."[49]

A full discussion of this issue goes far beyond the scope of this essay. However, in view of Martin's pessimistic conclusion I will hazard a more optimistic suggestion. It may prove to be true that in its own fashion Western science, particularly ecology and the life sciences, but also physics and cosmology, is contributing to the development of a *new* Western world view remarkably similar in *some* ways (but only in some) to that more or less common to American Indian cultures. Science in the twentieth century has retreated from its traditional mechanistic and materialistic biases; indeed, twentieth-century science has been, just in this respect, "revolutionary." Popular Western culture still lags behind. Europeans and Euro-Americans remain, for the most part, nominally Christian and unregenerately materialistic and mechanistic, but the new biocentric and organic world view (embedded in a holistic cosmology and coupled with a field-theory ontology) has already begun to emerge. And there is, further, every reason to expect that eventually it will fully flower in the form of a wholly new popular culture. Present interest in environmental pollution, endangered species, popularized ecology, *and* American Indian environmental attitudes and values are all harbingers of this emerging consciousness.

By the foregoing criticisms I certainly do not intend to belittle Calvin Martin's major achievement in the main body of *Keepers of the Game*, which is a monumental contribution to the recent effort to reconstruct the outlines of the traditional American Indian outlook upon the world. Tom Regan, in a discussion which is very dependent upon Martin's, takes a step toward articulating the very real philosophical problem which Martin may have felt, but was able neither coherently to state nor effectively to resolve. According to Regan, "There is always the possibility that it was fear of the keepers [spiritual wardens of game animals in woodland Indian metaphysics], not appreciation of nature's inherent values, that directed these people's behavior."[50] Regan, therefore, believes that this consideration contributes "an ineradicable layer of ambiguity to the respectful behavior of Native Peoples [toward nature]."[51]

With Regan's observations before us we can now formulate what may have been the actual basis of Martin's reluctance to call American Indian attitudes toward nature "ethical" or "moral." Indian self-interest alone may have dictated deference toward nature, since if such restraint were not forthcoming, nature, everywhere spiritually enlivened, as they believed, would withhold its sustenance or, worse, actively retaliate and the Indians would woefully suffer. Now, any pattern of behavior motivated by mere selfishness on all accounts (including Hume's, to say nothing of Kant's) is certainly not properly described as moral or ethical. Hence, for all their touted spiritualizing of nature and reverence and restraint in taking game and gathering plants, perhaps "there is nothing here to suggest morality," to quote Martin again.

Regan quite fairly points out that "the ambiguity of Amerind behavior is the ambiguity of human behavior, the ancient puzzle over whether, as humans, we are capable of acting out of disinterested respect for what we believe has value in its own right or whether, beneath all manner of ceremony, ritual and verbal glorification of the objects of our attention, there resides, in Kant's memorable words, 'the dear self', the true, the universal sovereign of our wills.'"[52] As this observation clearly suggests, to describe *any* human behavior whatsoever as "ethical" or "moral" may be naive and incautious. Personally, I think Regan and perhaps Martin (if this is in fact the basis of the latter's reservations) are being overly cynical about human nature. I am more inclined to agree with Hume when he says, respecting human motives of behavior, that while

> we may justly esteem our *selfishness* the most considerable, I am sensible, that, generally speaking, the representations of this quality have been carried much too far; and that the descriptions, which certain philosophers delight so much to form of mankind in this particular, are as wide of nature as any accounts of monsters, which we meet with in fables and romances. So far from thinking that men have no affection for anything beyond themselves, I am of opinion, that tho' it be rare to meet with one, who loves any single person better than himself; yet 'tis rare to meet with one, in whom all the kind affections taken together, do not over-balance all the selfish.[53]

Human beings are not, I think, incapable of acting from motives of affection, sympathy, regard, respect, fellow-feeling, reverence, and so on, as well as from purely selfish motives; thus, I think human beings per se are not incapable of ethical or moral behavior.

Most folk ethics (as distinct from formal, philosophical theories) take account of and play upon both our moral and our selfish sentiments. Take the familiar Christian ethic as an example. We are urged to love God and to love our neighbor as ourselves. Those whose moral sentiments overbalance the selfish probably do genuinely behave respectfully, for the most part, toward other persons because they love God and at least sympathize with (if not love) one another. On the other hand, there is an appeal to the dear self. If you do not obey God's commandments and at least act *as if* you respected other persons, God will punish you.

In this respect it seems to me that Indian land ethics are precisely analogous to Western humanitarian ethics. Nowhere in this discussion have I claimed that traditional American Indians were morally better than Westerners in the sense that they were more altruistic, and Europeans and Euro-Americans more selfish. Rather, I have claimed that these two broad *cultural traditions* provide very different views of nature and thus very differently excite or stimulate the moral sentiments of their members. In persons belonging to both cultures there is, we may be sure, a mixture of selfishness and altruism. The ratio does not vary so much from culture to culture as from individual to individual. Some individuals in any culture may be very nearly devoid of benevolent feelings, while others are so filled with them that they willingly sacrifice themselves for the sake of their fellows. Hence Indian land ethics, like the humanitarian religious folk ethic of Western culture appeal to both our noble sentiments and selfish fears.

In traditional American Indian cultures the animals and plants were commonly portrayed as fellow members of a Great Family or Great Society. They were "persons" worthy of respect, even affection. But if there were individuals (and in every human group there always are) incapable of other-oriented feelings, people who were narrowly selfish, then an appeal to fear of punishment was included, as it were, as a backup motivation to the same forms of action that others were motivated to do because of *moral* sentiments. Noble and generous American Indians would have been mortified to slaughter game animals wantonly and needlessly for sport alone, since the animals were fellow members of an extended family or extended society and had themselves been so generous and cooperative. On the other hand, less noble Indians might have been induced to submit to similar restraints because of fear of retribution. This retributive factor does not suggest, to me at any rate, that American Indian *world views* did not, therefore, include a land ethic (Martin's claim), or even that there is, therefore, an "ineradicable layer of ambiguity" in the average, manifestly restrained, behavior of traditional Indians toward nature (Regan's claim), an ambiguity which makes it impossible for us to decide if their restrained relations with nature were genuinely moral or merely selfish. Such restraints were doubtless of both the moral and selfish sorts, and the balance between these two behavioral poles varied from person to person and, with respect to a given person, probably from time to time. The point is, American Indian *cultures* provided their members with an environmental ethical *ideal*, however much it may have been from time to time or from person to person avoided, ignored, violated or, for that matter, grudgingly honored because of fear of punishment.

# 11

## American Indian Land Wisdom?: Sorting Out the Issues

### Introduction

Simultaneous with the popularization of ecology and public awareness of the "environmental crisis," traditional American Indian cultures came to symbolize a lost but not forgotten harmony of human beings with nature. This most recent Indian mystique blends nostalgia and optimism. It expresses, iconographically, regret and outrage for the despoliation of a biotically rich and diverse continent. And it expresses hope that contemporary Euro-American society will emulate the ideal of a fitting human-nature relationship represented by traditional Native American peoples.

It is as difficult precisely to specify as it is historically to corroborate, however, anything so diffuse and fatherless as an image in the collective contemporary consciousness. A putative American Indian "land or environmental wisdom"—which may serve as a kind of generic term—resolves, upon closer scrutiny, into several distinct and apparently disparate types. And since there is, so to speak, a documentary horizon at roughly A.D. 1492 beyond which we cannot directly look, claims that one sort of environmental wisdom or another prevailed among traditional American Indian peoples are difficult to sift and verify. On the one hand, the manifest biotic capital of North America at first European landfall and, on the other, archeological evidence of occasional wastage and the extinction of a large number of species of large mammals provide ambiguous indications of traditional American Indian environmental *behavior*. And the connection between cognitive culture and cultural behavior is complex and tenuous. Cultural ideals serve to guide and inspire personal and collective behavior; they do not determine it. Conversely, episodes of behavior in violation of cultural norms do not necessarily invalidate or impugn them. Some method, or triangulation by means of several methods, is needed more directly to assay the environmental *beliefs, attitudes,* and *values* existing among traditional American Indian peoples.

Such systematic and empirical studies are perhaps now more needed than ever. The dialectics of contemporary popular mythology are such that a backlash repudiation of the image of traditional American Indians as native environmentalists may be expected to occur sooner or later as a matter of course. It will likely be sooner if Rudolf Kaiser's exposé of the spurious origins of what is surely the most celebrated example of American Indian land wisdom becomes widely known in this country—the famous oration of Chief Seattle during the Port Elliot treaty negotiations of 1854–55.[1] Seattle almost certainly uttered an oration in his native language during these events. His speech was reconstructed in English, we cannot know how accurately, by Henry A. Smith, M.D., who was present on the occasion of its delivery.[2] But the version of the speech (or, as it is sometimes called, letter) of Chief Seattle (to President Franklin Pierce), which has in recent years been quoted so ubiquitously, is not even the Smith rendition of unknown veracity. "I have seen a thousand rotting buffalos on the prairie, left by the white man who shot them from a passing train. I am a savage and do not understand how the smoking iron horse can be more important than the buffalo that we kill only to stay alive.... If we sell you our land, love it as we've loved it. Care for it as we've cared for it.... How can you buy or sell the sky, the warmth of the land?...The idea is strange to us."[3] These are familiar words, virtually household American Indian environmental rhetoric, but they, along with the other ecological and environmental pieties attributed to Seattle, were actually composed by one Ted Parry as a film script for a movie called "Home" produced by the Southern Baptist Convention in 1971–72 and interpolated into William Arrowsmith's redaction of Henry A. Smith's nineteenth-century rendition of Seattle's words—whatever they may have been.

But this is only one, particulary sordid, example of the casual way in which the idea of a traditional American Indian land wisdom has been propagated in contemporary culture. Its critics have been equally irresponsible. For example, Daniel Guthrie in an especially scurrilous ar-ticle published in *Bioscience* cited, among other equally irrelevant circumstances, the environmental and ecological conditions on pres-ent-day Indian reservations as evidence that pre-contact American Indian peoples (who, in his view, represent "primitive man") were as environmentally and ecologically insensitive as their Euro-American successors.[4]

Guthrie also voices the argument—often thought to be fatal to the "romantic" notion of an American Indian land wisdom—that the In-dian impact on the North American environment was limited by Tech-nology, not ideology. The proof? First, a thinly populated continent at

European landfall—suggesting that American Indian subsistence methods were so meager as to keep Indians well below the carrying capacity of the land, even for gatherer-hunters. And second, the historical fact that when better technologies became available—the steel trap, knife and axe, the rifle, the chain saw, the snow mobile, etc., etc., etc.—the Indian did not hesitate to use them. And to full advantage. I deal with the latter "evidence" subsequently in this discussion. I argue there that to adopt a technology is, insidiously, to adopt the world view in which the technology is embedded. Here I might add, conversely, that the adoption by Indians of Western technologies was accompanied by massive and aggressive disruption of their traditional belief systems by Europeans and Euro-Americans. If the white man had landed in North America, off-loaded cargoes of axes, knives, iron kettles, and so on, and then turned around and left, it remains a moot question whether or not these allegedly more efficient means of environmental exploitation would have been embraced and abused by the recipients—or even used at all.

The exploitative potential of native technologies is an empirical question of a different sort, for which there is very little hard data—one way or the other. It has remained a Western chauvinist's article of faith, going back to Thomas Hobbes and John Locke, that the subsistence technologies of non-civilized peoples can only afford them the barest hold on life—a life, to quote Hobbes, which is at best "poor, nasty, brutish, and short" (if not "solitary"). And Locke stated, categorically and without a shard of fact to back his claim, that an Indian "King [sic] of a large and fruitful Territory there [in America] feeds, lodges, and is clad worse than a day Labourer in *England*."[5] Calvin Martin, in *Keepers of the Game*, reviews a wide range of literature that bears on the subject—everything from Henry Dobyns's revised pre-Columbian population estimates (which take account of the decimation of European diseases on aboriginal American populations) to Marshall Sahlins's revised portrait of gatherer-hunter affluence—and concludes that "the impression we are left with, based on studies of modern hunter-gatherers using aboriginal tools, is that these people indeed have had the technological capacity to exert greater pressure on their faunal and floral resources than they have chosen to do.... [Thus, extrapolating from observation of modern gatherer-hunters to those of the past] the Indian, equipped with his traditional tools in protohistoric times, was quite capable of inflicting greater damage on game resources than he apparently did.... Need, then, not technology was the overriding factor, and need was determined by the great primal necessities of life as these were understood and regulated by cultural considerations."[6]

William Cronon, in a more recent and geographically focused (as well as less controversial) study, corroborates Martin's conclusion: "On the coast were fish and shellfish, and in the salt marshes were migratory birds. In the forests and lowland thickets were deer and beaver; in cleared upland fields were corn and beans; and everywhere were the wild plants whose uses were too numerous to catalog. For New England Indians, ecological diversity, whether natural or artificial, meant abundance, stability, and a regular supply of the things that kept them alive.... If the Indians considered themselves happy with the fruits of relatively little labor, they were like many peoples of the world as described by modern anthropologists."[7]

The argument that American Indians lacked the technology for massive environmental destruction, and hence had no need of an environmental ethic, is often offered—once again, Daniel Guthrie provides a good example—in the same breath with the claim that Indians were no better in their treatment of the environment than their Euro-American successors because their remote ancestors (!) have been implicated in the otherwise mysterious extinction of a number of genera of large mammals at the end of the Pleistocene. Paul S. Martin argued that these extinctions were not merely coincidental with the arrival of big game hunters from Siberia, but were directly caused by the original discoverers of America.[8] Martin's thesis has been contested, but supposing he is right, one cannot have it both ways. It cannot both be true that Pre-Columbian American Indian technology was so ineffective as to be incapable of palpable environmental destruction and that a more primitive Paleo-Indian technology was so effective as to have been responsible for more North American extinctions than followed upon the rediscovery of the continent by modern Europeans.

Paul S. Martin himself hints at a historical dialectic that could make his overkill hypothesis the basis of a historical argument for, rather than against, the eventual evolution by eventual American Indians of a land wisdom: "With the extinction of all but the smaller, solitary, and cryptic species, such as most cervids, it seems likely that a more normal predator-prey relationship would be established. Major cultural changes would begin. Not until the prey populations were extinct would the hunters be forced, by necessity, to learn more botany. Not until then would they need to readapt to the distinctive biomes in America...."[9]

Among the major cultural changes and part of the process of readaptation to the distinctive biomes in America may just have been the evolution of a land wisdom. Why should "major cultural changes" be confined to material culture? After all, learning more botany is as much a conceptual as behavioral accomplishment. Learning to respect the land—however that might have been cognitively codified—might have gone hand in hand with learning more botany. Natural selection may have favored those Native American descendents of the remnant populations of Siberian immigrants who evolved an ideology which helped them avoid the pattern of overexploitation that brought to an end to the ultimately ruinous *modus vivendi* of their ancestors.

In any case, in general, arguments for an against an American Indian land wisdom have been so distanced from specific cognitive cultural materials as to be virtually *a priori* in character. Nor has it even been at all clear exactly what is at issue. In the following discussion, I first offer conceptual clarification of the question at hand; second, a method for its resolution third an application of that method in a particular cultural context; and finally some concluding remarks.

### An American Indian Land Wisdom Typology

Four distinct types of American Indian land wisdom have been proffered in the literature so far: utilitarian conservation, religious reverence, ecological awareness, and environmental ethics.

In the 1930s William C. McCleod and Frank G. Speck attempted to persuade the literate public that principles of conservation were practiced among traditional American Indian peoples.[10] To my knowledge theirs are the earliest, and still among the best informed, arguments for an American Indian environmental wisdom. By "conservation" Speck and McCleod expressly meant utilitarian conservation as it was understood and implemented in the thirties and as it had been previously defined by Gifford Pinchot—the rational, prudent exploitation of natural resources to obtain from them maximum sustained yield. Indeed, Speck explicitly employed evidence of conservation among American Indians to reach a more general conclusion, namely, that the then common racist stereotype of traditional American Indians as peoples languishing at a subrational level of consciousness was erroneous. In other words, aboriginal conservation, the rational use of resources, Speck averred, proved that traditional American Indians were *eo ipso* rational.

Speck and McCleod based their conclusions on ethnographic observations of post-contact American Indians living in relative isolation from Euro-American civilization and practicing an apparently traditional way of life. Both Speck and McCleod relied heavily upon the *contemporary* institution of the family hunting territory and its division into annually rotated quarters—to permit the recovery of populations game animals—as incontrovertible evidence of conservation among *aboriginal* northern woodland hunting-gathering peoples. Such an institution would certainly suggest a careful, quantitative, empirical census

of game resources and a management plan for their systematic exploitation—the basic elements of utilitarian conservation principles.

McCleod, however, is expressly aware that some question might
be raised about the provenance of the family hunting territory system
—that it might have been a response to the European fur trade and
thus also ancillary to European economic concepts of natural resources,
private property, supply, demand, and so on, or even that conservation
was expressly taught to the Indians by whites. Still he insists that "there
seems to be no doubt of its originality."[11] Subsequent research, of course,
inclines to the opposite opinion—that the family hunting territory, with
its cognitive correlates, was a post-contact development.[12]

The distinctly cognitive, as opposed to behavioral, evidence for
conservation marshaled by McCleod and Speck actually points to a
second, completely different sort of environmental wisdom—which
they identify as a "religious" reverence for nature and nonhuman
natural entities. Speck rehearses miscellaneous examples of ceremonies, legends, and ritual practices among Algonkian hunter-
gatherers and sums up his observations with this famous remark:
"With these people no act of this sort is profane, hunting is not a war
upon the animals, not a slaughter for food or profit, but a *holy
occupation*."[13] And in a decidedly less dramatic style McCleod notes that
"spiritual motives may have played a large part in giving rise to
conservation. To primitive man there is a soul in all things animate and
(to us) inanimate. ... [Thus] they appear to have rationalized [*sic*] their
rude conservation in spiritual terms."[14]

As McCleod, more clearly than Speck, seems to realize, "conservation" of "natural resources" may have been more a side effect of
animism and religious veneration than a consciously envisioned goal.
According to Speck and McCleod, wastage and/or immoderate harvest
of plants and animals was offensive to their spirits or spirit-wardens.
Hence without explicitly intending to conserve resources—their intent
being rather not to offend nature spirits—the woodland hunter-
gatherers whom Speck described might have achieved the same
results adventitiously.

Indeed, it would seem that the complex of concepts constituting
deliberate utilitarian conservation would be cognitively dissonant
with an alleged religious veneration of the environment. Speck con-
cisely sums up the latter attitude as follows:

> The hunter's virtue lies in respecting the souls of the animals
> necessarily killed, in treating their remains in prescribed manner and
> in particular, in making use of as much of the carcass as is possible.
> These observances constitute religious obedience. The animals slain
> under the proper conditions and treated with the consideration due

them return to life again and again. They furthermore indicate their whereabouts to the "good" hunter in dreams resigning themselves to his weapons in a free spirit of self-sacrifice.[15]

To look upon animal and plant persons as impersonal material resources, to observe the details of their distribution, growth recruitment, breeding habits and seasons, and so on, with an eye to harvesting as many as prudently possible, that is, to coldly calculate the maximum or even optimum sustained yield of these "resources," would seem in and of itself to represent a dangerously irreverent attitude toward their spirits. Further, as more a matter of logic than likelihood, to believe that beaver, moose, and other slain animals returned to life upon proper disposal of their skeletons would seriously confound the calculations which are an essential element in the conservation cognitive complex.

Speck attributes to the American Indians he studied yet a third species of land wisdom which is more ideologically consonant with a religious veneration of nonhuman natural entities than utilitarian conservation is, but which—because it may exist apart from a religious framework of belief and practice—represents a distinct type. He says, "The idea of treating animals and plants after the principle of the *Golden Rule* was so typical of the killing and gathering methods of the eastern Indians that they literally used their privilege of hunting, fishing, and collecting, as though they were treating animals and plants with *the same thought and consideration offered to human beings.*"[16] Speck here attributes to woodland hunter-gatherers an ethical attitude—as distinct from an attitude of religious reverence—toward nonhuman natural entities. An ethical attitude toward certain beings may exist in the absence of worship, veneration, or reverence for them. We do not worship, venerate, or reverence other people, though we may respect them. As modern secular ethics illustrate, ethical attitudes may be divorced from a religious or supernatural system of belief altogether. Irving Hallowell's extensive and extremely sympathetic and reflective work among the Ojibwa, an Algonkian people, provides ample evidence that the Ojibwa regarded animals, plants, and assorted other natural things and phenomena as persons with whom it was possible to enter into complex social intercourse. And social interaction is, as it were, the matrix from which morality is forthcoming and in which it is in the first exercised. ( I shall comment more fully on Hallowell's observations and analyses as they bear on an American Indian land wisdom in the next section of this discussion).

A fourth distinct kind of land wisdom, recently the one most commonly attributed to pre-Columbian American Indians, is ecology.

According to Stewart Udall (who also attributes an environmental ethic to American Indians), Fred Fertig, J. Donald Hughes, Terrence Grieder, G. Reichel-Dolmatoff, William A. Ritchie and Thomas W. Overhold (to mention only a few) and "ecological awareness" among American Indians inhibited their potential despoliation of the environment.[17]

The term "ecology," of course, has become more and more diluted as it has become more and more popular. It is often now used most loosely to mean roughly the same thing as "natural environment"—as in the sentence, "Strip-mining is bad for the ecology." Correlatively, anyone who strongly advocates environmental protection may be called an "ecologist," no matter how limited his or her training or even literacy in biology. Ecology, *sensu stricto*, is a subdiscipline of biology, and an ecologist is someone with an advanced degree (or at least a strong track record of professionally respectable amateur research) in that field. Thus, to say that American Indians were native, intuitive, natural, original ecologists could mean, most loosely, that they were strong advocates of environmental protection or, most strictly, that they had advanced degrees in a subdiscipline of biology. The former notion is a historical-political anachronism and the latter is absurd.

More generously interpreted, those who claim that American Indians possessed an ecological awareness may be taken to mean that American Indians had a thorough and systematic knowledge of the biota of their respective environments and, more especially, of the dynamic interactions, dependencies, and relationships among the several constituents of their environments. Such sophisticated knowledge is not at all unlikely to have accumulated among peoples living in an intimate, direct, and dependent relationship with nature. And that such knowledge actually exists among contemporary American Indians living in traditional life ways is amply supported by ethnographic investigation.[18]

Unfortunately, not all contemporary scientific ecologists are environmentalists. Just as modern ecology may be put to use in service of strictly economic ends, so may native ecology have been. From the existence of an ecological awareness among American Indians, nothing follows about their attitudes and values respecting ecosystems.

### Methods for Discovering an American Indian Land Wisdom

These four basic types of putative environmental wisdom prevailing among traditional American Indians—conservation, religious reverence, environmental ethics, and ecological awareness—are very often confused or conflated by a single author in a single discussion. J. Donald Hughes, for example, promiscuously attributed all four forms of environmental wisdom (as well as feminism) to northeastern hunter-gatherers in "Forest Indians: The Holy Occupation."

The means of substantiating the notion that a land wisdom of one or another sort existed among traditional American Indians are equally varied and uncritical. The more popular discussions pay little attention to cultural specificity and rely primarily on what might be called testimonials for evidence or support. The previously mentioned (apocryphal) Chief Seattle, Chief Joseph, Neihardt's Black Elk, Brown's Black Elk, Luther Standing Bear, Lame Deer, Vine Deloria and a number of other more or less recent Indian spokespersons are indiscriminately quoted as evidence for traditional American Indian conservation, ecology, environmental religion, or land ethics. Although I am personally not unmoved by these testimonials, a less sympathetic critic might dismiss them on several counts. They are, for the most part, relatively very recent (mid-nineteenth-century or later), they may be idiosyncratic (rather than a genuine reflection of shared cultural values), and they may be (quite understandably and justifiably, but nonetheless, merely) nostalgic. As one is forcibly dispossessed of one's ancestral lands, it is natural to feel both outrage at colonial usurpers and nostalgia for one's rightful natural heritage. The tender sentiments for the environment in the testimonials one finds in such eclectic collections as T.C. McLuhan's *Touch the Earth* or Peter Nabokov's *Native American Testimony* may only be a personal reaction and cultural afterthought, a natural response to cultural oppression and personal dispossession.[19]

A second approach to the question of a traditional American Indian land wisdom bases conclusions on what might be called descriptive ethnography. From a critical point of view, this method constitutes a quantum leap in sophistication and reliability in comparison with the testimonial technique.

The descriptive ethnographic method provides a firsthand account of the environmental behavior of contemporary remnants of hunter-gatherer cultures and a record of their accompanying beliefs, attitudes, and values as expressed both discursively and symbolically in ceremony, song, story, myth, and legend. Two outstanding examples of this method are Adrian Tanner's *Bringing Home Animals* and Richard Nelson's *Make Prayers to the Raven*.[20] Such accounts are culturally specific—often, as Tanner's work with the Mistassini Cree, subspecific—and critically disciplined.

The painstaking empirical research, dedication, and sympathy of contemporary ethnographers—whose work requires them to live in circumstances of hardship in necessarily remote and inhospitable environments—fills me, an armchair scholar, with unbounded respect and admiration. Still, the degree to which these contemporary accounts may be generalized not only across contemporary cultural boundaries, but across several centuries into the pre-Columbian past of the *same* culture, is problematic. The influence of global technological civilization and the ideology which engendered it and in which it remains grounded is (except perhaps among a few Amazonian peoples) inescapable. It is also insidious. Technologies are never cognitively and axiologically neutral. They are embedded in an engendering and sustaining system of ideas. To buy guns, motors, and mackinaw jackets is to buy, however unintentionally, a world view to boot. Both the Koyukon and the Mistassini Cree use guns and steel traps in taking game, wear some store-bought clothes, and to one degree or another are influenced by Christianity, modern science, Western medicine, money, and materialism.

On the other hand, what other assumption may be made than that those cultural elements not identifiably Western in origin must be at least a *legacy* of the aboriginal cultural past, if not identical with it? Still, an implacable skeptic might argue that the apparently reverential or ethical attitudes (whether express or implied) toward nonhuman natural entities are a consequence of Western influence no less than self-conscious conservation principles and practices like the family hunting territory. As I earlier suggested, conservation is comprised of a complex of ideas deeply intertwined with the foundational cognitive elements of the Western world view. Reverential or ethical attitudes could be interpreted, on the other hand, as a dialectical reaction to typical Western attitudes of indifference and brutality toward nature. And, as a bottom line, the interests of the ethnographer, his or her research agenda, the questions she or he poses to herself or himself or asks his or her informants may subtly shape the conclusions of his or her research. Contemporary ethnographers, it is pleasing to note, are very often also dedicated environmentalists. A critic might argue that research results documenting the existence of ethnic environmental attitudes and values congenial with the environmental attitudes and values of the investigator may be as much the product of a natural human bias and selectivity as of objective, disinterested, and balanced reportage.

To obviate at least some of the uncertainties of the descriptive ethnographical approach to the verification of the hypothesis that there existed some sort of environmental wisdom among traditional American Indians, Calvin Martin in *Keepers of the Game* employed a methodology which he called ethnohistory.[21] He suggested complementing ethnographic reports with historical documents—the letters, reports, chronicles, records and so on, of explorers, traders, missionaries, European captives who lived among natives, acculturated natives, and so on—as close to the documentary horizon as possible. Such documents portray Indian material and cognitive culture at first contact or more or less soon thereafter, prior to generation upon generation of ever-increasing cultural influence from Europeans. The often casual and unsystematic and always ethnocentric and distorted quality of these early documents can then be compared and cross-checked with the more systematic and objective, but always relatively recent, ethnographic accounts in such a way that ideally they mutually correct, supplement, enrich, and illuminate one another. Martin, in my opinion, makes very effective and persuasive use of this method to reconstruct a portrait of a "land ethic" type of land wisdom pervasive among Eastern subarctic hunter-gatherers on the eve of European contact. (It is unfortunate that Martin discredited his own constructive profile of an aboriginal American Indian land ethic, however, with his eccentric and entirely speculative hypothesis of a war between Indians and animals and his petulant and self-contradictory effort to discredit the "myth" of an American Indian land wisdom perpetrated by contemporary environmentalists.)

Finally, Thomas W. Overholt and I, in our book, *Clothed-in-Fur and Other Tales*, followed a method first proposed by A. Irving Hallowell similar to the methods of philosophical analysis and literary critisicm.[22] A putative traditional American Indian land wisdom in any interesting sense, from the point of view of contemporary environmentalism, would not be the personal wisdom of an exceptional Indian sage or philosopher, but the collective environmental ethos of a community. Such an ambient and possibly implicit aspect of a cultural world view is borne, as all other aspects of cognitive culture, by an ambient and communal vehicle—a culture's language.

While language is routinely used on a day-to-day basis to convey personal meanings and messages, it is also the repository of a common system of cultural meanings and a common narrative heritage. Hence, the systematic study of a culture's common medium (language per se) and narrative heritage (its general fund of myths, legends, and tales) should provide a reliable and objective method for a recovery of its common beliefs, attitudes, and values, including environmental beliefs, attitudes, and values. And, although this necessarily remains a speculative matter, this method should give us a glimpse beyond the documentary horizon—to the extent that a culture's language survives and its narrative heritage lives on. Stories have, as it were, a life of their own. They persist with only incidental changes, through radically changed cultural circumstances. Consider the Euro-American oral heritage of fairy tales. They are about princes and princesses living in castles, knights in shining armor, magical swords, witches, sorcerers, and trolls. They hark back to another physical and psychic world. Yet they live on, relatively unchanged in the retelling, in our own world of skyscrapers, airplanes, computers, and technocrats.

Unlike Frank Speck, Irving Hallowell does not appear to have been especially interested in environmental issues or American Indian environmental attitudes and values. Hence, his semantic analyses of the Ojibwa language cannot be impugned as consciously or unconsciously biased in favor of one or another type of American Indian land wisdom. Overholt and I undertook a reexamination of Hallowell's analysis of Ojibwa semantic categories with an eye to applying them to the question of an Ojibwa land wisdom. According to Hallowell, the formal Ojibwa linguistic distinction between animate and inanimate (analogous to gender distinctions in Romance languages) does not correspond to scientifically informed Western intuitions.[23] For example, some stones (flint), certain kinds of shells (the *megis* shell of the *Midewiwin,* for instance), thunder, various winds, and so on, as well as plants, animals, and human beings fall into the animate linguistic class. Further, the category of *person,* according to Hallowell, is not coextensive with the category *human being* in Ojibwa semantic discriminations as it is in English and other modern Western languages.[24] Animals, plants, stones, thunder, water, hills, and so on may be persons in the Ojibwa linguistic organization of experience.

Now, as Hallowell points out, there is an intimate link in Ojibwa, as in English, between persons and a complex network of social interaction. Since nature is more broadly animate and personal in the traditional Ojibwa world than in the contemporary Western world, "the world of personal relations," according to Hallowell, "in which the Ojibwa live is a world in which vital social relations transcend those which are maintained with human beings."[25] The Ojibwa cycle of myths detail, elaborate, and amplify the personal and social organization of nature and of human-nature interaction structurally represented in Ojibwa semantic discriminations. Using William Jones's extensive and remarkable collection of stories, *Ojibwa Texts,* Overholt and I found that the Ojibwa narratives consistently represent the natural world as a world of other-than-human persons organized into a congeries of societies.[26] Plant and animal species are, as it were, other tribes or nations. Human economic intercourse with other species is not represented as the exploitation of impersonal, material natural resources, but as reciprocal gift-giving or bartering, in which both the human and nonhuman parties to the exchange benefit. Game animals give their skins and flesh to human beings, who in return give the animals tobacco and other desirable cultivars and artifacts. The slain animals are reincarnated in the most literal sense of that term— reclothed in flesh and fur—and thus come back to life to enjoy their humanly bestowed benefits.

The *nomoi*, the rules or customs governing human-nature realtionships among the Ojibwa, are thus of an essentially social-ethical sort. The animal spirits are not worshiped in any religious sense of the term; rather, like members in good standing of a human society, they are respected. Their personal interests and feelings are taken into account. As in any social ethic, the rules or conventions serve to formalize and articulate this affective moral posture of respect for persons and to provide behavioral guidance.

Most interestingly we found a correspondence in abstract form between the Ojibwa environmental ethic and the Aldo Leopold land ethic, which is the most celebrated and appealing version of environmental ethics in contemporary environmental thought.[27] The principle idea upon which Leopold rests his land ethic is the ecological concept of a biotic community:

> All ethics so far evolved rest upon a single premise: that the individual is a member of a community of interdependent parts.... The land ethic simply enlarges the boundaries of the community to include soil, waters, plants, and animals, or collectively: the land.[28]

The detailed representations of the personal-social order of nature among the Ojibwa, on the one hand, and among contemporary ecologists like Aldo Leopold, on the other, are, of course, vastly different. The one is mythic and anthropomorphic, while the other is scientific and self-consciously analogical. Nevertheless, when the mythic and scientific detail is stripped away from either, respectively, an identical abstract structure—an essentially social structure—constitutes the core conceptual pattern of the totemic natural community of the Ojibwa and the biologist's economy of nature. In form, thus, the Ojibwa land ethic and the Aldo Leopold land ethic are identical.

## Conclusion

On the basis of these reflections what conclusions may be reached? Did traditional American Indians possess an environmental wisdom? If so, of what type? How can we be sure whether they did or not, at this distance from a past which we cannot autopsy?

To take up the last question first, contemporary descriptive ethnography, ethnohistory, and ethnolinguistic/narrative analysis are all useful methods, and may be cooperatively brought to bear on the question of a traditional American Indian land wisdom. For example, in the tradition with which I am most familiar, the Algonkian ethnographies of Speck and more recently Tanner, the Eastern subarctic ethnohistory of Martin, the more analytic ethnometaphysical studies of the Ojibwa by Hallowell, and the Ojibwa texts of Jones, all agree in fundamental particulars about the cognitive organization of the Ojibwa and, more generally, of the Algonkian world. Nonhuman natural entities are personal beings, socially organized into families, clans, and nations not unlike the traditional Algonkians themselves. Relations with these other-than-human persons are, accordingly, socially structured. They are courteous, cautious, mutual, reciprocal, deferential, diplomatic—forms of conduct which must be maintained to sustain the interspecies social structure and, so to speak, international balance of power. From a sociobiological point of view, this is the sum and substance of an ethic—an American Indian land or environmental ethic.

To generalize a priori beyond the Ojibwa and Algonkian cultural materials I have mentioned would not be warranted. A similar collection and comparison of ethnography, early historical documents, semantic and mythic analyses from other American Indian cultures would almost certainly reveal very different cognitive organizations of phenomenal experience and correspondingly and proportionately different attitudes and values respecting nature. What was the traditional Papago, Shoshone, Hopi, or Cherokee land wisdom, if any, like? If a concerted and systematic effort were undertaken, an ethnographic map of types of American Indian land wisdom might gradually be built up and, moreover, correlated with the biogeographical map of North America, in the way Nelson has suggested, to develop a kind of North American ecology of mind.[29]

To speculate briefly on other Plains cultures, if the Lakota world view familiar to everyone from *Black Elk Speaks* withstands critical scrutiny, then the Sioux pictured nature as more like a vast extended family than a congeries of societies. Such a world view appears to be corroborated by the Lakota mythic materials collected in the 1890s by James R. Walker.[30] An environmental wisdom is certainly immediately inferrable from such a representation, but it would not be very precisely described as an ethic. One's familial duties, it seems to me, go beyond ethics. Ethics suggests, at least to me, a formality inappropriate to intimate familial relations. No matter how such tender environmental sentiments as those Black Elk expresses may be labeled, however, there seems to me to be an important environmental consciousness and conscience implicit in them.

As a philosopher, professionally concerned not only with conceptual analysis and clarity, but also with consistency, I am inclined to think that conceptually inconsistent environment attitudes cannot be credibly attributed to a single people. In particular, I would suppose, as I remarked earlier, that prudential utilitarian conservation, since it is conceptually dissonant with either a religious or an ethical intellectual orientation to nature, could not be autochthonous to a culture in which a religious or ethical orientation to nature was manifest. Reflection stimulated by correspondence with Richard Nelson, however, has convinced me that this judgment is wrong. In a letter to me, Nelson wrote,

> Regarding empirical knowledge of ecological processes, sustained yield practices based on such knowledge, and deliberate conservation of resources, my experiences with Koyukon people especially (and Kutchin to a lesser degree) convince me that they had a well-developed, empirically based system of ecological knowledge and conservation prior to contact with Europeans. It is definitely my impression that people like the Koyukon approach their environment as much from a scientific, empirical point of view, as from an animistic and symbolic perspective. This includes not only the practical, technical processes of locating and obtaining food, but also the longer range processes of maintaining food resources. For the Koyukon and Kutchin, conservation of these resources is definitely a conscious goal.[31]

Nelson here says in effect that the traditional Koyukon and Kutchin were ecologically informed, deliberate conservationists, as well as animistic environmental ethicists. But how could such disparate beliefs coexist in one world view?

A little reflection on the Western world view to which I was enculturated suggested that such conceptual incongruities may be, despite philosophers' apparently aberrant passion for consistency, the human norm. Christianity coexists more or less comfortably with modern science. Euro-Americans function in an empirical, technical, material, and mechanical world, and at the same time many believe in God, heaven, hell, miracles, possessions, the power of prayer, life after death, and the other general doctrines of Christianity.

Why should I be reluctant to suppose, therefore, that the traditional Koyukon or Ojibwa could at once represent their environments as animate, personal, and social *and* as a systemically integrated pool of impersonal resources which must be calculatively sustained and prudently conserved? A typical modern Euro-American can believe that a rich man has as little chance to enter heaven as a camel to pass through the eye of a needle and still spend his or her life in pursuit of the Almighty Dollar. At least among the Koyukon and Ojibwa the behavioral implications of conservation and land ethics converge, however dissonant their cognitive foundations. Both serve to inhibit thoughtless destruction and overexploitation of nature. They are behaviorally complementary, if not conceptually consistent. On the other hand, Western religious beliefs and Western scientific-technological materialism are often contradictory in their practical implications as well as mutually inconsistent in their cognitive foundations. But that doesn't stop may Euro-Americans from espousing both.

Of the several kinds of land wisdom attributed to traditional American Indian cultures, I am most skeptical of the religious reverence type, at least as applied to the Ojibwa and other similar Indian world views. I wish to emphasize immediately, however, that my concerns are more terminological than substantive. To say that American Indians had a spiritual representation of nature is misleading because of the *usual connotation* of the term "spiritual," which suggests an other-worldly and eschatological orientation of mind. To believe that animals, plants, wind, thunder, rocks, mountains, the sun and moon, and so on are conscious and communicative persons, like ourselves, and to hypostatize or reify such consciousnesses, including our own, as owing to the presence of souls, spirits, or *manitous* is not quite the same as a "spiritual" orientation to life in the ordinary Western sense of the term. Western religious thought has been overwhelmingly dualistic. The spirit and flesh are not only ontologically distinct, they are morally opposed, from the point of view of traditional Western religious thought. Hence, the term "spiritual" ordinarily implies an antinatural moral opposition to the "carnal," "brute," physical world—as it is regularly stigmatized from a conventional "spiritual" point of view. It is equally misleading, I think, to characterize the means of communicating with nature spirits—dreams, visions, divination, and ceremonials—as "religious rites," given the usual connotation of the term "religious." Hence, for all its rhetorical power and stylistic appeal, Speck's declaration that hunting was a "holy occupation" among Algonkian hunter-gatherers misses the mark. From the data he provides, it seems to have been, rather, a magical and moral occupation. Human life in nature from the perspective of the Lakota organization of experience as portrayed in *Black Elk Speaks* and *The Sacred Pipe,* on the other hand, might more accurately be characterized as religious or holy, since prayers and worshipful rites seem to figure more prominently in the Lakota ideal of human-nature relationships than in the Algonkian.

Finally, we may ask, can a traditional American Indian land wisdom help to guide the United States and other modern nations out of the present environmental malaise? I think certainly it can. If Richard Nelson is correct to suppose that some traditional American Indian peoples practiced conservation complemented by a land ethic and maintained a long-term balance between themselves and nature, then in his words, "if they can do it, so can we."[32] Their example, I think we may be confident, represents hope. It also represents a role model, despite Calvin Martin's disclaimer, which we can relate to and emulate. If Overholt and I are right to suppose that some American Indian peoples portrayed their relationship with nature as essentially social and thus, by implication, as essentially moral, then their rich narrative heritage could provide, ready-made, the myths and parables missing from abstract articulations of biosocial environmental ethics like Aldo Leopold's.

A traditional American Indian land or environmental wisdom is not a neoromantic invention. But we are just beginning to explore what it actually amounted to, and only in some cultures and in some bioregions. More careful, systematic, and critical research will almost certainly prove to be enormously rewarding and, ultimately, of perhaps the greatest possible practical benefit to contemporary society.

# V

## Environmental Education, Natural Aesthetics, and E.T.

# 12

## Aldo Leopold on Education, as Educator, and His Land Ethic in the Context of Contemporary Environmental Education

Aldo Leopold was truly a watershed figure in the history of American conservation. His slim volume of elegant essays, *A Sand County Almanac*, is comparable to the work of Henry David Thoreau, George Perkins Marsh, and John Muir, and represents indeed the most recent development of the fundamental scientific and philosophical ideas in that great literary tradition. Roderick Nash, in *Wilderness and the American Mind*, correctly credits Aldo Leopold with powerfully advocating for the first time in Western intellectual history, broad human ethical responsibility to the nonhuman natural world.[1] This radical proposal may be found latently present in some of the essays of John Muir, but Muir neither fully articulated nor fully grounded it, as Leopold did, in a supporting matrix of ideas.

Aldo Leopold's contribution to environmental thought and value, moreover, is recognized and acknowledged not only in this country, but internationally as well. For example, systematic environmental philosophy is pursued more vigorously in Australia today than in the United States, and among Australian philosophers Aldo Leopold's land ethic is accepted both as a seminal contribution to contemporary environmental ethics and as a continuing model for their own work.[3]

Although an ethic may be articulated and persuasively advocated by a single creative individual, it will remain ineffectual unless it becomes generally distributed in the population, unless, indeed, it becomes a firmly entrenched cultural institution. Aldo Leopold's own literary mode of expression, a style at once simple but profound, concrete yet reaching the most abstract and subtle domains of thought and feeling, has shepherded the land ethic in its first steps toward broad cultural currency. But a wider effort is required if Leopold's dream of a national, even eventually global, ecological conscience is to be realized. The task is primarily one of environmental education and it falls squarely upon the shoulders of educators.

Accordingly, the general theme of these remarks will be education and the land ethic. This discussion is in three parts. The first topic is Leopold's own reflections on ecological education, as they are revealed in *A Sand County Almanac*. Aldo Leopold was himself an educator, a professor of game management, an academic discipline which he pioneered, at the University of Wisconsin. He made a deep impression on his students. The second topic is Aldo Leopold's own practical approach to education. To learn what his style and methods were as a teacher I have consulted several of his former students, men and women who have themselves gone on to distinguished careers in wildlife biology.[3] The conclusion reflects on a general educational stratagem to impart the land ethic and develop an ecological conscience in contemporary educational circumstances. The approach which I shall recommend is implied by the conceptual foundations of the land ethic itself.

### Aldo Leopold on Education

Aldo Leopold had a lot to say about education, and most of it was gently but sharply critical. Indeed, one complete essay in the more recent, expanded edition of *A Sand County Almanac*, "Natural History" is a short dissertation on the state of the art, its past, and its future.[4] There he develops more specifically and systematically certain themes that surface as occasion dictates throughout the other essays in the book.

In biological education particularly, Leopold is concerned that laboratory biology has usurped the place of natural history. Laboratory biology involves such things as "memorizing the names of the bumps on the bones of a cat."[5] It is pursued indoors and involves dead animals. Natural history, on the other hand, involves the living animal and more importantly its living context. Leopold felt that given a limited curriculum and limited schedule of classes, biology students are better served by more field-oriented courses, more natural history, and less laboratory technique.

There is another more deeply theoretical tension at which Leopold hints in this discussion lurking beneath these manifest indoor/outdoor, dead/alive dichotomies. Natural history, he remarks, suffered some loss of ground earlier in the history of biological education because it then consisted largely of "labeling species and amassing facts about food habits without interpreting them."[6] But "modern natural history deals only incidentally with the identity of plants and animals, and only incidentally with their habits and behaviors. It deals principally with their relations to each other, their relation to the soil and water in which they grew, and their relations to the human beings who sing about 'my country' but see little or nothing of its inner workings."[7] There was, in other words, within natural history itself theoretical conflict between taxonomy and ecology. Ecology is built upon taxonomy as upon a foundation, but ecology is a more advanced development in biological theory.

Taxonomy, the art of labeling and classifying plants and animals according to an elaborate conceptual schematism consisting of species, genus, family, order, class, and so on, originated as a formal study with Aristotle, the founder of Western biology, and has remained the backbone of the biological sciences ever since. Ecology, of course, is, relatively speaking, a newcomer. Taxonomy gets along well enough with dead specimens, but that is not its most serious shortcoming as a science which is supposed to deal with living nature. Rather, since the taxonomical identity of an animal or plant locates it within a highly formal and largely abstract system of organization, preoccupation with this system tends to obscure the actual and concrete system of living ecological relations among animals and plants. A plant or animal's taxonomical niche, in other words, conceptually connects it to other phylogenetically similar species, while its ecological niche may place it in an altogether different pattern of relations. As Leopold remarked, for purposes of ecological understanding, "The species of a [trophic] layer are alike not in where they came from or in what they look like, but rather in what they eat."[8] A clear example is afforded by the few species of plankton-feeding shark which are, of course, phylogenetically and taxonomically related to other sharks but which ecologically more closely resemble baleen whales. Filter-feeding sharks, in other words, pursue the same "profession" in the "economy of nature" as the mysticeti. The exclusive attention paid to taxonomical classification for many centuries may have been a necessary state in the development of biological theory but, ironically, tended to make biologists and biology blind to ecological relations, and resulted in a picture of the living world as so many logically determined species loosed on the landscape to relate haphazardly with one another catch-as-catch-can.

This observation has direct and concrete implications for contemporary environmental education. Take the ubiquitous nature walk as a case in point. Practically all of those I have ever been guided along consisted of an endless catalogue of species. It usually goes something like this: "There's an indigo bunting; here a red oak, yonder a white oak, to the left spiderwort, to the right butterfly weed; on the branch above your head, a vireo; and high in the sky there's a hawk! Is it a red-tail or sharp-shin?" and so on and on. But how all these species are connected to the sandy loam on which I stand, its proximity to the water table, the mean annual temperature and rainfall, the velocity and direction of prevailing winds, frost-depth and snow cover in winter, and hundreds of other affective features of the landscape, are things I am left to wonder about, while my fellow amblers do not think of them at all. They are merely dazzled or bored by the naturalist's display of mnemonics. Knowing the names and pedigrees of our nonhuman neighbors is a foundational accomplishment which I do not intend at all to demean, but that should be the beginning, not the end, of a naturalist's lore. How to create a really ecological ecology walk is a question I can't answer, but it is a problem which should be high on the priority list in the field of outdoor environmental education.

Another recurrent theme in Aldo Leopold's philosophy of education is summed up in the following remark: "Education, I fear, is learning to see one thing by going blind to another."[9] For example, he writes, "I once knew a lady, banded by Phi Beta Kappa, who told me that she had never heard or seen the geese that twice a year proclaim the revolving seasons to her well-insulated roof. Is education possibly a process of trading awareness for things of lesser worth? The goose who trades his is soon a pile of feathers."[10] Here again is the indoor/outdoor dichotomy, but with a different spin.

Achievement in modern American education, as certified by Phi Beta Kappa, is measured almost exclusively in terms of literacy. Learning in general is equated, in other words, with book learning. Therefore, it follows, the more learned we are, the less aware we are of things other than the pages of a book, since time spent reading is time spent with our eyes darting across a line of type, and our other senses idling. Aldo Leopold had the daring to ask pointedly if the benefits of this practically universal educational assumption are worth the price.

In order to counter this assumption or, perhaps better, in order to deflect it in a way useful to environmental education, Leopold often employs the concept of reading as a metaphor. Just as reading a book is a process of interpreting signs and recreating a world in imagination, so nature is an open and ever-present book for those who can read her signs and who possess an active intelligence. Why should not education consist as much in learning to read the land as in learning to read books? Here are a few illustrations. "He who owns a veteran bur oak owns more than a tree. He owns a historical library, and a reserved seat in the theatre of evolution. To the discerning eye, his farm is labeled with the badge and symbol of the prairie war."[11] Following the destruction of prairie flora by the mindless mowing of a cemetery, Leopold remarks, "If I were to tell a preacher of the adjoining church that the road crew has been burning history books in his cemetery, under the guise of mowing weeds, he would be amazed and uncomprehending.

How could a weed be a book?"[12] But to those who are literate in this broader sense, to those who can read the land, silphium, dock, and bluestem are intelligible runes and teach a lesson in history as well as botany. Again, he writes, "Every farm is a textbook on animal ecology; woodsmanship is the translation of the book."[13]

Book learning versus a broader kind of awareness should not be construed as simply a matter of either one or the other, but not both. Leopold does in fact say of woodsmanship that "this skill is rare, and too often seems to be inverse to book learning,"[14] but literacy in the ordinary sense is crucially important: indeed, book learning may be foundational to learning to read the land. Daniel Boone was, for his time, a peerless woodsman, but "Boone saw only the surface of things. The incredible intricacies of the plant and animal community—the intrinsic beauty of the organism called America then in the full bloom of her maidenhood—were ... invisible and incomprehensible to Daniel Boone."[15] That's because "Daniel Boone's reaction depended not only on the quality of what he saw, but on the quality of the mental eye with which he saw it. Ecological science has wrought a change in the mental eye."[16] But science is historically a product of literacy and depends upon letters for its transmission and development.

Leopold also seems to have been ahead of his time in advocating what is now called interdisciplinary education. I believe that this is a natural consequence of his ecological habit of mind. Ecology stresses the relationships among plants and animals and the physical and chemical factors of their environments. It is natural, thus, that an ecological biologist such as Aldo Leopold would be more sensitive to and concerned with relations and connections in general. In terms of higher education, this would translate into an emphasis on the relations and connections between and among academic disciplines rather than on their separateness and autonomy. This is what I have referred to as an ecological approach to education (although for doing so I have been chastised by my ecologist colleagues who charge me with vulgarizing their good name).

In any case, Aldo Leopold gently satirized, with his characteristic wry wit, what I shall call (at the further risk of antagonizing my colleagues in ethology) the "academic territorial imperative." In "Song of the Gavilan" Leopold expanded and made explicit the familiar metaphor, the "harmony" of nature: "its score inscribed on a thousand hills, its notes the lives and deaths of plants and animals, its rhythms span ... the seconds and the centuries."[17] He then goes on to make the following comment.

There are men charged with the duty of examining the construction of the plants, animals, and soils which are the instruments of the great orchestra. These men are called professors. Each selects one instrument and spends his life taking it apart and describing its strings and sounding boards. This process of dismemberment is called research. The place for dismemberment is called a university.

A professor may pluck the strings of his own instrument, but never that of another, and if he listens for music he must never admit it to his fellows or to his students. For all are restrained by an ironbound taboo which decrees that the construction of instruments is the domain of science, while the detection of harmony is the domain of poets.[18]

Here clearly Leopold chides his colleagues for their failure to make scientific education something whole and constructive rather than something endlessly analytic, a discontinuous series of fragments. He further suggests that science in isolation from the humanities, from poetry, music, literature, art, and philosophy, is something barren and even destructive. A good scientist must understand the whole picture of nature into which his specialty fits and, more expansively still, a good scientist must be sensitive to the wider emotional, evaluative, and philosophical implications of scientific investigation and discovery. It has always been especially significant to me that "The Land Ethic" begins with an allusion to Homer's *Odyssey* and contains a fragment from Aristotle's *Nichomachean Ethics*. Clearly Leopold himself was a broadly cultured man.

With respect first to tearing down artificial walls between academic disciplines, he comments in "The Land Ethic" that

one of the requisites for ecological comprehension is an understanding of ecology, and this is by no means co-extensive with 'education'; in fact, much higher education seems deliberately to avoid ecological concepts. An understanding of ecology does not necessarily originate in courses bearing ecological labels; it is quite as likely to be labeled geography, botany, agronomy, history, or economics.[19]

And with respect, secondly, to the integration of ecological understanding with the humanities, he comments that

no important change in ethics was ever accomplished without an internal change in our intellectual emphasis, loyalties, affections, and convictions. The proof that conservation has not yet touched these foundations of conduct lies in the fact that philosophy and religion have not yet heard of it.[20]

At least this circumstance has now been remedied. Religion heard about conservation in 1967 with the publication in *Science* of Lynn White Jr.'s controversial classic, "The Historical Roots of Our Ecologic Crisis," in which he traced human arrogance, self-importance, and the consequent "ecological crisis" to the basic tenets of the Judeo-Christian religious tradition.[21] He succeeded in provoking a vigorous debate in religion and theology which has considerably broadened environmental concerns. And during the last decade environmental ethics has become a recognized and well-established subdiscipline in academic philosophy.

To sum up: Aldo Leopold advocated more field and outdoor education and less passive and sedentary indoor study. He stressed the importance of the study of *live* plants and animals in their living environments as well as the study of dead ones in sterile and artificial laboratory environments. Above all he believed that biological education should be ecological, that is, it should strive to impart to students an understanding of the actual living relationships of plants and animals rather than only their pigeonholes in the abstract conceptual scheme of taxonomical categories. He suggested that the ability to read the land was every bit as important as the ability to read books and that too much of the latter could be worse than none at all. Finally, he understood that science and poetry are not antagonistic orientations of the mind. As any reader of *A Sand County Almanac* knows, Leopold was accomplished in both. He knew that the human mind and spirit are one and that latent in the emerging science of ecology were vast implications for philosophy and religion. Higher education, he insisted, must recognize this wholeness and courageously explore the connections across disciplinary boundaries, even though some sacred cows may be sacrificed in the process.

## Aldo Leopold as Educator

In her recent book, *Strictly for the Chickens,* Frances Hamerstrom wrote, "Aldo Leopold was known by many of his students simply as 'The Professor' as though there were no other professors on the University of Wisconsin campus. ... In those days not everybody knew that Aldo Leopold was a great man, but his students did."[22]

Aldo Leopold was not only a great man, as measured by his contribution to the republic of letters and the environmental consciousness (and conscience) of the Western world, he was also a great teacher, as measured by the respect, veneration, affection, and, not least, accomplishment of his erstwhile students.

What were the qualities, exactly, that made The Professor a person of such profound impact upon his students? I went to visit several of his students and one of his own children to inquire. I expected, I must admit, to hear from them the adjectives commonly used to characterize a memorable teacher—dynamic, enthusiastic, spellbinding, and so on. Robert McCabe, who joined him in 1939, continued as his "assistant" until his death in 1948, and eventually headed the department which he founded, expressly denied that he was an especially dynamic lecturer. That is not to say that he was dull or boring. He was always interesting, according to McCabe, but eschewed the theatrics that lecturers of lesser substance sometimes use to purchase the interest of their students. According to McCabe, Leopold never used a lectern; rather, he sat on the desk, smoked his pipe, and made his point in an unpretentious anecdotal style.

He treated each student as an individual person. He called on students in class to answer questions. These classroom questions and his test questions never emphasized rote memory but did require thoughtful integration of information. By all accounts, although he was always probing and questioning his students, he was unfailingly gentle and always kind. Nevertheless, according to Robert McCabe, he was not an easy touch for a good mark. His tests were never true/false or multiple choice. They consisted of essay questions, and he fully justified his evaluation in marginal notes.

His graduate students were personally selected by The Professor. He seems to have looked for students who were strongly field-oriented and showed promise in field techniques. He did not hold his graduate students at arm's length. Indeed, he developed warm personal and enduring relationships, at least with some of them. His daughter, Nina, told me that he practically considered his graduate students as part of the family. Nevertheless, as a graduate student you didn't go to The Professor's office to shoot the breeze. He regarded himself as busy, as indeed he was. Frederick Hamerstrom remembers that when you paid him an office visit, you had his full and complete attention, but Robert McCabe adds that neither did you waste his time. He was warm, but serious, just as he was gentle, but demanding.

Nina Leopold Bradley described for me a typical workday in her father's life. He was an early riser and reached his office by six in the morning or even earlier. He said that he did his best work before eight. His day was filled with appointments, lecture preparations, classes, and the usual paper work and routine business of university professors. He would arrive home at five for supper. He did not bring his work home. He engaged with his family in intelligent and stimulating supper conversation. He asked the children about their day and listened attentively to their thoughts and accounts. He and his wife, Estella, often read aloud or listened to classical music in the evenings. They retired early.

On Monday nights seminars were held, after which, by tradition, apples were served for refreshment. Frances Hamerstrom remembers the seminar discussions as being sharply critical. Professor Leopold's questions were always probing, but again, he was never harsh, unkind, or overbearing. Neither did he dominate or overtly direct discussion. His aim was to draw things out of the seminar presenters and stretch their powers of thought and analysis as far as possible and to encourage a critical attitude on the part of all participants.

His conversation apparently had the same mastery of the language that is so amply evident in his writing. His vocabulary was rich, his syntax clear, his diction precise, and he assiduously avoided pedantic speech. According to Frances Hamerstrom, Leopold asked that his students take similar pains to express themselves clearly and directly and always to care deeply for the language. He encouraged them to give radio talks, garden club lectures, and so on, to promote public awareness of wildlife and conservation. Field work was only part of the campaign; communication was also vitally important to him.

Frederick Hamerstrom recalls that he had contempt for what he called "College English"—inflated, muddy, and fatuous prose—and that he often criticized the narrowness of many professionals to whom he disparagingly referred as "first-generation scientists." These were scientists who were so narrowly specialized that they lacked breadth of interest and overall cultural background. Leopold himself displayed an extraordinary breadth of interest and he was a charming, interesting, and interested conversationalist.

It is difficult for even the most articulate and reflective of students to say exactly what qualities make a great teacher like Leopold. I suppose, as in many things human, there is an ineffable something, a bit of magic, an unusual and fortuitous blend of qualities, something hard to pin down. Nonetheless, several characteristics were reiterated by all my informants.

The first requirement of a good teacher is to know something worth imparting to others. Leopold's knowledge and talents in his field were nothing short of astonishing, and they have now become legendary. Robert McCabe once said that The Professor could pick up a handful of forest soil, filter it through his fingers, smell it, and without having previously taken a census of the area, give a remarkably accurate prediction of the flora and fauna that could be found there. Frances Hamerstrom records in her book an equally impressive vignette. While helping the Hamerstroms dig an outhouse (to ordinary folk a grimy, boring, mindless task) The Professor took the occasion, as each layer of soil was exhumed, to speculate extemporaneously on its origin and subsequent history, from relatively recent timber fires all the way back to the glacial incursion some ten thousand years before. These are just two illustrations of his uncanny ability to "read the land."[23]

A second characteristic was his genuine interest in his students. He was by all accounts generous, kind, gentle, warm, and caring. Students can immediately sense indifference, and an inability to relate personally and become genuinely involved with students will always seriously inhibit the transmission of skill and information.

Finally, as Nina Bradley recounted, as a teacher her father exercised restraint. He was keenly aware of the thrill of personal discovery and did not rob those around him of the pleasure of learning. His method of teaching was, in other words, essentially Socratic. Socrates, if we may trust Plato's portrait of him, though always a paragon of virtue and usually good-humored, could also be a truculent, abrasive, and occasionally unscrupulous quibbler. I certainly do not mean to suggest that Aldo Leopold was like Socrates in these particulars. But Socrates realized a fundamental educational truth, that the best teachers provide their students with a standard of personal and professional excellence and with a stimulating and encouraging environment in which to learn. A good teacher is rather like a catalyst in a chemical reaction. There is the body of information, technique, and theory, and there is the student. The good teacher brings the two together and enables the reaction to take place.

Charles Bradley previously set out this comparison of Aldo Leopold with Socrates. As he wrote in a brief memoir, "then I would remember the gentle pressure of the questions coming at me and realize the extent to which my mind had been pushed: pushed for clarity, pushed for accuracy, pushed for depth of understanding, pushed to the point where ignorance emerged as the limiting factor to that line of conversation."[24] While Socrates might have gone further and embarrassed his interlocutor, Aldo, mercifully, "just changed the subject when he felt any trace of defensiveness."[25] This Socratic core of the The Professor's teaching technique seems to be confirmed by Robert McCabe and the Hamerstroms. McCabe implied that Leopold was in fact notorious for asking his graduate students unexpected but penetrating questions about their field research during their regular reports to his office. Indeed, one student who was not identified to me by name, according to McCabe, lived in chronic fear (which became acute as the hour arrived) of those periodic interviews.

Some very revealing actual questions of this "modern Socrates" (in Mr. Bradley's insightful characterization) are found in the essay "Natural History."

> To visualize more clearly the lopsidedness and sterility of biological education as a means of building citizens let's go afield with some typical bright student and ask him some questions. We can safely assume he knows how plants grow and cats are put together, but let us test his comprehension of how the land is put together.
>
> We are driving down a country road in northern Missouri. Here is a farmstead. Look at the trees in the yard and the soil in the field and tell us whether the original settler carved his farm out of prairie or woods? Did he eat prairie chicken or wild turkey for Thanksgiving? What plants grew here originally which do not grow here now? Why did they disappear? What did the prairie plants have to do with creating the corn-yielding capacity of this soil? Why does this soil erode now, but not then?
>
> Again, suppose we are touring the Ozarks. Here is an abandoned field in which ragweed is sparse and short. Does this tell us anything about why the mortgage was foreclosed? About how long ago? Would this field be a good place to look for quail? Does short ragweed have any connection with the human story behind yonder graveyard? If all the ragweed in the watershed were short, would that tell us anything about the future of floods in the streams? About the future prospects for bass and trout?
>
> Many students would consider these questions insane, but they are not. Any amateur naturalist with a seeing eye should be able to speculate intelligently on all of them, and have a lot of fun doing it [26]

It is easy to see how a safe-and-sure student lulled into complacency and intellectual torpor by rote learning might have dreaded going afield with The Professor. On the other hand, imagine the excitement, the sheer exhilaration the same experience would afford an intellectually active and genuinely curious student. These questions and others like them engage the imagination. What can be seen is interesting not only in its own right but as an indication of what cannot be seen. They conjure the past and the future and that which is present, but hidden from view. An apparently static and plain landscape by these questions comes alive with drama, heritage, and portent. Perhaps in just this direction lies the solution to our earlier problem: how, in outdoor education, can we transform the passive taxonomical nature walk into the imaginatively active, participatory, ecology walk? Here may be an alternative not only to the point and name school but to the blindfold, ropes, and other gimmicks of the Climatization school. The latter may stimulate the senses and entertain, but it does little or nothing to stimulate the mind and promote country literacy, the skill in reading the land.

## The Land Ethic in Contemporary Environmental Education

Aldo Leopold's teaching and research field was game management or wildlife ecology. (As the field matured, its name changed.) He was its founder. He wrote the book, both figuratively and literally. Yet, if this were his single or greatest achievement, he would be remembered fondly only by his family and students and venerated as founding father by succeeding generations of fellow professionals in this special and somewhat arcane field. What has propelled Aldo Leopold to posthumous international celebrity is his philosophical achievement, and especially his land ethic.

The land ethic is sorely needed in our time; indeed, in the long run, the viability of our civilization, even the future tenure of our species on the planet, may well depend upon the capacity of our now global culture to absorb it. Leopold himself, even in the late forties, was well aware of this necessity. "There is no other way," he wrote, "for land to survive the impact of mechanized man..."[27]

How can environmental education, then, contribute to the dissemination, the promulgation of the land ethic? It is a vitally important task, and it rests more squarely and directly with educators than with any other group or profession.

Everyone's experience will amply indicate, I think, that ethical education, generally speaking, must be indirect to be successful and lasting. One doesn't, in other words, get very far by climbing on a soap box and announcing, as if a message from heaven, addenda to the Ten Commandments or an emendation of the Golden Rule. Indeed, the evangelical approach is more likely to produce the opposite result. People, more commonly than not, react defiantly to self-righteous preaching. Aldo Leopold was as keenly aware of this feature of human psychology as anyone else and thus presented the land ethic, though in urgent (but not strident) tones, as a natural development in cultural evolution: "The extension of ethics to this third element [the land] in [the] human environment is, if I read the evidence correctly, an evolutionary possibility and an ecological necessity."[28]

In what sense and to what degree the advent of the land ethic is a cultural evolutionary possibility can be inferred from the theoretical foundations of the land ethic. And upon drawing out this inference we shall also discover the most effective educational approach for its promulgation.

The land ethic is biological in scope (that is, it includes plants and animals, soils and waters within its purview) and it is biological in its theoretical foundations. This gives it, apart from its other merits, a certain formal charm, a sort of cognitive harmony.

Where do ethics, generally speaking, come from? They are, after all, personally troublesome. Individually, it would seem, we would be better off without them, for an ethic is, in Leopold's words, "a limitation on freedom of action in the struggle for existence."[29] Primitive people solved this mystery as most others with a stock reply: Ethics like other profound goods and evils in human life come from the gods or God (depending on the particulars of theology). In our own Judeo-Christian tradition, for example, we have the vivid and dramatic image of Moses going up on Mount Sinai to receive directly from Jehovah the Ten Commandments.

And why would a person accept moral limitations on his or her freedom of action? The god-given explanation of the origin of ethics also answers this question with equal alacrity. If one doesn't follow the limitations imposed by the gods (or God), then the gods (or God) will sorely punish one. It is better to humor the whims of the gods (or God) than to risk their (or His) terrible wrath.

Philosophical humanism long ago abandoned the divine-origin theory of ethics in favor of one more subtle but equally speculative. Morality is, according to general philosophical consensus, a product of reason. Reason issues moral commandments and every other faculty in the human frame either obeys the dictates of reason or rebels against them. If the former, we are moral; if the latter, immoral.

Natural science cannot accept either of these traditional theories of the origin of ethics. The first is ruled out because it attributes a supernatural cause to a natural phenomenon. The second is ruled out because reason is apparently a recently acquired and very delicate and variable human faculty, itself in some ways dependent upon ethics. The standard philosophical explanation, in short, puts the cart before the horse.

Darwin was the first to tackle the problem from a natural-history point of view in his second great work, *The Descent of Man*. At first glance it would seem that ethical behavior would be weeded out of the gene pool by the inexorable operation of the principle of natural selection, the fundamental mechanism of evolutionary biology, since it is a limitation on freedom of action and thus apparently advantageous to everyone but the agent himself. Evolutionary theory would seem to require, indeed, that as time goes on, human beings should become more and more aggressive, competitive, mutually hostile, and narrowly selfish, since it is the victors in life's *struggle* who live to pass on their traits to succeeding generations. Yet what we actually find is that through time, moral behavior has become more complex, broader, and more refined. We are faced, thus, with a paradox, an anomaly. How can evolutionary *theory* be squared with the manifest *fact* of human moral behavior, the universal acceptance of "limitation[s] on freedom of conduct in the struggle for existence"?

Darwin's solution is in principle both direct and simple. Many species of animals, Homo sapiens conspicuously among them, survive and flourish better in social organizations than as solitaries. Social existence, however, is not possible unless individuals relinquish certain liberties, unless individuals are to some degree mutually deferential, cooperative, and considerate of one another's welfare. In short, accepting ethical limitations on behavior is the dues one pays in order to join society. These limitations in human societies are articulated in a code or body of custom or usage which we call, in sum, ethics or morality. As Leopold points out, we might alternatively define an ethic as "a differentiation of social from antisocial conduct."[30]

This natural-history explanation of the origin of ethics, to which Leopold alludes toward the beginning of "The Land Ethic," clearly issues in a fundamental principle, that ethical relations and social organization are correlative. The details of our ethic reflect the structure of our society and, more importantly for the land ethic, the perceived boundaries of our society are also the perceived boundaries of the extent of our moral obligations.

History amply confirms this relationship between social boundaries and the extent of moral obligation. When societies were small, merely clan or tribal organizations, an individual's ethical obligations extended only to members of his or her own clan or tribe; anyone else was dealt with according to the dictates of expediency, not conscience. As society grew in extent, as tribes merged into nations, the extent of ethical obligations grew apace. We now live in what Marshall McLuhan has aptly styled a "global village." Those who acknowledge their membership in this single global human community also acknowledge moral obligations to all members of the community—that is, to all human beings—nationality, race, or other previously socially sorting characteristics notwithstanding.

The land ethic in Aldo Leopold's great vision is the next step in this process of social-ethical evolution. He writes, "All ethics so far evolved rest upon a single premise: that the individual is a member of a community of interdependent parts. ... The land ethic simply enlarges the boundaries of the community to include soils, waters, plants, and animals, or collectively: the land."[31]

But how can we help to bring this next step in the ethical sequence to pass? The answer to this question should now be very direct and clear: it is simply through promoting extensive and intensive *ecological understanding.* As Leopold has pointed out, "that land is a community is the basic concept of ecology. ..."[32] Educating people in ecology is, therefore, teaching them to understand and to perceive the natural world as "one humming community." It is, moreover, fostering the perception of ourselves and the human economy as but one part of the larger society and economy of nature. Ecology is not just one science among many; it is a habit of mind and a way of experiencing. The end result of genuine ecological education is a complete reorientation of a person to his or her surroundings.

When ecological understanding and awareness become generally distributed in our culture, then the land ethic will follow as a natural and psychologically necessary consequence. Evolution has endowed us with what we might call, following Hume, a set of "moral sentiments" which are, so to speak, triggered by the recognition of a fellow member of our society or community. The basic concept of ecology is that the myriad nonhuman natural beings—soils and waters, plants and animals—are functioning members of a single natural community to which we also belong and upon which we utterly depend for the means to life. When this basic concept of ecology is taught at all levels of education, from story and song in early childhood education to abstract, theoretical mathematics, science, and philosophy in higher education, the land ethic may be transformed from one man's dream to all mankind's reality.

# 13

## Leopold's Land Aesthetic

Aldo Leopold is perhaps America's most distinguished conservationist. He is especially renowned as the forerunner of all contemporary environmental ethics.[1]

Leopold also expressed a definite "land aesthetic." Although his
land aesthetic has not enjoyed as much attention as the land ethic, it
could prove to be more inspirational to private landowners.

Leopold's land ethic is yet another set of rules or limitations. It calls
for obligation, self-sacrifice, and restraint and thus could be unappeal-
ing to farmers and landowners. This is especially true at a time when
agriculture is beset by economic hardship and bureaucratic interfer-
ence.

The land aesthetic, on the other hand, might be more palatable
since it emphasizes assets and rewards. Yet it also fosters conservation:
"If the private owner," Leopold wrote, "were ecologically minded, he
would be proud to be the custodian of a reasonable proportion of such
areas [wetlands, woodlots, native prairies, etc.] which add diversity and
beauty to his farm."[2]

### Appreciating things unseen

Leopold wrote explicitly about natural aesthetic value in his classic, *A Sand County Almanac.*

Leopold's land aesthetic, like his land ethic, is derived from evolutionary and ecological biology. Earlier theories of natural aesthetics
were also associated with larger complexes of ideas. Landscape archi-
tecture during the European Enlightenment, formalism, was based
upon Euclidean geometry and associated with the mechanistic model
of nature.[3] The natural aesthetic still popular today—the scenic or
picturesque aesthetic—originated with the romantic movement.[4] The
scenic natural aesthetic idolizes essentially alpine *vistas*—mountain
peaks, valleys, waterfalls, and the like. It was best expressed in this
country by the writings of John Muir and the landscape painting of

Thomas Cole and the Hudson River School.

Leopold's land aesthetic, on the other hand, recognizes the beauty of neglected natural environments. It emphasizes less the directly visible, scenic aspects of nature and more the conceptual—diversity, complexity, species rarity, species interactions, nativity, phylogenetic antiquity—the aspects of nature revealed by evolutionary and ecological natural history.

Leopold remarks that "our ability to perceive quality in nature begins, as in art, with the pretty." Examples of pretty landscapes might be golf links, Kentucky bluegrass horse farms enclosed by white fences, and the like. "It proceeds through successive stages of the beautiful"— let's say, for example, the Yosemite Valley, the Grand Canyon, sequoia groves, etc.—"to values as yet uncaptured by language."[5] Leopold then goes on to capture, in his own compact, descriptive prose, the beauty in a landscape that the conventional scenic natural aesthetic finds plain, if not odious: a crane marsh.

He draws an analogy to art appreciation. Among gallery-goers there are also those whose taste is limited to the pretty—to naive, realistic still life or portrait painting, for example. Then there are those capable of appreciating successive stages of the beautiful present in "fine art," whether pretty or not. And finally there are serious and studied aesthetes who are alert to values beyond the beautiful: such subtler aesthetic qualities in painting are composition, color combination, technique, expression, humor, historical allusion, and so forth. It is the same with land: to get beyond the pretty and the beautiful requires some *cultivation* of sensibility. One must *acquire* "a refined taste in natural objects":

> The taste for country displays the same diversity in aesthetic competence among individuals as the taste for opera, or oils. There are those who are willing to be herded in droves through "scenic" places: who find mountains grand if they be proper mountains with waterfalls, cliffs, and lakes. To such the Kansas plains are tedious.[6]

For Leopold the Kansas plains are aesthetically exciting less for what is directly seen than for what is *known* of their history and biology. "They see the endless corn, but not the heave and the grunt of ox teams breaking the prairie ... They look at the low horizon, but they cannot see it, as de Vaca did, under the bellies of the buffalo."[7]

In "Marshland Elegy" Leopold beautifully illustrates the impact of an evolutionary understanding on perception. Wisconsin's first settlers called sandhill cranes "red shitepokes" for the rusty clay stain their "battleship gray" feathers acquire in summer.[8] Like Daniel Boone, who "saw only the surface of things," the Wisconsin homesteaders saw red shitepokes as merely large birds in the way of farm progress. But evolutionary literacy can alter and deepen perception:

> Our appreciation of the crane grows with the slow unraveling of earthly history. His tribe, we now know, stems out of the remote Eocene. The other members of the fauna in which he originated are long since entombed within the hills. When we hear his call we hear no mere bird. He is the symbol of our untamable past, of that incredible sweep of millenia which underlies the daily affairs of birds and men.[9]

Ecology, as Leopold pictures it, is the biological science that runs at right angles to evolutionary biology. Evolution lends to perception a certain depth, "that incredible sweep of millennia," while ecology provides it with breadth. Wild things do not exist in isolation from one another. They are "interlocked in one humming community of co-operations and competitions, one biota.[10] Hence the crane confers "a paleontological patent of nobility" on its marshy habitat.[11] We cannot love cranes and hate marshes. The marsh itself is now transformed by the presence of cranes from a "waste," "God-forsaken" mosquito swamp, into a thing of precious beauty.

Ecology, history, paleontology, and geology each penetrate the surface of direct sensory experience and supply substance to scenery. The romantic, scenic aesthetic, by comparison with the ecological land aesthetic, is superficial and uninformed. "In country . . . a plain exterior often conceals hidden riches."[12] To get at these hidden riches takes more than a gaze through a car window. To promote appreciation of nature is "a job not of building roads into lovely country, but of building receptivity into the still unlovely human mind."[13]

## The Physics of Beauty

The general emphasis of Leopold's land aesthetic is on what has been called "biological literacy." In addition, Leopold formulated a quite specialized and somewhat technical natural aesthetic category: the *noumenon*. Here is how he introduces the term in *A Sand County Almanac:*

> The physics of beauty is one department of natural science still in the Dark Ages. Not even the manipulators of bent space have tried to solve its equations. Everybody knows, for example, that the autumn landscape in the north woods is the land, plus a red maple, plus a ruffed grouse. In terms of conventional physics, the grouse represents

only a millionth of either the mass or the energy of an acre. Yet subtract the grouse and the whole thing is dead. An enormous amount of some kind of motive power has been lost.

It is easy to say that the loss is all in our mind's eye, but is there any sober ecologist who will agree? He knows full well that there has been an ecological death, the significance of which is inexpressible in terms of contemporary science. A philosopher has called this imponderable essence the *noumenon* of material things. It stands in contradistinction to *phenomenon,* which is ponderable and predictable, even to the tossings and turnings of the remotest star.

The grouse is the noumenon of the north woods, the blue jay of the hickory groves, the whiskey-jack of the muskegs, the piñonero of the juniper foothills. . . .[14]

And one could go on: the cutthroat trout of high mountain streams, the sandhill crane of northern bogs and marshes, the prong-horn antelope of the high plains, the alligator of southeastern swamps. These noumena might be called, more precisely though less arrest-ingly, "aesthetic indicator species." They supply the hallmark, the imprimatur to their respective ecological communities. If they are missing, then the rosy glow of perfect health is absent from the land-scape. Like the elusive mountain lion and timber wolf, they need not be seen to grace and enliven the countryside. It is enough merely to *know* that they are present.

## Trade-offs of progress

The prevailing pre-Darwinian natural aesthetic, the scenic or pic-turesque aesthetic, frames nature, as it were, and deposits it in gal-leries—the national parks—for most ordinary folk, far from home. We herd in droves to Yellowstone, Yosemite, and the Smokies to gaze at natural beauty and, home again, ignore or despise the river bottoms, fallow fields, bogs, and ponds on the back forty. The land aesthetic enables us to mine the hidden riches of the ordinary. It ennobles the commonplace. It brings natural beauty literally home from the hills.

Natural beauty, therefore, might become a new farm product for home consumption. Most farmers I talk with tell me they farm for reasons that go beyond profits. Among the noneconomic reasons I hear most frequently expressed are being "your own boss," getting "plenty of fresh air and sunshine," doing "honest work" in an environment fostering "traditional family values." These are all psychic-spiritual rewards. Another reason for preferring rural to urban life could be the natural aesthetic stimulation of the agrarian landscape.

For better or worse, the trend in agriculture is toward increased mechanization accompanied by a consequent diminution in all the values of rural life *except* profits. Leopold comments that a gradual, insidious mechanization has spoiled the satisfactions of hunting particularly and outdoor recreation in general.[15]

The same phenomenon has perhaps also eroded the noneconomic satisfactions of farming. Chemical pesticides and herbicides have made the environment less healthful. Heavy machinery has reduced back-breaking labor, but at the price of making farm work no less tedious and not much different than factory work. Woodlots, wetlands, and wildlife are just relic curiosities, like the yokes and harnesses hanging in a dark corner of the barn. Kitchen gardens, brood hens, porkers, beefers, milk cows, berry patches, beehives, sugar bushes, and orchards are all inefficient, uneconomical, and time-consuming sources of foods. It is certainly easier and often cheaper for the farmer to get his groceries, like everyone else, at the supermarket. The typical farm and suburban households today differ only in driving time to the nearest shopping mall. Perhaps *quality* of life is the trade-off for efficiency.

The new humane, environmental, and conservation *ethics* would impose new obligations and restraints on the hapless farmer. In my area, central Wisconsin, farming has been revolutionized recently by center-pivot irrigation. Blonde sands in the outwash plain of the Valders incursion of the Wisconsin glacier once barely supported modest herds of dairy cows. They now produce, with the help of fertilizer, fossil fuels, and a vast subsurface aquifer, a virtually hydroponic cash crop of potatoes, green beans, peas, and corn. With the new profits and prosperity have come aerial spraying of pesticides, fungicides, and herbicides, clearing of woodlots and windbreaks, draining of wetlands, and aldicarb in well water.

Environmentalists expect the farmer to subsidize public health. Conservationists expect him to subsidize wildlife (and open his land to public hunting). And animal libbers expect him to subsidize their tender sensibilities. Many farmers are understandably angry. Their overhead and taxes go up while prices for their products go down. Adding insult to injury, they are asked to make costly changes in their method of production for the sake of everyone else's quality of life.

The land ethic and its more recent academic derivatives emphasize the negative. They are a new set of "thou shalt nots."[16] An ethic, indeed, by its very definition, according to Leopold, is constraining—"a limitation on freedom of action in the struggle for existence." The land *aesthetic*, on the other hand, emphasizes the positive. It emphasizes the *private*, not the public, *benefits* of both conservation and environmental quality. Leopold illustrated this point with the following anecdote.

> One Saturday night not long ago, two middle-aged farmers set the alarm clock for a dark hour of what proved to be a snowy, blowy Sunday. Milking over, they jumped into a pickup and sped for the sand counties of central Wisconsin, a region productive of tax deeds, tamaracks, and wild hay. In the evening they returned with a truck full of young tamarack trees and a heart full of high adventure. The last tree was planted in the home marsh by lantern-light. There was still the milking.
>
> In Wisconsin "man bites dog" is stale news compared with "farmer plants tamarack." Our farmers have been grubbing, burning, draining, and chopping tamarack since 1840. In the region where these farmers live the tree is exterminated. Why then should they want to replace it? Because after twenty years they hope to reintroduce spagnum moss under the grove, and then lady's-slippers, pitcher plants, and the other nearly extinct wildflowers of the aboriginal Wisconsin bogs.
>
> No extension bureau had offered these farmers any prize for this utterly quixotic undertaking. Certainly no hope of gain motivated it. How then can one interpret its meaning? I call it Revolt—revolt against the tedium of the merely economic attitude toward land. We assume that because we had to subjugate the land to live on it, the best farm is therefore the one most completedly tamed. These two farmers have learned from experience that the wholly tamed farm offers not only a slender livelihood but a constricted life. They have caught the idea that there is pleasure to be had in raising wild crops as well as tame ones. They propose to devote a little spot of marsh to growing native wildflowers. Perhaps they wish for their land what we all wish for our children—not only a chance to make a living but also a chance to express and develop a rich and varied assortment of inherent capabilities, both wild and tame. What better expresses land than the plants that originally grew on it?

## Rewards, not restrictions

The land aesthetic cannot redress, at least not directly, all the environmental ills of modern agriculture. Excessive nitrates and dangerous levels of chemical pesticides in groundwaters are problems with essentially agronomic, not aesthetic, solutions. The same may be said of the problems of soil erosion and sedimentation of surface waters.

The land aesthetic, rather, is addressed more directly to the subtle but pervasive problem of rural biological impoverishment.

Wildlife and the native flora are being crowded out by a variety of human activities, agriculture among them. Some species are being displaced to the point of local extirpation in many areas. And some species, like the black-footed ferret, the prairie grouse, and the Furbish lousewort, are threatened with total extinction. It is certainly debatable, but the extreme loss of biotic diversity and complexity is perhaps more insidious than chemical pollution or soil erosion. The latter are reversible processes, but, as the saying goes, "extinction is forever."

The land aesthetic calls attention to the psychic-spiritual *rewards* of maintaining the biological integrity and diversity of the rural landscape. The integration into the farmstead of natural biotic communities, with their full complement of characteristic species, provides color, interest, variety, diversion, excitement, sport, and dietary variety for the farm family that gauges its wealth by these standards as well as by those usual in the marketplace.

The addition of noneconomic values into the calculation of wealth inherent in the land aesthetic might even *indirectly* help to solve soil erosion and water pollution problems. By emphasizing noneconomic values, the land aesthetic helps to expand our concept of quality of life. The distinct rewards of rural life can be completed and perfected only when a lasting partnership with the land is worked out. The land aesthetic could be a first step toward that ideal.

### The good old days again?

Leopold died in 1948. Since then, things have changed. Farming is not what it used to be. It has become agribusiness. It is as competitive as any other industry (perhaps more so). What two farmers in revolt did in Leopold's day may no longer be possible in present circumstances. Competition drives agribusinessmen to turn a profit from every acre. Woodlots, tamarack-spagnum bogs, marsh hay, deer beds, tall-grass prairies, and trout streams are a luxury today's agribusinessmen may simply be unable to afford.

One proof that farmstead conservation is affordable for the average farmer is that an average farmer can, in fact, afford it. It is fundamentally a question of preference, not of economics. Would you rather eat store-bought or homegrown? Would you rather rise to roosters crowing and birds singing or to the alarm clock? Do you want to have woods for your children to play in or roller rinks? Would you rather provide your family with the chance to see woodcock, prairie grouse, and muskrat or more Disneylands and movies? Would you like to look at the sky from your tractor seat and see an occasional hawk and heron or just powerlines and crop dusters?

I would have been inclined to acquiesce to the argument that farmstead diversity and beauty are now unaffordable, if I were not acquainted with a latter-day farmer in revolt against agrarian impoverishment (in the larger sense of the word). My farmer friend, Justin Isherwood, is a modern, big-time agribusinessman. He, his father, and two brothers grow 600 or 700 acres of potatoes, corn, and other cash crops by modern, mechanical methods. They make a good living. Still they are able to keep more than 200 acres of woods and swamp out of production, because they like woods and wildlife. And, too, they get their fuelwood and some sawlogs out of them.

Justin's house is set in a sugar bush, and he makes 40 or 50 gallons of maple syrup every spring before planting—not because he can't buy Aunt Jemima, but because he prefers pure maple and enjoys sugaring. Instead of going bowling he and his family go berry-picking. In preference to Monday-night football, farmer Isherwood makes elderberry, blackberry, and dandelion wine down cellar. His wife, Lynn, grows a quarter-acre kitchen garden. They keep chickens. She cans, dries, pickles, and freezes the surplus. Supper at the Isherwood's is an object lesson in stylish subsistence. Everything is homegrown or homemade. The chicken is tougher, but tastier. The wine murker, but also headier. The potatoes are the farm product. The pickled green tomatoes have no taint of monosodium glutamate. The ice cream, which you have worked for yourself, seems sweeter for the effort—sweeter still, drenched in maple syrup, glistening with crisp spring sunshine.

I have visited the magical Isherwood woods. Its soils are low and damp. They support oak, maple, aspen, basswood, ash, and a comparable variety of softwoods. The mature canopy keeps the second growth widely spaced, straight, and wiry. The matted carpet of damp detritus is broken by fiddlehead ferns, raspberry briers, skunk cabbage, marsh marigold, and trillium. It is big enough for a farm boy to explore new continents haunted by strange natives. And after the onset of adolescence (and a smattering of Emerson, Thoreau, and Muir) the same farm boy may await his religious experience sitting against the broad trunk of a great white pine, basking in the warmth of the slanting October sun, surrounded by the "psalm-singing" hardwoods.

Practically every other agribusinessman in the "golden sands" (the name once referred to the color of the poor soil of the outwash plain—now it means something else) has cut his woods to make more field to grow more potatoes, to bank more profits. But what about the trade-off? How can kids be pioneers in a potato patch or form a conception of divinity by contemplating an irrigation rig? Leopold asks:

> Is it profitable for the individual to build a beautiful home? To give his children a higher education? No it is seldom profitable, yet we do both. These are in fact ethical and aesthetic premises which underlie the economic system....
>
> It of course goes without saying that economic feasibility limits the tether on what can or cannot be done for land. It always has and it always will. The fallacy the economic determinists have tied around our collective necks is the belief that economics determines *all* land use. This is simply not true. An innumerable host of actions and attitudes, comprising perhaps the bulk of all land relations, is determined by the land-users' tastes and predilections, rather than purse.[18]

For natural aesthetic tastes and predilections to become refined, is it necessary that the farmer take a Ph.D. in natural history? Refined taste in natural things is as much an intellectual as an emotional and sensory accomplishment. It is, therefore, partly a product of education. But overeducation, as Leopold remarks, can be as deadening as undereducation.[19]

Agribusinessmen and women are just as smart and just as well educated as businessmen and women in any industry. To stay afloat in a competitive, sophisticated industry, they have to be. Native intelligence, a general liberal education, and innate common sense and intuition are more than enough ingredients to make for good land aesthetics. Moreover, agrarian traditions of self-sufficiency and abundant subsistence, with the agrarian diversification and conservancy they imply, supply a supporting heritage of ways and means.

Because beautiful land and its psychic rewards are not consumable industrial products, they are not pushed by Madison Avenue advertising. Agrarian landowners, like everyone else, are sold instead hollow mechanical pleasures, passive entertainment, and nutrition-poor convenience foods. A counter-advertising campaign as well as an ecological education and a recollection of the good old days may be needed for the agrarian landowner to reap the aesthetic harvest for home consumption that his uncultivated land is capable of producing.

# 14

## Moral Considerability and Extraterrestrial Life

### I

Let me first ask what extraterrestrial life is and then go on to ask upon what conceptual foundations its moral considerability may be based.

In the still-vital mythic human mind of the present age, the Space Age as it is often called, space exploration is portrayed essentially as a geometric and technological projection of the European expeditions to the New World in the fifteenth, sixteenth, and seventeenth centuries just as those explorations were mythically portrayed by the explorers themselves and their contemporaries in terms of still earlier paradigms.[1] Columbus, Cortez, and De Soto saw themselves as knights embarked upon a quest—if not for the Holy Grail, then for the fabulous wealth of the Orient, the Fountain of Youth, or the lost Eden. They traversed a relatively vast ocean in relatively primitive and puny craft. The bold imagination and heroic temerity of the discoverers paid off, though not in terms of what they themselves actually sought. In fact they found vast new lands, populated by exotic flora and fauna and strange human beings. The fabulous medieval-biblical mythic portrayal of the discovery of the New World eventually gave way to the pedestrian reality of conquest, colonization, domestication, exploitation, and intercontinental commerce.

Today we see interplanetary space as a larger, emptier ocean, our current spacecraft as the Nina, Pinta, and Santa Maria and the planets as so many new continents. We expect to find no fountains of youth, cities of gold, or Edenic paradises (silly illusions of a bygone age) on Venus, Mars, or the moons of Jupiter and Saturn, but we do seriously entertain the expectation of farming, mining, and colonizing our Sun's planets or those of some other star. We project routine transport and commerce between worlds.[2] Why? Partly just because we can, or think we can, but more practically because we must if our civilization is to

249

have the resources and the real estate to continue to grow. Just like Europeans of the previous centuries who, after overpopulating Europe and overtaxing the natural resources of that continent, moved their operations to the Americas and Australia and so avoided the consequences, we will, upon overpopulating and exhausting Earth's resources, move our operations to new New Worlds with the same impunity.

I personally regard the prevailing notions of routine space travel and extraterrestrial resource and real-estate development with their implicit supposition of a throwaway Earth as illusions no less vacuous and no less potentially tragic than those of the most extravagant Spanish conquistadores.[3] The reality our adventures in space will disclose, I predict—and the sooner we realize it the better—is that we are, for all practical purposes, Earth-bound. Human life is evolved from, specifically adapted to, presently embedded in, integrated with, and utterly dependent upon the exact and unimaginably complex physical, chemical, and biological conditions of the planet Earth. The realization and affirmation of our earthiness, our inseparability from the Earth, should be, and hopefully soon will be, the biggest payoff of space exploration. Europeans readily adapted North America to European patterns of settlement, methods of agriculture, and manufacturing. South America and Australia have been somewhat less tractable. Humans will not find the Sun's other planets even remotely so hospitable and submissive.[4] And interstellar exploration, discovery, and colonization is, as I shall explain, ruled out by the limitations of physical laws, the statistical improbability of Earthlike planets in accessible regions of the galaxy, and the sheer immensities of cosmic spatio-temporal dimensions in proportion to the relatively brief duration of a human lifetime.

I begin with this prevailing contemporary mythic representation of space travel and planetary exploration as a projection of earlier ocean navigation and continental exploration, because I believe it substantially shapes our uncritical expectation of what it would mean to find and interact with extraterrestrial life. In the most puerile and jejune science fiction—the pervasive popularity of which suggests, however, an implicit general credulity of its structural premises—our "starships" (with such revealing names as *Enterprise*) island-hop among an archipelago of planets inhabited by only slightly strange-looking *people* in futuristic get-ups, or in period costumes as the case may be. These planets and their unfortunate populations are often ruled by merciless, unearthly Oriental potentates or beautiful, but bad, Eurasian seductresses. Our guys vanquish theirs and thus help make the universe safe for democracy and for either native or colonial bourgeois developers and entrepreneurs.

But these silly fantasies occur only in the Buck Rogers, Flash Gordon, Star Trek, and Star Wars type of science fiction, don't they? They also occur in the supposedly more sophisticated specimens of the genre, of which *Dune* is the most celebrated representative.[5] What is more astonishing and irresponsible, since it is not represented as science fiction but as science per se, is that equally fantastic notions are rife at the highest levels of scientific inquiry into the possibility of extraterrestrial life. Notice how A. Thomas Young, formerly Deputy Director of NASA's Ames Research Center and later Director of Goddard Space Flight Center, conflates life with human life:

> We know of only one existence of life in the universe—that being ourselves on planet Earth. We know that our Earth is an enormously small part of our Universe. A perplexing question evolves as to whether life abounds [in the universe] or are we unique.[6]

Actually, it is most probably the case both that we—human beings— are unique and that life abounds elsewhere in the universe. Young seems not only not to have thought of this possibility, but he gives no thought either to the ten to thirty million other species that with us comprise life on this planet. The explanation for this omission, I conjecture, lies probably in Young's participation in the now-obsolete mechanistic world view pioneered by Descartes, whose conceptual segregation of living mankind from merely mechanical plants and animals has been compounded by subsequent militant humanism and human technological self-insulation from nature.

John A. Billingham, Chief of the Extraterrestrial Research Division of NASA's Ames Research Center, acknowledges the possible existence of other-than-human extraterrestrial life but seems to think of it as it may exist on other worlds only as the staging ground for the organic evolution of humanoid intelligence and, upon that, the cultural evolution of "technological civilizations." Writes Billingham:

> Modern astrophysical theory predicts that planets are the rule rather than the exception. Planets are therefore likely to number in the hundreds of billions in our Galaxy alone. Given a suitable location and environment for any single planet, current theories of chemical evolution predict that life will begin. And given a period of billions of years of comparative stability life will sometimes evolve to the stage of intelligence. The next step may be the emergence of a technological civilization, and it is possible that civilizations may be in communication with each other.[7]

If so, of course, we want to be in on the fun.

In the face of this sort of giddy enthusiasm for communicating with "intelligent life" on other planets, it is both sobering and irritating to observe that those involved in SETI, the search for extraterrestrial intelligence, have not first established—as a kind of preliminary benchmark or data base, so that they would have some idea of what communicating with an exotic intelligence would be like—communication with nonhuman forms of intelligent life on Earth. Cetaceans carry the biggest brains on this planet, with richly fissured cerebral cortexes and a brain-to-body weight ratio comparable to that of humans.[8] Like us they are social mammals. But they live in an environment, relatively speaking, very different from ours. Hence, theirs is a world apart from ours, a terrestrial analogue of an extraterrestrial environment. And they engage, apparently, in complex vocal communication, of which we to date understand not one word—or rather click, grunt, or whistle.[9] What this omission reveals is not only an arrogant disregard for nonhuman terrestrial intelligence; it also clearly shows that by extraterrestrial intelligence those involved in SETI mean something very like, if not identical to, human intelligence.

The distinguished Harvard astrophysicist Eric J. Chaisson takes us from Billingham's idle but relatively modest proposal—to search the skies in hopes of eavesdropping on the interstellar communications of extraterrestrial technological civilizations—to the stock, infantile, science-fiction fantasies of universal conquest and dominion. Chaisson points out that in the moments following the big bang, radiation dominated matter and then, after a relatively short time, matter became predominant over energy. Now, listen to what will follow this:

> One thing seems certain [certain?!]: we on Earth, as well as other intelligent life forms throughout the Universe, are now participating in a fantastically important [fantastic, indeed!] transformation—the second most important transformation in the history of the Universe. ...Matter is now losing its total dominance, at least in those isolated locations where technologically intelligent life resides....Together with our galactic neighbors, should there be any, we may be in a position some day to gain control of the resources of much of the Universe, rearchitecturing it to suit our purposes, and in a very real sense, ensuring for our civilization a measure of immortality.[10]

One wants to know how it is possible for these scientists to say such things among their colleagues and maintain their professional credibility. Some might contend that Young, Billingham, Chaisson, Carl Sagan, and others who write in a similar vein do so deliberately to pander to our vanities of glory and greed in order to dupe us into allocating public funds to finance their very expensive but very speculative research and development projects. Without the prospect of rearchitecturing the universe and ensuring ourselves a measure of immortality, public support for astrophysics, exobiology, and NASA might dry up. But I just cannot bring myself to believe that such simple, base, and cynical motives are really the explanation.

I rather think that what we find here is a sincere and not uncommon mixture of science and myth. In addition to the mythic projection into outer space of the heroic adventures of Renaissance European mariners and the complementary post-Renaissance doctrines of mechanism and humanism, we can identify several deeper strata of obsolete dogma, in these conceptual core samples, mined from past Western culture. Oparine and Fessenkov have identified one key element— essentially a residue of Aristotelian and Thomistic teleology—namely, the belief that somehow we ourselves, intelligent (human) life, are the *telos*, the goal of God's creation now transposed into the (no doubt divinely planned and directed) evolution of the universe.[11] Hence, given the spatio-temporal vastness of the universe, it would be surprising, indeed, if nature did not at every suitable location achieve its natural purpose: us or something very like us—intelligent (humanoid) life.

In addition to the tendency to assume that the probable existence of life on other worlds must eventuate in human or humanlike intelligent life, there is the tendency to assume that human or humanlike intelligent life on other planets will inevitably be culturally similar to twentieth-century Western civilization or some more "advanced" version of the same. The myth of teleological organic evolution is compounded, in other words, by the myth of teleological cultural evolution. The theoretical paradigm of teleological cultural development is E. B. Tylor's Victorian anthropological scenario—according to which mankind began its tenure on Earth in a state of abject "savagery," progressed through "barbarism," and arrived at last at a state of civilization (of which, of course, Anglo-American civilization is the most perfect stage)—now, in the inevitable course of things, become technological.[12]

One thing we can be sure of, I suggest in sum, is that extraterrestrial life, if found at all, will not be found to be anything resembling human life. The embarrassingly wide supposition to the contrary seems attributable to unconscious residues of earlier Western religious and philosophical notions of teleological evolution, both natural and cultural, to Western religious and philosophical humanism, to Western cultural chauvinism, and to an uncritical extraterrestrial extrapolation of recent terrestrial history. Furthermore, to the extent that the hypotheses of the existence of "intelligent" extraterrestrial life and extraterrestrial "technological civilization" are either defined or tacitly understood in anthropomorphic terms (and how else could they be defined or understood?), we can also be confident that such life does not exist beyond Earth.

Anthropologist C. Owen Lovejoy has elegantly and authoritatively summed up the case against the existence of extraterrestrial humans (and with it intelligent, technological, anthropomorphic civilzations) as follows:

> Man is a highly specific, unique, and, unduplicated species. If we wish to make probability estimates of the likelihood that cognitive ...life has evolved on other suitable planets, the simplest and most direct question we may pose is: What is the probability that cognitive life would evolve on *this* planet, were not man already a constituent of its biosphere? From what we know of the human evolutionary pathway and of the critical elements that have directed it, the odds against its reexpression are indeed remote, if not astronomical. ...What is the probability that any named species, be it mammal, reptile, or mollusk, would evolve again on this planet [let alone some other]? ... I think it is quite reasonable to suppose that despite the immensity of the known Universe, the specificity of the physiostructure of any organism is so great and its immensely complex pathway of progression so ancient that such probabilities are simply infinitesimal.[13]

Thus not only is it very unlikely that there are any other people out there, and, in the absence of people or people-like creatures, any other "technological civilizations" (not to mention how unlikely it is that even if there were humanlike extraterrestrials, their cultural sequence would duplicate the Western model and culminate in a technological civilization); it is also, by exactly the same evolutionary-ecological reasoning, very unlikely that there are any Earthlike species whatever on other planets. It is therefore unlikely that there are—and almost a certainty that we shall never find—Earthlike planets uninhabited by humanlike creatures (analogous to lush, uninhabited tropical islands in the contemporary mythic mind), that is, planets with familiar species (minus *Homo sapiens*) interacting in familiar ecological patterns, on which we might establish colonies.

## II

Having thus dispelled the science-fiction aura from the question, what is extraterrestrial life? Let us consider a less fictional, more scientific approach to its answer.

Biology, the science of life, has been heretofore confined to the study of terrestrial life. Unlike physics and chemistry, which are, historically, cosmic in scope and compass, biology is a local science.[14] Therefore, to the extent that life is a well-defined scientific term in biology (the science of life, which has so far been limited to a study of terrestrial life), the very concept of extraterrestrial life is problematic, even paradoxical.

However, there is a certain unity in the sciences generally and, more particularly, a continuity between chemistry and biology, both historically (or evolutionarily) and conceptually (or theoretically). Life on Earth, in other words, evolved upon a chemical base, and, as systematic conceptual constructs, organic chemistry and biology are bridged by biochemistry. Life, therefore, may be generically characterized without prejudice to its location or accidental specificity.[15]

Yale biophysicist Harold Morowitz has provided, in the concept of *negentropy*, perhaps the most general parameters for exobiology:

> Life as we know it . . . is not a property of the universe as a whole, but of planetary surfaces. These surfaces are not at equilibrium . . . because they constantly receive radiant energy from their central star and reradiate energy to outer space. . . . Therefore . . . the molecular organization of planetary surfaces, which we know as evolution involves no violation of thermodynamic principles.[16]

As Morowitz points out, however, the concept of life involves something more than mere molecular order that every planetary surface would, to one degree or another, exhibit. Self-organization (growth and development) and self-replication (reproduction) are, perhaps, the most general characteristics of a minimally "living" concatenation of molecules.[17]

We might also wish to add self-disintegration (death), if self-organization and self-replication themselves would not quickly end in self-stultification. Self-disintegration or death, in other words, seems to be a condition for the indefinite duration of self-organization and self-replication.

A planetary surface on which there existed growing, reproducing, and dying complex molecular structures would also be one on which there could occur natural selection, evolutionary elaboration, and ecosystemic complication and integration.[18]

If we go further and require that a properly living structure be cellular, with a membrane and well-articulated nucleus, we would almost certainly price ourselves out of the solar system. Such life would be possible only on a liquid-water planet, and the only such planet in the solar system is the Earth.

The remarkable bonding properties of carbon provide the most general chemical basis for the emergence and evolution of the complex self-organizing and self-replicating structures on Earth. But even to define life in terms of hydrocarbon polymers may be too restrictive. As early as 1940, English astronomer H. Spencer Jones pointed out that in certain extraterrestrial environments silicon could play a role similar to the role of carbon on Earth.[19] Life on other planets, particularly on other planets in our solar system, then, if it exists at all, may not only be rudimentary or primitive; it may be, depending upon how generous we wish to be with the concept of life, based upon an altogether different biochemistry than life as we know it on Earth.

### III

Ethics is more a normative than a descriptive study of human behavior. That is, in ethics we want to know less how people *might* than how they *should* or *ought to* act, do, treat, or live. The sense of *norm* in *normative* is not the sense of norm in the vulgar meaning of *normal*—that is, average, mean, lowest common denominator. Rather, *norm* in *normative* (and in the medical meaning of *normal*) connotes a benchmark, a standard, an ideal.

The *ethical* question at the heart of this essay is how to treat extraterrestrial life—if there is any and if we ever find any. As an ethicist, I am not competent to predict how we will in fact treat extraterrestrial life if and when we encounter it. However, as it seems to me, an untrained observer, the human track record—average, or in that sense, normal human behavior—does not bode well for any extraterrestrial life unfortunate enough to be discovered by us. I am not at all sure that, as an ethicist, I can even address with confidence the question how we *ought to* treat extraterrestrial life. The question is made remote and speculative by two general uncertainties, one metaethical, the other epistemic.

Firstly, while today almost everyone of sound mind and good will agrees that *human* life without qualification is the subject of unambiguous and incontrovertible moral concern, there is by no means general agreement that other-than-human *terrestrial* life should be the subject of a similar concern. The suggestion that other-than-human terrestrial life possesses moral value—value, that is, apart from its utility to serve human ends—is greeted at best with skeptical indulgence and at worst with impatient ridicule, not only by popular moralists and their constituents, but more especially by mainstream Western moral philosophers.[20] In the prevailing contemporary ethical climate, the hypothesis

that we might even entertain just the possibility of human moral obligations to *extra*terrestrial life, assuming that it is not anthropomorphic,
therefore will likely be regarded as so absurd as to be beneath contempt.[21] Animal liberation/rights moral philosophers, who attempt to
extend moral considerability to a narrow range of our closest terrestrial
nonhuman relatives, are by their own estimation at the leading edge of
ethical theory and, by the estimation of their mainstream philosophical
critics, muddled sentimentalists.[22]

The chilly reception greeting even such comparatively modest
proposals as animal welfare ethics for a more generous and expansive
provision of moral considerability for nonhuman life forms cannot be
attributed simply to the churlishness and/or niggardliness of reactionary guardians of the Western moral tradition. Rather, Western
moral thought from Plato and St. Paul to Tillich and Hare provides few
conceptual resources to underwrite theoretically such generosity of
spirit and to effect rigorously such an expansion. But a more embracing
ethic, to be a proper ethic, must have a sound conceptual basis and
logical rigor, and it must somehow connect with historical moral
theory. A life-centered—a literally biocentric—ethic discontinuous
with traditional moral philosophy would not be recognizable as a
species of ethics, and so could not be seriously entertained or critically
appraised.

Secondly, not only is the very concept of extraterrestrial life problematic—because of the aforementioned local character of biology—
but a critical exploration of the hypothesis that extraterrestrial life
exists leads to an even more confounding paradox. Venus and Mars,
the most likely planetary hosts for extraterrestrial life in our solar
system, have been visited by unpeopled probes with disappointing
results.[23] If life, however broadly defined, does not exist in the solar
system—and it now seems more probable that it does not than that it
does—may we suppose that it exists in the galaxy of which our solar
system is a member?[24]

We know that our galaxy alone contains literally billions of stars.
Thus, if our star, the Sun, is not unique or especially extraordinary in
possessing a family of planets, and if we assume that life (defined so as
not to be conceptually too terramorphic) is a natural, perhaps inevitable, stage in the progressive ordering of mature, suitably endowed and
situated planetary surfaces, then the probability that extraterrestrial
life exists in our galaxy beyond our solar system approaches unity and,
thus, certainty.

But what of our chances to positively or empirically confirm this
convincing a priori argument? Our spiral galaxy, the Milky Way, is on
the average approximately 100,000 light years wide and 5,000 light

years thick.[25] Exobiologist Valdemar Firsoff estimates there to be about two life-supporting planets per million cubic light years.[26] Let us now imagine ourselves actually setting out to find the other life-supporting planet in our million-cubic-light-year district. It ought to be only forty to sixty light years away.

The speed of light, however, is a limiting velocity—nothing can exceed it. And only particles of zero rest mass can actually attain the speed of light. Massy objects like spaceships are limited in principle to several fractional factors less than the speed of light. For purposes of calculating a time-and-energy budget for interstellar space exploration, Hewlett-Packard engineer Bernard Oliver suggests we generously posit a ship speed "far beyond our present technology," of one-fifth the speed of light.[27] At that rate an expedition sent to our nearest stellar neighbor, Alpha Centauri, four light years away, would arrive in twenty years. In the forty-year working lifetime of a highly trained crew only the next closest star beyond Alpha Centauri, regardless of its qualifications, could be visited and examined—and this assumes that our astronauts would be willing never to return home, would be willing to undertake, in effect, a suicide mission.[28] A search of a few more stars might be undertaken in a century by unpeopled probes, depending upon how many we sent and how far away their targets were. What would be the probability of finding in this way the other life-supporting planet in our million-cubic-light-year district in a thousand years or a hundred thousand or a million, and at what expense of energy and other terrestrial resources?[29] My guess is that it would be very small, and prohibitively expensive.

Hence, and here is the epistemological paradox, we may take it as very nearly certain—given our knowledge of the size and stellar population of the galaxy, our understanding of biochemistry and organic evolution, and the reasonable assumption that our solar system is neither unique nor extraordinary—that life abounds in the galaxy. But this knowledge has no, or very nearly no, positive significance or operational translatability. To the extent that scientific epistemology remains positivistic, the seemingly very innocent and reasonable hypothesis that life abounds in the Milky Way turns out to be as scientifically nonsensical as the hypothesis that an electron has both a definite location and a definite velocity. The hypothesis is unverifiable in principle primarily because of the limitations on our autopsy imposed by Einstein's constant $c$, the speed of light, which functions in the large arena of interstellar space somewhat like Planck's constant, $h$, the quantum, in the small arena of subatomic space. An uncertainty principle, in other words, is operative in very large dimensions of space-time as it is in very small, at least in respect to the search for extraterrestrial life.

The metaethical and epistemological uncertainties surrounding the ethical question posed here lead to a third, more practical uncertainty: Can there be, really, any serious justification for this exercise? If animal welfare ethics are controversial, if terrestrial biocentric and ecocentric environmental ethics are contemptuously ignored or ridiculed, isn't the construction of an ethic for the treatment of something we-know-not-what-or-whether-it-may-be more than just a little fatuous?

Right now, right here on Earth, anthropogenic species extinction grinds on at a catastrophic pace.[30] While we are wondering how to treat hypothetical life that may, for better or worse, lie forever beyond our ken, let alone our actions, the life we do partially understand and certainly know to exist is being stamped out—often without notice or comment and with very little remorse or protest—under our noses. Shouldn't we get our intellectual priorities straight, and worry first about the treatment of terrestrial life, which is presently under such extreme and actual duress? Once we've got a persuasive ethic worked out to help address the more pressing real-world problem of wholesale terrestrial biocide, then maybe we can think about how we ought to treat extraterrestrial life—if there is any, if we should recognize it when we see it, and if we should ever encounter it!

I am not convinced by this criticism of the present enterprise, even though I have stated it as strongly as I can. It sounds a lot like the stock liberal diatribe against the Apollo project in the sixties: As a nation, so that argument went, we are allocating huge sums of money to put a man on the Moon, while here on Earth socioeconomic conditions for the urban minority underclasses in affluent America grow daily more desperate, and, in the oppressed and impoverished Third and Fourth Worlds, the "wretched of the Earth" die daily of preventable disease and outright starvation. Shouldn't we put our moral and financial resources to work addressing these earthly social problems before we consider a hollow technological vanity like putting a man on the Moon?

I thought then, and still think now, that even so the Apollo project was morally defensible and economically worthwhile, not so much because of the official rationale—the technical and scientific harvest forthcoming from lunar exploration—but primarily because of the impact of Apollo on human consciousness here on Earth.[31] We have known since the centuries of Copernicus and Galileo that the Earth is a planet and the Moon its satellite. But for one of us to stand on the Moon, look upon a distant Earth, and return to the rest of us photographs of our own small and very precious planet, translated heretofore mere propositional knowledge into palpable human experience. We all participated vicariously in that experience. It was, indeed, a most signal event in the collective mind of mankind. Neil Armstrong was the Archimedes of human consciousness. Given the Moon to stand on, he moved the Earth. His lever was a camera. More than any other single phenomenon, those photographs of a soft, lake-blue planet, coyly swirled about with flouncy clouds, floating in empty space—with the utter desolation of the moonscape in the foreground—precipitated the ecological and environmental decade that immediately followed.[32] The photographs of the Earth taken from the Moon also helped bring to the forefront of social consciousness the concept of universal human community. We could all *see* our world as one. The concept of universal human rights immediately became public-policy rhetoric. We were all fellow citizens of a single small world, fellow passengers with all the other water-planet creatures on what then became spaceship Earth. Our indivisible collective dependency on Earth and its luxuriant life-forms was made poignantly visceral by the empathy we all felt for the ill-fated *Apollo 13* astronauts—their tenuous and precarious existence in space modules and spacesuits—on their desperate journey home to Earth.

The discussion of environmental ethics in the solar system, if not in the cosmos beyond, in a less far-reaching and certainly less dramatic way, might have a similar reflexive impact. To seriously entertain the ethical question, how ought we to treat extraterrestrial life?, may put into proper perspective the more immediate and pressing question, how ought we to treat life on Earth? To entertain a noble moral stance toward extraterrestrial life might help to shame us into taking more seriously a noble moral stance toward terrestrial life. And, as I have elsewhere argued, the Copernican revolution (made palpable by the Apollo project) is as much a conceptual foundation of environmental ethics as the subsequent Darwinian and ecological revolutions in thought.[33] Hence, reminding ourselves from time to time of these larger spatial and temporal parameters may be conceptually important for terrestrial environmental ethics.

And who knows, somewhere in the solar system we just might find some extraterrestrial life. In case we do, it would be better for us, wouldn't it, to be morally prepared for our first close encounter with extraterrestrial life than to shoot first and ask questions later?

Let me conclude these penultimate observations with the following ethical thought experiment. Imagine our astronauts finding something that seems to be more than just a mineral configuration of matter somewhere off the Earth. After performing some tests and consulting some criteria, they determine that they have indeed found extraterrestrial life or "living things." They then systematically eradicate all of it (or them) within reach. There seems to be something morally wrong, with such an act of destruction—something more wrong than if the astronauts had found, say, some interesting patterns etched by solar winds on a planet's lifeless surface and erased them. Let us begin with this hopefully shared moral intuition as a touchstone and ask ourselves why we feel that the former act of otherworldly vandalism would be morally worse than the latter.[34]

## IV

The most popularly known but philosophically least cultivated environmental ethic, the Leopold land ethic, provides little help for conceptually articulating our hopefully shared moral intuition respecting extraterrestrial life. The land ethic conceptually bases moral considerability for Earth's complement of animals, plants, waters, and soils upon evolutionary kinship and ecological community.[35] In other words, the land ethic confers moral standing on terrestrial plants and animals in part because they share with us a common evolutionary heritage. They are "fellow-voyagers ... in the Odyssey of evolution"— indeed, perhaps we and they ultimately evolved from a single parent cell.[36] And Earth's plants and other animals along with the elemental components of Earth's biosphere are all, in Leopold's representation, also presently working members in good standing of Earth's biotic community. That is, terrestrial plants, animals, soils, and waters are ecologically integrated and mutually interdependent. This wholesale symbiosis of Earth's biota, by a moral logic that I have elsewhere elaborated, generates for us, according to Leopold, ethical duties and obligations to the ecosystem as a whole and to its members severally.[37] Extraterrestrial life forms, assuming that they were not of Earthly origin and inoculated somehow on some foreign body, or vice versa, would not be our kin—that is, descendants of a common paleontological parent stock—nor would they be participants in Earth's economy of nature or biotic community. Hence they would lie outside the scope of Leopold's land ethic.

Pursuant to the general reflexive motif of this discussion, the consideration of the moral standing of extraterrestrial life sheds an interesting and very valuable light on Leopold's land ethic. It reveals the limitations of its conceptual foundations and thus highlights and more sharply defines its outlines. With our imaginations limited, as they often are in ethics and more especially in environmental ethics, by terrestrial horizons, Leopold's land ethic, which "enlarges the boundaries of the [biotic/moral] community to include soils, waters, plants, and animals, or collectively: the land," may seem to include everything "under the Sun" and thus to effectively include nothing; to be, in other words, impossibly dilute.[38] However, from the point of view of the Copernican spatio-temporal dimensions of our present discussion—the solar system, the galaxy, and the universe at large—the land ethic seems almost parochial in extent and even tribal in nature because it restricts itself to local—that is, terrestrial—beings, and rests their moral value on kinship and mutual dependency. The very failure of the land ethic to provide moral considerability for extraterrestrial life reveals at once its strength for Earth-oriented environmental ethics—which is of course the only variety of environmental ethics with any genuine practical interest or application.

The land ethic, thus, could fairly be called a case of Earth chauvinism or terrestrialism. But unlike male chauvinism and racism, the land ethic is not anti-anything—extraterrestrial life in this case. It would not, in other words, encourage or necessarily sanction the suppression, enslavement, or destruction of extraterrestrial life. The land ethic simply has nothing to say about extraterrestrial life. If pressed to respond to the possibility that extraterrestrial life may exist in the solar system, that it may be found by human beings, and that it may be affected by human actions, an exponent of the land ethic might suggest that something analogous to diplomatic relations between autonomous and independent gens would be implied by it. But such an extension of the land ethic to moral problems with which it was not designed to deal is too speculative to matter to be pursued with confidence.

The advent and academic notoriety of the animal liberation/rights ethics set in motion an intellectual dialectic that led to the development of an apparently novel life-principle ethic by Kenneth Goodpaster, building on suggestions of Joel Feinberg, and a revival of interest in Albert Schweitzer's popularly known reverence-for-life ethic.[39]

Animal liberationist Peter Singer argued that animals ought to be extended the same moral consideration as people because animals have the same capacity as people for suffering.[40] For Singer, sentiency, the capacity to experience pleasure and pain, should be the criterion for the moral considerability of beings.[41]

As this is obviously an inadequate basis for an environmental ethic, since most environmental entities are not sentient—all forms of plant life, for example, and many kinds of animals are not—Goodpaster attempted to extend Singer's moral logic a step further.[42] Sentiency, he argued, ought not to be the criterion for moral considerability, because sentiency exists in some beings only as a means to another end—life.[43] Life, therefore, being the end in reference to which sentiency evolved as a means, ought to be the characteristic in reference to which moral considerability should be conferred.

As I have elsewhere pointed out, Goodpaster's life-principle ethic and Schweitzer's reverence-for-life ethic, though they differ primarily in vocabulary, rhetoric, and historical resonance, have in the abstract a common metaethical foundation.[44] In the last analysis, both defend the moral considerability of living beings because they are conative (a capacity logically parallel to sentiency).

The Goodpaster life-principle and Schweitzer reverence-for-life ethics urge that we extend moral considerability to (and/or reverence for, in Schweitzer's case) only terrestrial life. I do not mean to suggest that either Goodpaster or Schweitzer expressly exclude extraterrestrial life; it is just clear that, quite naturally, the only life they are thinking about is terrestrial life, since that's all the life anyone knows to exist or imagines that she or he might actually affect.

But extraterrestrial life would be conative. I mean I guess it would be minimally conative—that is, in Feinberg's by now classical definition of conative, in possession of at least one of the following characteristics: "conscious wishes, desires, and hopes; or urges and impulses; or unconscious drives, aims, and goals; or latent tendencies, directions of growth and natural fulfillments."[45] Anything having the minimal characteristics of life sketched in the second section of this essay a growing, reproducing, dying thing—would have, it would seem necessarily, at least latent tendencies, directions of growth, and natural fulfillments if not unconscious drives, aims, and goals or conscious wishes, desires, and hopes. Such a thing would have therefore a "'good' of its own, the achievement of which can be its due," in Feinberg's words, and thus moral rights, as Feinberg grounds rights, or at least moral considerability, in Goodpaster's terms—if there is any significant difference between the possession of moral rights and moral considerability.[46]

Similarly, upon Schweitzer's more voluntarist and mystical rendering of conativity, I would suppose that extraterrestrial life, no less than terrestrial life, would be possessed by the will-to-live and therefore, according to Schweitzer, "just as in my own will-to-live there is a yearning for life, ... so the same obtains in all the will-to-live around me, equally whether it can express itself to my comprehension or whether it remains unvoiced." Schweitzer then goes on to say, "Ethics thus consists in this, that I experience the necessity of practising the same reverence for life toward all will-to-live, as toward my own."[47]

The life-principle/reverence-for-life ethics are, as it were, tailor-made for conceptually articulating and grounding our hopefully shared moral intuition that extraterrestrial life should be treated with respect, or reverence, if and when we may encounter it. The life-principle/ reverence-for-life ethics, however, have a foible symmetrical with but opposite to that of the Leopold land ethic. The land ethic is, because of its holistic or ecosystemic value orientation, practicable as a terrestrial environmental ethic, but, because of its conceptual foundations and logical structure, incapable of transference to life off the Earth. The life-principle/reverence-for-life ethics are, because of their conceptual foundations and logical structures, capable of transference off the Earth, but, because of their individualistic or atomic biases, impracticable as terrestrial environmental ethics.[48] In other words, the life-principle/reverence-for-life ethics are serviceable as extraterrestial environmental ethics, but, ironically, fail miserably as terrestrial environmental ethics.

Let me elaborate. Only individual living things are conative, at least as Feinberg and Schweitzer variously understand this shared basic idea. Populations, species, biocenoses, ecotones, biomes, and the biosphere as a whole are not. Hence, only individual living things are properly rights bearers (Feinberg), morally considerable (Goodpaster), or objects of reverence and respect (Schweitzer). To consistently practice the life-principle/reverence-for-life ethics at home on Earth would require a life style so quiescent as to be suicidal, as Schopenhauer clearly recognized and affirmed.[49] To live is necessarily to exploit other living beings. Since we are integrated members of the terrestrial bioeconomy in which the life of one thing is purchased by the death of another, the exponents of life-principle/reverence-for-life ethics at home on Earth are caught in an unavoidable practical conundrum at every turn. However, since our astronauts would not be integrated members of some extraterrestrial ecosystem and would be bringing with them their own terrestrial foodstuff and other necessities of life, the life-principle/reverence-for-life ethics would be practicable, without continuous compromise between principle and necessity, in respect to life on other bodies in the solar system—should there be any and should our astronauts ever encounter it. Without the need to eat or otherwise to exploit extraterrestrial life our astronauts could categorically respect and/or revere it.

But there is both a rational philosophical demand and a human psychological need for a self-consistent and all-embracing moral theory. We are neither good philosophers nor whole persons if for one purpose we adopt utilitarianism, for another deontology, for a third animal liberation, for a fourth the land ethic, and for a fifth a life-principle or reverence-for-life ethic, and so on. Such ethical eclecticism is not only rationally intolerable, it is morally suspect—as it invites the suspicion of ad hoc rationalizations for merely expedient or self-serving actions.

Let me therefore recommend an environmental ethic that is sufficiently inclusive and consistent to provide at once for the moral considerability of extraterrestrial as well as of terrestrial life without neglecting the practical primacy of human life, human needs, and human rights.

Bryan G. Norton has distinguished between strong and weak anthropocentrism.[50] Anthropocentrism is the view that there exists no value independent from human experience. Whether such a view is ultimately justifiable or not, it seems to be the prevailing view in Western axiology.[51] In Norton's terms, strong anthropocentrism takes any valued human experience as in principle equal to any other— push-pin is as good as poetry, bird-shooting as good as botanizing, and dune-buggying as good as desert pup-fish habitat restoration. Nonhuman beings are merely resources for valued human experiences, and no constraints—except essentially economic constraints—are warranted when those resources are consumed or destroyed in the process of using them to satisfy human preferences. From the point of view of strong anthropocentrism, if when human astronauts encounter life on another planet they are more amused to eradicate it then to leave it alone, and a majority of the rest of us feel better off or at least no worse off for their having done so, then that is what they should do.

Weak anthropocentrism on the other hand, the *locus classicus* of which Norton finds in Thoreau, regards certain uses of things as transforming and ennobling human nature.[52] Some human experiences, therefore, are better than others because they expand and enlarge human consciousness, in short because they make better beings of us.[53] Thus it is better to botanize than bird-shoot, better to save desert pup-fish than dune-buggy, and better to write poetry than play pushpin because push-pin, bird-shooting, and dune-buggying stultify the human spirit and stupefy the human mind while literature, science, and species conservation elevate the human spirit and enlighten the human mind.

Now, as it seems to me, weak anthropocentrism would govern our use of extraterrestrial as well as terrestrial life all to the greater good of mankind. I can think of nothing so positively transforming of human consciousness as the discovery, study, and conservation of life somewhere off the Earth. It would confirm experientially, palpably, viscerally what we presently believe in the abstract: that life is the expression of an inherent potentiality in physical nature. Such an event would immeasurably advance the ongoing process of the demystification of human consciousness, which is presently progressing all too slowly. And to find life off the Earth, to discover a wholly exotic biology, to cherish it and try to understand something about it would, I believe, transform our present view of life on Earth. In relation to extraterrestrial life, terrestrial organisms, ourselves included, comprise one great family, one gens. The current myopic prejudices regarding terrestrial species as somehow alien or exotic forms would perforce melt away in comparison with truly alien or exotic life forms. In short, the Archimedean adventure of the Apollo Project would thereby be completed.

# Notes

## Introduction: The Real Work

1. The subtitle of this introduction alludes to Gary Snyder, *The Real Work: Interviews and Talks: 1964–1979* (New York: New Directions, 1980).

2. Kristin Shrader-Frechette epitomizes this approach. See K.S. Shrader-Frechette, *Environmental Ethics* (Pacific Grove: Boxwood Press, 1981), *Nuclear Power and Public Policy: Social and Ethical Problems with Fission Technology* (Boston: D. Reidel, 1980) and "Environmental Ethics and Global Imperatives" in Robert Repetto, ed., *The Global Possible* (New Haven: Yale University Press, 1985). John Passmore, *Man's Responsibility for* [n.b., not "to"] *Nature: Ecological Problems and Western Traditions* (New York: Charles Scribner's Sons, 1974) is an apologetical tour de force for anthropocentrism.

3. The most notable representatives of this approach are Peter Singer, *Animal Liberation: A New Ethics for Our Treatment of Animals* (New York: The New York Review, 1975); and Tom Regan, *All That Dwell Therein: Animal Rights and Environmental Ethics* (Berkeley: University of California Press, 1982) and *The Case for Animal Rights* (Berkeley: University of California Press, 1983).

4. Singer's is limited to sentient animals, Regan's to mammals.

5. Technically speaking, there is a difference between "animal liberation" (Singer's theory) and "animal rights" (Regan's theory).

6. A notable example of ecocentrism is Holmes Rolston, III, *Philosophy Gone Wild: Essays in Environmental Ethics* (Buffalo: Prometheus Books, 1986) and "Duties to Ecosystems" in J. Baird Callicott, ed., *Companion to A Sand County Almanac: Interpretive and Critical Essays* (Madison: University of Wisconsin Press, 1987).

7. For a systematic discussion of the metarational character of Deep Ecology see Warwick Fox, *Approaching Deep Ecology: A Response to Richard Sylvan's Critique of Deep Ecology* (Hobart: University of Tasmania Environmental Studies Occasional Paper 20, 1986) and Michael Zimmerman, "Quantum Theory, Intrinsic Value, and Panentheism," *Environmental Ethics* 10 (1988), 3–30. For the opinion that, from the point of view of oriental thought, philosophy itself is part of the problem, not the solution, see David L. Hall, "On Seeking a Change of Environment," Roger T. Ames, "On Putting the *Te* back into Taoism" and Gerald James

Larson, " 'Conceptual Resources' for 'Environmental Ethics' " in J. Baird Calli-cott and Roger T. Ames, eds., *Environmental Philosophy: The Asian Traditions* (Albany: SUNY Press, 1989).

8. The invocation of Wittgenstein, the fly, and the bottle is in Larson, " 'Conceptual Resources'."

9. Biographical studies of Aldo Leopold are Susan Flader, *Thinking Like a Mountain: Aldo Leopold and the Evolution of an Ecological Attitude toward Deer, Wolves, and Forests* (Columbia: University of Missouri Press, 1974) and Curt Meine, *Aldo Leopold: His Life and Work* (Madison: University of Wisconsin Press, 1988).

10. Paul W. Taylor, *Respect for Nature* (Princeton: Princeton University Press, 1986).

## Animal Liberation: A Triangular Affair

1. Aldo Leopold, *A Sand County Almanac* (New York: Oxford University Press, 1949), pp. 202–3. Some traditional Western systems of ethics, however, have accorded moral standing to nonhuman beings. The Pythagorean tradition did, followed by Empedocles of Acragas; Saint Francis of Assisi apparently believed in the animal soul; in modern ethics, Jeremy Bentham's hedonic utilitarian system is also an exception to the usual rule. John Passmore ("The Treatment of Animals," *Journal of the History of Ideas* 36 [1975], 196–218) provides a well-researched and eye-opening study of historical ideas about the moral status of animals in Western thought. Though exceptions to the prevailing attitudes have existed, they are exceptions indeed and represent but a small minority of Western religious and philosophical points of view.

2. The tag "animal liberation" for this moral movement originates with Peter Singer whose book *Animal Liberation* (New York: New York Review, 1975) has been widely influential. "Animal rights" have been most persistently and unequivocally championed by Tom Regan in various articles, among them: "The Moral Basis of Vegetarianism," *Canadian Journal of Philosophy* 5 (1975): 181–214, "Exploring the Idea of Animal Rights" in *Animal Rights: A Symposium,* ed. D. Patterson and R. Ryder (London: Centaur, 1979); "Animal Rights, Human Wrongs," *Environmental Ethics* 2 (1980): 99–120. A more complex and qualified position respecting animal rights has been propounded by Joel Feinberg, "The Rights of Animals and Unborn Generations" in *Philosophy and Environmental Crisis,* ed. William T. Blackstone (Athens: University of Georgia Press, 1974), pp. 43–68, and "Human Duties and Animal Rights, " in *On the Fifth Day,* ed. R. K Morris and M. W. Fox (Washington: Acropolis Books, 1978), pp. 45–69. Lawrence Haworth ("Rights, Wrongs and Animals," *Ethics* 88 [1978]: 95–105), in the context of the contemporary debate, claims limited rights on behalf of animals. S. R. L. Clark's *The Moral Status of Animals* (Oxford: Clarendon Press, 1975) has set out arguments which differ in some particulars from those of Singer, Regan, and Feinberg with regard to the moral considerability of some nonhuman

animals. In this discussion, as a tribute to Singer, I use the term *animal liberation* generically to cover the several philosophical rationales for a humane ethic. Singer has laid particular emphasis on the inhumane usage of animals in agribusiness and scientific research. Two thorough professional studies from the humane perspective of these institutions are Ruth Harrison's *Animal Machines* (London: Stuart, 1964) and Richard Ryder's *Victims of Science* (London: Davis-Poynter, 1975), respectively.

3. Peter Singer and Tom Regan especially insist upon *equal* moral *consideration* for nonhuman animals. Equal moral *consideration* does not necessarily imply equal *treatment*, however, as Singer points out, cf. Singer, *Animal Liberation*, pp. 3, 17–24, and Singer, "The Fable of the Fox and the Unliberated Animals," *Ethics* 88 (1978): 119–20. Regan provides an especially clear summary of both his position and Singer's in "Animal Rights, Human Wrongs," pp. 108–12.

4. We have Richard Ryder to thank for coining the term *speciesism*. See his *Speciesism: The Ethics of Vivisection* (Edinburgh: Scottish Society for the Prevention of Vivisection, 1974). Richard Routley introduced the term *human chauvinism* in "Is There a Need for a New, an Environmental Ethic?" *Proceedings of the Fifteenth World Congress of Philosophy* 1 (1973): 205–10. Peter Singer ("All Animals Are Equal," in *Animal Rights and Human Obligations*, ed. Tom Regan and Peter Singer [Englewood Cliffs, N.J.: Prentice-Hall, 1976], pp. 148–62) developed the egalitarian comparison of speciesism with racism and sexism in detail. To extend the political comparison further, animal liberation is also a reformist and activist movement. We are urged to act, to become vegetarians, to boycott animal products, and so forth. The concluding paragraph of Regan's "Animal Rights, Human Wrongs" [p. 120] is especially zealously hortatory.

5. Leopold, *Sand County Almanac*, p. 204.

6. Ibid., pp. 201–3. A more articulate historical representation of the parallel expansion of legal rights appears in C. D. Stone's *Should Trees have Standing?* (Los Altos: William Kaufman, 1972), pp. 3–10, however without specific application to animal liberation.

7. Leopold, *Sand County Almanac*, p. 203.

8. Ibid., p. 204.

9. Ibid., p. 221 (trees); pp. 129–133 (mountains); p. 209 (streams).

10. John Benson ("Duty and the Beast," *Philosophy* 53 [1978]: 547-48) confesses that in the course of considering issues raised by Singer et al. he was "obliged to change my own diet as a result." An elaborate critical discussion is Philip E. Devine's "The Moral Basis of Vegetarianism" (*Philosophy* 53 [1978]: 481–505).

11. For a biography of Leopold including particular reference to Leopold's career as a "sportsman," see Susan L. Flader, *Thinking Like a Mountain* (Columbia: University of Missouri Press, 1974).

12. See especially, Leopold, *Sand County Almanac*, pp. 54–58; 62–66; 120–22; 149–54; 177–87.

13. A most thorough and fully argued dissent is provided by John Rodman in "The Liberation of Nature," *Inquiry* 20 (1977): 83–131. It is surprising that Singer, whose book is the subject of Rodman's extensive critical review, or some of Singer's philosophical allies, have not replied to these very penetrating and provocative criticisms. Another less specifically targeted dissent is Paul Shepard's "Animal Rights and Human Rites" (*North American Review* [Winter, 1974]: 34–41). More recently Kenneth Goodpaster ("From Egoism to Environmentalism" in *Ethics and Problems of the 21st Century,* ed. K. Goodpaster and K. Sayre [Notre Dame: Notre Dame University Press, 1979], pp. 21–35) has expressed complaints about the animal liberation and animal rights movement in the name of environmental ethics. "The last thing we need," writes Goodpaster, "is simply another 'liberation movement'" (p. 29).

14. Singer, "All Animals Are Equal" (p. 159), uses the term *humanist* to convey a speciesist connotation. Rationality and future-conceiving capacities as criteria for rights holding have been newly revived by Michael E. Levin with specific reference to Singer in "Animal Rights Evaluated," *The Humanist* (July/August, 1977): 14–15. John Passmore, in *Man's Responsibility for Nature* (New York: Charles Scribner's Sons, 1974), cf., p. 116, has recently insisted upon having interests as a criterion for having rights and denied that nonhuman beings have interests. L. P. Francis and R. Norman ("Some Animals are More Equal than Others," *Philosophy* 53 [1978]: 507–27) have argued, again with specific reference to animal liberationists, that linguistic abilities are requisite for moral status. H. J. McCloskey ("The Right to Life," *Mind* 84 [1975]: 410–13, and "Moral Rights and Animals," *Inquiry* 22 [1979]: 23–54), adapting an idea of Kant's, defends, among other exclusively human qualifications for rights holding, *self*-awareness. Richard A. Watson ("Self-Consciousness and the Rights of Nonhuman Animals and Nature," *Environmental Ethics* 1 [1979]: 99–129) also defends self-consciousness as a criterion for rights holding, but allows that some nonhuman animals also possess it.

15. In addition to the historical figures, who are nicely summarized and anthologized in *Animal Rights and Human Obligations,* John Passmore has recently defended the reactionary notion that cruelty towards animals is morally reprehensible for reasons independent of any obligation or duties people have to animals as such (*Man's Responsibility,* cf., p. 117).

16. "Humane moralists" is perhaps a more historically accurate designation than "animal liberationists." John Rodman, "The Liberation of Nature" (pp. 88–89), has recently explored in a programmatic way the connections between the contemporary animal liberation/rights movements and the historical humane societies movement.

17. Tom Regan styles more precise formulations of this argument, "the argument from marginal cases," in "An Examination and Defense of One Argument Concerning Animal Rights," *Inquiry* 22 (1979): 190. Regan directs our attention to Andrew Linzey, *Animal Rights* (London: SCM Press, 1976) as well as to Singer, *Animal Liberation,* for paradigmatic employment of this argument on behalf of moral standing for animals (p. 144).

18. A particularly lucid advocacy of this notion may be found in Feinberg, "Human Duties and Animal Rights," especially p. 53ff.

19. Again, Feinberg in "Human Duties and Animal Rights" (pp. 57–59) expresses this point especially forcefully.

20. John Rodman's comment in "The Liberation of Nature" (p. 91) is worth repeating here since it has to all appearances received so little attention elsewhere: "If it would seem arbitrary ... to find one species claiming a monopoly on intrinsic value by virtue of its allegedly exclusive possession of reason, free will, soul, or some other occult quality, would it not seem almost as arbitrary to find that same species claiming a monopoly on intrinsic value for itself and those species most resembling it (e.g., in type of nervous system and behavior) by virtue of their common and allegedly exclusive possession of sentience?" Goodpaster ("From Egoism to Environmentalism," p. 29) remarks that in modern moral philosophy "a fixation on egoism and a consequent loyalty to a model of moral sentiment or reason which in essence generalizes or universalizes that egoism ... makes it particularly inhospitable to our recent felt need for an environmental ethic ... For such an ethic does not readily admit of being reduced to 'humanism'—nor does it sit well with any class or generalization model of moral concern."

21. John Rodman, "The Liberation of Nature" (p. 95), comments: "Why do our 'new ethics' seem so old? ... Because the attempt to produce a 'new ethics' by the process of 'extension' perpetuates the basic assumptions of the conventional modern paradigm, however much it fiddles with the boundaries." When the assumptions remain conventional, the boundaries are, in my view, scalar. But they are triangular when both positions are considered in opposition to the land ethic. The scalar relation is especially clear when two other positions, not specifically discussed in the text, the reverence-for-life ethic and pan-moralism, are considered. The reverence-for-life ethic (as I am calling it in deference to Albert Schweitzer) seems to be the next step on the scale after the humane ethic. William Frankena considers it so in "Ethics and the Environment," *Ethics and Problems of the 21st Century*, pp. 3–20. W. Murry Hunt ("Are Mere *Things* Morally Considerable," *Environmental Ethics* 2 [1980]: 59–65) has gone a step past Schweitzer, and made the bold suggestion that *everything* should be accorded moral standing, pan-moralism. Hunt's discussion shows clearly that there is a similar logic ("slippery slope" logic) involved in taking each downward step and thus a certain commonality of underlying assumptions among all the ethical types to which the land ethic stands in opposition. Hunt is not unaware that his suggestion may be interpreted as a *reductio ad absurdum* of the whole matter, but insists that that is not his intent. The land ethic is not part of this linear series of steps and hence may be represented as a point off the scale. The principal difference, as I explain below, is that the land ethic is collective or "holistic" while the others are distributive or "atomistic." Another relevant difference is that moral humanism, humane moralism, reverence-for-life ethics, and the limiting case, pan-moralism, either openly or implicity espouse a pecking-order model of nature. The land ethic, founded upon an ecological

model of nature emphasizing the contributing roles played by various species in the economy of nature, abandons the "higher"/"lower" ontological and axiological schema, in favor of a functional system of value. The land ethic, in other words, is inclined to establish value distinctions not on the basis of higher and lower orders of being, but on the basis of the importance of organisms, minerals, and so on to the biotic community. Some bacteria, for example, may be of greater value to the health or economy of nature than dogs, and thus command more respect.

22. Rodman, "The Liberation of Nature" (p. 86), says in reference to Singer's humane ethic that "the weakness ... lies in the limitation of its horizon to the late eighteenth and early nineteenth century Utilitarian humane movement [and] its failure to live up to its own noble declaration that 'philosophy ought to question the basic assumptions of the age'."

23. Leopold, *Sand County Almanac*, pp. 224–25.

24. Anthropologist Clifford Geertz ("Ethos, World View, and the Analysis of Sacred Symbols, in *The Interpretation of Culture*, ed. Clifford Geertz [New York: Basic Books, 1973], p. 127) remarks that in cultures the world over "the powerfully coercive 'ought' is felt to grow out of a comprehensive factual 'is'.... The tendency to synthesize world view and ethos at some level, if not logically necessary, is at least empirically coercive; if it is not philosophically justified, it is at least pragmatically universal." Rodman, "The Liberation of Nature" (p. 96), laments the preoccupation of modern moral philosophy with the naturalistic fallacy, and comments that "thanks to this, the quest for an ethics is reduced to prattle about 'values' taken in abstraction from the 'facts' of 'experience' the notion of an ethics as an organic ethos, a way of life, remains lost to us."

25. By "first-," "second-," and "third-" order wholes I intend, paradigmatically, single cell organisms, multicell organisms, and biocenoses, respectively.

26. "Some Fundamentals of Conservation in the Southwest," composed in the 1920s but unpublished until it appeared last year *(Environmental Ethics* 1 [1979]: 131–41), shows that the organic analogy, conceptually representing the nature of the whole resulting from ecological relationships, antedates the community analogy in Leopold's thinking, so far at least as its moral implications are concerned. "The Land Ethic" of *Sand County Almanac* employs almost exclusively the community analogy but a rereading of "The Land Ethic" in the light of "Some Fundamentals" reveals that Leopold did not entirely abandon the organic analogy in favor of the community analogy. For example, toward the end of "The Land Ethic" Leopold talks about "land health" and "land the collective organism" (p. 258). William Morton Wheeler, *Essays in Philosophical Biology* (New York: Russell and Russell, 1939), and Lewis Thomas, *Lives of a Cell* (New York: Viking Press, 1974), provide extended discussions of holistic approaches to social, ethical, and environmental problems. Kenneth Goodpaster, almost alone among academic philosophers, has explored the possibility of a holistic environmental ethical system in "From Egoism to Environmentalism."

27. Jeremy Bentham, *An Introduction to the Principles of Morals and Legislation* (Oxford: Clarendon Press, 1823), chap. 1, sec. 4.

28. This has been noticed and lamented by Alistaire S. Gunn ("Why Should We Care About Rare Species?" *Environmental Ethics* 2[1980]: 36) who comments, "Environmentalism seems incompatible with the 'Western' obsession with individualism, which leads us to resolve questions about our treatment of animals by appealing to the essentially atomistic, competitive notion of rights. ..." John Rodman, "The Liberation of Nature" (p. 89), says practically the same thing: "The moral atomism that focuses on individual animals and their subjective experiences does not seem well adapted to coping with ecological systems." Peter Singer has in fact actually stressed the individual focus of his humane ethic in "Not for Humans Only: The Place of Nonhumans in Environmental Issues" (*Ethics and Problems of the 21st Century*, pp. 191–206) as if it were a virtue! More revealingly, the only grounds that he can discover for moral concern over species, since species are per se not sensible entities (and that is the extent of his notion of an ethically relevant consideration), are anthropocentric grounds, human aesthetics, environmental integrity for humans, and so forth.

29. Leopold, *Sand County Almanac*, pp. 223 and 209.

30. Edward Abbey, *Desert Solitaire* (New York: Ballantine Books, 1968), p. 20.

31. Garrett Hardin, "The Economics of Wilderness," *Natural History* 78 [1969]: 173–77. Hardin is blunt: "Making great and spectacular efforts to save the life of an individual makes sense only when there is a shortage of people. I have not lately heard that there is a shortage of people" (p. 176).

32. See, for example, Garrett Hardin, "Living on a Lifeboat," *BioScience* 24 (1974): 561–68.

33. In *Republic* 5 Plato directly says that "the best governed state most nearly resembles an organism" (462D) and that there is no "greater evil for a state than the thing that distracts it and makes it many instead of one, or a greater good than that which binds it together and makes it one" (462A). Goodpaster in "From Egoism to Environmentalism" (p. 30) has in a general way anticipated this connection: "The oft-repeated plea by some ecologists and environmentalists that our thinking needs to be less atomistic and more 'holistic' translates in the present context into a plea for a more embracing object of moral consideration. In a sense it represents a plea to return to the richer Greek conception of man by nature social and not intelligibly removable from his social and political context though it goes beyond the Greek conception in emphasizing that societies too need to be understood in a context, an ecological context, and that it is this larger whole that is the 'bearer of value.'"

34. See especially *Republic* 4.444A–E.

35. For a particularly clear statement by Plato of the idea that the goodness of anything is a matter of the fitting order of the parts in relation to respective wholes see *Gorgias* 503D–507A.

36. Cf., *Republic* 5.461C (infanticide); 468A (disposition of captives); 3.416D–406E (medicine).

37. Cf., *Republic* 5.459A–406E (eugenics, nonfamily life and child rearing), *Republic* 3.416D–417B (private property).

38. Cf., *Republic* 4.419A–421C and *Republic* 7.419D–521B.

39. After so much strident complaint has been registered here about the lack freshness in self-proclaimed "new" environmental ethics (which turn out to be "old" ethics retreaded) there is surely an irony in comparing the (apparently brand new) Leopold land ethic to Plato's ethical philosophy. There is, however, an important difference. The humane moralists have simply revived and elaborated Bentham's historical application of hedonism to questions regarding the treatment of animals with the capacity of sensibility. There is nothing new but the revival and elaboration. Plato, on the other hand, never develops anything faintly resembling an *environmental* ethic. Plato never reached an ecological view of living nature. The wholes of his universe are body, soul, society and cosmos. Plato is largely concerned, if not exclusively, with moral problems involving individual human beings in a political context and he has the temerity to insist that the good of the whole transcends individual claims. (Even in the *Crito* Plato is sympathetic to the city's claim to put Socrates to death however unjust the verdict against him.) Plato thus espouses a holistic ethic which is valuable as a (very different) paradigm to which the Leopold land ethic, which is also holistic but in a relation to a very different whole, may be compared. It is interesting further that some (but not all) of the analogies which Plato finds useful to convey his holistic social values are also useful to Leopold in his effort to set out a land ethic.

40. Leopold, *Sand County Almanac*, p. ix.

41. See John Muir, "The Wild Sheep of California," *Overland Monthly* 12 (1874): 359.

42. Roderick Nash (*Wilderness and the American Mind*, rev. ed. [New Haven and London: Yale University Press, 1973], p. 2) suggests that the English word *wild* is ultimately derived from *will*. A wild being is thus a willed one—"self-willed, willful, or uncontrollable." The humane moralists' indifference to this distinction is rather dramatically represented in Regan's "Animal Rights, Human Wrongs" (pp. 99–104) which begins with a bid for the reader's sympathy through a vivid description of four concrete episodes of human cruelty toward animals. I suspect that Regan's intent is to give examples of four principal categories of animal abuse at the hands of man: whaling, traffic in zoo captives, questionable scientific experimentation involving unquestionable torture, and intensive meat production. But his illustration, divided according to precepts central to land ethics, concern two episodes of wanton slaughter of *wild* animals, a blue whale and a gibbon, aggravated by the consideration that both are specimens of disappearing species, and two episodes of routine cruelty toward *domestic* animals, a "bobby calf" (destined to become veal) and a laboratory

rabbit. The misery of the calf and the agony of the rabbit are, to be sure, reprehensible, from the perspective of the land ethic, for reasons I explain shortly, but it is, I think, a trivialization of the deeper environmental and ecological issues involved in modern whaling and wildlife traffic to discuss the exploitation and destruction of blue whales and gibbon apes as if they are wrong for the same reasons that the treatment of laboratory rabbits and male dairy calves is wrong. The inhumane treatment of penned domestics should not be, I suggest, even discussed in the same context as whaling and wildlife traffic; it is a disservice to do so.

43. John Rodman, "The Liberation of Nature" (p. 101), castigates Singer for failing to consider what the consequences of wholesale animal liberation might be. With tongue in cheek he congratulates Singer for taking a step toward the elimination of a more subtle evil, the genetic debasement of other animal beings, that is, domestication per se.

44. A particularly strong statement of the ultimate commitment of the neo-Benthamites is found in Feinberg's "Human Duties and Animal Rights" (p. 57): "We regard pain and suffering as an intrinsic evil ... simply because they are pain and suffering.... The question 'What's wrong with pain anyway?' is never allowed to arise." I shall raise it. I herewith declare in all soberness that I see nothing wrong with pain. It is a marvelous method, honed by the evolutionary process, of conveying important organic information. I think it was the late Alan Watts who somewhere remarks that upon being asked if he did not think there was too much pain in the world replied, "No, I think there's just enough."

45. Paul Shepard, "Animal Rights and Human Rites" (p. 37), comments that "the humanitarian's projection onto nature of illegal murder and the rights of civilized people to safety not only misses the point but is exactly contrary to fundamental ecological reality: the structure of nature is a sequence of killings."

46. This matter has been ably and fully explored by Paul Shepard, *The Tender Carnivore and the Sacred Game* (New York: Scribner's Sons, 1973). A more empirical study has been carried out by Marshall Sahlins, *Stone Age Economics* (Chicago: Aldine/Atherton, 1972).

47. The expression "meat from God" occurs twice in *Sand County Almanac*, p. viii and p. 166. The expression is usually given a spiritual-metaphorical interpretation: In the Foreword Leopold writes, "It is here [at the shack] that we seek—and still find—our meat from God"—that is, spiritual satisfaction. Read in light of the second occurrence its meaning more probably is: It is here at the shack that we go hunting—successfully—despite the general decline in game elsewhere. Leopold mentions "organic farming" as something intimately connected with the land ethic; in the same context he also speaks of "biotic farming" (p. 222).

## Review of Tom Regan, *The Case for Animal Rights*

1. See Ernest Partridge's excellent review, *Environmental Ethics* 7 (1985): 81–86.

2. Peter Singer, "Ten Years of Animal Liberation," *New York Review of Books* (17 January 1985): 46–52.

3. David L. Hull, "A Matter of Individuality," *Philosophy of Science* 45 (1978): 335–60.

4. Mark Sagoff, "Animal Liberation and Environmental Ethics: Bad Marriage, Quick Divorce," *Osgoode Hall Law Journal* 22 (1984): 306, p. 26.

5. Steve S. Sapontzis, "Predation," *Ethics and Animals* 5 (June, 1984): 27–36.

6. Henry Beston, *The Outermost House: A Year of Life on the Great Beach of Cape Cod* (New York: Viking Press, 1971), p. 25, emphasis added.

7. Tom Regan, "An Examination and Defense of One Argument Concerning Animal Rights," in *All That Dwell Therein* (Berkeley: University of California Press, 1982), pp. 113–47.

8. To my knowledge Tom Regan has never addressed the thoughtful and telling critique of animal rights developed by John Rodman who makes this point in "The Liberation of Nature," *Inquiry* 20 (1977): 83–131. Does Regan's neglect of Rodman's critique mean that he cannot answer it?

9. Beston, *Outermost House,* p. 221.

10. Mary Midgley, *Animals and Why They Matter* (Athens, Ga.: University of Georgia Press, 1983), pp. 112-24.

## Animal Liberation and Environmental Ethics: Back Together Again

1. J. Baird Callicott, "Animal Liberation: A Triangular Affair," *Environmental Ethics* 2 (1980): 311–228. Reproduced herein, pp. 15–38.

2. Mary Anne Warren, "The Rights of the Nonhuman World" in Robert Elliot and Arran Gare, *Environmental Philosophy: A Collection of Readings* (University Park: The Pennsylvania State University Press, 1983), pp. 109–131.

3. Ibid., pp. 130–131.

4. Ibid., p. 131.

5. Tom Regan, *The Case for Animal Rights* (Berkeley: University of California Press, 1983), pp. 362–363. For a discussion see my review in *Environmental Ethics* 7 (1985): 365–372. Reproduced herein, pp. 39–47.

6. Mark Sagoff, "Animal Liberation and Environmental Ethics: Bad Marriage, Quick Divorce," *Osgoode Hall Law Journal* 22 (1984): 306.

7. Mary Midgley, *Animals and Why They Matter* (Athens: University of Georgia Press, 1983), p. 112.

8. Ibid., pp. 130, 131.

9. Peter Singer, *Animal Liberation: A New Ethics for Our Treatment of Animals* (New York: Avon Books, 1977), pp. xi-xiii. Sympathy has recently been defended as an appropriate foundation for animal welfare ethics by John A. Fischer, "Taking Sympathy Seriously," *Environmental Ethics* 9 (1987): 197-215.

10. Kenneth Goodpaster, "From Egoism to Environmentalism" in K. Goodpaster and K. Sayre, eds., *Ethics and Problems of the 21st Century* (Notre Dame: Notre Dame University Press, 1979), 21-35.

11. David Hume, *A Treatise of Human Nature* (Oxford: The Clarendon Press, 1969), p. 487.

12. My most comprehensive statement to date is "The Conceptual Foundations of the Land Ethic," in J. Baird Callicott, ed., *Companion to A Sand County Almanac: Interpretive and Critical Essays* (Madison: University of Wisconsin Press, 1987), 186-217. Reproduced herein, pp. 75-99.

13. Peter Singer, *The Expanding Circle: Ethics and Sociobiology* (New York: Farrar, Straus, and Giroux, 1982).

14. Aldo Leopold, *A Sand County Almanac* (New York: Oxford University Press, 1949), p. 216.

15. Peter Singer toys with this idea in *Animal Liberation:* "It must be admitted that the existence of carnivorous animals does pose one problem for the ethics of Animal Liberation, and that is whether we should do anything about it. Assuming that humans could eliminate carnivorous species from the earth, and that the total amount of suffering among animals in the world were thereby reduced, should we do it?" (p. 238). Steve Sapontzis in "Predation," *Ethics and Animals* 5 (1984) concludes that "where we can prevent predation without occasioning as much or more suffereing than we would prevent, we are obligated to do so by the principle that we are obligated to alleviate avoidable animal suffering" (p. 36). I argue in "The Search for an Environmental Ethic," in Tom Regan, ed. *Matters of Life and Death*, 2nd Edition (New York: Random House, 1986), pp. 381-423, that both Singerian animal liberation and Reganic animal rights imply the ecological nightmare of a policy of predator extermination.

16. See Holmes Rolson III, "Beauty and the Beast: Aesthetic Experience of Wildlife" in D. J. Decker and G. R. Goff, eds., *Valuing Wildlife: Economic and Social Perspectives* (Boulder: Westview Press, 1987), pp. 187-196.

17. David Hume, *An Enquiry Concerning the Principles of Morals* (Oxford: The Clarendon Press, 1777), p. 219, emphasis added.

18. Charles Darwin, *The Descent of Man and Selection in Relation to Sex* (New York: J. A. Hill and Company, 1904), p. 120.

### Elements of an Environmental Ethic: Moral Considerability and the Biotic Community

1. Richard Routley, "Is There a Need for a New, an Environmental Ethic?" in Bulgarian Organizing Committee, ed., *Proceedings of the Fifteenth World Congress of Philosophy* I (Sophia, Bulgaria: Sophia-Press, 1973), pp. 205–10.

2. Ibid., p. 207.

3. Routley's limiting case paradigms (as I call them) are more intuitively than logically compelling. Just what religious and philosophical ethical systems belong to the "dominant" tradition of Western ethical thought? (Indeed, what is Western and what Eastern?) Without being certain that we have enumerated them all and taken up each separately, it cannot be *proved* that Western moral thought does not. On the other hand, it is a challenge, which I have been unable to meet, to find a major European ethical system, classical or modern, which meets the test of Routley's limiting case paradigms. In every system it is at best other persons, and often only the agent's own self, which count for something, while nonhuman natural entities are included in moral reckoning only in relation to persons as property or as being involved in a general and vague conception of the quality of (human) life. Holmes Rolston, III, "Is There an Ecological Ethic?" *Ethics* 85 (1975): 101, appears to concur: "Our ethical heritage largely attaches values and rights to persons, and if nonpersonal realms enter, they enter only as tributary to the personal."

4. Aldo Leopold, "The Conservation Ethic," *Journal of Forestry* 31 (1933): 634–643. *A Sand County Almanac*, (New York: Oxford University Press, 1949), pp. 201–226.

5. Ibid., p. 203

6. Ibid., p. 202.

7. Charles Darwin, *Descent of Man and Selection in Relation to Sex* (New York: J. A. Hill and Co., 1904) chaps. 4, 5. "No tribe," Darwin writes, "could hold together if murder, robbery, treachery, etc., were common; consequently such crimes, within the limits of the same tribe 'are branded with everlasting infamy'..." Petr Kropotkin in *Mutual Aid: A Factor of Evolution* (London: W. Heinemann, 1902) extended the same principle to other species.

8. Edward O. Wilson, *Sociobiology: The New Synthesis* (Cambridge: Harvard University Press, 1975).

9. Leopold, *Sand County Almanac*, p. 204.

10. That a proper ethic must be evenhanded, that duties must be reciprocal and rights mutual, has been used recently as an avenue for criticism of environmental ethics; for example, Michael Fox, " 'Animal Liberation': A Critique," *Ethics* 88 (1978): 112.

11. Leopold, *Sand County Almanac*, p. 203.

12. Ibid., p. 209–10.

13. Ibid., p. 223.

14. Ibid., p. 224.

15. John Passmore, *Man's Responsibility for Nature: Ecological Problems and Western Traditions* (New York: Charles Scribner's Sons, 1974), p. 116.

## The Conceptual Foundations of the Land Ethic

1. Wallace Stegner, "The Legacy of Aldo Leopold"; Curt Meine, "Building 'The Land Ethic' "; both in J. Baird Callicott, ed., *Companion to A Sand County Almanac: Interpretive and Critical Essays* (Madison, Wis.: University of Wisconsin Press, 1987). The oft-repeated characterization of Leopold as a prophet appears traceable to Roberts Mann, "Aldo Leopold: Priest and Prophet," *American Forests* 60, no. 8 (August 1954): 23, 42–43; it was picked up, apparently, by Ernest Swift, "Aldo Leopold: Wisconsin's Conservationist Prophet," *Wisconsin Tales and Trails* 2, no. 2 (September 1961): 2–5; Roderick Nash institutionalized it in his chapter, "Aldo Leopold: Prophet," in *Wilderness and the American Mind* (New Haven: Yale University Press, 1967).

2. John Passmore, *Man's Responsibility for* [significantly not "to"] *Nature: Ecological Problems and Western Traditions* (New York: Charles Scribner's Sons, 1974).

3. H. J. McCloskey, *Ecological Ethics and Politics* (Totowa, N.J.: Rowman and Littlefield, 1983), p. 56.

4. Robin Attfield, in "Value in the Wilderness," *Metaphilosophy* 15 (1984), writes, "Leopold the philosopher is something of a disaster, and I dread the thought of the student whose concept of philosophy is modeled principally on these extracts. (Can value 'in the philosophical sense' be contrasted with instrumental value? If concepts of right and wrong did not apply to slaves in Homeric Greece, how could Odysseus suspect the slavegirls of 'misbehavior'? If all ethics rest on interdependence how are obligations to infants and small children possible? And how can 'obligations have no meaning without conscience,' granted that the notion of conscience is conceptually dependent on that of obligation?)" (p. 294). L. W. Sumner, "Review of Robin Attfield, *The Ethics of Environmental Concern*," *Environmental Ethics* 8 (1986): 77.

5. Aldo Leopold, *A Sand County Almanac* (New York: Oxford University Press, 1949). Quotations from *Sand County* are cited by in the text of this essay by page numbers in parentheses.

6. Edward O. Wilson, *Sociobiology: The New Synthesis* (Cambridge: Harvard University Press, 1975), p. 3. See also W. D. Hamilton, "The Genetical Theory of Social Behavior," *Journal of Theoretical Biology* 7 (1964): 1–52.

7. Charles R. Darwin, *The Descent of Man and Selection in Relation to Sex* (New York: J. A. Hill and Company, 1904). The quoted phrase occurs on p. 97.

8. See Adam Smith, *The Theory of the Moral Sentiments* (London and Edinburgh: A. Millar, A. Kinkaid, and J. Bell, 1759) and David Hume, *An Enquiry Concerning*

*the Principles of Morals* (Oxford: The Clarendon Press, 1777; first published in 1751). Darwin cites both works in the key fourth chapter of *Descent* (pp. 106 and 109, respectively).

9. Darwin, *Descent,* pp. 98ff.

10. Ibid., pp. 105ff.

11. Ibid., pp. 113ff.

12. Ibid., p. 105.

13. See, for example, Elman R. Service, *Primitive Social Organization: An Evolutionary Perspective* (New York: Random House, 1962).

14. See Marshall Sahlins, *Stone Age Economics* (Chicago: Aldine Atherton, 1972).

15. Darwin, *Descent,* p. 111.

16. Ibid., pp. 117ff. The quoted phrase occurs on p. 118.

17. Ibid., p. 124.

18. See Donald Worster, *Nature's Economy: The Roots of Ecology* (San Francisco: Sierra Club Books, 1977).

19. Charles Elton, *Animal Ecology* (New York: Macmillan, 1927).

20. Aldo Leopold, *Round River* (New York: Oxford University Press, 1953), p. 148.

21. Kenneth Goodpaster, "On Being Morally Considerable," *Journal of Philosophy* 22 (1978): 308–25. Goodpaster wisely avoids the term *rights,* defined so strictly albeit so variously by philosophers, and used so loosely by nonphilosophers.

22. Kenneth Goodpaster, "From Egoism to Environmentalism" in *Ethics and Problems of the 21st Century,* ed. K. E. Goodpaster and K. M. Sayre (Notre Dame, Ind.: University of Notre Dame Press, 1979), pp. 21–35.

23. See Immanuel Kant, *Foundations of the Metaphysics of Morals* (New York: Bobbs-Merrill, 1959; first published in 1785); and Jeremy Bentham, *An Introduction to the Principles of Morals and Legislation,* new edition (Oxford: The Clarendon Press, 1823).

24. Goodpaster, "Egoism to Environmentalism." Actually Goodpaster regards *Hume* and Kant as the cofountainheads of this sort of moral philosophy. But Hume does not reason in this way. For Hume, the other-oriented sentiments are as primitive as self-love.

25. See Peter Singer, *Animal Liberation: A New Ethics for Our Treatment of Animals* (New York: Avon Books, 1975) for animal liberation; and see Tom Regan, *All That Dwell Therein: Animal Rights and Environmental Ethics* (Berkeley: University of California Press, 1982) for animal rights.

26. See Albert Schweitzer, *Philosophy of Civilization: Civilization and Ethics,* trans. John Naish (London: A & C. Black, 1923). For a fuller discussion see J. Baird Callicott, "On the Intrinsic Value of Non-human Species," in *The Preservation of Species,* ed. Bryan Norton (Princeton: Princeton University Press, 1986), pp. 138–72.

27. Peter Singer and Tom Regan arc both proud of this circumstance and consider it a virtue. See Peter Singer, "Not for Humans Only: The Place of Nonhumans in Environmental Issues" in *Ethics and Problems of the 21st Century,* pp. 191–206; and Tom Regan, "Ethical Vegetarianism and Commercial Animal Farming" in *Contemporary Moral Problems,* ed. James E. White (St. Paul, Minn.: West Publishing Co., 1985), pp. 279–94.

28. See J. Baird Callicott, "Hume's Is/Ought Dichotomy and the Relation of Ecology to Leopold's Land Ethic," *Environmental Ethics* 4 (1982): 163–74, reproduced herein, pp. 117–127; and "Non-anthropocentric Value Theory and Environmental Ethics," *American Philosophical Quarterly* 21 (1984): 299–309, for an elaboration.

29. Hume, *Enquiry,* p. 219, emphasis added.

30. Darwin, *Descent,* p. 120.

31. I have elsewhere argued that "value in the philosophical sense" means "intrinsic" or "inherent" value. See J. Baird Callicott, "The Philosophical Value of Wildlife," in *Valuing Wildlife: Economic and Social Values of Wildlife,* ed. Daniel J. Decker and Gary Goff (Boulder, Col.: Westview Press, 1986), pp. 214–221.

32. See Worster, *Nature's Economy.*

33. See J. Baird Callicott, "The Metaphysical Implications of Ecology," *Environmental Ethics* 8 (1986): 300–315, for an elaboration of this point. Reproduced herein, pp. 101–115.

34. Robert P. McIntosh, *The Background of Ecology. Concept and Theory* (Cambridge: Cambridge University Press, 1985).

35. Aldo Leopold, "Some Fundamentals of Conservation in the Southwest," *Environmental Ethics* I (1979): 139–40, emphasis added.

36. Arthur Tansley, "The Use and Abuse of Vegetational Concepts and Terms," *Ecology* 16 (1935): 292-303.

37. Harold J. Morowitz, "Biology as a Cosmological Science," *Main Currents in Modern Thought* 28 (1972): 156.

38. I borrow the term "devolution" from Austin Meredith, "Devolution," *Journal of Theoretical Biology* 96 (1982): 49–65.

39. Holmes Rolston, III, "Duties to Endangered Species," *BioScience* 35 (1985): 718–26. See also Geerat Vermeij, "The Biology of Human-Caused Extinction," in Norton, *Preservation of Species,* pp. 28–49.

40. See D. M. Raup and J. J. Sepkoski, Jr., "Mass Extinctions in the Marine Fossil Record," *Science* 215 (1982): 1501–3.

41. William Aiken, "Ethical Issues in Agriculture," in *Earthbound: New Introductory Essays in Environmental Ethics,* ed. Tom Regan (New York: Random House, 1984), 269. Tom Regan, *The Case for Animal Rights* (Berkeley: University of California Press, 1983), 262, and "Ethical Vegetarianism," 291. See also Eliott Sober, "Philosophical Problems for Environmentalism," in Norton, *Preservation of Species,* 173–94.

42. I owe the tree-ring analogy to Richard and Val Routley (now Sylvan and Plumwood, respectively), "Human Chauvinism and Environmental Ethics," in *Environmental Philosophy,* ed. D. Mannison, M. McRobbie, and R. Routley (Canberra: Department of Philosophy, Research School of the Social Sciences, Australian National University, 1980), pp. 96–189. A good illustration of the balloon analogy may be found in Peter Singer, *The Expanding Circle: Ethics and Sociobiology* (New York: Farrar, Straus and Giroux, 1983).

43. For an elaboration see Thomas W. Overholt and J. Baird Callicott, *Clothed-in-Fur and Other Tales: An Introduction to an Ojibwa World View* (Washington, D.C.: University Press of America, 1982).

44. J. Baird Callicott, "Traditional American Indian and Western European Attitudes toward Nature: An Overview," *Environmental Ethics* 4 (1982): 163–74. Reproduced herein, pp. 177–201.

45. Ernest Partridge, "Are We Ready for an Ecological Morality?" *Environmental Ethics* 4 (1982): 177.

46. Peter Fritzell, "The Conflicts of Ecological Conscience," in J. Baird Callicot, ed., *Companion to A Sand County Almanac: Interpretive and Critical Essays* (Madison, Wis.: University of Wisconsin Press, 1987), pp. 128–153.

47. See Worster, *Nature's Economy.*

48. Scott Lehmann, "Do Wildernesses Have Rights?" *Environmental Ethics* 3 (1981): 131.

## The Metaphysical Implications of Ecology

1. See for example E. A. Burtt, *The Metaphysical Foundations of Modern Science* (Garden City, N.Y.: Anchor Books, 1954) and Ernest Nagel, *The Structure of Science* (New York: Harcourt, Brace and World, 1961).

2. The term "New Ecology" was first used in H. G. Wells, with Julian Huxley and G. P. Wells, *The Science of Life* (New York: Garden City Publishing Co., 1939), p. 961, to characterize ecology after the quantifiable ecosystem model was developed by Arthur Tansley in 1935. See Warwick Fox, "Deep Ecology: A New Philosophy of Our Time?" *The Ecologist* 14 (1984): 994–200, and J. Baird Callicott,

"Intrinsic Value, Quantum Theory, and Environmental Ethics," *Environmental Ethics* 7 (1985): 257–275, for a discussion of the convergence and complementary characteristics of the New Physics and New Ecology. Reproduced herein, pp. 157–174.

3. John Gribbin, *In Search of Schrodinger's Cat: Quantum Physics and Reality* (New York: Bantam, 1984), claims that while "Newton had it [atomism] in mind in his work on physics and optics, atoms only really became a part of scientific thought in the latter part of the eighteenth century when the French chemist Antoine Lavoisier investigated why things burn" (p. 19). But according to Thomas Kuhn, *The Copernican Revolution: Planetary Astronomy and the Development of Western Thought* (Cambridge, Mass.: Harvard University Press, 1957), whose historical point of view is somewhat broader than Gribbin's, "early in the seventeenth century atomism experienced an immense revival.... Atomism was firmly merged with Copernicanism as a fundamental tenet of the 'new philosophy' which directed the scientific imagination" (p. 237).

4. "Primary" and "secondary" qualities were terms given to Galileo Galilei's distinction between putative actual and nonactual qualities of the elements by John Locke, *Essay Concerning Human Understanding* (New York: E. P. Dutton and Co., 1961). Locke attempted to ground the distinction empirically rather than theoretically; the futility of this attempt was subsequently demonstrated by Berkeley. The revealing terms, "the full" and "the empty," are attributed to the fifth-century-B.C. atomists by Aristotle, *Metaphysica*, 985b4.

5. See G. S. Kirk and J. E. Raven, *The Presocratic Philosophers: A Critical History with a Selection of Texts* (Cambridge: Cambridge University Press, 1962), and Burtt, *Metaphysical Foundations of Modern Science*.

6. Ibid.

7. See Nagel, *The Structure of Science*.

8. Ibid.

9. For Democritus's materialistic psychology, see W. K. C. Guthrie, *A History of Greek Philosophy*, vol. 2 (Cambridge: Cambridge University Press, 1965), for Lucretius's see Titus Lucretius Carus, *De Rerum Natura*, trans. Robert Latham (Harmondsworth: Penguin, 1951); and for Hobbes's see Thomas Hobbes, *Leviathan* (New York: Collier Books, 1962). For Pythagoras's dualism see W. K. C. Guthrie, *A History of Greek Philosophy* (Cambridge: Cambridge University Press, 1962), Vol. 1; for Plato's see especially *Phaedo* in *Plato I: Euthyphro, Apology, Crito, Phaedo, and Phaedrus with an English Translation by Harold Fowler North* (London: William Heineman Ltd. for The Loeb Classical Library, 1914); and for Descartes' see *Meditations on First Philosophy* in E. S. Haldane and G. R. T. Ross, trans., *The Philosophical Works of Descartes* (Cambridge: Cambridge University Press, 1911), vol. 1.

10. There is remarkable unanimity of thought on this point among Pythagoras, Plato, and Descartes, the West's most influential dualists.

11. See Thomas Hobbes, *Leviathan*.

12. See Immanuel Kant, *Foundations of the Metaphysics of Morals* (New York: Bobbs-Merrill Co., 1959).

13. See especially Plato, *Phaedo*.

14. See *De Partibus Animalium* and *Politicus* in *The Basic Works of Aristotle*, edited by Richard McKeon (New York: Random House, 1941), pp. 643–661 and 1127–1316 respectively.

15. Ibid.

16. Anthony Quinton, "The Right Stuff," *The New York Review of Books* 32 (Dec. 5, 1985): 52.

17. See Ernst Haeckel, *Generelle Morphologie der Organismen*, 2 vols. (Berlin: Reimer, 1966); and Carl Linnaeus, "Specimen Academicum de Oeconomia Naturae," *Amoenitates Academicae* II: Holmae (Lugdoni Batavorum: Apud Cornelium Haas, 1751).

18. Donald Worster, *Nature's Economy: The Roots of Ecology* (Garden City, N.Y.: Anchor Books, 1979).

19. See Gilbert White, *The Natural History of Selborne* (New York: Harper, 1842).

20. See John Burroughs, "The Noon of Science" in *The Writings of John Burroughs*, vol. 17: *The Summit of the Years* (Boston: Houghton Mifflin and Company, 1913) and Frederick E. Clements, *Research Methods in Ecology* (Lincoln, Nebraska: University Publishing Co., 1905).

21. See R. Tobey, *Saving the Prairies: The Life Cycle of the Founding School of American Plant Ecology, 1895–1955* (Berkeley: University of California Press, 1981) and Robert P. McIntosh, *The Background of Ecology: Concept and Theory* (Cambridge: Cambridge University Press, 1985).

22. See Charles Elton, *Animal Ecology* (New York: Macmillan, 1927).

23. See Arthur G. Tansley, "The Use and Abuse of Vegetational Concepts and Terms," *Ecology* 16 (1935): 292–303.

24. Worster, *Nature's Economy*, p. 303.

25. Ibid, p. 332.

26. See Aldo Leopold, *A Sand County Almanac* (New York: Oxford University Press, 1949). For a discussion of the ecological and evolutionary foundations of the land ethic see J. Baird Callicott, "The Conceptual Foundations of the Land Ethic" in J. Baird Callicott, ed., *Companion to A Sand County Almanac: Interpretive and Critical Essays* (Madison: University of Wisconsin Press, 1987), pp. 186–215. Reproduced herein, pp. 75–99.

27. See Aldo Leopold, "Some Fundamentals of Conservation in the Southwest," *Environmental Ethics* 1 (1979): 131–148.

28. Leopold, *Sand County Almanac*, p. 216.

29. Paul Shepard, "A Theory of the Value of Hunting," *Twenty-Fourth North American Wildlife Conference* (1957): 505–6.

30. Harold J. Morowitz, "Biology as a Cosmological Science," *Main Currents in Modern Thought* 28 (1972): 156.

31. Arne Naess, "The Shallow and the Deep, Long-Range Ecology Movement: A Summary," *Inquiry* 16 (1973): 98.

32. Ibid., p. 95.

33. Werner Heisenberg, *Physics and Philosophy: The Revolution in Modern Science* (New York: Harper and Row, 1958), remarked, "We may say that all elementary particles consist of energy. This could be interpreted as defining energy as the primary substance of the world.... The elementary particles are certainly not eternal and indestructible units of matter, they can actually be transformed into each other.... Such events have been frequently observed and offer the best proof that all particles are made of the same substance: energy" (pp. 70-71).

34. Gary Snyder, "Song of the Taste," in *Regarding Wave* (New York: New Directions, 1967), p. 17.

35. See Naess, "The Shallow and the Deep, Long-Range Ecology Movement."

36. Eliot Deutsch, "Vedanta and Ecology" in T. M. P. Mehederan, ed., *Indian Philosophical Annual* 7 (Madras: The Center for Advanced Study in Philosophy, 1970). 1 10

37. Paul Shepard, "Ecology and Man: A Viewpoint" in P. Shepard and D. McKinley, eds., *The Subversive Science: Essays toward an Ecology of Man* (Boston: Houghton Mifflin Co., 1967), p. 3.

38. Fritjof Capra, *The Tao of Physics: An Exploration of the Parallels between Modern Physics and Eastern Mysticism* (Boulder: Shambala, 1975), pp. 30–31.

39. Deutsch, "Vedanta and Ecology," p. 4.

40. See Kenneth Goodpaster, "From Egoism to Environmentalism," in K. Goodpaster and K. Sayre, eds., *Ethics and Problems of the 21st Century* (Notre Dame: University of Notre Dame Press, 1979), pp. 21–35.

41. Paul Shepard, "Ecology and Man: A Viewpoint," p. 2.

42. See Alan Watts, *The Book on the Taboo against Knowing Who You Are* (New York: Pantheon Books, 1966).

43. Holmes Rolston, III, "Lake Solitude: The Individual in Wildness," *Main Currents in Modern Thought* 31 (1975): 122.

44. Paul Shepard, "Ecology and Man: A Viewpoint," p. 4

45. See Paul Shepard, *Thinking Animals: Animals and the Development of Human Intelligence* (New York: The Viking Press, 1978).

46. See Jonathan Powers, *Philosophy and the New Physics* (London: Methuen, 1982).

47. See J. Baird Callicott, "Intrinsic Value, Quantum Theory, and Environmental Ethics."

48. See Goodpaster, "From Egoism to Environmentalism."

49. Aldo Leopold, *A Sand County Almanac with Essays on Conservation from Round River* (New York: Ballantine Books, 1966), p. 197.

50. John Seed, "Anthropocentrism," Appendix E in Bill Devall and George Sessions, *Deep Ecology: Living as if Nature Mattered* (Salt Lake City, Nev.: Peregrin Smith Books, 1985), p. 243.

## Hume's *Is/Ought* Dichotomy and the Relation of Ecology to Leopold's Land Ethic

1. Aldo Leopold, *A Sand County Almanac* (New York: Oxford University Press, 1949), pp. viii, ix.

2. Holmes Rolston, III, "Is There an Ecological Ethic?" *Ethics* 85 (1975): 93–109; "Values in Nature," *Environmental Ethics* 3 (1981): 113–28; "Are Values in Nature Subjective or Objective?" *Environmental Ethics* 4 (1982): 125–151.

3. Don E. Marietta, Jr., "The Interrelationship of Ecological Science and Environmental Ethics," *Environmental Ethics* 2 (1979): 195–207; "Knowledge and Obligation in Environmental Ethics: A Phenomenological Approach" *Environmental Ethics* 4 (1982): 153–162. Tom Regan, "On the Connection Between Environmental Science and Environmental Ethics," *Environmental Ethics* 2 (1980): 363–66.

4. J. Baird Callicott, "Elements of an Environmental Ethic: Moral Considerability and the Biotic Community," *Environmental Ethics* 1 (1979): 71–81. Reproduced herein, pp. 63–73.

5. Anthony Flew, *Evolutionary Ethics* (London: Macmillan, 1967), p. 59.

6. Cf. David Hume, *A Treatise of Human Nature* (Oxford: Clarendon Press, 1960), bk. 3, pt. 3, sec. 1, pp. 469–70.

7. Charles Darwin, *Descent of Man,* 2nd ed. (New York: J. A. Hill and Co., 1904), p. 107, Cf. Hume, *Treatise,* pp. 577–78.

8. George Edward Moore, *Principia Ethica* (Cambridge University Press, 1903), chap. 1, sec. B, no. 9 ff.

9. For example (representing environmental ethics) John Rodman, "The Liberation of Nature?" *Inquiry* 10 (1977): 83–131, writes, "First, there is the powerful prohibition of modern culture against confusing 'is' and 'ought,' the 'natural' with the 'moral'—in short the taboo against committing 'the natural-

istic fallacy'." Anthony Flew writing in a more traditional context, provides another example in "On Not Deriving 'Ought' from 'Is'" in *The Is/Ought Question*, ed., W. D. Hudson (London: Macmillan, 1969) in which "naturalistic fallacy" and *"is/ought* dichotomy" are used interchangeably. William Frankena in a very thorough analysis of Moore ("The Naturalistic Fallacy," *Mind* 48 [1949]: 464–77) very convincingly argues that the is/ought dichotomy and the naturalistic fallacy are two distinct issues and that the naturalistic fallacy is not a *fallacy* in the proper sense of the word.

10. Hume, *Treatise*, p. 469.

11. Ibid., p. 469.

12. Regan, "On the Connection between Environmental Science and Environmental Ethics," p. 363.

13. Commenting on Hume's ethical theory, Philippa Foot writes, "Between these calm and indolent judgments [of reason] and the assertion that something should be done there is, Hume thinks, the famous gap between *is* and *ought*. Hume thought he himself had hit on the perfect solution to the problem. The new element in a proposition about virtue was the reference to a special sentiment of approbation: nothing new in the object, but something in ourselves," "Hume on Moral Judgment," *David Hume: A Symposium*, ed. D. F. Pears (London: Macmillan and Co., 1963), pp. 73–74. Foot, thus, has anticipated me in believing that Hume himself regarded the *is/ought* logical lacuna to be bridged by a premise referring to passion, sentiment, or interest. A more elaborate and detailed argument along similar lines may be found in A. C. MacIntyre, "Hume on 'Is' and 'Ought'" in *The Is/Ought Question*. As MacIntyre sums up his argument, "one has to go beyond the [is/ought] passage . . .; but if one does so, it is plain that we can connect the facts of the situation with what we ought to do only by means of one of those concepts which Hume treats under the heading of the passions . . ." (p. 48).

14. Immanuel Kant, *Foundations of the Metaphysics of Morals*, trans. Lewis White Beck (New York: Bobbs-Merril, 1959), p. 34. Philippa Foot develops this line of thought in "Morality as a System of Hypothetical Imperatives," *Philosophical Review* 81 (1972): 303–16.

15. For a particularly candid, indeed unabashed, statement of this sort of attitude see Gene Spitler, "Sensible Environmental Principles for the Future," *Environmental Ethics* 2 (1980): 339–52.

16. Leopold, *Sand County Almanac*, p. 204.

17. Ibid., p. 208

18. Ibid., p. 204.

19. Hume, *Treatise*, pp. 486–87.

20. Ibid., pp. 484–85.

21. Leopold, *Sand County Almanac*, p. 109.

22. I have reversed the order of the premises (1) and (2) in the general format as previously employed in deference to MacIntyre's discussion, "Hume on 'Is' and 'Ought'," which refers to a suppressed "major premise" which appropriately formulates an agent's sentiments. In the previous examples the premise containing reference to the agent(s)' feelings(s) was indexed "(2)" since it was in fact suppressed and "bridged" the *is* premise and the *ought* conclusion.

23. J. Baird Callicott, "Animal Liberation: A Triangular Affair," *Environmental Ethics* 2 (1980): 319, n. 21. Reproduced herein, pp. 15–38. It has been traditionally associated with Albert Schweitzer and recently systematically expounded by Kenneth Goodpaster, "On Being Morally Considerable," *Journal of Philosophy* 75 (1978): 308–25.

24. Cf. Callicott, "Elements of an Environmental Ethic."

25. Leopold, *Sand County Almanac*, pp. 224–25.

26. Hume himself, of course, did not discuss the evolution of the moral sentiments or passions. He wrote before Darwin and the evolutionary habit of mind. However, see Anthony Flew's comment in *Evolutionary Ethics*, p. 59.


## On the Intrinsic Value of Nonhuman Species

1. See George M. Woodwell, "The Challenge of Endangered Species," in *Extinction Is Forever*, edited by Ghillian Prance and Thomas Elias (New York: New York Botanical Garden, 1977), p. 5

2. See Thomas Eisner et al., "Conservation of Tropical Forests," *Science* 213 (1981): 1314, and Thomas E. Lovejoy, "Species Leave the Ark One by One," in Bryan G. Norton, ed., *The Preservation of Species* (Princeton, NJ: Princeton University Press, 1986), pp. 13–27.

3. See International Union for Conservation of Nature and Natural Resources (IUCN), *Red Data Book* (Morges, Switzerland: IUCN, 1974) and Norman Myers, "An Expanded Approach to the Problem of Disappearing Species," *Science* 193 (1976): 198–201.

4. Norman Myers, *The Sinking Ark: A New Look at the Problem of Disappearing Species* (New York: Pergamon Press, 1979), p. 4. This seemingly preposterous rate is based upon the assumption that systematic deforestation of moist tropical forests could result in the loss of one million species by the turn of the century (see Eisner et al., "Conservation of Tropical Forests"). Considering how close we are to 2000 A.D., the rate of 100 per day actually appears conservative. An average of more nearly 150 species extinctions per day would have to take place if one million species were to become extinct between now and the year 2000.

5. Eisner et al., "Conservation of Tropical Forests"; Myers, *Sinking Ark*, p. 5.

6. A. R. Wallace, *The Geographical Distribution of Animals* (London: Macmillan, 1876), p. 150.

7. This and other questions in the paragraph are routinely posed rhetorical questions. Should the figure of 90 + percent be doubted, however, see David M. Raup, "Size of the Permo-Triassic Bottleneck and Its Evolutionary Implications," *Science* 206 (1979): 217–18.

8. See Normal D. Newell, "Crises in the History of Life," *Scientific American* 208 (1963): 76–92; David M. Raup and J. John Sepkoski, Jr., "Mass Extinctions in the Marine Fossil Record," *Science* 215 (1982), 1501–03.

9. Two recent works, Myers, *Sinking Ark,* and Paul and Anne Ehrlich, *Extinction: The Causes and Consequences of the Disappearance of Species* (New York: Random House, 1981), are in large part convenient catalogues of utilitarian or, more accurately, "homocentric" arguments for species preservation. Also see Norton, *Preservation of Species* and Alastair S. Gunn, "Preserving Rare Species," in *Earthbound, New Introductory Essays in Environmental Ethics* edited by Tom Regan (New York: Random House, 1984), pp. 289–335. Gunn provides a taxonomy and critical discussion of utiltarian or homocentric arguments for species preservation.

10. As a system of philosophical ethics, utilitarianism does not posit human happiness or human well-being as the *summum bonum.* Rather, Jeremy Bentham and John Stuart Mill, the founders of utilitarianism, declared that pleasure is good and pain is evil and that it is the duty of a moral agent to maximize the one and minimize the other no matter where located, that is, no matter by whom experienced. Cf. Jeremy Bentham, *Introduction to the Principles of Morals and Legislation,* New Edition (Oxford: The Clarendon Press, 1823), chap. I, secs. I and X, and John Stuart Mill, *Utilitarianism* (New York: Library of Liberal Arts, 1957), chap. 2. The implications of this view for animal liberation and the preservation of species are discussed below.

11. Woodwell, "The Challenge of Endangered Species," p. 5, and Howard S. Irwin, *Extinction Is Forever,* Preface, p. 2. Cf. also Michael Soule's comment in *Proceedings of the U.S. Strategy Conference on Biological Diversity, Nov. 16–18, 1981* (Washington, D.C.: Department of State Publication 9262, 1982), p. 61: "It is regrettable that we must all pretend to be concerned exclusively with man and his welfare and put nearly all of our arguments for conservation for biological diversity in terms of benefit for man. When [will we] admit in public that conservation is not only for people, something most of us already admit in private?"

12. William Godfrey-Smith, "The Rights of Non-humans and Intrinsic Values," in *Environmental Philosophy,* edited by Don Mannison, Michael McRobbie, and Richard Routley (Canberra: Australian National University, 1980), p. 31, shares my suspicions: "Although environmentalists often use the rare herb argument, it seems to me that it is really only a lever; it does not express a very significant component of their thinking." See also Alastair S.

Gunn, "Why Should We Care About Rare Species?" *Environmental Ethics* 2 (1980): 17–37.

13. Examples, in chronological order, are: John Muir, *Our National Parks* (Boston: Houghton Mifflin, 1901), p. 57, and *A Thousand-Mile Walk to the Gulf* (Boston: Houghton Mifflin, 1916), p. 98; Aldo Leopold, *A Sand County Almanac* (New York: Oxford University Press, 1949), pp. 210, 211; Charles Elton, *The Ecology of Invasions by Animals and Plants* (London: Methuen, 1958), p. 144; David Ehrenfeld, "The Conservation of Non-Resources," *American Scientist* 64 (1976): 654; Bruce MacBryde, "Plant Conservation in the United States Fish and Wildlife Service," in *Extinction Is Forever*, p. 70; Ehrlich and Ehrlich, *Extinction*, p. 48; Roger E. McManus and Judith Hinds, eds., *The Endangered Species Act Reauthorization Bulletin 1* (Washington, D.C.: Center for Environmental Education, Dec. 1981), p. 3.

14. Gunn, "Preserving Rare Species," p. 330.

15. Mark Sagoff, "On the Preservation of Species," *Columbia Journal of Law* 7 (1980): 64, claims that "we enjoy an object because it is valuable; we do not value it merely because we enjoy it. . . Esthetic experience is a perception as it were, of a certain kind of worth." For a similar judgment about aesthetic experience as applied to the question of species preservation see Lilly-Marlene Russow, "Why Do Species Matter?" *Environmental Ethics* 3 (1981): 101–12. William F. Baxter, *People or Penguins: The Case for Optimal Pollution* (New York: Columbia University Press, 1974), p. 5, however, turns this argument on its head: "Damage to penguins, or sugar pines, or geological marvels is, without more, simply irrelevant. One must go further . . . , and say: Penguins are important because people enjoy seeing them walk about rocks. . ." Ehrenfeld, "The Conservation of Non-Resources," p. 654, discusses the aesthetic rationale for species preservation and concludes that "it is rooted in the homocentric, humanistic world view," since it appeals, finally to what "is stimulating to man." He finds the aesthetic rationale incompatible with the "humility-inspiring discoveries of community ecology or with the sort of ecological world view, emphasizing the connectedness and immense complexity of man-nature relationships, that now characterize a large bloc of ecological thought." This is also the case, I think, with Donald Regan's novel argument for the intrinsic value of experiences regarding nonhuman species in "Duties of Preservation," *Preservation of Species*, edited by Norton, pp. 195–220. The "organic unity" of the "complex" consisting of a natural object, human knowledge of a natural object, and the human pleasure taken in that knowledge notwithstanding, upon Regan's argument nonhuman species remain only instrumentally valuable as *epistemic resources;* the value Regan finds in nonhuman species is formally the same as aesthetic value, since species are valuable according to his account as objects of epistemic experience rather than as objects of aesthetic experience. The putative intrinsic value he claims for nonhuman species is susceptible to reduction to mere instrumental value. As either aesthetic or epistemic objects, nonhuman species are valued only as means to an intrinsically valuable state of human consciousness, or so either Baxter or Ehrenfeld might insist.

16. See, for example, Holmes Rolston, III, "Are Values in Nature Subjective or Objective?" *Environmental Ethics* 4 (1982): 125–51; and Don E. Marietta, Jr., "Knowledge and Obligation in Environmental Ethics: A Phenomenological Approach," *Environmental Ethics* 4 (1982): 153–62.

17. See for example, Christopher Stone, *Should Trees Have Standing? Toward Legal Rights for Natural Objects* (Los Altos: William Kaufman, 1974), for an "operational" definition. It may be worth noting that the Endangered Species Act of 1973 confers rights upon specimens of endangered species according to Stone's operational criteria, although the Act does not specify "rights" per se and grounds its protection for endangered species exclusively in utilitarian terms.

18. See H. L. A. Hart, "The Ascription of Responsibility and Rights," in *Logic and Language,* edited by Anthony Flew (Garden City: Anchor Books, 1965), pp. 151–74.

19. John Rodman, "The Liberation of Nature," *Inquiry* 20 (1977): 108, agrees with this analysis of the popular preservationist usage of "rights": "To affirm that 'natural objects' have 'rights' is symbolically to affirm that all natural entities, including humans, have intrinsic worth simply by virtue of being." Nicholas Rescher, "Why Save Endangered Species?" in *Unpopular Essays on Technological Progress* (Pittsburgh: University of Pittsburgh Press, 1980), agrees that species per se cannot be coherently attributed rights. He also asserts that we have an ethical duty to save endangered species because they possess a metaphysical intrinsic value. He does not, however, undertake to provide a *theory* of intrinsic value or detail a metaphysics which conceptually grounds the intrinsic value of species.

20. David L. Hull, "A Matter of Individuality," *Philosophy of Science* 45 (1978): 335–60.

21. For a general discussion, see Michael Ruse, "Definitions of Species in Biology," *The British Journal for the Philosophy of Science* 20 (1969): 97–119. For a critical discussion of Hull's views see D. B. Kitts and D. J. Kitts, "Biological Species as Natural Kinds," *Philosophy of Science* 46 (1979): 613–22, and Arthur L. Caplan, "Back to Class: A Note on the Ontology of Species," *Philosophy of Science* 48 (1981): 130–40.

22. In the interests of both contemporary relevance and saving space I shall *not* discuss those classical moral metaphysics which might provide for the intrinsic value of nonhuman species but which have few contemporary exponents. An example of one such theory is G. E. Moore's Intuitionism in which value or "goodness" is alleged to be an objective, but "non-natural," quality which one may discern by one's unaided moral sensibilities.

23. Ehrenfeld, "The Conservation of Non-Resources," p. 654.

24. Ibid., p. 655. Similar ideas are expressed in his "What Good Are Endangered Species Anyway?" *National Parks and Conservation Magazine* 52 (October 1978): 10–12; and *The Arrogance of Humanism* (New York: Oxford University Press, 1978), pp. 207–11.

25. See John Passmore, "The Treatment of Animals," *Journal of the History of Ideas* 36 (1975): 195–218, for a definitive discussion.

26. Lynn White, Jr., "The Historical Roots of Our Ecologic Crisis," *Science* 155 (1967): 1203–7. White does not consider an alternative, environmentally more sympathetic interpretation of the verses in question, generally referred to as "stewardship." According to the stewardship interpretation of Scripture, man's superiority implies not only privilege but responsibility. For a scholarly elaboration and defense of a stewardship reading of Genesis 1:26–30 see James Barr, "Man and Nature: The Ecological Controversy and the Old Testament," *Bulletin of the John Rylands Library* (1972): 9–32.

27. Lynn White, Jr., "Historical Roots," p. 1205.

28. It should be kept in mind that the idea that human beings possess moral or natural rights was initially defended by John Locke in his quaint *First Treatise of Government* in scriptural terms. God, according to Locke, conferred rights upon Adam and his descendants. In this connection we should remind ourselves of Thomas Jefferson's famous words in the Declaration of Independence: "all men .. *are endowed by their Creator* with certain inalienable rights," emphasis added. Human worth and dignity thus were once commonly grounded in a theocentric moral metaphysic.

29. Muir, *Our National Parks,* p. 57, emphasis added.

30. Muir, *Thousand-Mile Walk,* pp. 98–99.

31. Arthur Weiser, *The Old Testament: Its Formation and Development,* D. Barton (New York: Association Press, 1961).

32. Ibid., p. 77.

33. See F. M. Cornford, *Principia Sapientia* (Cambridge: Cambridge University Press, 1952), chap. 11, for a detailed discussion.

34. Cf. "The Tübingen School," most notably, H. J. Kramer, *Arete bei Platon und Aristoteles: zum Wesen und zur Geschichte der platonischen Ontologie* (Heidelberg: Heidelberger Akademie, 1959); cf. also Konrad Gaiser, *Platons ungeschriebene Lehre* (Stuttgart: E. Klept, 1963); Konrad Gaiser, ed., *Das Platonbild* (Hildesheim: G. Olms, 1969) and J. N. Findlay, *Plato: The Written and Unwritten Doctrines* (London: Routledge and Kegan Paul, 1974).

35. See Plato, *Gorgias* 503e–508c, for a reasonably clear and explicit statement of the nature of goodness (i.e., value).

36. G. W. v. Leibniz, "Monadology," no. 58 in G. R Montgomery, trans., *Leibniz* (LaSalle, Ill.: Open Court, 1962), p. 263.

37. G. W. v. Leibniz, "Discourse on Metaphysics," sec. 6, in *Leibniz,* p. 11.

38. See, for example, Noel J. Brown, "Biological Diversity: The Global Challenge," in *Proceedings of the U.S. Strategy Conference on Biological Diversity* (see n. 11 above).

39. Leopold, *Sand County Almanac,* p. 224.

40. Peter Miller, "Value as Richness: Toward a Value Theory for an Expanded Naturalism in Environmental Ethics," *Environmental Ethics* 4 (1982): 103.

41. See Leibniz, "Monadology," nos. 53–59, for an explicit discussion of these conditions. In addition to order and variety, Leibniz also includes in the concept of value the tantalizingly "organic" characteristics of "interconnection," "relationship," "adaptation," and "universal harmony." For a fuller discussion see Walter H. O'Briant, "Leibniz's Contribution to Environmental Philosophy," *Environmental Ethics* 2 (1980): 215–20.

42. See Leibniz, "Discourse on Metaphysics," sec. 5, where he compares God to "an excellent Geometer" and to "a good architect." He goes on to say, "that the reason [God] wishes to avoid multiplicity of hypotheses or principles [is] very much as the simplest system is preferred in Astronomy" (*Leibniz,* pp. 8–9).

43. Kenneth Goodpaster, "From Egoism to Environmentalism," in *Ethics and Problems of the 21st Century,* edited by Kenneth Goodpaster and Kenneth Sayre (Notre Dame: Notre Dame University Press, 1979), pp. 21–35.

44. Kant provides the clearest possible illustration: "Its [the categorical imperative's] foundation is this, that rational nature exists as an end in itself. Man necessarily conceives his own existence this way, and so far this is a subjective principle of human action." In Kant's view this subjective principle becomes (relatively) "objective" by generalization: "But in this way also every other rational being conceives of his own existence, and for the very same reason; hence the principle is also objective, and from it, as the highest practical ground, all laws of the will must be capable of being derived." John Stuart Mill, Bentham's utilitarian protégé, employs the same general strategy as Kant to transcend egoism. According to Mill, "the happiness [previously defined in terms of pleasure and pain] which forms the utilitarian standard of what is right in conduct is not the agent's own happiness but that of all concerned. As between *his own* happiness and that of others, utilitarianism requires him to be as strictly impartial as a disinterested and benevolent spectator." Immanuel Kant, *Foundations of the Metaphysics of Morals,* trans. by John Watson (Glasgow: Jackson, Wylie and Company, 1888), second section, and John Stuart Mill, *Utilitarianism* (New York: Bobbs-Merrill, 1957), chap. 2, emphasis added.

45. Kant, *Foundations,* second section: "And even beings whose existence depends upon nature [including thus animals and plants], not upon our will have only relative value as means [i.e., instrumental value]." For a more elaborate statement see "Duties to Animals and Spirits," in Immanuel Kant, *Lectures on Ethics,* trans. by Louis Infield (New York: Harper and Row, 1963), pp. 239–41.

46. Jeremy Bentham, *An Introduction to the Principles of Morals and Legislation,* new edition. (Oxford: Oxford University Press, 1823), chap. xvii, sec. 1.

47. J. Baird Callicott, "Animal Liberation: A Triangular Affair," *Environmental Ethics* 2 (1980): 311–38. Reproduced herein, pp. 49–59. See also similar views

expressed by R. and V. Routley, "Human Chauvinism and Environmental Ethics," in Mannison et al., eds., *Environmental Philosophy*, pp. 96–189 (see n. 12 above).

48. Peter Singer, "Not for Humans Only: The Place of Nonhumans in Environmental Issues," in Goodpaster and Sayre, eds., *Ethics and Problems of the 21st Century*, pp. 191–206. Tom Regan has expressed a similar view in *The Case for Animal Rights* (Berkeley: University of California Press, 1983), p. 360: "...the reason we ought to save the members of endangered species of animals is not because the species is endangered but because the individual animals have valid claims and thus rights."

49. In response to this concern which I first expressed as an "irony" of animal liberation in "A Triangular Affair," animal liberationist Edward Johnson saw nothing wrong with it. According to Johnson, "the crucial point, though, is that there is no 'irony' here even if a species does become extinct, since it is not the species that is being liberated, but individual members of the species." Edward Johnson, "Animal Liberation Versus the Land Ethic," *Environmental Ethics* 3 (1981): 267.

50. Sagoff, personal communication.

51. Arthur Schopenhauer, *The World as Will and Idea*, trans. Haldane and Kemp (Garden City: Doubleday, 1961); see also, "Transcendent Considerations Concerning the Will as Thing in Itself," in *The Will to Live: Selected Writings of Arthur Schopenhauer*, ed. Richard Taylor (New York: Frederick Unger, 1962), pp. 33–42.

52. "Just as in my own will-to-live there is a yearning for more life... so the same obtains in all the will-to-live around me, equally whether it can express itself to my comprehension or whether it remains unvoiced." Schweitzer here says in effect, my essence and for me the source of my own preciousness is the will to live, but the same thing, a striving for life, is in every other living thing. There follows the transition from egoism to altruism: "Ethics thus consists in this, that I experience the necessity of practicing the same reverence for life toward all will-to-live, as toward my own." Albert Schweitzer, *Civilization and Ethics*, trans. John Naish, reprinted in Regan and Singer, eds., *Animal Rights and Human Obligations* (Englewood Cliffs: Prentice-Hall, 1976), p. 133.

53. H. J. McCloskey holds such a position in "Rights," *Philosophical Quarterly* 15 (1965): 115–27. See also Meredith Williams, "Rights, Interests, and Moral Equality," *Environmental Ethics* (1980): 149–61. For the general relationship between interests and rights see also Joel Feinberg, "The Nature and Value of Rights," *Journal of Value Inquiry* 4 (1970): 243–57, and Bryan Norton, "Environmental Ethics and Non-human Rights," *Environmental Ethics* 4 (1982): 17–36.

54. Peter Singer, *Animal Liberation: A New Ethics for Our Treatment of Animals* (New York: New York Review, 1975) p. 8, writes, "The capacity for suffering and enjoying things is a prerequisite for having interests at all, a condition that must be satisfied for having interests at all." See also Tom Regan, "The Moral Basis of Vegetarianism," *Canadian Journal of Philosophy* 5 (1975): 181–214; and

William Frankena, "Ethics and the Environment," in Goodpaster and Sayre, eds, *Ethics of the 21st Century*.

55. Joel Feinberg, "Can Animals Have Rights?" in Regan and Singer, eds., *Animal Rights and Human Obligations*, p. 191. Paul W. Taylor, in "The Ethics of Respect for Nature," *Environmental Ethics* 3 (1981)· 199–200, without using the term "conation," appears to understand "interests" along lines similar to Feinberg's: "We can act in a being's interest or contrary to its interest without its being interested in what we are doing to it. It may, indeed, be wholly unaware.... When construed in this way, the concept of a being's good [i.e., interest] is not coextensive with sentience or the capacity for feeling pain."

56. Kenneth Goodpaster, "On Being Morally Considerable," *Journal of Philosophy* 75 (1978): 306–25. Goodpaster here wisely avoids a discussion of rights. In his view rights would involve something more (what more, he does not say) than interests. J. Kantor, "The 'Interests' of Natural Objects," *Environmental Ethics* 2 (1980): 163–71, also draws attention to Feinberg's inconsistency in defining "interest" in terms of conation and then denying interests to plants. In Kantor's view plants may have interests. However, he does not think that the interests of plants can serve as the basis of rights; siding with Singer and Regan, he thinks that in addition a being must consciously suffer from having its interests harmed in order to be accorded rights.

57. Schweitzer, *Civilization and Ethics*, p. 136; Goodpaster, "Being Morally Considerable," p. 324. For a discussion of Schweitzer on this problem see William T. Blackstone, "The Search for an Environmental Ethic," in Tom Regan, ed., *Matters of Life and Death* (New York: Random House, 1980), pp. 299–335.

58. Goodpaster, "Being Morally Considerable," p. 313.

59. Schweitzer, *Civilization and Ethics*, p. 137.

60. Donald VanDeVeer, "Interspecific Justice," *Inquiry* 22 (1979): 55–79, has made an attempt to do just this.

61. Doubts concerning the serviceability of the predominant individual-egalitarian bias of moral metaphysics in the modern tradition vis-à-vis environmental ethical problems have been publicly expressed by John Rodman, "Liberation of Nature"; Bryan Norton, "Environmental Ethics and Non-Human Rights"; Richard and Val Routley, "Human Chauvinism"; Peter Miller, "Value as Richness"; Tom Regan, "The Nature and Possibility of an Environmental Ethic," *Environmental Ethics* 3 (1981): 19–34; and J. Baird Callicott, "Animal Liberation."

62. Cf. David Hume, *A Treatise of Human Nature* (Oxford: The Calrendon Press, 1960), bk. III, pt. I.

63. Charles Darwin, *The Descent of Man and Selection in Relation to Sex*, 2nd ed. (New York: J. A. Hill, 1904), p. 97.

64. Ibid., p. 107.

65. Ibid., p. 118.

66. Ibid., p. 124.

67. Darwin seems both aware and forthright about his dependence on the concept of group selection in his account of the origin and evolution of morals: "We have now seen that actions are regarded by savages, and were probably so regarded by primeval man, as good or bad, solely as they obviously affect the welfare of the tribe—not that of the species, nor that of the individual member of the species. This conclusion agrees well with the belief that the so-called moral sense is aboriginally derived from the social instincts, for both relate at first exclusively to the community" (ibid., p. 120). V. C. Wynne-Edwards, *Animal Dispersion in Relation to Social Behavior* (Edinburgh: Oliver and Boyd, 1962), provides the most celebrated recent support for group selection. Wynne-Edwards was refuted to the satisfaction at least of most biologists by G. C. Williams in *Adaptation and Natural Selection: A Critique of Some Current Evolutionary Thought* (Princeton: Princton University Press, 1966) and ever since, the concept of group selection has been avoided by most evolutionary theorists and certainly by sociobiologists. For a recent summary discussion see Michael Ruse, *Sociobiology: Sense or Nonsense?* (Boston: D. Reidel, 1979).

68. Most notably by W. D. Hamilton, "The Genetical Theory of Social Behavior," *Journal of Theoretical Biology* 7 (1964): 1–32; R. L. Trivers, "The Evolution of Reciprocal Altruism," *Quarterly Review of Biology* 46 (1971): 35–57; Edward O. Wilson, *Sociobiology: The New Synthesis* (Cambridge: Harvard University Press, 1975). Ruse, *Sociobiology: Sense or Nonsense?* provides a thorough bibliography.

69. Leopold, *Sand County Almanac*, p. 202.

70. Ibid.

71. Ehrlich and Ehrlich, *Extinction*, p. 48.

72. Ibid., pp. 50–51.

73. Hume, *Treatise*, pp. 484–85.

74. Darwin, *Descent*, p. 122.

75. Leopold, *Sand County Almanac*, p. 204.

76. See the discussion of Hume in W. D. Hudson, *Modern Moral Philosophy* (Garden City: Anchor Books, 1970), for a good summary of professional opinion.

## Intrinsic Value, Quantum Theory, and Environmental Ethics

1. Richard Routely, "Is There a Need for a New, an Environmental Ethic?" in Bulgarian Organizing Committee, ed, *Proceedings of the Fifteenth World Congress of Philosophy I* (Sophia Bulgaria: Sophia Press, 1973), pp. 205–10.

2. Tom Regan, "The Nature and Possibility of an Environmental Ethic," *Environmental Ethics* 3 (1981): 34. For an insightful critical discussion of Regan's essay, generally supportive of the subjectivist approach to a theory of inherent value in nature outlined in this section, see Evelyn B. Pluhar, "The Justification of an Environmental Ethic," *Environmental Ethics* 5 (1983): 47–61. For a dissenting opinion on the centrality of the problem of establishing intrinsic value in nature see Bryan Norton, "Environmental Ethics and Weak Anthropocentrism," *Environmental Ethics* 6 (1984): 131–48.

3. See Kenneth Goodpaster, "On Being Morally Considerable," *Journal of Philosophy* 75 (1978): 308–25.

4. Regan, "Nature and Possibility," p. 33.

5. Peter Miller, "Value as Richness: Toward a Value Theory for the Expanded Naturalism in Environmental Ethics," *Environmental Ethics* 4 (1982): 101–14.

6. David Hume, *A Treatise of Human Nature*, bk. 3, p. 1, sec. 1 (Oxford: The Clarendon Press, 1988), pp. 468–89. My interpretation of Hume in this and earlier papers owes much to J. L. Mackie's *Hume's Moral Theory* (London: Routledge and Kegan Paul, 1980). For a full-scale metaethical development of the Humean subjectivist axiology outlined in this section see J. L. Mackie, *Ethics: Inventing Right and Wrong* (New York: Penguin Books, 1977).

7. *Webster's Seventh New Collegiate Dictionary* (Springfield: G. & C. Merriam Company, 1972).

8. Robin Attfield has also recently developed a distinction between intrinsic, inherent, and instrumental value in the context of environmental ethics. Cf. Robin Attfield, *The Ethics of Environmental Concern* (New York: Columbia University Press, 1983), pp. 140–53. Attfield defines *intrinsic value* as a Benthamic naturalist. Not disallowing that other things may be intrinsically valuable, he asserts, I suppose after consulting his inner axiological oracle (see note 12 below), that "nevertheless pleasure and pain remain of positive and negative value in themselves." Attfield endorses C. I. Lewis's definition of *inherent value* as "the value which an object has through its ability to contribute to human life by its presence ... [such as] things whether alive or not which are interesting to watch or study or beautiful to contemplate, or which heal us when we are with them." As I have here defined *inherent value*, the value an object has through its ability to contribute to human life by its presence, as an object to watch or study, is *not* a case of inherent value. Rather, such value remains instrumental value, as I have defined it, since the object is the means to preferred experiences of the valuer. Neither Attfield nor Lewis before him provide a concept, however it may be labeled, of inherent value, as here set out. For Attfield, thus, a plant species, like the giant sequoia, lacks intrinsic value since it lacks sentiency, but possesses what he calls inherent value and what I would call psycho-spiritual instrumental value. Hence, as Attfield himself admits, Routley's last man would do nothing wrong were he deliberately to extirpate the giant sequoia if he were not interested in watching or studing the trees, but only in taking perverse pleasure in the extermination of their species. Attfield

also cites W. K. Frankena, "Ethics and the Environment," in Goodpaster and Sayre, eds., *Ethics and Problems of the 21st Century* (Notre Dame: Notre Dame University Press, 1979), p. 13, as endorsing Lewis's conception of inherent value. Cf. C. I. Lewis, *The Ground and Nature of the Right* (New York: Columbia University Press, 1955), p. 69. In reaction to the naturalistic value theory of Bentham's classical utilitarianism, namely that pleasure is intrinsically valuable, Tom Regan has cut a distinction between intrinsic and inherent value along yet other lines. Regan allows intrinsic value to attach to pleasure. In this he is in agreement with Attfield and Bentham and Bentham's many exponents. According to Regan's stipulation, *inherent* value accrues to individual beings. Regan's understanding of inherent value is formally the same as his understanding of intrinsic value. Both designate the objective value of something in and for itself. Inherent and instrinsic value differ, according to Regan, rather, in extension or denotation: "(1) the value of individuals and (2) the value of mental states or states of affairs," respectively. Tom Regan, *All That Dwell Therein* (Berkeley: University of California Press, 1982), p. 115. Regan's concern is that if only pleasure, let's say, is intrinsically valuable, that is valuable in and for itself, then classical utilitarianism is obliged to treat individuals as, so to speak, disposable receptacles of the precious commodity. Hence, some individuals may be treated abominably for the sake of maximizing the intrinsically valuable commodity reposing in other containers. See also Tom Regan, *The Case for Animal Rights* (Berkeley: University of California Press, 1983), pp. 235–56.

9. Richard and Val Routley, "Human Chauvinism and Environmental Ethics," in Mannison, McRobbie, and Routley, eds., *Environmental Philosophy* (Canberra: Australian National University, 1980), pp. 96–189, provide an extended argument to show that though there may be no value without valuers, it does not follow either that only valuers are valuable or that only the preferred experiences of valuers are valuable.

10. For a representative opinion, see Brand Blanchard, *Reason and Goodness* (New York: Macmillan, 1961), chap. 4. For a summary of opinion see Jonathan Harrison, "Ethical Subjectivism," in Paul Edwards, ed., *The Encyclopedia of Philosophy* (New York: Macmillan, 1967), 3:78–81.

11. Edward O. Wilson, personal communication. Cf. Edward O. Wilson, *Sociobiology: The New Synthesis* (Cambridge: Harvard University Press, 1975); W. D. Hamilton, "The Genetical Theory of Social Behavior," *Journal of Theoretical Biology* 7 (1964): 1–32; and R. L. Trivers, "The Evolution of Reciprocal Altruism," *Quarterly Review of Biology* 46 (1971): 35–57. Edward O. Wilson, *On Human Nature* (New York: Bantam Books, 1979), claims that "Science may soon be in a position to investigate the very origin and meaning of human values.... Philosophers..., most of whom lack an evolutionary perspective, have not devoted much time to the problem.... Like everyone else, philosophers measure their personal emotional responses to various alternatives as though consulting a hidden oracle.... Human emotional responses and the more general ethical practices based on them have been programmed to a substantial degree by natural selection over thousands of generations" (pp. 5–6).

12. Callicott, "On the Intrinsic Value of Nonhuman Species."

13. Holmes Rolston, III, "Values in Nature," *Environmental Ethics* 3 (1981): 114.

14. Ibid.

15. Peter Miller, personal communication.

16. Warwick Fox, "Deep Ecology: A New Philosophy of Our Time?" *The Ecologist* 14 (1984): 194–200.

17. Don E. Marietta, Jr., "The Interrelationship of Ecological Science and Environmental Ethics," *Environmental Ethics* 1 (1979): 195–207. A similar thought is implicitly present in Alan R. Dregson, "Shifting Paradigms: From the Techno-cratic to the Person-Planetary," *Environmental Ethics* 2 (1980): 221–40.

18. Richard and Val Routley, "Human Chauvinism and Environmental Ethics," 155. See also R. and V. Routley, "Semantic Foundations of Value Theory," *Nous* 17 (1983): 441–56.

19. Holmes Rolston, III, "Are Values in Nature Subjective or Objective?," *Environmental Ethics* 4 (1982): 127. Jay McDaniel in "Physical Matter as Creative and Sentient," *Environmental Ethics* 5 (1983): 291–317, also relates quantum theory to the fact-value dichotomy in value theory, but he does so in a way fundamentally different from that suggested by Marietta and Rolston and developed here. McDaniel, integrating Whiteheadian metaphysics with quantum theory, grounds the intrinsic value of physical matter in the "creative sentience" he believes to reside in physical matter. McDaniel, thus, assumes an axiological naturalism not unlike Bentham's. He assumes, in other words, that experience (whether pleasant or not) is valuable: "the fact that energy composing a rock exhibits unconscious reality-for-itself [elsewhere called 'non-conscious sentiency'] means that the rock has intrinsic value, for *intrinsic value* is nothing else than the reality a given entity has for itself, independently of its reality for the observer" (p. 315).

20. Rolston, "Subjective or Objective," p. 129.

21. Cf. Werner Heisenberg, *Physics and Philosophy: The Revolution in Modern Science* (New York: Harper and Row, 1962), chap. 2.

22. Rolston, "Subjective or Objective," p. 127. Rolston cites Samuel Alexander, *Beauty and Other Forms of Value* (New York: Thomas Crowell Company, 1968).

23. Ibid., p. 129.

24. Werner Heisenberg, a founder of the Copenhagen Interpretation, comments in *Physics and Philosophy* that "we can say that the matter of Aristotle, which is mere 'potentia,' should be compared to our concept of energy, which gets into 'actuality' by means of the form, when the elementary particle is created" (p. 160).

25. Fritjof Capra, *The Tao of Physics* (Boulder: Shambala Publications, 1975), pp. 68–69.

26. Paul Shepard, "Ecology and Man—A Viewpoint," in Shepard and McKinley, eds., *The Subversive Science* (Boston: Houghton Mifflin, 1969), p. 2.

27. Ibid., p. 3.

28. Ibid., p. 4. Arne Naess in "The Shallow and the Deep, Long-Range Ecology Movement: A Summary," *Inquiry* 16 (1973): 95, in a single short paragraph captured the structural similarity between ecology and quantum theory and suggested that both imply a doctrine of real internal relations: "Deep ecology [involves] rejection of the man-in-environment image in favor of *the relational, total-field image*. Organisms [are] knots in the biospherical net or field of intrinsic relations. An intrinsic relation between two things A and B is such that the relation belongs to the definitions or basic constituents of A and B, so that without the relation, A and B are no longer the same things. The total field model dissolves not only the man-in-environment concept, but every compact thing-in-milieu concept—except when talking at a superficial or preliminary level of communication."

29. Shepard, "Ecology and Man," p. 3. Shepard cites Alan Watts, *The Book on the Taboo Against Knowing Who You Are* (New York: Pantheon, 1966).

30. Kenneth Goodpaster, "From Egoism to Environmentalism" in *Ethics and Problems of the 21st Century*, pp. 21–35.

31. Callicott, "Non-anthropocentric Value Theory and Environmental Ethics," n. 33.

32. Richard and Val Routley, "Human Chauvinism and Environmental Ethics," p. 152.

33. For a compendium of such theorists, see David P. Gauthier, ed., *Morality and Rational Self-Interest* (Englewood Cliffs: Prentice Hall, 1970). Notable among contemporary moral philosophers who appear to equate rationality with self-interest are John Rawls and Garrett Hardin. Cf. John Rawls, "Distributive Justice," in Laslett and Runciman, eds., *Philosophy, Politics and Society* (Oxford: Basil Blackwell, 1969), pp. 58–82; and Garrett Hardin, "The Tragedy of the Commons," *Science* 162 (1968): 1243–48.

34. Aldo Leopold, "The Round River," in *A Sand County Almanac, with Essays on Conservation from Round River* (New York: Ballantine Books, 1970), p. 197.

## Traditional American Indian and Western European Attitudes Toward Nature: An Overview

1. Joseph E. Brown, "Modes of Contemplation through Action: North American Indians," *Main Currents in Modern Thought* 30 (1973–74): 60.

2. Calvin Martin, *Keepers of the Game: Indian-American Relationships and the Fur Trade* (Berkeley and Los Angeles: University of California Press, 1978), p. 186.

3. W. Vernon Kinietz, *Indians of the Western Great Lakes, 1615–1760* (Ann Arbor: University of Michigan Press, 1965, p. 115).

4. Thomas S. Kuhn, *The Copernican Revolution: Planetary Astronomy and the Development of Western Thought* (Cambridge: Harvard University Press, 1957), p. 237.

5. H. Paul Santmire, "Historical Dimensions of the American Crisis," reprinted from *Dialog* (Summer 1970) in *Western Man and Environmental Ethics*, ed. Ian G. Barbour (Menlo Park: Addison-Wesley Publishing Co., 1973), pp. 70–71.

6. Empedocles, *Purifications*, DK 31 B 121, in *An Introduction to Early Greek Philosophy*, trans. John Mansley Robinson (New York: Houghton Mifflin, 1968), p. 152.

7. Aldo Leopold, *A Sand County Almanac* (New York: Oxford University Press, 1949), p. 215.

8. Richard Erdoes, *Lame Deer: Seeker of Visions* (New York: Simon & Schuster, 1976), pp. 108–09.

9. Ibid., p. 101.

10. Ibid., p. 124.

11. Ibid., pp. 102–03.

12. John G. Neilhardt, *Black Elk Speaks* (Lincoln: University of Nebraska Press, 1932), p. 3.

13. Ibid., p. 6.

14. Ibid., p. 7.

15. N. Scott Momaday, "A First American Views His Land," *National Geographic* 149 (1976): 14.

16. Ruth M. Underhill, *Red Man's Religion: Beliefs and Practices of the Indians North of Mexico* (Chicago: University of Chicago Press, 1965), p. 40.

17. Diamond Jenness, *The Ojibwa Indians of Parry Island, Their Social and Religious Life,* Canadian Department of Mines Bulletin no. 78, Museum of Canada Anthropological Series no. 17 (Ottawa, 1935), pp. 20–21. The (Parry Island) Ojibwa, Jenness earlier details, divided spirit into two parts—soul and shadow—though, as Jenness admits, the distinction between the soul and shadow was far from clear and frequently confused by the people themselves.

18. A. Irving Hallowell, "Ojibwa Ontology, Behavior, and World View," *Culture in History: Essays in Honor of Paul Radin,* ed. S. Diamond (New York: Columbia University Press, 1960), p. 26.

19. Kinietz, *Indians of the Western Great Lakes,* p. 126.

20. Hallowell, "Ojibwa Ontology," p. 19.

21. Ibid., p. 41.

22. Ibid., p. 32.

23. Ibid., p. 35.

24. Ibid., p. 47, emphasis added.

25. Brown, "Modes of Contemplation," p. 64.

26. Ian McHarg, "Values, Process, Form," from *The Fitness of Man's Environment* (Washington, D.C.: Smithsonian Institution Press, 1968), reprinted in Robert Disch, ed., *The Ecological Conscience* (Englewood Cliffs: Prentice-Hall, 1970), p. 25.

27. Ibid., p. 98.

28. Leopold, *Sand County Almanac,* pp. 225–26.

29. Yi-Fu Tuan, "Discrepancies between Environmental Attitude and Behavior," in *Ecology and Religion in History,* eds. D. Spring and I. Spring (New York: Harper and Row, 1974), p. 92.

30. Ibid., p. 98.

31. Stewart Udall, "First Americans, First Ecologists," *Look to the Mountain Top* (San Jose: Gousha Publications, 1972), p. 2.

32. Neihardt, *Black Elk Speaks,* p. 212.

33. Momaday, "First American Views," p. 18.

34. The most scurrilous example of this sort of argument with which I am acquainted is Daniel A. Guthrie's "Primitive Man's Relationship to Nature," *BioScience* 21 (July 1971): 721–23. In addition to rotting buffalo, Guthrie cites alleged extirpation of pleistocene megafauna by Paleo-Indians, c. 10,000 B.P. (as if that were relevant), and his cheapest shot of all, "the litter of bottles and junked cars to be found on Indian reservations today."

35. Martin, *Keepers,* p. 187, emphasis added.

36. Ibid., p. 186, emphasis added.

37. Ibid., p. 187.

38. Ibid., p. 71.

39. Ibid., p. 77.

40. Ibid., p. 116. Martin is here quoting Adrian Tanner *Bringing Home Animals: Religious Ideology and Mode of Production of the Misstassini Cree Hunters* (New York: St. Martin's Press, 1979) with approval.

41. Leopold, *Sand County Almanac,* p. 204.

42. Ibid., p. 203.

43. Ibid., p. 227.

44. Cf. J. Baird Callicott, "Animal Liberation: A Triangular Affair," *Environmental Ethics* 2 (1980): 311–38. Reproduced herein, pp. 15–38.

45. Cf. ibid., p. 324.

46. Leopold, *Sand County Almanac,* p. 204.

47. Marin, *Keepers,* p. 188, emphasis added.

48. Kenneth M. Morrison, *American Indian Culture and Research Journal* 3 (1979): 78.

49. Martin, *Keepers,* p. 188.

50. Tom Regan, "Environmental Ethics and the Ambiguity of the Native American Relationship with Nature," in Tom Regan, *All That Dwell Therein: Animal Rights and Environmental Ethics* (Berkeley, University of California Press, 1982), p. 234. Martin does, of course, mention such fears (see n. 38), but does not pursue the line of thought this psychological element suggests to Regan

51. Ibid.

52. Ibid., p. 235.

53. David Hume, *A Treatise of Human Nature* (Oxford. Clarendon Press, 1960), pp. 486–87.

## American Indian Land Wisdom?: Sorting Out the Issues

1. Rudolf Kaiser, "Chief Seattle's Speech(es): American Origins and Euro pean Reception—Almost a Detective Story," paper presented to European Association for American Studies Biennial Conference, Rome, Italy, 1984. See also, Rudolf Kaiser, "A Fifth Gospel, Almost: Chief Seattle's Speech(es). American Origins and European Reception," in Christian Feest, ed., *Indians and Europe: An Inter-disciplinary Collection of Essays* (Aachen, Federal Republic of Germany: Rader Verlag, 1987).

2. See Luke Starnes, "The Saga of Seattle," *Golden West* Vol. 4, #2 (Jan. 1968): 34–37, 60–64.

3. Kaiser, "Chief Seattle's Speeches," Appendix 3.

4. Daniel Guthrie, "Primitive Man's Relationship to Nature," *BioScience* 21 (1971): 721–723.

5. John Locke, *Two Treatises of Government;* quoted by William Cronon, *Changes in the Land: Indians, Colonists, and the Ecology of New England* (New York: Hill and Wang, 1983) p. 79.

6. Calvin Martin, *Keepers of the Game: Indian-Animal Relationships and the Fur Trade* (Berkeley: University of California Press, 1978) pp. 16, 17, 33. See Henry F.

Dobyns, "Estimating Aboriginal American Population: An Appraisal of Techniques with a New Hemispheric Estimate," *Current Anthropology* 7 (1966): 395–412; Marshall D. Sahlins, *Stone Age Economics* (Chicago: Aldine Atherton, 1972). Also see John Witthoft, "The American Indian Hunter," *Pennsylvania Game News* (April, 1953): 8–13.

7. Cronon, *Changes in the Land,* pp. 53, 80.

8. Paul S. Martin, "The Discovery of America," *Science* 179 (1973): 969–974.

9. Ibid., p. 972.

10. William Christie McCleod, "Conservation among Primitive Hunting Peoples," *The Scientific Monthly* 43 (1936): 562–566; Frank G. Speck, "Aboriginal Conservators," *Bird-Lore* 40 (1938), 258–261; and "Savage Savers," *Frontiers* 4 (Oct. 1939): 23–37.

11. McCleod, "Conservation among Primitive Hunting Peoples," p. 564.

12. See Eleanor Leacock, "The Montagnais 'Hunting Territory' and the Fur Trade," *American Anthropological Association Memoir* No. 78 (vol. 56, no. 5, part 2, Oct. 1954), and Charles A. Bishop, "The Emergence of Hunting Territories among the Northern Ojibwa," *Ethnology* 9 (1970): 1–5.

13. Speck, "Aboriginal Conservators," p. 260.

14. McCleod, "Conservation," p. 562.

15. Speck, "Savage Savers," p. 23.

16. Ibid., emphasis added.

17. Stewart Udall, "First Americans, First Ecologists," in Charles Jones, ed., *Look to the Mountain Top* (San Jose, Cal.: The H. M. Gousho Co., 1972) pp. 2–12; J. Donald Hughes, "Forest Indians: The Holy Occupation," *Environmental Review* 2 (1977): 2–13; Terrence Grieder, "Ecology Before Columbus," *Americas* 22 (1970): 21–28; G. Reichel Dolmatoff, "Cosmology as Ecological Analysis: A view from the Rainforest," *Man* 2 (1976): 307–318; William A. Richie, "The Indian and His Environment," *New York State Conservationist Journal* 10 (1955–56): 23–27; Thomas W. Overholt, "American Indians as Natural Ecologists," *American Indian Journal* 5 (September 1979): 9–16.

18. See, for example, Richard K. Nelson, "A Conservation Ethic and Environment: The Koyukon of Alaska," in Nancy Williams and Eugene Hunn, eds., *Resource Managers: North American and Australian Hunter-Gatherers* (New York: American Association for the Advancement of Science, 1982), pp. 211–228.

19. T. C. McLuhan, ed., *Touch the Earth: Native American Testimony* (New York: Harper and Row Publishers, 1978).

20. Adrian Tanner, *Bringing Home Animals: Religious Ideology and Mode of Production of the Mistassini Cree Hunters* (New York: St. Martin's Press, 1979); Richard K. Nelson, *Make Prayers to the Raven: A Koyukon View of the Northern Forest* (Chicago: University of Chicago Press, 1983).

21. Calvin Martin, *Keepers of the Game,* p. 10.

22. Thomas W. Overholt and J. Baird Callicott, *Clothed-in-Fur and Other Tales: An Introduction to An Ojibwa World View* (Washington, DC: University Press of America, 1982); A. Irving Hallowell, *Culture and Experience* (Philadelphia: University of Pennsylvania Press, 1955).

23. A. Irving Hallowell, "Ojibwa, Ontology, Behavior, and World View" in Stanley Diamond, ed., *Culture in History: Essays in Honor of Paul Radin* (New York: Columbia University Press, 1960), pp. 23–24. See also Mary B. Black, "Ojibwa Taxonomy and Percept Ambiguity," *Ethos* (1977): 90–118.

24. Ibid., p. 21.

25. Ibid., p. 43.

26. William Jones, *Ojibwa Texts,* 2 vols. (Leyden and New York: Publications of the American Ethnological Society, 1917, 1919, respectively).

27. Also see J. Baird Callicott, "Traditional American Indian and Western European Attitudes toward Nature: An Overview," *Environmental Ethics* 4 (1982): 293–318. Reproduced herein, pp. 177–201.

28. Aldo Leopold, *A Sand County Almanac* (New York: Oxford University Press, 1949), p. 204.

29. Nelson, "A Conservation Ethic."

30. See James R. Walker, *Lakota Belief and Ritual,* ed. Raymond J. DeMallie and Elaine Jahner (Lincoln: University of Nebraska Press, 1980).

31. Richard K. Nelson, personal communication (May 2, 1985).

32. Ibid.

## Aldo Leopold on Education

1. Roderick Nash, *Wilderness and the American Mind,* revised ed. (New Haven: Yale University Press, 1973), ch. 11.

2. D.S. Mannison, M.K. McRobbie, and R. Routley, ed., *Environmental Philosophy: Ethics, Political Philosophy, Social Theory* (Canberra: The Australian National University, 1980).

3. Frederick and Frances Hamerstrom, Wisconsin Department of Natural Resources (ret.) and Adjuct Professors, University of Wisconsin-Stevens Point; Robert S. McCabe, Professor of Wildlife Ecology, University of Wisconsin-Madison; Charles Bradley and Nina Leopold Bradley, directors of the Aldo Leopold Fellowship Program at the Leopold Memorial Reserve.

4. Aldo Leopold, *A Sand County Almanac, With Essays on Conservation from Round River* (New York: Ballantine, 1970): 202–210.

5. Ibid., p. 205.

6. Ibid., p. 207.

7. Ibid., p. 209.

8. Ibid., p. 252.

9. Ibid., p. 168.

10. Ibid., p. 20.

11. Ibid., p. 30.

12. Ibid., pp. 49–50.

13. Ibid., p. 86.

14. Ibid., p. 225.

15. Ibid., p. 291.

16. Ibid.

17. Ibid., p. 158.

18. Ibid., p. 162.

19. Ibid., p. 262.

20. Ibid., p. 246.

21. Lynn White, Jr., "The Historical Roots of Our Ecologic Crisis," *Science* 155: 1203–1207.

22. Frances Hamerstrom, *Strictly for the Chickens* (Ames: Iowa State University Press, 1980), pp. 26, 28.

23. Ibid., p. 38.

24. Charles Bradley, "A Short History of a Man Hunt," *Wisconsin Academy Review* (December 1979), p. 7.

25. Ibid.

26. Aldo Leopold, *Sand County Almanac,* pp. 208–9.

27. Ibid., p. xix.

28. Ibid., p. 239.

29. Ibid., p. 238.

30. Ibid.

31. Ibid., p. 239.

32. Ibid., p. xix.

33. Ibid., p. 193.

## Leopold's Land Aesthetic

1. See J. Baird Callicott, ed., *Companion to A Sand County Almanac: Interpretive and Critical Essays* (Madison: University of Wisconsin Press, 1987).

2. Aldo Leopold, *A Sand County Almanac, With Essays on Conservation from Round River* (New York: Ballantine, 1970) p. 249.

3. See Ian McHarg, *Design with Nature* (Garden City, NJ: Doubleday, 1971) and J. Baird Callicott, "The Land Aesthetic," *Companion to A Sand County Almanac*, pp. 157–171.

4. See Roderick Nash, *Wilderness and the American Mind*, revised ed. (New Haven: Yale University Press, 1973).

5. Aldo Leopold, *A Sand County Almanac*, p. 102.

6. Ibid., pp. 179–80.

7. Ibid., p. 180.

8. Ibid., p. 105.

9. Ibid., pp. 102 3.

10. Ibid., p. 193.

11. Ibid., p. 103.

12. Ibid., p. 180.

13. Ibid., p. 295.

14. Ibid., pp. 146–47.

15. Ibid., pp. 214–15.

16. See Callicott, *Companion to A Sand County Almanac*.

17. Leopold, *Sand County Almanac* p. 238.

18. Ibid., pp. 202–203.

19. Ibid., pp. 262–63.

20. See J. Baird Callicott, "Aldo Leopold on Education, as Educator, and His Land Ethic in the Context of Contemporary Environmental Education," *Journal of Environmental Education* 14 (1982): 34–41. Reproduced therein, pp 223–237.

## Moral Considerability and Extraterrestrial Life

1. See for example Charles L. Sandford, *The Quest for Paradise* (Urbana, Ill.: The University of Illinois Press, 1961) and Daniel S. Boorstin, *The Discoverers: A History of Man's Search to Know His World and Himself* (New York: Random House, 1983) for an account of the self-image of Renaissance discoverers. See William K. Hartmann, "Space Exploration and Environmental Issues," *Environmental Ethics* 6 (1984): 227–39, for an explicit, self-conscious projection of the Renaissance discovery, exploration, and exploitation of the New World into a new interplanetary frontier.

2. See Hartmann, "Space Exploration and Environmental Issues," for a recent example of seriously entertaining these things. Ian McHarg, *Design with Nature* (Garden City, N.Y.: Doubleday, 1969), rather elaborately and very convincingly makes the point that to successfully design a self-sustaining space colony, which Hartmann also envisions, we would have to recreate the Earth.

3. Ibid. Hartmann denies that extraterrestrial resource development and colonization, which he enthusiastically recommends, would lead to a " 'disposable planet mentality' " (p. 229). Yet he apparently forgets this disclaimer and later writes, "the possibilities of self-sustaining colonies of humans ... on other planetary surfaces are really increasing the chances for survival of the human race against [political and environmental] disasters." If we think we can escape these disasters by emigrating off the Earth, we shall have less incentive to try to avert them.

4. Ibid. Hartmann calls Earth "a Hawaii in a solar system of Siberias." More apt, but not nearly apt enough, would be a Hawaii in a solar system of Antarcticas. Hartmann goes on to say immediately, "Earth is the only known place where we can stand naked in the light of a nearby star and enjoy our surroundings." It is the only known place we can stand wearing anything less than a spacesuit, and most other known planets provide no place to stand or, if they do, even a spacesuit would not be protection enough from solar radiation.

5. Frank Herbert, *Dune* (New York: Chilton Books, 1956). In *Dune* we are to imagine a desert planet without oceans or extensive forests but with, nevertheless, an apparently breathable atmosphere containing, we must therefore suppose, free oxygen—and this is touted to be an ecologically well-informed science fiction!

6. A. Thomas Young, "Conference Overview," in John Billingham, ed., *Life in the Universe* (Cambridge, Mass.: Massachusetts Institute of Technology Press, 1982), p. xi.

7. Billingham, "Preface," in *Life in the Universe*, p. ix.

8. See Peter Morgane, "The Whale Brain: The Anatomical Basis of Intelligence," in Joan McIntyre, ed., *Mind in the Waters* (New York: Scribner's, 1974), pp. 84–93.

9. See Peter Warshall, "The Ways of Whales," in *Mind in the Waters*, pp. 110–40.

10. Eric J. Chaisson, "Three Eras of Cosmic Evolution," in *Life in the Universe*, pp. 15–16.

11. A. Oparine and V. Fessenkov, *La Vie dans l'Universe* (Moscow: Editions en Langues Etrangères, 1958), translated from the French and quoted by V. A. Firsoff, *Life beyond the Earth: A Study in Exobiology* (New York: Basic Books, 1963), p. xii.

12. E. B. Tylor, *Anthropology: An Introduction to the Study of Man and Civilization* (New York: Appleton, 1897).

13. C. Owen Lovejoy, "Evolution of Man and Its Implications for General Principles of the Evolution of Intelligent Life," in *Life in the Universe*, pp. 317–29. It should be pointed out that Carl Sagan, in *The Dragons of Eden: Speculations on the Evolution of Human Intelligence* (New York: Ballantine, 1977), asserts that "evolution is adventitious and not foresighted" (p. 8), but he remains undaunted in his belief in the existence of anthropomorphic extraterrestrial intelligence, even though he "would ... not expect their brains to be anatomically or physiologically or perhaps even chemically close to ours" (p. 243). How then could their functions be close to ours? Sagan's answer is that "they must still come to grips with the same laws of nature" (p. 242). The laws of nature are objective realities, like Platonic forms, Sagan seems to think—as opposed to Kantian descriptions of our own subjective ordering of experience—and evolutionary development from widely divergent points of departure and following radically different pathways will converge upon a mental representation of them, not as target, but as a selective end result. "Smarter organisms by and large survive better and leave more offspring than stupid ones" (p. 241). Granted. But Sagan's argument turns on an ambiguity in the concept of "smarter organisms" coming "to grips with the same laws of nature." Cetaceans, who own brains very like ours in chemistry, anatomy, and physiology, have come to grips with the laws of nature governing the propagation, reflection, and detection of sound waves, but no one supposes that their evolution and intelligent deployment of echolocation entails that they have mastered the science of wave mechanics. Birds do not need to know aerodynamics to fly or optics to see. Survival intelligence, the evolutionary equivalent of street smarts, is not necessarily the same as theoretical intelligence. In sum and in short, it is not necessary, in order to come to grips with the laws of nature on a practical basis, that an organism theoretically represent to itself the laws of nature or even be cognizant that natural laws as such exist—if in fact as such they do exist.

14. See J. D. Bernal, "Molecular Structure, Biochemical Function, and Evolution," in T. H. Waterman and H. J. Morowitz, eds., *Theoretical and Mathematical Biology* (New York: Blaisdell Publishing Co., 1965), chap. 5, for an explicit comparison of biology with physics and chemistry in this context.

15. See Peter Shuster, "Evolution between Chemistry and Biology," *Origins of Life* 14 (1984): 3–14, for a recent summary discussion.

16. Harold J. Morowitz, "Biology as a Cosmological Science," *Main Currents in Modern Thought* 2 (1972): 153.

17. See Firsoff, *Life Beyond the Earth*, p. 4.

18. See Sherwood Chang, "Organic Chemical Evolution," in *Life in the Universe*, pp. 21–46; and F. Raulin, D. Gautier, and W. H. Ip, "Exobiology and the Solar System: The Cassini Mission to Titan," *Origins of Life* 14 (1984): 817–24.

19. See Sir H. Spencer Jones, *Life on Other Worlds* (London: English Universities Press, 1940).

20. For an extended discussion ranging from skeptical indulgence to impatient ridicule see John Passmore, *Man's Responsibility for Nature: Ecological Problems and Western Traditions* (New York: Scribner's 1974).

21. I was interested to learn that Michael Tooley, "Would ETIs Be Persons?" in James L. Christian, ed., *Extraterrestrial Intelligence: The First Encounter* (Buffalo, NY: Prometheus Books, 1976), provides, by applying the usual ethical categories of mainstream Western moral thought, moral considerability for extraterrestrial intelligent beings of sci-fi fantasy, provided they are also conative, self-conscious, and envisage the future. Tooley does not address (and his discussion suggests he would not philosophically support) moral considerability for mere life—extraterrestrial or otherwise.

22. Peter Singer, *Animal Liberation: A New Ethics for Our Treatment of Animals* (New York: The New York Review, 1975), writes, "Philosophy ought to question the basic assumptions of the age" (p. 10), as if his extension of moral considerability to animals were really radical. See H. J. McCloskey, "Moral Rights and Animals," *Inquiry* 22 (1979): 23–59, for a humanistic rejection of animal liberation/rights.

23. Paul M. Henig, "Exobiologists Continue to Search for Life on Other Planets," *BioScience* 30 (1980), quotes physicist William G. Pollard as saying of exobiology that it is "a branch of science so far without content" (p. 9). Exobiologist Richard S. Young, "Post-Viking Exobiology," *BioScience* 28 (1978), makes the essentially logical (and thus largely formal) point that "the absence of evidence of life [on Mars] should not necessarily be construed as evidence of the absence of life" (p. 502).

24. For a discussion of the shift of informed opinion toward skepticism regarding extraterrestrial life, see Paul M. Henig, "Exobiologists Continue to Search for Life on Other Planets."

25. These dimensions are supplied by Firsoff, *Life Beyond the Earth*, p. xi.

26. Ibid.

27. Bernard M. Oliver, "Search Strategies," in *Life in the Universe*, p. 352.

28. Ibid. Oliver entertains the possibility of a search voyage spanning several generations requiring thus "nursery and educational facilities [which adds

weight and increases energy requirements]. .... The longer time," he realistically reminds us, "also increases the risk of disaffection or actual mutiny by the crew: the parents were presumably screened for psychological stability; the children are not" (pp. 354–55). Incidentally, Oliver's calculations do not neglect the time-dilating effects of speeds approaching the speed of light in relativity theory; his time calculations are given in the ship-time reference frame.

29. Ibid. Oliver calculates (p. 354) the energy required to accelerate a starship of 1,000 tones to one-fifth the speed of light in multiples of units of millennia of U.S. energy consumption—that is, in units equivalent to 1,000 years of total energy consumption by the United States.

30. See Norman Myers, *The Sinking Ark: A New Look at the Problem of Disappearing Species* (New York: Pergamon Press, 1979), for an authoritative scientific account. For a philosophical-ethical response, see Bryan G. Norton, ed., *The Preservation of Species* (Princeton, N.J.: Princeton University Press, 1986).

31. Hartmann, in "Space Exploration and Environmental Issues," very nicely summarizes and documents this impact. Hartmann's central practical concern seems to be that environmentalists not add their opposition to that of socialists, fiscal conservatives, and others who hope to see space exploration projects scrapped. Although I do not share Hartmann's mythic vision of space colonies and space resource development, I am not opposed to space exploration, since I think that the more we explore space, the more deeply impressed we will be with our embeddedness in and dependence upon Earth.

32. Ibid. Hartmann agrees, "It is no coincidence that the first Earth Day, in 1970, came soon after these pictures became available."

33. See, for example, J Baird Callicott, "On the Intrinsic Value of Nonhuman Species," in Norton, *The Preservation of Species*, pp. 138–72. Reproduced herein, pp. 129–155.

34. The role of intuition in ethics is controversial. Tom Regan, *The Case for Animal Rights* (Berkeley: University of California Press, 1983), pp. 133ff., provides a recent summary, a sorting of the issues, and a defense for the utility of moral intuitions such as this one as a point of departure for further ethical analysis.

35. For a schematic analysis of the land ethic, see J. Baird Callicott, "Elements of an Environmental Ethic: Moral Considerability and the Biotic Community," *Environmental Ethics* 1 (1979): 71–81. Reproduced herein, pp. 63–73.

36. Aldo Leopold, *A Sand County Almanac and Sketches Here and There* (New York: Oxford University Press, 1949), p. 109. Lewis Thomas, *The Lives of a Cell: Notes of a Biology Watcher* (New York: Viking Press, 1974), p. 5, notes that there is a "high probability that we derived from some single cell, fertilized in a bolt of lightning as the Earth cooled."

37. See Leopold, "The Land Ethic" in *A Sand County Almanac*, and J. Baird Callicott, "Elements of an Environmental Ethic" and "The Search for an Envir-

onmental Ethic," in Tom Regan, ed., *Matters of Life and Death,* 2nd ed. (New York: Random House, 1986), pp. 381–423.

38. Leopold, "The Land Ethic," p. 204.

39. Joel Feinberg, "The Rights of Animals and Unborn Generations," in William T. Blackstone, ed., *Philosophy and Environmental Crisis* (Athens: University of Georgia Press, 1974), pp. 43–68; Kenneth Goodpaster, "On Being Morally Considerable," *Journal of Philosophy* 22 (1978): 308–25; Albert Schweitzer, "The Ethic of Reverence for Life" in Tom Regan and Peter Singer, eds., *Animal Rights and Human Obligations* (Englewood Cliffs, N.J.: Prentice-Hall, 1976), pp. 133–38. For a discussion of the dialectic see Kenneth Goodpaster, "From Egoism to Environmentalism," in K. E. Goodpaster and K. M. Sayre, eds., *Ethics and Problems of the 21st Century* (Notre Dame, Ind.: University of Notre Dame Press, 1979); pp. 21–35.

41. Ibid.

42. Kenneth Goodpaster, "On Being Morally Considerable."

43. Ibid., p. 316.

44. J. Baird Callicott, "On the Intrinsic Value of Nonhuman Species."

45. Joel Feinberg, "The Rights of Animals and Unborn Generations," p. 49. Italics added.

46. Ibid., p. 50. Goodpaster, in "On Being Morally Considerable," wisely steers clear of the intellectual quagmire of the nature of rights and the qualifications of rights holders.

47. Albert Schweitzer, "The Ethic of Reverence for Life," p. 133.

48. Kenneth Goodpaster, in "From Egoism to Environmentalism," provides a very clear and illuminating discussion of the moral reasoning, the logic, of all ethics that rest on a criterion for moral standing/moral rights, such as rationality, sentiency, conativity, and the like.

49. Both Schweitzer and Goodpaster admit the strict impracticability of their conation-centered ethics. Goodpaster, in "On Being Morally Considerable," writes, "The clearest and most decisive refutation of the principle of respect for life is that one cannot *live* according to it, nor is there any indication in nature that we were intended to." And Schweitzer, in "The Ethic of Reverence for Life," writes, "It remains a painful enigma how I am to live by the rule of reverence for life in a world ruled by creative will which is at the same time destructive will...." For a fuller discussion see J. Baird Callicott, "On the Intrinsic Value of Nonhuman Species."

50. See Arthur Schopenhauer, *The World as Will and Idea,* trans. R. B. Haldane and J. Kemp (Garden City, N.Y.: Doubleday, 1961), pp. 297ff.

51. Bryan G. Norton, "Environmental Ethics and Weak Anthropocentrism," *Environmental Ethics* 6 (1984):131–48.

52. Ibid., p. 136.

53. For a historical analysis see J. Baird Callicott, "Intrinsic Value, Quantum Theory, and Environmental Ethics," *Environmental Ethics* 7 (1985): 257–75. Reproduced herein, pp. 157–174.

# Index

## (Notes Excluded)

315